MAHAD
The Making of the First Dalit Revolt

MAHAD

The Making of the First Dalit Revolt

with the Account of

Comrade R.B. More, the Chief Organizer of the First Conference

Anand Teltumbde

MAHAD: The Making of the First Dalit Revolt
Anand Teltumbde

First Published 2016

ISBN 978-93-5002-398-3 (Hb)

Published by
AAKAR BOOKS
28 E Pocket IV, Mayur Vihar Phase I, Delhi 110 091
Phone: 011 2279 5505 Telefax: 011 2279 5641
aakarbooks@gmail.com.com; www.aakarbooks.com

Type Set at
Arpit Printographers, Delhi 110 092

Printed at
Sapra Brothers, Delhi 110 092

To

Babasaheb Ambedkar

and all the other heroes, known and unknown of Mahad
—who seeded the Dalit Movement with their sacrifices

&

Valjibhai Patel

of the Council for Social Justice, Ahmedabad
—one such hero who has been carrying on the legacy of the Mahad struggle in these depressing times

Preface

This book was primarily inspired by the account of the first Mahad Conference by Comrade R.B. More, who was the chief organizer of the conference that led to the epic struggle of Dalits for their civil rights. Com. More had written a long article in Marathi, reminiscing nearly 35 years later how he came to conceive an idea of the Mahad Conference, which was published in the *Annual* of Babasaheb Ambedkar College, Mahad. It was later published in a booklet form but had limited circulation, and even the Marathi readership did not know about it. It was felt that this historical document should be made available to a wider readership, which might be interested to know about the making of this first struggle of Dalits. It was, therefore, translated into English.

Babasaheb Ambedkar himself had written detailed editorials on this struggle in *Bahishkrut Bharat,* the organ of the Bahishkrut Hitkarini Sabha that he founded for the upliftment of the Untouchables. These editorials also provide a good deal of information on and around the Mahad Conference and the subsequent Satyagraha, which unfortunately is still confined to texts written in Marathi. Some parts of it have, however, been printed in volume 17 of the *Dr. Babasaheb Ambedkar Writings and Speeches* published by the Maharashtra Government. There is another important source, which is the multi-volume biography in Marathi written by C.B. Khairmode. The importance of these volumes is that they contain a lot of raw material in the original on important events in the life of Dr. Ambedkar, without authorial interpretation or editorial polish. Besides, there are stray accounts in Marathi such as the biography of A.V. Chitre, one of the main organizers of the Mahad Conference as well as the Satyagraha, which provide information on aspects missing in others. Alongside, we sensed that the State Archives would also have records on this struggle. Our search confirmed availability of a fairly large amount of documents in the Archives, particularly after the First Conference and on the conduct of the Second Conference, which was called the Satyagraha Conference. It reflected the importance with which the colonial administration looked at these struggles. These documents provided an administrative perspective on the struggles, and were therefore considered important. All this material was used in constructing the accounts of the First and Second Mahad Conferences.

It is unlikely that the full significance of the Mahad Conferences can be realized without understanding what the caste system of India is. Also, it is equally vital to understand historical resistance movements against castes which preceded the Mahad struggle. A chapter was, therefore, added to elicit its evolutionary character in a broad-brush manner beginning with the misty times of the origin of castes and ending with the incipient movements of Dalits that had sprung up in various parts that preceded Mahad. Likewise, another chapter was added at the end to provide a hindsight view of the Mahad struggle that will link it to the experiential aspects of the contemporary Dalit movement. Both these chapters are meant to situate Mahad within its historical context.

The credit for this book truly lies elsewhere. Basically, my friend Dr Shridhar Pawar had brought out a translation of Comrade R.B. More's Marathi booklet on Mahad Satyagraha to me for review. It was done collectively by him, Sanober Keshwar, Shailendra Mehta and Niranjani Shetty. While discussing the form in which to publish this article length booklet, it was felt that I should write a comprehensive introduction to it. The process of writing this introduction has basically extended to make it a book that you are reading. Shridhar painstakingly collected archival materials and made them available to me. The other person is Subodh More, who has been carrying the legacy of activism from his two generations, viz., his father Comrade Satyendra More and his grandfather Comrade Ramchandra Babaji (R.B.) More. He provided me with reference material that I needed from time to time, and also got me some of the bio-sketches of important personalities associated with the Mahad Conference and the Satyagraha. Later, my activist friend Veera Sathidar, Prof. Prahlad Jogdand of the University of Mumbai, and Prof. Vilas and Usha Wagh, both of Sugawa Prakashan also helped me by providing reference material as and when needed. Obviously, contributions of all these friends go beyond formal acknowledgement. My contribution rather has been in delaying the publication by almost four years in doing my part of the job.

I, however, wish to acknowledge the generous help of some people. Among them is my erstwhile colleague Anitha Aranha in Petronet India for voluntarily typing out my handwritten notes and my family, daughters Rashmi and Prachi; and wife Rama in miscellaneous tasks. My thanks are also due to my erstwhile colleague Arvind Krishnaswamy, and friend and comrade S.V. Rajadorai who have gone through the text and suggested changes. In the end, sporadic assistance came from friends, Devendra Ingle and Milind Bhawar, in providing referencing details whenever I sought them.

I thank Prof. John Douglas of JJ School of Fine Arts, Mumbai for providing beautiful sketches of some prominent heroes of Mahad as you see them in Appendix 8. My friend Sudharak Olwe, a renowned photographer, provided a photograph of the commemorative mural erected at the Chavadar tank at Mahad, which has been creatively used by another friend, Uttam Ghosh, in designing the beautiful cover. I gratefully acknowledge their friendly contributions.

Thanks are also due to the team of Aakar Books for producing the book in this attractive form.

14 April 2015

Anand Teltumbde
B-243, IIT, Kharagpur 721 302

Contents

1

Introduction: The Importance of Mahad

We learn from history that we never learn anything from history.

–Hegel

Mahad*, in the folklore, is associated with the Chavadar tank Satyagraha, which actually never took place. The Dalit march to the tank and drinking its water in assertion of their civil rights happened during the first conference (on 20 March 1927), which was not a Satyagraha; it was a Depressed Classes Conference that had decided spontaneously to exercise their right just the previous night. The Second Conference, a sequel to the first one, in response to the vehement opposition of the caste Hindus, was consciously planned as a Satyagraha Conference and had plans to burn the *Manusmruti* and start an agitation at the Chavadar tank till it was opened to Dalits. However, because of the court injunction against it, fraudulently managed by some orthodox caste Hindus just before the Conference, the latter programme was suspended. These two conferences being collectively referred to as Satyagraha is thus erroneous. What was Mahad then? What exactly happened in Mahad? Why does it assume so much importance in the Dalit universe? What is its legacy to the contemporary Dalit movement? And what are its lessons to posterity? These are some of the questions that are dealt with in the following pages.

Indeed, Mahad is permanently engraved in the collective consciousness of Dalits as a glorious chapter of their liberation

* Mahad is used in the text symbolizing both the conferences that happened in 1927 in addition to the name of the town where they took place.

struggle. It represents the first collective articulation of their civil rights and clear resolve to assert them. Before Mahad the acts of violation of the caste code had begun happening either by individual Dalits or by their collectives but unfortunately they were not noted as such beyond their locale. Here, the most notable mention must be made of the militant movement of Pulayas (Dalits in Kerala) spearheaded by a remarkable person, Mahatma Ayyankali (1863-1941), which had won the Dalits of Travancore the right to walk along public roads in 1900 and to admit their children into public schools in 1907, more than two decades before Mahad.[1] Unfortunately, it remained unknown beyond south Kerala, so much so that even Dr Ambedkar did not know of it. Other initiatives were led or mediated by upper caste men. This was the first time that the Dalits had consciously gathered to assert their civil rights on their own. The mainstream scholarship is reluctant to call Mahad a civil rights struggle. These days, it has evolved a new 'casteist' terminology referring to anything connected with Dalits with a prefix 'Dalit'. The civil rights of Dalits then become Dalit rights; writing by a Dalit becomes Dalit writing, and even the public positions if their occupants are Dalit are very innocuously referred to by the latter's caste[2]. Even the so-called progressives are seen falling into this ditch of retrogression and unknowingly expose the limits of their progressiveness. The Mahad struggle as such is never referred to as the civil rights struggle in generic terms as for instance the struggle of the African Americans has been. It was basically meant for the assertion of civil rights not of any Dalit imagination but as established by law. And as such it should have been rightfully recognized as one of the first major battles for civil rights in modern times anywhere in the world. Arguably, it precedes the civil rights movement in the United States by a quarter of a century.[3] Dalits refer to it as *mukti-sangram* (battle for freedom), and as a *kranti* (a revolution). Babasaheb Ambedkar had himself compared it with the constitution of the National Assembly or Storming of the Bastille, the critical instances in the French Revolution that mark the definitive high point in history of the world. In contrast to this mega-portrayal by Dalits, it remains completely ignored by the mainstream historians in the country.[4] As a result, the world has been largely oblivious of this important marker in the annals of the human rights struggle of the oppressed humanity.

Was Mahad really a revolution? Obviously, it was neither aimed at nor did it achieve any overthrow of the government or power structure, as did the French Revolution. Was it as momentous as the constitution of the National Assembly by the Third Estate (working classes) in France or storming of the Bastille, the dreary symbol of the French feudalism in 1789? What change did it accomplish? The French Revolution saw the demise of monarchy in France and the establishment of a republic. What did the Mahad struggle achieve? Did it give civil rights to Dalits? How does it compare with the recognized civil rights movement of the African Americans? These and other such are obvious questions that arise in relation to it. They may be properly reflected upon by readers, perhaps after reading this book.

But before considering them, one has to necessarily understand the caste system against which this revolt was organized. Without understanding this context readers may not find anything spectacular in the entire episode and may fail to grasp its importance. Beyond the caste system, they will have to understand the custom of untouchability, essentially an offshoot of the former but assuming an independent existence with a menacing prowess to ostracize over a sixth of the Indian population that denied them even basic human identity. This abominable system of graded inequality and untouchability never faced any organized challenge over its history of more than two milleniums before Mahad. It had hegemonized the entire subcontinent and almost become a life-world of people including the victims. Why and how did the Dalits, who were hollowed out of any strength over such a long period suddenly rise in revolt against this hegemonic system? Unless one appreciates that the Indian caste system is a unique system of social stratification, with a unique feature of self-organization and self-regulation, one may not understand why the people internalized their own immobile stature, however lowly or pitiable, in the caste hierarchy. Unlike political structures, caste pervaded every sphere of social life and made the structure impervious to any fundamental change. Threatening such a system from within, therefore, becomes a significant act in itself.

Uniqueness of Castes

The caste system in India is one of the forms of social stratification. All civilizations had developed some kind of stratification in society, commensurate with the scale of their surplus production. In small-scale and low-technology societies, stratification is limited by low levels of accumulation and usually organized in terms of age, gender, and kinship position. In contrast, large-scale, wealthier societies are more likely to be stratified into enduringly complex groups or classes reproducing themselves. Stratification involves not only the forms of discrimination that stand in the way of egalitarianism but also the structure of rewards and punishment that characterize economy and the larger social order. Sociologists commonly identify three major forms of stratification in complex societies: *caste* systems, with rigid borders, highly differentiated statuses, and limited possibility of mobility; the system of *estates* characteristic of European feudal societies, which distinguished between the clergy, the nobility, and the broad category of peasants, merchants, and artisans; and *class systems*, more common in modern societies.[5] The first two systems are dominated by ascribed status, or status into which one is born.[6] Class systems, in contrast, provided a greater space for mobility for achieved status. In the class system, the contemporaneous meritocratic ideal placed a premium on achievement, in spite of economic, cultural, and institutional pressures for general reproduction of structures of inequality.

Estates were part of European feudalism, but also existed in many other traditional civilizations in varying forms.[7] Estate systems were found in societies ranging from pre-state socio-economic formations to politically organized pre-capitalist societies such as Ancient Rome and Medieval Europe. The feudal estates consisted of strata with differing obligations and rights, some of these differences being established by law. In

Europe, the highest estate was composed of the aristocracy and gentry. The clergy formed another estate, having lower status but possessing various distinctive privileges. Those who came to be called the 'third estate' were the commoners—serfs, free peasants, merchants and artisans. The features of each estate system varied, but they all shared one trait in common: in estate societies, there was a direct homology between stratification and relations of production. The estates were closely aligned with the classes; they differed from classes primarily because they crystallized into a structure with corresponding political and economic processes, supported by an ideology which justified inequality as a natural, inherited reality. While the class system was structurally mobile in the estate system the king was usually the final determinate of who was who.

Max Weber made an absolute distinction between class and estate (status group) as between economy on the one hand and 'honour' and 'social intercourse' on the other.[8] Class is the social structural position groups relative to the economic, social, political, and cultural resources of society. It is highly significant in determining one's life chances. Being a structural phenomenon, unlike estate or castes, class cannot be directly observed. The class system is based on partly 'achieved' status, whereas both estate and caste systems are based on purely 'ascribed' status. Nonetheless, you can "see" class through various indicators that people project, often unintentionally, about their class status. The clothing you wear, the car you drive or, for that matter, whether you have a car or use a bus, are the indicators which project class to others as a symbol of our presumed worth in society. The class system became the dominant system under capitalism. Although it is extremely exploitative, within it individuals are basically free units who can strive to overcome their exploitation if they so desire and transcend their class. In contrast to this Weberian conception, Karl Marx, who saw capitalism as the first mode of production in history throwing up two basic classes, viz. proletariat and bourgeois, viewed classes purely in terms of relations of production.

The caste system completely denies mobility. A person born

in a caste finds his life chances frozen by his caste. Dr. Ambedkar gave a succinct definition of caste: "A caste is an enclosed class".[9] This definition clarifies the distinction between class and caste. The essential element in the caste system is the division of society into many mutually exclusive groups called castes. The caste into which a person is born defines his or her social status through life, and prescribes the group within which that person could marry. Caste represents an extreme case when its separation is secured not only through convention and laws but also ritually (impurity through contacts)[10] supported by religion. The concept of pollution governs relations between different castes. This concept is absolutely fundamental to the caste system and along with the concepts of *karma* and *dharma* it has contributed to making caste a unique institution.[11] The caste system, as it evolved, represents a continuum of infinite castes strung within a fluid hierarchy that while collectively maintaining its macro structure unleashes incessant contention within its class. This feature imparts the caste system its unique oppressive prowess as well as longevity.

However, many people including G.S. Ghurye, the doyen of Indian sociology, argue that the caste system is not unique to India. For instance, he argues that birth and status distinctions are not uncommon in other societies, "well-marked status groups within a society, distinguished from one another by rights and disabilities, separated from one another by the absence of freedom of intermarriage may therefore, be considered to be a common characteristic of the mental background and social picture of the Indo-European cultures".[12] Indeed, the features that Ghurye speaks about are found in other societies too but whether they adequately map the Indian caste system is the real question. Ghurye's perspective on caste based on status groups, rights, disabilities, unfreedoms, etc., is too constricted to confirm his own account characterized by certain notions of Hinduism such as, allegiance to racial theory; a search for certain unrealistic features of caste in terms of status; an acute focus on the boundary and divisions and subdivisions within caste groups resulting in the view that sub-castes are the "real" castes; and future directions of caste. As Bose (1996) observed, "this perspective would tend to contradict the racial view of caste because in the racial view, caste would be a unique feature of a particular society associated with the unique racial features."[13] These scholars have reduced castes to their skeleton devoid of flesh and blood, and their dynamics that makes them a life-world of people conditioning their social relations. There is no system in the world that reflects this dynamic feature of castes.

There are many countries where caste-like features are encountered. The Osu people in Nigeria and southern Cameroon are treated by the Igbo indigenous religious system to be a 'living sacrifice', an outcaste, Untouchable and sub-human people.[14] An ordinary Igbo person would not marry or permit any of his relations to marry an Osu person. If they married, they are also regarded as Osu. Once born into the Osu caste, the Nigerian is an outcaste with limited opportunities or acceptance, regardless of his or her ability or merit.[15] There is another caste-like system among the Mande societies in Senegal, Gambia, Guinea, Sierra Leone, Liberia, Ivory Coast, and Ghana, previously Ancient Manden, where people have traditionally been divided by occupation and ethnic ties.[16] The highest hierarchy in the *Mande* caste system, the Horon (nobles/ freeborn), are traditionally farmers, fishermen, warriors, and animal breeders; the lowest caste are the Jonow (meaning slave) made up of people whose ancestors were enslaved by other Africans during tribal wars. An important feature of this system is castes based on trade, such as blacksmiths and griots.[17] Besides, there are several other caste-like stratifications such as Wolof in Senegal and Fulani in West Africa. Wolof lived in highly stratified societies based primarily on blood relationships. There were three highly separated castes: freemen (*gor* or *jambur*); those of slave descent (*jaam*); and artisans (*ñeeño*). Intermarriage rarely took place between these castes.[18] Fulanis are a nomadic Muslim ethnic group located primarily in present-day Burkina-Faso, Mali, and Niger. The Fulanis continue to adhere to a fairly rigid caste system. The major castes, in their order of stature are the nobility, the traders, the tradesmen, and the descendants of slaves.[19] There is a varna like system among the Borana in north-east Kenya and southern Ethiopia wherein Borana Gutu (pure) are treated as the highest, followed by Gabbra, Sakuye, and Watta, a traditional hunter-gatherer caste, being the lowest. The Watta are considered unwanted, worthless, and condemned to lifelong servitude for members of the higher castes.[20] The inter-caste clashes between castes, particularly between Barana and Gabbra, the two upper caste groups, continue even today.[21] In Yemen there exists a caste-like system that keeps the Al-Akhdam (Arabic word Akhdam means servants) social group as the perennial manual workers (scavengers) for the society through practices that mirror untouchability. Though practising Islam over 1,000 years, they are treated quite like Dalits, and like Dalits they prefer to be called *Al Muhamasheen*, or 'marginalized ones'. They are believed to be the descendants of Abyssinian soldiers from Ancient Ethiopia who stayed in Yemen after a failed invasion in the 6th century AD. They were so hated that they were forced to accept the worst jobs, such as transporting and disposing of human sewage and collecting garbage.[22] Likewise, there are people in Japan known as Burakumin (*Buraku*, meaning community or hamlet, and *min*, meaning people), or *Hisabetsu Buraku* meaning "discriminated communities/discriminated hamlets"). Studies comparing the caste systems in India and Japan have noted similar discriminations.[23] Like the Burakumins, the *Baekjeong* were an "Untouchable" outcaste group of Korea.[24] The condition of the *Baekjeong* in pre-colonial Korean society was quite similar to the Dalits under the rule of the *Peshwas*. They were seen as a contemptible and polluted group of people that others feared and avoided meeting. If they saw *Yangban* (the higher caste), even their children, along the road they were expected to bow and pay respect. Like Dalits they too began their resistance movement beginning in the late 19th and early 20th centuries, firstly aimed at reform and later a more radical change. The system, however, disappeared in the turbulence the Korean society underwent.[25]

Some people, noting such instances of stratifications and discriminatory practices, tend to liken these societies with that of India. They forget the fact that not just these but all the societies sometime in the past had some kind of stratification and discriminatory practices. However, as they evolved, most of them discarded these practices depending on the rate of development, and the residue of the old structure and practices only survived in a few. In a superficial way, they may seem like India's caste system but they are essentially different. They feature in a small section of the society and apply to a minority as in the case of the *Barakumin* and are not a pervasive feature like the Indian caste system. The Indian caste system is not just based on stratification but is a continuum of infinite castes strung loosely within the four-fold varna framework which is vested with divine sanction. Although classically not a part, but it includes and as its distinguishing aspect, the class the people who are completely segregated as Untouchables, but themselves divided into numerous castes mirroring the hierarchy of the classical structure. Therefore, the Indian caste system becomes a gigantic, complex, and intricately evolved continuum of simultaneously loose and rigid hierarchy—rigid in the macro framework of varna and loose within it—pervasively practised over a vast geographical area as the life-world of the people. Thus, it differs from others both in qualitative as well quantitative terms.

Caste and Slavery

Another system that is often compared with the Indian caste system, particularly at the level of its outcastes, is the institution of slavery, commonly found in the old world. There is no doubt that slavery was hugely oppressive and violated human rights, but it may still not compare well with the caste oppression of the Dalits in India.

Slavery refers to the practice of owning people as property, and forcing them to work without compensation. While the practice of slavery evokes intense disgust in modern times, slavery was an accepted institution in the old world. Slavery was practised in Ancient Mesopotamia, Egypt, Greece, Israel, Persia, Rome, and Byzantium, as well as among the Chinese, Mayans, Aztecs, Indians and a number of Africans, Polynesians and Melanesians.[26] The invention of agriculture 10,000 years ago led to surplus production and engendered conflicts among people to control it. The birth of the state as a control apparatus was the byproduct of this process. Those who succeeded in overpowering others in this conflict had surplus with which they could make other people work for them. This was the rudimentary form of slavery. The power dynamics that set into motion necessitated ever increasing power to sustain it. Since land was the main biotic source of surplus in those times and hence a source of power, people set out to conquer lands from other people. The vanquished people in such wars became the big source of slaves for the victors to till these lands and, thus, came into being the institution of slavery. The other sources were the fugitive, delinquents, and outlaws from within the society. The offspring of these enslaved people became slaves themselves and provided a vast workforce.[27]

While this was the approximate origin of slavery anywhere, in each country it appears to have developed specific features depending upon the physical endowments of those countries. Scholars have studied many of these civilizations in order to understand the specificities of slavery in them with varying degree of success. For instance, in Mesopotamia, they significantly found that although slaves under the code had the status of property or merchandize (meaning they could be traded), they had rights. Slaves were permitted to own property, conduct business, and even marry free women.[28] Manumission was allowed through both self-purchase or adoption by the owner. They did not find any racial component to Egyptian and Roman slavery. Many of the slaves in Egypt were Israelite Jews and neighbouring African blacks while those in Rome t were drawn from blonde, blue-eyed Anglo-Saxons from Britannia or Blacks from Sahara as well as every other racial type including those of Italian stock.[29]

Although, there was a notion of slaves being inferior in most civilizations, generally speaking, the ancient world does not seem to have had racial association with inferiority.[30] There are even references from the past which suggest that slaves were indistinguishable from other people.[31] For instance, although the Romans felt the need to distinguish them with distinctive appearance for control purposes, they could not do so for the fear that this identity might induce unity among slaves and inspire them to revolt.[32] Roman history is still littered with slave rebellions, particularly in the 1st and 2nd centuries BC, in some of which slaves managed collectively to free themselves from their masters.[33] There are references to slavery in India in literary sources during the 6th century BC to the beginning of the Christian era. Thereafter the references disappear indicating that it might have been replaced by a more intricate and efficient caste system. Again, the reference to slavery surfaces during the Islamic period.[34] Generally, when the Muslims arrived as per their customs they would have imported African slaves to India. There is no further information on Indian slavery beyond the bonded labour system, which still prevails in India. It can be clearly seen as an outgrowth of the caste system, as most bonded labourers belong to the Dalit communities.[35] A report by the Anti-Slavery International in 2008 revealed that Dalit bonded labourers are employed to carry out the most physically straining and menial types of work in industries such as silk farms, rice mills, salt pans, fisheries, quarries and mines, tea and spice farming, brick-kilns, textile industry, and domestic work.[36]

In any case, the reference to slavery in its comparison with the caste system is of a general nature, as discussed above. It shows that although slaves were treated as property or merchandize, they could themselves own property, conduct business, marry free women, buy their freedom from their legal owners, and even purchase other slaves or hire free individuals to work in their own households.[37] Also, while they were treated as inferior in the society, there was no racial stigma associated with their status. The European slave was relatively undifferentiated, constituting thereby a single class. In the Indian caste system, however, since the direct producers were split up into different castes and *jatis*, the division remained deeply hierarchical. Most importantly, slavery did not rob them of their consciousness of their human selves, which occasionally erupted into revolts. While such revolts are found aplenty in the history of slavery, there is not a single comparable instance in the long history of the caste system in India. Although castes also did not have racial association, in the microcosm of villages that they operated, everybody's caste was known. Even in the modern urban setting, which provides a huge space for anonymity, Dalits can barely hide their castes. As in the case of slavery, the caste system also granted caste-specific rights to people; the uppermost caste having all of them and the lowest ones without any. Unlike a slave, who could set himself free, a caste man could never escape his destiny. Moreover, caste consciousness, unlike consciousness of a slave that impels him to rebel against slavery, further enslaves a person into his caste. In slavery, there is an intrinsic hope of transcending the system, whereas in the caste system one does not have any such hope.

Dr. Ambedkar himself elaborately compared the situation of slaves in classical Rome and in Europe and the Americas with that of the Untouchables in India and established that untouchability was much worse than slavery. For instance, to cite one of the passages from his voluminous exposition on this subject:

> ...there are differences between untouchability and slavery, which makes untouchability a worse type of an un-free social order. Slavery was never obligatory. But untouchability is obligatory. A person is *permitted* to hold another as his slave. There is no compulsion on him if he does not want to. But an Untouchable has no option. Once he is born an Untouchable, he is subject to all the disabilities of an Untouchable. The law of slavery permitted emancipation. 'Once a slave always a slave', was not the fate of slaves. In untouchability there is no escape. 'Once an Untouchable always an Untouchable!' The other difference is that untouchability is an indirect and, therefore, the worst form of slavery. The deprivation of a man's freedom by an open and direct way is a preferable form of enslavement. It makes the slave conscious of his enslavement and to become conscious of slavery is the first and most important step in the battle for freedom. But if a man is deprived of his liberty indirectly he has no consciousness of his enslavement. Untouchability is an indirect form of slavery. To tell an Untouchable 'you are free, you are a citizen, you have all the rights of a citizen', and to tighten the rope in such a way as to leave him no opportunity to realize the ideal is a cruel deception.

> It is enslavement without making the Untouchables conscious of their enslavement. It is slavery though it is untouchability. It is real though it is indirect. It is enduring because it is unconscious. Of the two orders, untouchability is beyond doubt the worse.[38]

The worst feature of the caste system vis-à-vis slavery is the opposite consciousness they produce and also their processes of production. While caste consciousness strengthens the caste system, slave consciousness resists the system of slavery. Dr. Ambedkar once said, "Tell a slave, he is a slave and he will rise in revolt." This was not possible with Untouchables, who willingly endured their untouchability for centuries. Untouchability induced a sense of self-deprecation in Untouchables, and this killed their spirit of revolt. The process of producing this consciousness basically differs because of the differential structures of the two systems. In slavery, the system has two dominant parts in contradiction: slaves and masters. The structure of the caste system depicts a continuum that obviates the neat division between the oppressor and the oppressed. The contradiction is pushed down to the local levels, not for elimination of the oppression but for becoming an oppressor. The castes contend within their locale with the castes which suffer similar oppression as them, for superiority. This eliminates the possibility of any rebellion against the system as a whole.

Racism and Casteism

Beyond slavery, the caste system gets compared with racism practised in the Western world, particularly in the United States in respect to the Blacks. The Blacks also faced discrimination and humiliation from the white majority and had to wage a very long battle for securing their civil rights. Provoked by the continuing discrimination and police oppression, a section of their youth had taken to a militant path in the 1960s and formed a Black Panther party, an African-American revolutionary left-wing organization working for the self-defence for Black people.[39] The similarity between their struggles is perceived and emulated by none other than the Dalit youth in the form of Dalit Panthers in 1972.[40] While in some sense, the racial oppression appears severer than caste oppression, simply because a Black man cannot escape his physical identity, whereas a lower caste person can easily do that, there is more to the caste oppression than meets the eye. Like the visibility of race, the racial oppression is also visible; the caste oppression is deep drawn, subtle and, therefore, far more vicious.

On the experiential plane caste discrimination is quite like racial discrimination and, hence, there is a vocal tendency among Dalit activists to treat caste as race. The first loud representation of it was heard in the 2001 World Conference against Racism (WCAR) in Durban. Another trend is the *Mulnivasi* movement launched by a section of Dalits which racially segregates all the lower castes as the indigenous people and the upper castes as outsiders. These people tacitly take a cue from Mahatma Phule who professed that *arya bhat* Brahmans were a foreign element who installed themselves as the rulers by attacking the dasyus, the original inhabitants of India, who were the *shudras* and *atishudras* and reduced them to subservience. There is an obvious strategic value in the racial conception of caste but there should not be much dispute that castes were not races. Dr. Ambedkar had rejected the idea that caste was race. He wrote that "The Brahman of Punjab is racially of the same stock as the Chamar of Punjab. The caste system does not demarcate racial division. The caste system is a social division of people of the same race."[41] Actually, writing at another level he refutes the theory of racial purity proffered by some people in support of castes:

> Some have dug a biological trench in defence of the Caste System. It is said that the object of Caste was to preserve purity of race and purity of blood. Now ethnologists are of the opinion that men of pure race exist nowhere and that there has been a mixture of all races in all parts of the world. Especially is this the case with the people of India." Mr. D.R. Bhandarkar in his paper on *Foreign Elements in the Hindu Population* has stated that "There is hardly a class, or Caste in India which has not a foreign strain in it.[42]

Many scholars also dispute the claim that casteism is akin to racism. Sociologist M.N. Srinivas has debated the question of rigidity in caste[43], whereas others have applied theoretical models to explain mobility and flexibility in the caste system in India.[44] According to these scholars, groups of lower-caste individuals could seek to elevate the status of their caste by attempting to emulate the practices of higher castes; the oppressed race does not have such an option. Indeed, there are many differences between race and caste. Race relations are physical, whereas caste relations are cultural. As Cox (1945) observed, "As distinguished from a bipartite interracial adjustment, the caste system is ancient, provincial, culturally oriented, hierarchical in structure, status conscious, non-conflictive, non-pathological, occupationally limited, lacking in aspiration and progressiveness, hypergamous, endogamous and static."[45] There are fundamental differences in the ways in which race and caste relations are patterned, which produces a differential impact on society. Cox further observes:

> The structures of race and of caste relationship are incommensurable. Caste has reference to the internal social order of a society; race suggests a whole people, wherever found about the globe. A people in actual world dispersion will not conceive of themselves as members of a caste. While there may be rivalry for position among castes, between races in opposition there will be a struggle for power. Racial antagonism tends to divide the society vertically; the caste system tends to stratify it into a status hierarchy. ... The mobility which racial antagonism abhors is movement across a colour fence which surrounds each race regardless of the social position of the individual. The mobility which the caste system limits is movement from one corporate group into another within an assimilated society.[46]

Race sentiment and interest tend to be universal; while caste sentiment and interest tend to be circumscribed and localized. Unlike caste in India, the Blacks in America have been seeking to increase their participation and integration in the dominant culture. The absence of such striving is an inseparable feature of the caste system.[47] There is a sense of inferiority associated with the black race but the important thing is that it does not have any religious sanction as castes claim. The Blacks in America in a short time could dispel the notion of inferiority in them firstly with glorious resistance to Jim Crow legislations and later movements like the Garvey movement, by far the largest mass movement of Black Americans of the 1920s that challenged entrenched ideas of white supremacy and Black inferiority; spread the ideas that Black people, Black culture, Black history, and Africa were noble and Black people had created great civilizations that rivalled Western civilization on every front; the Harlem Renaissance which gave birth to their confident expression in the form of Black literature, music, drama and so on, and the movements like 'Black is Beautiful' in the 1960s that demolished the remnant traces of inferiority of 'black being ugly and low' and made the Blacks take pride in being Black. Unlike the Dalits in India, the Blacks no more carry any baggage of social disapproval. Therefore, they tend to strive for more and more participation in mainstream culture. It is relatively difficult for Dalits to shake off their baggage of inferiority in the social environment of pervasive caste prejudices. Cox again has a perceptive observation to make on this aspect of Black enterprise:

> If, for instance, the Negro-white relationship were a caste relationship, Negroes would not be aspiring towards the social position occupied by whites; their concern, rather, would be almost entirely with the development of a socially sufficient internal organization. It is this centrifugal cultural drive among Negroes which produces fear and antagonism among the white ruling class. Indeed, the most potent weapon of racial aggression—segregation—has been devised to inhibit it. Thus, the scheme of race relationship in America centres on attempts of Negroes to reach new levels of participation and opposition to these attempts by whites.[48]

Battle against the Caste System

The caste system had evolved into a formidable system of stratification wherein innumerable castes while bearing a definitive sense of varna hierarchy through their affiliation to one of the varnas, were strung in a fluid hierarchy within their varna. As a result, every caste essentially remained in contention for higher status with the caste in its vicinity. There were numerous such contentions at the micro level among the castes which not only left the macro structure unchallenged but also internalized its hierarchy and lent it legitimacy. Another operative feature of the caste system was that castes were held together in an interdependent relationship that ensured subsistence of all people albeit corresponding to their caste status. The system provided them with a sense of security; the only condition being the people abided by their caste dharma. Every caste had its psychological comfort or discomfort and differential benefits or loss. The exploitation and oppression was ingrained in the system but was so diffused that it was impossible to discern who precisely was the exploiter and who was the exploited. Even the Brahman varna, which was ensconced at the top of the varna hierarchy, had various Brahman subcastes which contended for higher status among themselves. And the situation was no different with the Untouchables, who even being *avarnas* mirrored the same contention. The division between the *dwija* castes, who did not live by the sweat of their brows and the Shudras and the Untouchables who were to slog in service to them, which could only be noted in the modern times, was not viable as it still is not. The structure did not permit emergence of any such broad division so as to directly challenge the caste system.

Such was the formidable system against which Mahad symbolized the rebellion of the lowest of the low. Unless this struggle is seen in the historical perspective of the caste system its importance may not be fully realized. The following chapter is devoted to build this perspective. It provides a synoptic view of the caste system right from its origin to the modern times. Although direct combat against the caste system as we may imagine in modern times did not happen, the resistance to it expectedly ran concurrent in varied forms all through its history of over two millenniums. The struggles against the caste system, mostly proxied by the rise against Brahmanism, began germinating in colonial times as a result of the congenial environment of the colonial regime and the economic upliftment of a section of urban Dalits with the help of education and economic opportunities. These struggles being immediate predecessors were also of vital importance for understanding

Mahad. The chapter thus provides a complete run up to the very eve of the Mahad struggle.

NOTES AND REFERENCES

1. Ayyan-Kali (biography). Available at http://www.ambedkar.org/books/AYYAN-KALI.htm. [Last accessed on 25 April 2015].
2. None other than K.R. Narayanan was usually referred to as Dalit President in the media.
3. The struggle for civil rights of the African Americans at the individual and collective levels may arguably be traced back to the 17th century, when they were brought to the Americas as slaves. Some scholars reckon it from the 'separate but equal' judgement in the 'Plessy versus Ferguson' case in 1896 (See Chapter 6). However, their struggles came to be known as the Civil Rights Movement from the Brown vs Board of Education, 1954, Montgomery Bus Boycott (1955-56), passing the Civil Rights Act of 1964, Martin Luther King's assassination and the Poor People's March, to Memphis, 1968.
4. When the struggle for civil rights is spoken about, they begin it from the post-Emergency agitations of people. See, Mohan Ram, Civil Rights Situation in India, in Desai, A.R., *Violations of Democratic Rights in India*, Vol. 2, Popular Prakashan, Mumbai, 1986, pp. 91-95. Also, Aswin K. Roy, Civil Rights Movement and Social Struggle in India, *Economic and Political Weekly*, Vol. XXI, No. 28, 12 July, 1986, pp. 1202-06.
5. Margaret L. Andersen and Howard Francis Taylor, *Sociology: The Essentials*, Thompson Wordsworth, Belmont, 2007, pp. 182, 213.
6. Jon Shepard and Robert W. Greene, *Sociology and You*. McGraw-Hill, Ohio, 2003, p. A–22.
7. Anthony Giddens, *Sociology*, Polity Press, Cambridge, 2006, p. 299.
8. Louis Dumont, *Homo Hirarchicus: The Caste System and Its Implications*, University of Chicago Press, Chicago, 1980.
9. B.R. Ambedkar, Castes in India: Their Mechanism, Genesis and Development, in Vasant Moon (Comp.), *Dr. Babasaheb Ambedkar: Writings and Speeches*, Vol. 1, Education Department, Government of Maharashtra, Mumbai, 1979, p. 15.
10. Louis Dumont, op. cit., p. 249.
11. M.N. Srinivas, *Religion and Society among the Coorgs of South India*, Oxford, 1952, p. 28.
12. G.S. Ghurye, *Caste and Race in India*, Popular Prakashan, Bombay, p. 159.

13. Pradip Kumar Bose, A Narrative of Caste: Ghurye on Caste and Race in India, in A.R. Momin (ed.), *The Legacy of G.S. Ghurye: A Centennial Festschrift*, Popular Prakashan, Bombay, 1996, p. 65.
14. It was brought to the fore in a novel by Chinua Achebe, *No Longer at Ease*, East African Educational Publishers Ltd., Nairobi, 1966. Also downloadable free from many sites such as *kickass.to/no-longer-at-ease-pdf-pld991-t7230365.htmlý*. [Last Accessed on 21 January 2014].
15. Victor Dike, Osu *Caste System Discrimination in Igbo Land: Impact On Igbo Culture and Civilization*, Iuniverse Inc., New York, 2007.
16. Barbara G. Hoffman, *Griots at War: Conflict, Conciliation, and Caste in Mande*, Indiana University Press, 2000, p. 280.
17. Ibid.
18. See http://wolofresources.org/newwolof.htm. [Last accessed on 21 January 2014]
19. Richard M. Juang, and Noelle Morrissette (eds.), *Africa and the Americas: Culture, Politics and History*, Vol. 1, ABC-Clio, Santa Barbara, 2008, p. 492.
20. Aneesa Kassam and Ali Balla Bashuna, Marginalisation of the Waata Oromo Hunter-Gatherers of Kenya: Insider and Outsider Perspectives, *Africa: Journal of the International African Institute*, Vol. 74, No. 2 (2004), pp. 194-216.
21. In early 2012, for instance, dozens had died in clashes between the Gabra and Borana communities in Moyale, in northern Kenya and some 40,000 Kenyans were displaced into Ethiopia following inter-ethnic fighting. See, Inter-ethnic fighting displaces 40,000 in Kenya, Africa Daily, http://www.africadaily.net/reports/ Inter-ethnic_fighting_displaces_40000_in_Kenya_aid_ groups_999.html [Last Accessed on 21 January 2014]
22. Abadjian, Marguerite, Caste In Yemen, http://www.counter currents.org/hr-marguerite250404.htm. [Last Accessed on 21 January 2015]
23. Nobuo Shimahara, Toward the Equality of a Japanese Minority: The Case of Burakumin, *Comparative Education*, Vol. 20, No. 3 (1984), pp. 339-353; Buraku Liberation League. *Current Conditions of Buraku and Distinguishing Features of Buraku Discrimination in Japan*, May 2002. 18 November 2005, http://blhrri.org/kokusai/ un/un_0007-2.htm. [Last Accessed on 21 January 2014]
24. *Korean Caste System: Baekjeong, Yangban, Bone Rank System, Chungin, Nobi, Hopae, Cheonmin, Sangmin*, General Books LLC, 2010.
25. Kim, Joong-Seop, 1999. In Search of Human Rights: The Paekchong Movement in Colonial Korea, in *Colonial Modernity in Korea* edited

by Gi-Wook Shin and Michael Robinson, Harvard University Asia Center, Cambridge, London, pp. 311–335.

26. Leonie Acher, *Slavery and Other Forms of Unfree Labour*, Routledge, London, 1988; Thom Hartmann, *The Last Hours of Ancient Sunlight*, Hodder & Stoughton, London, 1999.
27. Keith Bradley and Paul Cartledge (eds.), *The Cambridge World History of Slavery*, Vol. 1: *The Ancient Mediterranean World*, Cambridge University Press, 2011.
28. Janius P. Rodriguez, *The Historical Encyclopedia of World Slavery*, Vol. 1 and 7, ABC-CLIO, Santa Barbara, 1979, p. 67; Shilpa Mehta Jones, *Life in Ancient Mesopotamia*, Crabtree Publishing, Saint Catharines, 2004, p. 12.
29. Stratification. http://social.jrank.org/pages/2978/ stratification.html. [Last Accessed on August 16, 2010]
30. As one Trinidadian historian of slavery Eric Williams puts it: Slavery was not born of racism: rather, racism was the consequence of slavery, in Eric Williams, *Capitalism and Slavery*, Perigee Books, New York, 1980, p. 7. Also, one should note that while slavery existed as an economic system for thousands of years before the conquest of America, racism as we understand it today did not exist.
31. There was no visible marker to identify a slave. For instance, C.L.R. James writes, "Historically it is pretty well proved now that the ancient Greeks and Romans knew nothing about race. They had another standard—civilized and barbarian—and you could have white skin and be a barbarian and you could be black and civilized." C.L.R. James quoted in Pete Alexander, *Racism, Resistance and Revolution*, Bookmarks: London, 1987, p. 5.
32. William Blair writes, "A passage in Seneca, which alludes to a proposal once made, to distinguish slaves by a peculiar dress but abandoned, from the danger if showing the numbers of the free, conveys, necessarily an impression, that numerical excess was much on the side of slaves. William Blair, *An Inquiry into the State of Slavery Amongst the Romans: from the Earliest Period till the Establishment of the Lombards in Italy*, Native American Books Distributor, New York, 2007, p. 274.
33. The most famous rebellion of thousands of slaves in central Italy was led by the gladiator Spartacus in 73-71 BC. He had formed an army that defeated several Roman legions, and at one point threatened Rome itself. There were many such large-scale rebellions on the island of Sicily. Keith Bradley, Resisting Slavery in Ancient Rome, in Keith Bradley and Paul Cartledge (eds.), *The*

Cambridge World History of Slavery, Volume 1, op. cit.; Richard Hart documents the rebellions of Black slaves to end their slavery. Richard Hart, *Slaves Who Abolished Slavery: Blacks in Rebellion*, University of West Indies Press, Jamaica, 1985, pp. ix-xii.

34. There are many studies such as K.S. Lal, *Muslim Slave System in Medieval India*, New Delhi, 1994; Salim Kidwai, Sultans, Eunuchs and Domestics: New Forms of Bondage in Medieval India, in Utsa Patnaik and Manjari Dingwaney (eds.), *Chains of Servitude: Bondage and Slavery in India*, Madras, 1985; Anal Kumar Chattopadhyay, *Slavery in India*, Calcutta, 1959; Indrani Chatterjee, *Gender, Slavery and Law in Colonial India*, New Delhi, 1999; Utsa Patnaik and Manjari Dingwaney (eds.), *Chains of Servitude: Bondage and Slavery in India*, Sangam Books, Madras, 1985, on slavery in India under the Islamic period.
35. The Denmark-based International Dalit Solidarity Network cites cases of caste-based slavery in all the countries of the Indian subcontinent. See for example the section of Caste-Based Slavery on their web site: http://idsn.org/caste-discrimination/key-issues/bonded-labour/india/. [Last accessed on 21 January 2014.]
36. Krishna Prasad Upadhyaya, *Poverty, Discrimination and Slavery: The Reality of Bonded Labour in India, Nepal and Pakistan* by Anti-Slavery International, 2008.
37. The slavery systems in the Ancient world present ample variants but they cohere on the points that the slaves were not totally immobile. They lived like free men among themselves and could buy their freedom from their owners. Regarding the Babylonian slavery Muhammad A. Dandamaev and Vladimir G. Lukonin write, "In Babylonia there was a relatively large number of slaves who had families and owned houses and substanitial moveable property. Slaves could dispose of their own property, relatively freely.... Slaves not only participated in the economic life of the country, but also had their own seals and appeared as witnesses at the conclusion of various business deals by free men or slaves. In legal life slaves could act as free men and be tried in court among themselves... Slaves in Babylonia sometimes even purchased other slaves or hired free individuals to work in their own households." Muhammad A. Dandamaev and Vladimir G. Lukonin, *The Culture and Social Institutions of Ancient Iran*, Cambridge University Press, Cambridge, 1989, p. 154. A plethora of literature on the slavery in America also testifies to these facts. Although varing in degree depending upon where they lived, in the South or North, the slaves owned land, homes, businesses, and paid taxes. They could

become free by paying off their owners. Such free Blacks themselves owned slaves. There were examples of free Blacks owning slave holding plantations in Louisiana, Virginia, and South Carolina. See for instance "Free Blacks in the Antebellum Period" http://memory.loc.gov/ ammem/aaohtml/aopart2.html. [Last accessed on 21 January 2014].

38. B.R. Ambedkar, Untouchables or the Children of India's Ghetto, in Vasant Moon (ed.), *Dr. Babasaheb Ambedkar: Writings and Speeches*, Vol. 5, Government of Maharashtra, Mumbai, 1989, p. 15.
39. Founded in Oakland, California, by Bobby Seale and Huey P. Newton on 15 October, 1966, the Black Panthers initially set forth a doctrine calling primarily for the protection of African American neighbourhoods from police brutality. Their objectives and philosophy expanded and evolved rapidly to espouse socialist and communist (largely Maoist) doctrines.
40. In the wake of increasing atrocities on Dalits in Maharashtra and dejected by the splits and inaction of the Republican Party of India, the Dalit youth of Mumbai, following the militant Black Panthers in the USA, founded Dalit Panthers in 1972. Quite like Black Panthers, they also reflected the left radical orientation in their Manifesto, which soon however became the cause of their decimation. See Lata Murugkar, *Dalit Panther Movement in Maharashtra: A Sociological Appraisal*, Sangam Books, London, 1991.
41. B.R. Ambedkar, The Annihilation of Caste, in Vasant Moon (Comp.), *Dr. Babasaheb Ambedkar: Writings and Speeches*, Vol. 1, Education Department, Government of Maharashtra, Mumbai, 1979, p. 49.
42. Ibid., p. 48.
43. M.N. Srinivas, *Religion and Society Among the Coorgs of South India*, Oxford, 1952, p. 32; *Caste in Modern India and Other Essays*, Media Promoters & Publishers Pvt. Ltd., Bombay; First Published, 1962, 11th Reprint, 1994, p. 48.
44. James Silverberg, "Social Mobility in the Caste System in India: An Interdisciplinary Symposium", *The American Journal of Sociology* 75 (3): November 1969, 443–444.
45. Oliver C. Cox, Race and Caste: A Distinction, *The American Journal of Sociology*, Vol. 50, No. 5 (March 1945) pp. 360-368.
46. Ibid.
47. Ibid., p. 363
48. Oliver C. Cox, op. cit., p. 366.

2

The Run-Up to Mahad

The revolution is not an apple that falls when it is ripe. You have to make it fall.

–Ernesto Che Guevara

Any historical event inspires awe and starts appearing unreal if not seen in its evolutionary context and historical perspective. Mahad was not an ordinary event; it embodied epochal consequences. Though not widely known outside Dalit circles, it may be recognized as one of the first struggles for civil rights in modern times with the only respectable exception of the struggle of the African Americans.[1] Mahad is surely a marker of the beginning of the independent Dalit movement, permanently associated with Babasaheb Ambedkar and, hence, occupies emotional space in the Dalit universe. With its historic significance and emotional value to Dalits it has become a part of folklore with the associated embellishments of imagery. Mahad has a deep imprint not only on the psyche of Dalits but also on the entire ethos of the Dalit movement. Therefore, it becomes especially important to see Mahad within its historical context in order to understand its making, its accomplishment, and its significance to the ongoing struggles of the Dalits. The context for Mahad is mainly built up by the caste system and by the changes it underwent through history. The chapter, therefore, seeks to trace the journey of castes from its birth through some important nodes. The informed readers are facilitated by the modular structure of the chapter to skip the parts they think they already know enough about.

The Caste Code

The origins of the caste system are trapped in the interstices of myth and history. The mythologized history of ancient India does not let us know precisely how this system came into existence, and how it evolved surviving momentous political and religio-cultural upheavals through centuries. Despite huge scholarly interests in its study, there are no definitive conclusions on these aspects.[2] What is evident is that it continues to be a potent and pervasive socio-cultural force that impacts people according to their placement in social hierarchy, not only in India but in the entire subcontinent of South Asia. While there have been changes in the classical caste configuration, the most adversely impacted people continue to be Dalits, the ex-Untouchables who number over one-sixth of the total population.

The source of the caste code is contained in the amorphous ideology of Brahmanism and is typically traced to the *Purusha Sukta* of the Tenth Mandala of the *Rig Veda,* regarded as the earliest Hindu text. A hymn in it describes the *varnas* as originating from the limbs of the *virat purush*: Brahman from the mouth, Kshatriya from the arms, Vaishya from the thighs, and Shudra from the feet.[3] However, Phule, Walangkar and Ambedkar argued that the *Purusha Sukta* was a recent addition to the Rig Veda, since the Rig Veda made no mention of the fourth, degraded varna, the Shudras.[4] While social stratification was not uncommon across the world in ancient times, what was unique about the varna system was that it was attributed to a religious text, claimed to be of divine origination. How these four broad varna types evolved into innumerable castes (*jatis*) and entrenched notions of internal hierarchy is a bigger mystery. Moreover, this code did not allude to the existence of the fifth category—the *avarna* or *panchamas*, people without varna or outside the four-fold varna system, the Untouchables. Nor do we find any textual reference to or a cogent explanation for how this category evolved later. 'Three classes—brahman, kshatriya and vaisya—are twice-born; the fourth, has a single birth and there is no fifth varna.[6] The *Arthshastra,* has reference to outcastes (chandala, antavasayins) beyond the four varnas and to graded penalties according to the caste of a person.[7]

The Laws of Manu or the *Manusmruti* which scholars say was compiled and composed between 2nd century BCE and 3rd century CE, during a period of instability that resulted after the breakdown of the Maurya (321 BCE–185 CE) and Shunga (183–73 BCE) empires, further elaborates and rigidifies this code. It reiterates the Purusha Sukta theory of the origin of the four varnas, and reinforces their divine origin. It simultaneously gives it worldly justification explaining that it was "for the sake of the prosperity of the worlds"[8]; "in order to protect this universe", separate (duties and) occupations were assigned to the varnas.[9]

The *Manusmruti* renders the implicit hierarchy of the *Purusha Sukta* explicit and justifies by saying 'since the Brahman sprang from the (virat purusha's, i.e., god's) mouth, he was the first-born, possessed the *Veda*, and hence became by right "the lord of this whole creation."[10] To the Shudra, at the bottom, the god prescribed 'one occupation', i.e., to serve meekly the other three varnas.[11] A shudra, whether bought or un-bought, was compelled to do servile work as he was created by god to be the slave of Brahmans.[12] The Rig Veda period was characterized by a predominantly pastoral semi-sedentary economy, some division of labour but by no means hereditary specialization of functions and absence of any form of endogamy and fourfold *varna* system. Though the Vaishya and Shudra appear along with the Brahmana and the *Rajanya* (Kshatriya) in the *Purusha Sukta* in the Tenth Mandala, which belongs to the latest stratum of *Rig Veda* and presumably synchronizes with the later Vedic texts, there is absolutely no mention of the practice of untouchability in this text.[13]

While, the *Manusmruti* adheres to this *Purusha Sukta* formation of the four-fold varnas as stated above, in the section on mixed classes it talks about the origin of the *dasyus* (slaves) and others who are outside this four-fold structure. It is here that for the first time the *Manusmruti* alludes to the existence of a people beyond the four-fold varna system as *dasyus*, the tribes which were not included in the *varna* system, irrespective of whether they spoke the language of the *mlechchhas* (barbarians) or that of the Aryans.[14] Among those outside the system were groups produced by illicit union of the people of different *varnas*, who were mandated to "subsist by occupations reprehended by the twice-born, the three upper varnas".[15] Among these occupations were catching and killing of creatures living in holes, working in leather,[16] carrying out the corpses of persons without any kith or kin,[17] and executing criminals.[18]

These 'impure' groups were to live in remote, wild areas or near burial grounds.[19] They would wear garments of the dead, they would eat food in broken utensils, they would wear ornaments made of black iron, and they would be always wandering from place to place.[20] To have intercourse with them would be an irreligious act. They would have social transactions only among themselves, and marry only with their equals.[21] They would eat food given by others in a broken dish; they would not walk about in villages and in towns in night.[22] By CE 300, as Eleanor Zelliot observes, specific caste groups (*jati*) of 'Untouchables' had come into existence.[23] Although, the *Manusmruti* came to take note of them, the system continued to be referred to as *chaturvarna* or four-fold system insinuating the unworthiness of them to be called a varna. They remained *avarna* (sans varna), outside the formal social structure that reflected in their physical segregation in villages and total exclusion from civic transactions.

The *Manusmriti* coded supremacy of the Brahman varna, prescribing dos and don'ts for all other varnas and created a dump of people as Untouchables to which all defaulters could be relegated. The ideology of the *shrutis* (Vedas) and *smritis* (Vedic scripture) that informed this social order was called Brahmanism. To what extent these codes were observed over centuries is the moot question. But if we are to base our judgment on the basis of certain practices extant as late as the 19th century, it appears that latter-day societies—sometimes located far from Greater Punjab and the Indo-Gangetic plains, where the Vedas, *Manusmruti* and ideology of caste was born—even exceeded the excesses prescribed in the *Manusmruti*. For example, in places like Tamil Nadu and Kerala in the southern-most part of India and in Pune in the west, under the Peshwas, certain Untouchable castes were even considered unapproachable and even unseeable—such was the force of the social imperialism of Brahmanism.

Anti-Casteism in the Distant Past

Pervasive though, ideological influence of the caste system had not gone unquestioned.[24] The earliest resistance to castes can be traced to the native Shramana[25] or renunciate ascetic traditions from the middle of the first millennium BCE[26] in India that dated back at least to the advent of Brahmans, if not earlier. The Shramanas had a radical view of life and society, nearly opposite to that of Brahmanism, which they propagated among people wandering across the land. Their practice was typically of three kinds: austerities, meditation, and the production and dissemination of knowledge, both spiritual and temporal. Several strands of the Shramana movement[27] existed. Although the various constituent strands of this movement did not cohere into a single ideological stream, they all generally rejected a supreme god, such as Brahma, or any other form of a creator and stood for equality of all humans.[28] Much of their influence, it appears, was confined to the ideological sphere and did not as much impact the mundane life of people in society. These ideologies in the form of Buddhism (and also Jainism) gained royal (state) support, got institutionalized as religions and remained the dominant ideologies of the subcontinent for almost a millennium, but they, contrary to the commonplace notion, did nothing to root out the poison of caste from the society. They remained content with creating a no-caste island of their monastic order. Their anti-casteism remained a passive ideology and did not have much impact on society.

Buddhism, no doubt contributed profound insight to the world in terms of its tenets of *dukkha*, *anitya*, *anatma*, and *pratitsamutpada* which in my opinion creates a sustainability paradigm of the entire sentient world in the philosophical realm.[29] But in practice, Buddha avoided confronting the odds on ground and rather conducted himself in a conciliatory manner. Some critical scholars, therefore, dispute certain basic attributes of Buddhism such as atheism and anti-casteism. For example, Weber (2001) disputes Buddha's atheism because he finds "it was not the gods, Brahmans and people belonging to a different creed that harassed him. Only his own religious friends, his co-religious, Shramanas did it" and Weber reaches a very damaging conclusion: "early Buddhism did not worship the gods of the lower castes or the Dalits but the gods of the higher castes. The gods of the lower caste people like for example Siva, were always a thorn in their flesh to them and to the non-Buddhist high castes."[30] Similarly, he questions Buddhism's anti-caste credentials that beyond opening its *Sangha* to the lower castes, it did nothing to confront the caste hierarchy. He cites Hans Wolfgang Schumann who had statistically proven that almost all of Buddha's disciples were high caste people and that the Brahmans comprised the majority of the *Sangha*.[31] A more balanced opinion comes from Randall who writes,

> Certainly, Buddhism was a challenge to the traditional brahman practices, attacking its rituals and especially its sacrifices by the doctrine of ahimsa, non-harming. But Buddhism should be seen as more of a reform movement within the milieu of the educated religious people - who were mostly Brahmans - rather than a rival movement from outside. Thus, although the Buddha himself was a kshatriya the largest number of monks in the early movement were of Brahman origin. In principle, the Sangha was open to any caste; and since it was outside the ordinary world, caste had no place in it. Nevertheless, virtually all monks were recruited from the upper two classes. The biggest source of lay support, however, the ordinary donor of alms, were the landowning farmers.[32]

Castes co-existed with the rise of both Jainism and Buddhism. Therefore both of these religions could be easily overpowered by the resurgent Brahmanism after the advent of Adi Shankara in 788 AD. If their ideologies were entrenched in the societal structure, they would not have been erased like a pencil impression from the social slate.[33] If these ideologies had real sway over the society, the life-world of people, it is unlikely that the society would reassume hierarchical caste stratification.

The radical views of Buddha remained mutedly confined to the ideological sphere. Buddhism did impart rationalistic outlook to the society and gave fillip to the production of scientific knowledge, to the extent that most scientific discoveries and inventions that are attributed to India have happened during the period of its dominance. However, the life-world of common people reflected little influence of this sphere. With enrichment of monasteries, with large endowments coming from kings and rich people, some amount of degeneration had also set in the monastic life, which further thinned the interface between monks and the larger society. Between 400 and 700 AD Chinese pilgrims visiting India had noticed a decline in the Buddhist community and the beginning of the process of incorporation of relevant Buddhist thoughts by Hinduism. Among these pilgrim-travellers was Faxian (also spelt as Fa-Hien), who left China in 399 AD, crossed the Gobi Desert, visited various holy places in India, and returned to China with numerous Buddhist scriptures and statues.

The most famous of the Chinese travellers, however, was the 7th century monk Xuanzang. When he arrived in north-western India, he found 'millions of monasteries' reduced to ruins by the Hunas, a nomadic Central Asian people. By the 8th century, Buddhist establishment became so engrossed with the cerebral activity, producing intricate philosophies that had little to do with the mundane life of the people or the radical ideological identity of Buddhism. It is this development which paved the way for Shankara's coup and the eventual downfall of Buddhism. With the collapse of the Pala dynasty in the 12th century, Indian Buddhism suffered yet another setback, from which it did not recover. Although small pockets of influence remained, the Buddhist presence in India became negligible.

There is no unanimity among scholars on the factors that contributed to Buddhism's demise in its homeland. As the Chinese pilgrims noted, Buddhism was on decline in many parts of the subcontinent by the 7th and 8th centuries. The decisive blow was, however, cast by Sankara's counter-revolution, which began with an innocuous defeat of Buddhists in a religious debate but culminated into an all-out Brahmanical onslaught on Buddhism. It comprised plunder and destruction of Buddhist viharas, stupas, idols, etc.; converting viharas into temples, mixing Hindu doctrines with Buddhism and Jainism, marginalization and demonization of Buddhists and Jains, and physical extermination of hundreds of monks and laity. While Brahmanism was always engaged in a cold war against Buddhism right since the latter's rise, what enabled this counter-revolution was the inherent weakness of Buddhism. Despite Buddha's advice to the *bhikku*s to be wandering activists devoted to the happiness and welfare of many, Buddhism remained primarily a monastic movement with little contact with the masses. The composition of the Buddhist *Sangha,* with a majority of upper caste people, must have been responsible for this disconnect with the people. It took pride in philosophical pursuits without bothering about the problems faced by the people. Huge endowments from the kings and rich people to monasteries made them further slothful and detached.

Many monasteries employed indentured slaves and paid labourers to care for the monks and to tend the lands they owned. Thus, when it was attacked by its enemies the masses did not show much interest in resistance or later in its revival. On the other hand, Brahmanism employed its intricate stratagem to wipe it out completely. It shrewdly appropriated whatever that appealed to the lower castes from Buddhism to win them over. The final stroke consisted in propagating the myth of Buddha being merely another 'incarnation' (avatar) of the Hindu god Vishnu. Buddha was, thus, effortlessly turned into just another of the countless deities of the Brahmanical pantheon. There is no doubt that Buddhism was ideologically oriented against Brahmanism but to say that it fought against the caste system or for the lower caste people is not true.

Anti-Caste Developments in Medieval Times

The Islamic conquests in the subcontinent took place mainly between the 11th and 17th centuries. Though they had begun in the 7th century, they were sporadic and intermittent and, hence, did not leave a mark. Islam, as such, had entered India much earlier, almost during the Prophet's lifetime, through the Arab traders.[34] With them, and with the later conquerors, came the Sufis, the mystics of Islam, who played a vital role in spreading the new faith.[35] With their liberal spirituality and their preference for the company of the poor, they attracted a multitude of Shudras and *avarnas* to Islam. In concrete terms, Islam stood for an escape from caste tyranny, for it opened to the oppressed the realms of learning and metaphysics, from which Brahmanism excluded them, and offered an alternative framework with which to confront caste. A virtual exodus to Islam resulted with Hinduism losing almost a fifth of its followers.[36] While Islam in India had no reformist intent vis-à-vis Hinduism, its spread in the subcontinent was reflective of a surge of resistance against castes, evidenced by the success of its epoch-altering civilizational model. Islam attracted Untouchables and other low caste people in large numbers because of its egalitarianism. Arnold writes: 'Islam appealed to the people and it derived the great mass of its converts from the poor. It brought in a higher conception of God, and a nobler idea of the brotherhood of man. It offered to the teeming low castes of Bengal, who had sat for ages abject on the outermost pale of Hindu community, free entrance into a new social organization.'[37]

The Moplas of Malabar, where the earliest Muslims landed, and Chitgonians of East Pakistan (now Bangladesh) are the examples of early en masse conversion to Islam. However, the process of proselytization was never on an organized scale. People, mainly placed at the lower rungs of the Hindu society, gradually but willingly adopted Islam, attracted by its democratic structure and fraternal approach. Arnold points to causes for the rapid increase of the Muslim population in the subcontinent. 'The insult and contempt heaped upon the lower castes of Hindus by their co-religionists, and the impossible obstacles placed in the way of any member of these castes desiring to better his condition, show up in striking contrast the benefits of a religious system, which has no outcastes and gives free scope for the indulgence of any ambition...'[38]

Apart from the religio-cultural appeal of Islam to the lower castes, the Muslim rule brought advanced feudal system that systematized land revenue administration, promoted manufacturing guilds and established cities, which provided further avenues to the lower castes to escape the bondage of the village system. In addition to the alien civilizational model that did not have any birth based privileges, the very influx of the lower castes into Islam kept the upper castes away from it. But with stabilization of the Muslim rule, the upper castes were also lured by the possibility of material and political gains and many of them converted to Islam. They introduced the notion of hierarchy in the Muslim society. The ruling class Muslims may have seen the virtue of the hierarchical Hindu social order from the viewpoint of governance. Romila Thapar observed, 'Since caste loyalty was stronger than political loyalty the really significant impact of Islam was upon social structure, and was seen in the creation of new sub-castes and new sects within those castes most permeated with Islamic ideas. ... In spite of its egalitarian philosophy, the influence of Islam did not lead to the disappearance of caste. The fact that Islam in India succumbed to and accepted caste society reduced the social dynamism of Islam.'[39] Muslims also started observing discrimination on the basis of lineage and birth. They were later on, divided into three broad categories, viz. Ashraf, Ajlaf and Arzal. The Muslims who claimed the foreign breeds (Syed, Shaikh, Pathan, etc.) constituted the category of Ashraf. The Atraf or Ajlaf were the Muslims converted from low occupational castes of the Hindus. And the third, Arzals were those Muslims who were Untouchables prior to their conversion to Islam. In actual practice the Ashrafs and Atrafs maintained a social distance with the Arzals and observed many rituals of untouchability. Hence, the problem of exploitation and social discrimination continued to persist.[40] The ulamas, scholars of Islamic jurisprudence, then provided religious legitimacy to castes invoking the concept of kafa'a.[41] This defeated the very purpose for which the majority of low caste people embraced Islam.

The Hindutva brigade developed a theory that the Muslim rule has been responsible for the rigidity in the caste system. One of their websites claims that (and there are scores of them making similar point) 'after the invasion and subsequent rule of Muslims, life became more difficult and castes became more rigid to stop conversion by stealth.'[42] One of their authors elaborates the point:

> When Islamic invasions started from the 9th Century and slowly and steadily the Muslim invaders became the political masters of the Indian subcontinent, the Caste system of the Hindu society became its Defence Mechanism and as a consequence it became more and more rigid. Sociologists all the world over agree that if the Hindu society was saved from total conversion to Islam it was mainly because of the Caste system. Its rigidity successfully prevented penetration by a foreign religion which had a totally different social set-up.[43]

These people justify the caste system as a benign system which existed in the Hindu society until it had to assume rigidity under the threat from the Muslims. They do not explain how at the first instance a small band of Turks or Afghans could invade this country repeatedly over a millennium, not to add to them the earlier and later invasions of the outsiders, if the social structure was so benign and just to its people. The truth was that the caste system provided only a small people to wield weapon to defend the country and left most other people utterly alienated. It is a pity that they do not realize that it is the caste system which was firstly responsible for giving this vast subcontinent its history of slavery. As for the rigidity argument during the Muslim rule, it could be logically turned onto its head. The sheer size of Muslim population should be enough to indicate that there was a mass exodus of people from Hinduism that happened during the Muslim rule. Notwithstanding the proselytizing zeal of the Muslims, this cannot be done with sword. Nowhere in the world has it happened by sheer force. As for India, none other than Swami Vivekananda said that these conversions did not happen by the power of sword and rather were the response of the lower castes to the oppressive condition in the Hindu society. More the caste system became rigid, the more would the people be impelled to exit it.

During the same period, one more wave of anti-caste movement emerged in the form of the Bhakti movement, which originated in the South between the 6th and 10th centuries. While many scholars traced in this movement influence of the Semitic religions like Christianity and Islam which were well established in South by that time, insofar as its emphasis on monotheism; emotional worship; self-surrender; adoration of the teacher; indifference towards rituals and the caste system were noted, it appears to have drawn from diverse sources like Tamil literature and Buddhism as it evolved. The Bhakti movement was not a unified movement but in relation to caste, it reflected, at least in some of its radical strands like Kabir panth, individualistic and anti-corporatist rebellion against caste. It had raised many low caste individuals like Ravidas, Chokhamela to the stature of sainthood and did not distinguish people by caste. Though these individuals broke caste restrictions imposed upon the Dalit communities to become Bhaktas, they could only preach human equality and criticize caste practices. Their influence on the society was limited only to spiritualism and prescribed *moksha* as the path to salvation. The Bhakti mode was not sufficient for the emancipation of the Dalits' socio-economic problems as it searched for emancipation more on a spiritual plane. The most important contribution of the Bhakti movement was in recognizing these problems and thereby instilling hope among the Dalits.[44] Romila Thapar observed, "The lack of vertical mobility in caste society isolated the castes and by the same token isolated thinking within the castes. This made the Bhakti movement politically ineffective during this period."[45]

Later, in the 15th century, when Sikhism, assimilating the lofty ideals of the Bhakti movement and Islam, was born—directly promising the banishment of caste distinctions—Dalits in the Punjab region rushed in to embrace it. However, other than being bestowed with such new appellations as Mazhabi Sikhs and Ravidasis, Sikhism made no substantive difference to their lives. It proved that the ideology or religious tenets are incapable of arresting the material interests of people. The contradiction between the material interests of the erstwhile Jats, who constituted landed gentry and the Untouchables, the landless labourers inevitably revived the old Hindu caste system into Sikhism. Today, there is absolutely no difference between the Hindu and Sikh caste system. Interestingly, Babasaheb Ambedkar, after the declaration of his resolve not to live in Hinduism, had given serious consideration to *en masse* conversion of the Depressed Classes to Sikhism. He must have realized the existence of caste system in Sikhism to discard the idea and to embrace Buddhism after 20 years.

Unintended Colonial Boon

While India's contact with Europe went back to the times of Alexander the Great, who had conquered the North West and set up his satraps in 327-326 BC, albeit for a short time, and the Romans thereafter for a long time as traders, none had established their settlements in the subcontinent. However, from the 15th century onwards the trading expeditions from various European countries like Portugal, Denmark, Netherlands, France, and England became fiercely competitive and wanted to secure their competitive position by creating trading settlements. The catalyst was the lucrative trade in spices from India, which constituted one of the main trading sessions of the world economy. While the Portuguese were the first to have such a settlement at Kollam in Kerala in 1502, eventually the British established their supremacy by directly colonizing over two-thirds of India, leaving small pockets for the Portuguese and French. The British colonial rule, which lasted for more than two centuries, had great impact on the caste system mainly in two ways: One, it brought in western institutional framework of governance with its army, police, rule of law, judiciary, and modern education; and the Second, through capitalist development of infrastructure and industry creating huge employment opportunity. This was prompted by its own colonial logic. Though unintended, both hugely helped the lower castes in rising against their oppression.

The very advent of the colonialists had brought many employment opportunities to Dalits in army, colonial establishments, and their households to escape their caste bondage. Dalits in many parts of the country entered British Army and had the first brush with their own military prowess, when they won series of battles for the British. The historical battle at Bhima-Koregaon in 1818 in which a small band of spirited Mahar and Pariah soldiers, had defeated a much bigger army of the Peshawas heralding the end of the Peshawa rule and establishing the British control over unified India is by far the most famous example. The army and other avenues of employment certainly lifted the Dalits economically. But the big difference came in through the education they received in military schools. It opened up new horizons showing them a glimmer of hope for emancipation from their oppressive existence. For the general public, however, English education became available through labyrinthine policy over a much longer time. Before the government could make up its mind (whether to interfere with the Hindu religion contrary to their stand of so called religious neutrality and break the caste code by giving education to Dalits), the Christian missionaries had opened schools in a big way as a part of their evangelical activities, despite the British colonialists viewing them with disfavor. The missionary activities certainly helped Dalits in the matter of education awakening them to the evil of the caste system.

The history of missionary activities in India goes back to the 1st century, when one of the Apostles of Christ, Thomas, established a church in Kerala in 52 AD. He converted many to Christianity including members of the royal family. These early Christians retained their caste status and consciousness and are still considered as high castes in Kerala society.[46] During the later phase, Christianity came as a religion of the European powers, who gave considerable importance to evangelizing activities. Right from the landing of Fr. Pedro de Kovilaham, the first missionary along with the Portuguese sailor Vasco de Gama, on the Malabar Coast on 20 May 1498, one observes sustained missionary activity in India.[47] In respect of castes, the early missionaries had two sets of experience. Those who tried to convert the upper castes, following in the footsteps of Thomas, experienced frustration as the upper castes would not let go of their caste privileges by converting to Christianity and, hence, were defensive of their religion. It led the colonial rulers to be cautious in matters concerning Hindu religion as they feared that it would jeopardize their colonial project. The 17th century missionary and empiricist Abbe' Dubois felt that the Indians bore very hardened prejudices which 'no human effort will persuade them to give up, even (if) they (were) in their own interests'. He therefore had advised the Europeans not to "risk making the gentlest and most submissive people in the world furious and indomitable by thwarting them".[48] While this was the experience with the upper castes, that with the lower castes was opposite and encouraging. The 16th century, Jesuit missionary Francis Xavier, who landed in India (Goa) on 6 May 1542, had great success in evangelizing the lower castes and outcastes. Christianity was thought of by them as 'the religion of the poor'.[49] Majority of the missionaries, who worked among poor, therefore, were critical of the caste system[50] as being the largest obstacle in conversion. E.P. Rice of the London Missionary Society who served as *missionary* in Bangalore and Chikkaballapura during 1873-95 had identified the obstacles confronting the missionaries in the 19th century, all of which one way or the other, are linked to the caste system.[51] Some missionaries went as far as demanding the government to destroy the caste system, which of course would not be accepted.[52]

In Christianity, education occupied an important place because Christians are supposed to read the 'Word of God'.[53] Most missionaries who landed in India were educated men and zealous educationists. Beyond this religious belief, education along with health services was used as important instruments for evangelization.[54] Barring the early period, from the 17th century onwards, we find the colonial authorities paying attention to education. With the arrival of missionaries in the 18th century, we find them establishing schools from 1719 onwards in various parts of the country.[55]

Education got a big fillip with the arrival of William Carey, who is considered to be 'the father of Modern Missions' in 1793. He believed that schools were 'one of the most effectual means of spreading the light of the gospel through the world'.[56] The very next year he opened the first primary school at Mudnabati at his own cost. Another educationist missionary to come and contribute to education was Alexander Duff, who landed in India in 1830. He opened his school on 12 July 1830, with the help of Raja Rammohun Roy, a noted social reformer, whose support proved invaluable in attracting many pupils whose parents were sceptical of Duff's missionary motives.[57]

Initially the missionaries had targeted the upper classes for education in English language with a hope that its cultural influence would 'trickle down' to the lower classes. But it did not work out because although the upper classes would benefit from English education, they would resist its cultural influence as it implied a risk of losing their caste privileges. Even the colonial government did not like missionaries to create problems by meddling with these classes with whom it had business relations. Although, Dalits appear to be the first to convert to Christianity, their large scale conversion could only happen in the latter half of the 19th century. For example, when the London Missionary Society started its activities in South Travancore in 1806, its first convert was Pariah, but the conversion of the Untouchable castes did not take place until 1860. Similar experiences were noted elsewhere.[58] Even the missionaries were initially not enthusiastic about converting the Untouchable castes for the fear of alienating others and blemishing the Christian society in general. Therefore, they tried to first convert the upper castes and only after realizing that it was not possible, they started converting the lower castes, which actually meant the shudra castes (like the Ezhavas and Nadars in South) and not the Untouchable castes. Its reflections are seen in the field of education too. Though the missionary schools were open to all castes and classes, initially their students came mostly from the upper castes.

The admission of the Untouchable students meant accepting exodus of all the non-Dalit students and effectively reducing the school to be only for the Untouchables, which could be ill afforded in the formative days of the Mission. Still there were instances of missionaries admitting Untouchable students. Way back in 1838, John Anderson of Madras accepted three Pariah boys (who had deceitfully entered the school) at the expense of losing 100 out of the 270 boys.[59] Of course, the motivation was not any anti-caste zeal but the long-term prospects of conversion, as Anderson commented, "This caste dispute ...will prepare us for greater trials in the case of a conversion."[60] While there were many such examples, there were exceptions too. For instance, Robert Noble, a CMS (Church Missionary Society) missionary in Andhra Pradesh had refused to admit the 'outcastes' to his school.[61]

It is only after establishing these schools that the missionaries began admitting students from the Untouchable castes. It took almost half a century for the spread of education to begin among Dalits, and to manifest itself into modern cultural capital, thereby, germinating unease about the caste system. The ideology of many early anti-caste reformers was shaped by missionary education. Mahatma Jotirao Phule, who pioneered these anti-caste revolts himself was a product of missionary education. When he launched his 'non-Brahman' movement and established schools for the Untouchables between 1848 and 1852, the Free Church of Scotland and the American Marathi Mission (in Ahmednagar) had lent support to Phule's Society, incurring displeasure of the colonial government which had a policy of non-intervention in social affairs of the Indians. Phule was all praise for the missionary work and saw them as emancipators of the lower castes. Invoking the metaphor of Bali raja, he wrote:

> ...missionaries, followers of Baliraja in the West, that is Jesus Christ, came to this country...preached the true teachings of Jesus among the shudras (low-caste) and freed them from the deceit and slavery of [caste]... [62]

Babasaheb Amebdkar also praised the missionaries as the only source of education for the Dalits:

> The only agency which could take charge of the education of the Depressed Classes was that of Christian missionaries. In the words of Mount Stuart Elphinstone they "found the lowest classes the best peoples." But the Government was pledged to religious neutrality and could not see its way to support missionary schools, so much so that no pecuniary grant was made in this Presidency to any missionary school in the early part of this period although

> the Educational Despatch of 1854 had not prohibited the giving of grants to missionary schools.[63]

One must, however, be clear that the missionaries, except for a few exceptions of individuals like William Goudie, Adam Andrew,[64] and Rev. Hatch Rhenius[65] who constituted dissidence in the movement, most were primarily moved by their missionary objectives and not by any spiritual zeal for the emancipation of Dalits or transformative motive of fighting the caste system. So also, while converting to Christianity, Dalits were also not driven by any 'spiritual' thirst but their material needs like food, shelter, employment, treatment in sickness, and of course protection from caste oppression. Whatever benefits that accrued to Dalits were, thus, purely unintended consequence. As for the role of the colonial government in education of Indians, the East India Company officials had pursued a policy of conciliation towards the native elites and supported vernacular learning, founding institutions like the Madarsa Aliya, an institution in Calcutta in 1781 for the study of Arabic and Persian languages, and Islamic Law, the Benares Sanskrit College in Varanasi in 1791, the College of Fort William in Calcutta in 1800, the Poona Sanskrit College in Pune in 1821, and the Calcutta Sanskrit College in 1824. After 1813, when the Company's territories were opened to Christian missionaries, this policy came into conflict with the views of evangelists who had the support of Charles Grant, Chairman of the East India Company, and led to the establishment of many reputed colleges by the missionaries like Scottish Church College in Calcutta in 1830, Wilson College in Mumbai in 1832, Madras Christian College in 1837, and Elphinstone College in Mumbai in 1856. By the early 1830s, the Anglicists had gained the upper hand in devising education policy in India, which led to Thomas Babington Macaulay's Minute on Indian Education of 1835.[66] During 1852–1853 some citizens of Bombay sent petitions to the British Parliament in support of both establishing and funding university education in India, which resulted in the Education Dispatch of July 1854 sent by Sir Charles Wood, which outlined a broad plan of state-sponsored education for India.

This Despatch became the basis of the education policy of the English East India Company. Even after Wood's Despatch, the approach of the East India Company towards the Dalits was not favourable. The general attitude was still informed by conciliation with the native elites, which practiced virtual ban on Dalits in schools, lest the upper caste students should boycott the school leading to its closure. The issue was precipitated in the case of a Mahar boy from Dharwad who petitioned the government in June 1856 against the denial of admission to him in the government school on account of his caste. The case was hotly debated but ultimately the government had to declare in 1858 that all the schools receiving government grants should be open to all students irrespective of their caste or creed.[67] Dr. Ambedkar observes how the government had practiced exclusion of the Dalit students from education contrary to its own proclamation:

> Under these circumstances mass education as contemplated by the Despatch of 1854 was in practice available to all except the Depressed Classes. The lifting of the ban on the education of the Depressed Classes in 1854 was a nominal affair only. For, although the principle of non-exclusion was affirmed by the Government its practical operation was very carefully avoided; so that we can say that the ban was continued in practice as before.[68]

Another significant source of education of Dalits during colonial times was the recruitment into army and subsequent education in military schools. When the British came to India, the people who significantly manned their army were Dalits. The British had a policy to educate their soldiers and ran military schools for this purpose. Thousands of Dalit recruits got educated through these schools. In Maharashtra, the Mahars from Konkan and Western Ghats who joined the army in large numbers and got educated in military schools later played a major role in organizing the Dalit movement. For the Mahars, the access to education and increased social status due to army job were the most important benefits. Zelliot writes that Ambedkar's experiences were 'free from the traditional village role, his early life was spent among educated ex-army men, imbued with the pride of soldiers and acquainted with a more sophisticated

Hinduism than that found in the village.'[69] Dr. Ambedkar himself attributes much of the credit for the Dalit movement in Maharashtra to Mahar recruitment in the British Army. He maintained:

> Until the advent of the British, the Untouchables were content to remain Untouchables .... In the army of the East India Company there prevailed the system of compulsory education for Indian soldiers and their children, both male and female. The education received by the Untouchables in the army ... gave them a new vision and a new value. They became conscious that the low esteem in which they had been held was not an inescapable destiny but was a stigma imposed on their personality by the cunning contrivances of the priest. They felt the shame of it as they ever did before and were determined to get rid of it.[70]

The access to education during the colonial period has been the revolutionary development in the history of Dalits. Education opened up the world to them; made them understand their status vis-à-vis others; helped develop the consciousness of being wronged and lent them psychological strength to resist it. This is the precise process one finds in various agitations articulated by Dalits before Ambedkar.

Other Enabling Factors: Economic and Political

The advent of British colonialism brought many unintended opportunities to Dalits for escaping their caste bondage. With the spread of new ways of administration and communication, the Mahars' place in the village grew less important, pushing them out to seek new jobs.[71] Apart from the army, many jobs like domestic help in British homes, petty jobs in their clubs, etc. became available to Dalits. Military service provided important benefits to its soldiers in terms of good pay and pensions; access to education and/or specialized training, preferential access to employment, enhanced social status, self-confidence, and personal satisfaction. In addition to the material benefits, it became 'a significant part of caste élan and mythology,'[72] that they were a martial race. Later, when the British undertook infrastructure projects, such as building roads, railways, warehouses, ports, and cities purely prompted by their colonial logic, huge employment opportunities became available for Dalits. The Mahars, with their surplus population and declining importance in village system, jumped at these opportunities more than other Dalit castes. Because of the lack of resources, the migration of Dalits to the urban centers remained moderate initially but it soon overtook all others'. Morris David Morrios' account corroborates it when it observes:

> One would probably be safe to suggest as a first approximation from the census data that before 1864 Untouchables were much less likely to move to Bombay than other groups and that afterwards they tended to move in at a slightly more rapid rate than all other groups combined, at least until 1921.[73]

With the creation of infrastructure, capitalist industry began dotting the new cities like Bombay and Nagpur. The Mahars began to take employment in textile mills, ammunition factories, ship repairing docks, railway workshops, engineering factories, construction works, and so on. The 1921 Census records that only 13.5 percent of the Mahar working force of nearly 300,000 were employed in their traditional occupation even though most Mahars maintained strong ties with their ancestral village.[74] The Khandesh Gazetteer for 1880 interestingly notes Mahars' railway connection, saying that they 'make excellent railway gang labourers and have gained a near monopoly of the unskilled railway labour market...'[75] It also noted the implications of the occupational changes: 'Of late between landlords and village Mahars complaints and feuds have become very common... the railway has done much for the Mahars... Some of them, gathering capital as petty contractors and moneylenders, show much independence, and manage their business without the help of any high caste clerks. Of late too, they have begun to send their boys to school'.[76] The occupational change and consequent upward mobility of the Mahars was especially noticeable in the Vidarbha region where their population was far in excess of what could be absorbed as village servants by the village system. The Mahars of Vidarbha were commonly seen as weavers, petty traders, carpenters and cultivators.[77] Thousands of Mahars particularly from the Konkan region had got into the army and some of them rose to high non-commission ranks.[78] In course of time, as a result of this massive switch away from caste vocation enabled many of them to save money and to graduate to higher earning professions such as petty contractors, labour suppliers, vendors, shopkeepers, etc. Soon this process created a section among them in urban clusters which was rid of their caste obligations, was economically well off, educated, and which acutely sensed the disabilities the caste system heaped on it. It had the wherewithal to rise and remove these disabilities. This was the germination of the future Dalit movement.[79]

The Non-Brahman Movement

These processes worked still better for the shudra castes than the Dalits. As discussed above, since they did not carry the stigma of untouchability, their admission did not involve the risk of alienating high castes for the missionaries. As such, the benefits of education accrued to them almost 50 years before it started benefitting the Dalits. Naturally, the germination of consciousness against their caste oppression and capacity build-up for the struggle against it happened in them much earlier and it manifested in the rise of the first non-Brahman movement under the leadership of Jotiba Phule (1827-1890). The nuanced difference between the oppression of the shudras and Dalits was not an issue in relation to the upper castes at this point. Both of them were the victims of the caste oppression by the latter. As a matter of fact, all the ritual disabilities listed out in the scriptures were actually meant for the shudras, Dalits being the avarna and outcaste, were beyond their pale. Empirically, as the farming or farm-related laboring castes, they were exploited on the one hand by the upper caste landlords and moneylenders and on the other by the Brahman priests. The power of exploitation of these *shetjis* and *bhatjis*, as Phule would call them respectively, was their positional power in the Hindu social order.

Jotiba Phule struck the Hindu social order like a meteor. A mali (gardener) by caste, educated in Scottish Mission's High School at Poona, Phule, along with some of his school friends (like Sadashiv Ballal Govande and Moro Vitthal Valavekar, both poor Brahmans), was fired with ideas of liberating the country from foreign rule taking inspiration from the lives of Shivaji and George Washington.[80] He was deeply influenced by Thomas Paine's radical ideas in his famous books, 'Age of Reason' and 'The Rights of Man'. After his schooling, Phule took a job of a school teacher in a Christian school and then became an entrepreneur taking up an agency for type-moulds for printing presses, then becoming a contractor to the Public Works Department to earn a living. The turning point came in the form of an incident when while participating in a marriage ceremony of a Brahman friend he was roughly rebuked for daring to participate because of his low caste.[81] From his own experience, Phule diagnosed that the plight of the shudras and the Untouchables (whom he called *atishudra*s, and tried to bind them together into a conjoined category, *shudra-atishudra*, a union of the labouring people in India) was mainly due to the lack of education, which was denied to them by the Brahmans and their evil contrivance called Brahmanism. He, therefore, decided to educate them by opening schools. Identifying girls to be the worst victims, Phule opened a school for girls in Pune in August 1848[82] and prepared his wife Savitribai (1831-1897) to be a teacher to handle the school tasks.

Jotiba and Savitribai carried on with this work despite all kinds of odds created by the orthodox people. Next, he emphasized education for Dalits and opened schools for them. In 1853, while ill, he founded a 'Society for Increasing Education among Mahars, Mangs and Others' with his childhood friend Govande as its president. The society had opened three more schools in Pune. Phule had waged multidimensional battle against Brahmanism. He was so contemptuous of Brahmans that he denounced both Prarthana Samaj and Sarvajanik Sabha, despite their professed pro-non-Brahman stance, just because they were mostly manned by the Brahmans and accused them of being under Brahmanical control. His anti-Brahman views created a rift between the Brahman members, who were his long standing friends on the question whether the Brahmans were the sole cause for deprivation of the low caste people and also whether the latter should be given basic skills of reading and writing or a 'thorough education' that would make them able 'to distinguish between good and bad' as he insisted.[83] He took up the case of Brahman widows, who were also ostracized by Brahmans like Dalits in the name of religious custom, and actually sheltered them in his own house and adopted a child from one such widow as his own son. He exposed the intrigues of Brahmans through many a popular pamphlets, books, ballads, and plays to arouse masses against Brahman orthodoxy. His writings on social and political issues reflected deep influence of Christianity and the ideas of Thomas Paine, one of the founding fathers of the United States. He founded the *Satyashodhak Samaj* (Truth-seeking Society) in 1873, just before the Deccan riots and eventually wrote *Sarvajanik Satya Dharma Pustak* (A Book of True Religion for All People), published posthumously (1891), wherein he expressed his views on religion so as to create society based on liberty, equality, and fraternity.[84] Phule provided a comprehensive radical critique of the Hindu social order, which if followed, had potential to change the face of the country. Phule's wife Savitribai Phule, groomed initially by him to be a teacher, not only supported him in his activism but also left her mark in the radical movement as modern India's first woman teacher, a radical exponent of mass and female education, a champion of women's liberation, a pioneer of engaged poetry, a courageous leader who took on the forces of caste and patriarchy.[85]

While Phule's movement was shouldered mainly by people of his caste and supported by many upper caste people including Brahmans, he was particularly interested in preparing activists from among the Untouchables and consciously worked for the same. He used to often visit their *bastis*; pick up smart, intelligent and energetic youth and inspire them to work for the emancipation of the Untouchables. He used to train them in writing and making speeches. Gopalbaba Walangkar, who is acknowledged as the pioneer of the Dalit movement by none other than Babasaheb Ambedkar, was himself the product of this training. Phule had inspired and prepared Walangkar for social work, and continued to support him while he was alive.[86] After his death, however, his disciples failed to shoulder his anti-caste legacy. The entire movement splintered after his death in 1891. Walangkar himself became a victim of caste prejudice a few years later. In 1895, five years after Phule's death, the Samaj decided to ban Dalits— Chambhars, Dheds, Mahars, and Mangs from their meetings.[87] 'Samaj's expulsion of its Dalit members in 1895 was an early sign of fissures within this imagined community of the *shudra-atishudra.*'[88] Notably, a faction went over to the Congress Party and another joined the Communists. Phule's legacy was, however, carried on by his atishudras in the form of a Dalit movement under the leadership of Babashaeb Ambedkar.[89]

Political Environment

The dawn of the 20th century portended significant political turbulence in the country. Lord Curzon's partition of Bengal in 1905 had created strong reactions all over the country. In Bengal, the initial peaceful and constitutional reaction turned violent; the younger generation adopting boycott and terrorist methods with indiscriminate use of arms. The agitation soon took a turn towards anarchy and disorder with several assassinations and attempts on the lives of British officials. The militant movement reached alarming scale by 1908 and appeared to be spreading among youth all over the country. In order to restore order and ensure stability to the British Raj, it was thought that mere cracking down on terrorism might aggravate the disorder unless it was accompanied by measures that would win over the upper classes. With this strategic thinking, John Morley, the Liberal Secretary of State for India, and Earl of Minto, the Conservative Governor General of India, came out with a package of reforms, commonly known as the Morley-Minto Reforms, which were embodied in the Indian Councils Act 1909. This Act envisaged increased participation of Indians in governance of British India. Encouraged by these developments, both the major parties, viz., Indian National Congress and the Muslim League, essentially representing two large communities, Hindus and Muslims respectively, decided to have their 'self-government'. Interestingly, during this time, the Muslim League delegation had represented to Lord Minto that the lower castes were not

Hindus.[90] It was the first time that a separate political identity to Dalit was proposed in a major political forum. As for the League, its intention was to reduce the number of Hindus by excluding the tribes and the Depressed Classes and, thereby, enhancing their relative representation.

As such, when World War I broke out in 1914, both of them stressed on 'self rule' in exchange of full support to the war efforts. In the wake of this understanding, both the parties had their annual sessions in Lucknow in 1916, wherein they agreed on a scheme, which came to be known as the Lucknow Pact. This Pact conceded separate electorates for Muslims and representational weightage for the minorities in legislatures, whereby in the provinces where the Muslims were in minority, they would have slightly more representation than their percentage of population, while in Muslim dominated provinces like Bengal and Punjab they would get less representation than their population warranted. Happy with the Indian support to the British war efforts, by the end of World War I, the British came out with the second instalment of reforms, which, as Curzon put it, were for 'increasing association of Indians in every branch of the administration and the gradual development of self-governing institutions with a view to the progressive realization of responsible government in India as an integral part of the British Empire.'[91] The reforms formulated by Edwin Samuel Montagu, the Secretary of State for India and Lord Chelmsford, Viceroy of India and known, therefore, as Montagu-Chelmsford reforms were embodied in the Government of India Act of 1919. This time they extended minority status and associated protection to the Sikhs. These reforms represented the maximum concessions the British were prepared to make at that time but failed to satisfy the Indians. There were demonstrations against them all over the country. The British unleashed repression and introduced the much hated Rowlatt Act in 1919, provoking intense protests, which culminated in the Jallianwala massacre.[92]

The political environment had opened up spaces for communities in the governance of the country. However, the Untouchables, though distinct, segregated and excluded from all the recognized communities, did not have their own existence as a community. They were taken as part of the Hindus but neither theoretically nor empirically were they Hindus. This fact was used up by the delegation of Muslim community when they placed their demands before Minto, Viceroy and Governor General in 1906, under the leadership of Aga Khan. Accepting these demands, the census of 1910 for the first time showed Hindus divided under three separate categories: (i) Hindus, (ii) animists and tribals and (iii) the Depressed Classes or Untouchables.[93] Needless to say such division helped Muslims to ask for representation at augmented scale as the Hindu population was considerably reduced by excluding the animists, tribals and Untouchables. It is this development that prompted the Congress to think of the Untouchables which had anyway started showing the signs of awakening. Gandhi, after his return in 1915 from South Africa, realized it more acutely than anybody else. In June 1916, in one of his earliest public addresses, he spoke about the problem of untouchability in Ahmedabad. The Congress gave up its allergic attitude towards social issues only after the British pronouncement of its plan for devolution of power to Indians.[94] Until then, there was a virtual rift between the minority within the Congress, who stood for social reforms and the majority who detested it. The pro-social reforms minority had met separately as Social Conference in the Congress conferences right from 1887 until 1895. When the 11th Congress conference met in 1895 in Pune, the stronghold of the conservatives led by Tilak, the social-reformist faced such hostility from the former that they were forced to disassociate completely from the Congress venue.[95] The attitudinal change in the Congress towards social issues was forced by political developments. The power hungry Congress had patched up with Muslim League and forged the Lucknow Pact and now began to secure support from Dalits, who it realized, could upturn its applecart. After formal assumption of leadership by Gandhi in 1921, the Congress began to befriend Dalits with its religio-moralistic appeal. In 1922, the Congress Working Committee had constituted a four-member committee comprising Swami Shraddhanand, Sarojini Naidu, Indulal

Yagnik, and G.B. Deshpande to formulate schemes to better the condition of the Untouchables, granting them a sum of Rs 5 lakh. However, nothing came out of it. In May 1923, the Congress Working Committee assigned this task to a more conservative and militant Hindu organization, the Hindu Mahasabha, which also did nothing.

Pre-Ambedkar Dalit Movements

Before Dr. Babasaheb Ambedkar symbolically entered public life, with the launch of his Marathi weekly *Mooknayak* on 31 January 1920, there existed significant movements of Dalits in some parts of the country, both led by Dalits as well as non-Dalits. In the context of Mahad, mostly the ones in Maharashtra have been discussed below, except for the movements of Ayyankali in South Kerala, Swamy Acchhutanand Harihar in Uttar Pradesh and Babu Mangoo Ram in the Punjab, which belonged to the first category and the famous Vaikom Satyagraha, which belonged to the second.

Movements Led by Non-Dalits

The British Raj brought in not only new institutionalized structure of administration, legislation, trade, network of communications, industrialization and urbanization, but also scholars, educators and missionaries, modern education, European literature, western liberalism, rationalism and, thereby, a constellation of fresh ideas. They induced unease in the erstwhile ruling elites which resulted in two types of reactions. While the orthodox section resented them and turned more inward and defensive the relatively more enlightened, the English-educated intelligentsia felt the need for reforms in the Hindu society. Expectedly, the movement for these reforms began in Bengal where western ideas had first taken roots. Raja Rammohun Roy and Debendranath Tagore founded the Brahmo Samaj on 20 August 1828 as a reformation movement against the prevailing rules set by Brahmanism, especially its Kulin practices. It was an acculturist movement which responded to the two-fold cultural challenges of utilitarian reformism and Christian proselytism.[96] It reflected syncretic approach because it endeavoured to reform Hinduism by resorting to the precepts of Christianity and Western rationalism, projecting it to be derived from the indigenous Hindu tenet embodied in the Vedas and Upanishads.

Many more such reform movements sprang up in the country[97] but all these movements were acutely constricted by their upper caste perspectives. While they repudiated caste and untouchability as one of the evils, none of them really focused on the issues of the Untouchables. Brahmo Samaj, Arya Samaj and later Prarthana Samaj, all addressed the issues of the upper castes, while the appeal of the Arya Samaj was mainly to the intermediary castes. As a result, although all these three major reform movements spoke about opposition to caste, they were not concerned with the problems of the Untouchables and confined their activities to the upper castes and classes.[98] Either these upper caste movements were nostalgically oriented only to rid their communities of evils because of which they lost to the western colonialists or somehow preserve their religious-cultural heritage. Howsoever they spoke against castes or untouchability; the truth is that they did nothing about it. It is only when the shudra-atishudras themselves rose against this Brahmanical contrivance for their enslavement that the people from the upper castes somewhat seriously stood up against these evils in Hindu society. It was Mahatma Phule's revolt against Brahmanism in Maharashtra that jolted the society throwing up scores of liberal Brahmans from the otherwise land of orthodoxy. Hugely constrained by their own caste and class backgrounds, the people like poet Keshavsut (1866-1905)[99], R.G. Bhandarkar (1837-1925)[100], Mahadev Govind Ranade (1842-1901)[101], Gopal Ganesh Agarkar (1856-1895)[102], Hari Narayan Apte (1864-1919)[103], and some others created intellectual climate for the discourse on social reforms. Besides the Brahmans, there were many from the Chandraseniya Kayastha Prabhu (CKP), the next most educated caste to Brahmans, who also were supportive of social change.

One of the most important social and religious reformers of pre-Ambedkar times, who had significant work among the Untouchables, was Vitthal Ramji Shinde (1873-1944)[104]. A

Maratha by caste, an activist of the Prarthana Samaj and the Congress, Shinde was much influenced by the reforms of Raja Rammohun Roy and Dayananda Saraswati. He established a night school for the children of the Untouchables in Pune in 1905 and founded the Depressed Classes Mission in Mumbai in 1906, with the objective of getting rid of untouchability, providing educational facilities to the Untouchables, starting schools, hostels, and hospitals for them, and solving their social problems. Accordingly, many schools and hostels were founded by this mission. He had started a paper, *Somvanshiya Mitra Samaj* (Somvanshi refers to the people of Mahar caste, but probably he used it for entire Untouchables) in March 1907 with the aim of religious and social reforms, especially for the Untouchables. Shinde had reflected at length on the origin of untouchability and the problems of the Untouchables.[105] He was one of the first thinkers to argue that Untouchables had formerly been Buddhists and rulers of Maharashtra before they were subjugated by upper caste invaders.[106] It was due to his efforts that a resolution to remove disabilities of the Depressed Classes was passed in the annual meeting of the Congress in 1917 at Calcutta and later in 1920 annual meeting at Nagpur.[107] Basically, after the Lucknow Pact, he assumed great importance as a link between the Congress and the Untouchables.

Shinde had considerable following among the Mahars including Babasaheb Ambedkar in the initial days.[108] Ambedkar came into conflict with Shinde with regard to giving testimony before the Southborough Commission, which toured India to survey opinions of the Indians on the franchise in the wake of the Montagu-Chelmsford reforms. Considering the Depressed Classes Mission as the representative organization of the Intouchables, Shinde was invited by the government to give testimony on behalf of the Untouchables. Shinde proposed a general franchise but limited it to those who had education up to fourth standard. Ambedkar submitted his memorandum on his own, calling for separate electorates with eleven Untouchables to be selected by vote (with a much lowered franchise) from delineated constituencies in Bombay Presidency, who would then choose one representative to the legislature.[109]

In a three-day *Akhil Bharatiya Bahishkrut Parishad* (All India Conference of the Boycotted) held at Nagpur in 1920, presided over by Shahu Maharaj of Kolhapur, Ambedkar mounted severe attack on Shinde. He pushed a resolution against Shinde, arguing that Shinde's proposals would leave Untouchables under the domination of the upper castes. Ambedkar basically detested the paternalistic attitudes of the upper caste reformers towards Dalits[110] and came to insist that the Dalit emancipation could only be accomplished by Dalit themselves. Ambedkar believed that howsoever hard the caste Hindus worked for their upliftment, they could not truly represent their interests. This Nagpur conference gave him an opportunity of turning the eyes of the Untouchables from the Deppressed Classes Mission of Shinde towards him. Faced with the increasing distrust of the Untouchables, Shinde resigned from the Mission in 1923. Later, he participated in Gandhi's Civil Disobedience movement but was largely disillusioned with the increasing separatist attitude of Dalits and died in 1944 as unsung, unwept man. Though discredited by the Dalits it may be remembered that he may be the first notable reformer who had boldly stated, 'Eradication of untouchability can be done only by abolition of the hierarchical caste system.'[111]

As seen above, caste or untouchability was not an issue for the mainstream Congress leaders until it realized the importance of Untouchables in the constitution of 'Hindus' post-Lucknow Pact in 1916.[112] If the Untouchables were not duly taken care of, they could easily claim separate identity and thereby topple the Congress applecart vis-à-vis the Muslim League. The sudden love of the Congress for the Untouchables began from this point on with the ulterior motive of winning their support for the Congress-League Scheme. At least four conferences of the Depressed Classes took place to discuss this Scheme. The first conference attended by 2,500 people held on 11 November, 1917 under chairmanship of Sir Narayan Chandavarkar[113], while expressing support to the Congress-League Scheme, asked for a Congress resolution for the removal of disabilities of the Depressed Classes and for their rights to elect their own representatives to the Legislative Councils in proportion to their numbers, which was more or less carried verbatim in the Congress resolution of December 1917.[114] The second conference was held a week later in November 1917 under the non-Brahman Party leadership of Bapuji Namdeo Bagade, which was attended by 2,000 Untouchables. It opposed the pledged support of the first conference to the Congress-League Scheme and urged the British to continue until all classes and specifically the Depressed Classes rose to the level where they could effectively participate in the administration. It also stated that if the government had decided to give political concessions to the Indians, Untouchables should be granted their own representation in the legislative bodies to ensure their civil and political rights. Strikingly enough, and contrary to the resolutions passed in the first conference, this conference did not make any prayer to the Indian National Congress or the higher castes to remove the disabilities imposed on them by religion and custom and instead addressed the issue directly to the British government. The third conference was held in 1918 under the leadership of Subhedar Ganpatrao Govind Rokde, probably a Mahar, which opposed the transfer of power to the caste Hindus and appealed to the government to grant them the right to choose their own representatives to legislatures in proportion to their population[115]. By passing a special resolution it appealed to the government to protect the interest of the Untouchables by granting them separate electorates. The fourth conference was sponsored by V.R. Shinde's Depressed Classes Mission which was chaired by Maharaja Gaekwad of Baroda, which was attended by Lokmanya Tilak. It was here that Tilak had said, 'If a God were to tolerate untouchability, I would not recognize him as God at all.'[116] From 1918 to 1920, he went on to convening untouchability removal conferences, some of which were presided over by Mahatma Gandhi and Maharaja Sayajirao Gaekwad.

Influenced by the work of Mahatma Phule, some non-Brahman princes like Shahu Chhatrapati, Maharaj of Kolhapur, and Sayajirao Gaekwad of Baroda also contributed directly and indirectly to the cause of emancipation of Dalits. Shahu Maharaj of Kolhapur (1874-1922), himself an adherent of the

Satyashodhak Samaj, became the main patron of the non-Brahman movement in Maharashtra. A descendent of Shivaji, he became bitterly anti-Brahman because his family priest had refused to use rituals recognizing his kshatriya status.[117] He pioneered reservation system by issuing a government order on 26 July 1902 for the recruitment of only non-Brahmans into state service until they formed 50 per cent of the posts.[118] Shahu Maharaj had opened a series of hostels to enable the education of dozen castes, Muslims and Jains in his own princely state in early 20th century. It catalyzed a significant spread of education among the Untouchables as is evident from statistical records. The number of Untouchable students in elementary schools rose from 234 in 1894, the year of Shahu's accession, to 27,830 by 1921-22.[119] He also helped them set up small businesses such as tea shops. Whenever he returned from his hunting trips, he would stop at one such tea shop run by an Untouchable and force all his hunting companions of elite class to take tea with him. This role-modeling by a king was a veritable revolutionary step against the practice of untouchability. Babasaheb Ambedkar was much impressed by such practical actions towards removal of untouchability than the paternalistic attitudes of most non-Dalits towards the Untouchables. Shahu met Ambedkar in 1920, when he made him a donation to start a bimonthly, *Mooknayak*. He had also sponsored a two-day conference at Mangaon in Kolhapur state on 19 and 20 March 1920 felicitating Ambedkar and lent him money to return to England for completing his education.

Movements Led by Dalits

The early movements of Dalits were catalyzed by those who freed themselves from economic or psychological subservience of the village structure.[120] Small sections of educated and economically better-off Dalits, particularly Mahars, emerged in Marathi speaking areas of British India. They began to organize against the discrimination faced by the community in its advancement. Notable among them were Gopal Baba Walangkar (Konkan) and Shivram Janba Kamble (Pune) in Bombay province and Kisan Fagoji Bansode, Ganesh Akkaji

Gawai, and many others in Vidarbha area of CP & Berar. Dalits in other parts of India also had made similar attempts[121] but none was as sustained as the movement of the Mahars of Maharashtra.[122] Many reasons may be identified for this but the single biggest reason is the ideological soil provided by the pioneering movement of Mahatma Phule against castes and the emergence of its torch bearer among Mahars in the legendary persona of Dr. Babasaheb Ambedkar.

However, three movements, separated from each other by geography, ideology and mode of action that preceded Mahad may have to be taken note of not because they had or had not any influence on the Dalit movement in Maharashtra, but merely because as the precedent instance, they could constitute reference point to understand Mahad.

Mahatma Ayyankali (1863-1941)

Ayyankali, born on 28 August 1863 in Venganoor in the princely state of Travancore in a family belonging to *Pulayar* (Untouchable) caste, which, however, was relatively well off having been awarded five acres of land by a grateful landlord. In those days, Untouchables were not allowed to walk through public roads. Their women were not allowed to cover their breasts in public places. Their children were not allowed access to education. Although Ayyankali was uneducated, he was sensitive enough to note these unjust customs imposed by the upper castes. He decided to challenge them. In 1893, he bought two white bullocks and a cart; tied big brass bells around the animals' neck, wore a dhoti, wrapped *angavasthram* around his shoulders and tied a *thalppavu* (turban of sorts) and drove the cart up and down the small market. When stopped by the upper caste people, he pulled out a long dagger and jumped off the cart and scared them away. Though he could ride in a cart through the streets unobstructed thereafter, the other Pulayars were not allowed to even walk there. So he led a 'walk for freedom' of Pulayars to Puthen Market. An upper caste mob prevented them. A riot broke out in which both the parties drew blood in what should be called the first armed rebellion of Dalits. Inspired by this *Chaliyar Riot*[123], the Pulayars in the surrounding areas came out in defiance to ask for other freedoms and rights which were customarily denied to them. This movement won them the right to walk along public roads in 1900 and to admit their children into public schools in 1907 in Travancore.

Ayyankali, also pioneered a movement for the rights of workers. He, later, established *Sadhu Jana Paripalana Sangham* (Association for the Protection of the Poor) to help the Dalits by providing them education, finance and legal support, and gave a slogan *'Progress through education and organization'*. When his attempt to enrol a Pulayar girl in a government school met with violent resistance by the upper castes, he organised what may have been the first strike by agricultural workers, who withdrew their labour from the fields owned by the upper castes until the government acceded to a complete removal of restrictions on education.[124] This daring son of Kerala breathed his last on 18 June 1941.

Adi Movements

The neo-Vedantic and non-Brahmin movements played an important catalytic role in developing alternate religion oriented reform movements among Dalits in some parts of the country in the forms of *Adi*-movements (*Ad-Dharm* in Punjab, *Adi-Dharma* in Bengal, *Adi-Hindu* in Uttar Pradesh (UP), etc.).[125] One such movement that had gained prominence was launched by Swamy Achhutanand Harihar (1869–1933) in UP and another by Babu Mangoo Ram Mugowalia (1886–1980) in Punjab.[126]

Born on 6 May, 1869, and brought up at a military cantonment, where his father worked, Achhutanand was educated in a missionary school and had gained an extensive knowledge of religious texts[127]. He worked for the Arya Samaj from 1905 to 1917 and was honoured with the title of "Pandit Hariharanand" and made chief of Madhya Pradesh, Gujarat and Rajasthan units.

However, witnessing the subtle practice of untouchability in the Arya Samaj, he came out and adopted a title of "Swami Achchutanand Harihar" as a mark of his Untouchable identity. He formed the "Bharatiya Achhut Mahasabha" (The Indian Untouchables Conference) to address social, political and economic issues of the Untouchables and started a monthly magazine, *Achhut* (The Untouchable) from Delhi in November, 1917. He launched *Adi-Dharma* (the original religion of Indians) an alternative religion for the Untouchables and challenged every custom and law which considered the Untouchables as inferior. He propagated pragmatism, rationality, and scientific philosophy, and unity among the Untouchables and Shudra castes.

When the Prince of Wales came on official visit to India in 1922, Acchhutanand organized a conference at Purana Quila (Old Fort) with Prince as the chief guest and more than ten thousands Untouchables in attendance. He presented a 17-point charter of demands before the Prince, which included opening of schools for the Untouchables; law for eradication of untouchability; separate electorates for the Untouchables; legal provisions to ensure representation of the Untouchables in local bodies; appointments of educated Untouchables to gazetted posts; official policy to promote trade and business among the Untouchables; abolition of the custom of *begar* (free labour); protection of the rights of the Untouchables by the government; representation to the Untouchables in government and private controlled businesses in proportion to the population; scholarships to every Untouchable child; separate school for the Untouchables; recruitment of the Untouchables in police and armed forces; enhancement in wages; appointment of the Untouchables as watchmen in the villages; grant of the government lands to the Untouchables belonging to the Gram Sabhas; representation in State Assemblies to the Untouchables; and most interestingly, a demand against the exploitation of women belonging to the Brahmans and Kshatriyas.

Later, Acchhutanand became a follower of Dr. Ambedkar. It is said that Dr. Ambedkar met him and discussed the issues related to Untouchables before going to the Round Table Conference. When Gandhi went on an indefinite fast against the grant of separate electorates to the Untouchables, he organized protest rallies in Prayag, Etawah, Lucknow and Kanpur against his fast.[128]

Another *Adi* movement is associated with Babu Mangoo

Ram Mugowalia. He was born on January 14, 1886, in village Mugowal, Hoshiarpur. Mangoo Ram's father Harman Dass, had left his traditional Chamar caste occupation and started business in hides. After schooling, Mangoo Ram helped his father develop their leather trade for some time and then left for the United States in 1909. For four years he did various farm jobs and worked in a sugar mill in the San Joaquin valley of California. In 1913, when some of the Punjabi settlers in California formed the Ghadar Party, Mangoo Ram joined it as a full-time worker in San Francisco. In 1915, chosen by Sohan Singh Bakhna, a prominent leader of the Ghadar Party, he participated in an important mission involving smuggling of weapons from California to the Punjab. He nearly escaped death sentence at the hands of British allies. Thinking that he had died, his family remarried his wife to his brother.[129] After returning in 1925, and seeing the condition of Dalits in India, he was convinced that there was need for social change, and wrote to Ghadar Party headquarters in San Francisco about the difficult conditions of the Untouchables in India, announcing that their freedom was more important to him than that of the nation itself. The leaders of the Ghadar Party reportedly agreed and designated him to work for the uplift of the Untouchables. On June 11th and 12th 1926, he convened a meeting in a school in his village, where he had taken up a job as a teacher, and formally launched the *Ad Dharm* movement. Mangoo Ram was elected its first president, a title he was retained for the duration of the movement. Besides creating a separate identity for the Untouchables in terms of ideology and customs, the *Ad Dharm* movement did not accomplish much. Later, like Acchhutanand, Mangoo Ram also followed Dr. Ambedkar and remained Ambedkarite until his death on 22nd April 1980.

Interestingly, while the movement of Mahars in Bombay area appears directly inspired by Mahatma Phule's, (understandably for their physical proximity), the movements in the Vidarbha drew their inspiration from Chokhamela[130], a 16th century Bhakti saint of the Mahar caste. Since these movements were mostly leader-centric, we have to necessarily see them through the activities of the leaders.

Gopal Baba Walangkar

Gopal Baba Walangkar (1840-1900) was one of the Mahar military pensioners who had settled at Dapoli in Ratnagiri district.[131] Like many Mahars before him he joined the British Army after finishing schooling. After his retirement in 1886, he devoted himself to the work of emancipation of the Untouchables with the inspiration and support from Jotiba Phule.[132] He mobilized people and made them conscious of their human rights. He highlighted the grievances of the people by writing in *Dinbandhu* and *Sudharak*, the popular Marathi periodicals of those days, in which he argued that casteism and untouchability had no religious basis and they were the monsters created by Brahmans. He made a critical study of the religious scriptures and came to the conclusion that castes were nothing but the contrivance created by the Aryas to subjugate the vanquished Anaryas. To propagate his thesis he published a booklet titled *Vital Vidhvansak* on 1 August 1889, raising 26 questions to the Shankaracharya and other Hindu religious leaders. He introspectively observed that since 'we tolerated injustice, hence the Hindus perpetrated injustice; if we had countered it, we could have changed our world,'[133] and exhorted Dalits not to tolerate injustice. He challenged the Hindu establishment to consider the text and come out with its response within six months else they would approach the government with these demands. He also warned that they might consider leaving this country itself if the Hindus continued treating them Untouchable.[134]

In order to organize all Dalits under one banner and to bring about reforms in them, he founded a social organization named *Anarya Doshpariharak Mandali* (the non-Aryan committee for righting of the wrongs) at Dapoli in the year 1890.[135] Gopalbaba had taken up the then burning issue of the Untouchables cropped up by the British orders to stop their recruitment into the army. Earlier, the Mahars, Mangs, and Chambhars were recruited into the East India Company's army but around 1890-91 their recruitment was stopped with an alibi that they were not martial castes. Even those in service were asked to leave. Gopalbaba took an initiative and prepared a long petition arguing how the Untouchables had won the British several battles, how they have an edge over others in military service, how their characterization as Untouchables was deceitful, and how the claim of the others of being a martial race was false.[136] It basically compared Mahars with the higher castes in martial matters and requested restoration of their recruitment in the military. He tried taking signatures of the Mahar pensioners but none signed it for the fear of incurring wrath of the British government.[137] This appeal prepared in July 1894 was not submitted to the government but in a meeting of the Untouchables held at Dapoli on 4 March 1895, a decision was taken and accordingly Walangkar had posted it to the government on 6 March 1895.[138] The first and concluding part of final appeal was translated into English[139], which is said to be done jointly by Gopal Baba Walangkar and Subhedar Ramji Sakpal (Ambedkar's father) with the help of Justice M.G. Ranade.[140] This campaign was unsuccessful. However, Basham elaborates:

> The government of India took the petition seriously enough to request information about the Koregaon monument from the government of Bombay (presumably to verify the petitioners' claims). Eighteen months after the initial submission of the petition, the Indian government replied that it was "unable to rescind the orders which have been issued regarding the castes to be admitted to the Bombay Army.[141]

In response to the obsession of the Indian National Congress for political reforms as against social reforms, Gopalbaba had asked of the Congress way back in 1897, 'what right you have got to demand the political reforms if you do not accept to bring about social reforms', the precise argument Babasaheb Ambedkar would reiterate years later.

In recognition of his social work, the government had honoured Walangkar by nominating him a member of the local board of Mahad taluka. Such an honour was perhaps being accorded to an Untouchable for the first time in the country. It evoked hot debate in the news papers of those days. Expectedly, the upper caste members did not appreciate this move. They had boycotted the first meeting that was to be attended by

Gopalbaba. The surprising thing was that even the backward caste member and a Muslim member also absented themselves.[142]

Walangkar wrote many articles in the popular newspapers of those days like *Deenbandhu* and *Sudharak,* both to sensitize the society to the miserable state of the Untouchables and to spread awareness among the Untouchables about their human rights. Thus, he became the first Dalit journalist. He also wrote *Hindu Dharma Darpan* in 1894 and composed many *akhandas* for the awakening of people. The unsparing manner in which he wrote, he could be considered as the first rebel Dalit litterateur. Walangkar sincerely worked for bringing about unity of all the sub-castes of the Dalits. As a disciple of Phule, he held education to be the key to their emancipation. The writings of Gopalbaba claimed *kshatriyahood* and dominant status to Dalits before the advent of the Aryans, echoing the claims of many Dalits who wore *adi* identity (such as Adi-Dravida, original Dravid) before him. He used various pen names like 'kondiram', 'das', 'satyadas', and 'satyeshwardas', indicating in a way his ideological tie with the *Satyashodhak* tradition of Jotiba Phule.

Indeed, Walangkar remained a lifelong disciple of Mahatma Phule and followed the principles of the Satyashodhak Samaj. Unfortunately, after the demise of Mahatma Phule, the then members of the Satya Shodhak Samaj left its non-caste ideology to the extent that they refused to allow the members of the Untouchable caste to attend a meeting of the Samaj at Novelty theatre in Bhavanipeth, Pune on 15 September 1895. Gopalbaba Walangkar did not go to attend it but felt sorry for the defeat of Phule by his own disciples.[143] Gopalbaba breathed his last in the year 1900 at Raodul, his native place.

Shivram Janba Kamble

Shivram Janba Kamble (1875-1940) was a true inheritor of the legacy of Gopalbaba Walangkar. Unlike him, he did not come from army background, but had good interface with the Europeans. A son of a butler, he could not receive formal education because of poverty and, like his father, became a butler in the Masonic Hall in the Pune Cantonment. He learnt to read and write and developed high appreciation for European culture and civilization. Inspired by the thoughts and mission of Mahatma Phule and Lokhitwadi[144], he decided to work for the liberation of his people. Working for creating social awareness among the Untouchables, he wrote in *Deenbandhu* urging the Untouchables to educate their children and exhorted the government to recruit them in the police and military service. In 1903, he wrote *Soochi Patra,* a pamphlet and later started a monthly *Somvanshiya Mitra* from Pune in 1909, which within a short time achieved huge popularity.[145]

Kamble decided to pursue the matter of recruitment of Mahars in military from where it was left by Gopalbaba. He convened a two-day conference of Mahars at Saswad in the Purandar taluka of Pune district on 23-24 November 1903, presided over by Subhedar (captain) Bahadur Gangaram Krishnaji Ghatge.[146] This conference was attended by Mahars from 51 villages.[147] This was perhaps the first time that Dalits in such numbers had collected to publicly deliberate on an issue of their collective interests and democratically decided the action plan.[148] Kamble organized many more meetings to secure consent of people and eventually drafted a petition, which was sent to Lord Lamington, Governor of Bombay, with signatures of 1558 Mahars. The main demands were recruitment of the Untouchables in the lower services, the police department, the Indian Army and admissions to the Untouchable students in the public schools.[149] When he did not get satisfactory response from the Governor he represented to the Government of India in June 1905. The Indian government regretted that it would not be able to oblige as it faced flak from other people.[150] Instead of getting disheartened by such an answer, he held the second Mahar conference at Jejuri on 5 April 1910, and as decided there he sent a memorandum all the way to the Secretary of State for India on 10 December 1910.[151] Providing a list of 70 Mahars who became Subhedar and 33 Mahars who became Jamadars in the army, he demonstrated the military prowess of Mahar people and argued how unjust the decision to ban their recruitment to the army was. He pleaded that the government should not only restore their recruitment but also form separate battalion of

Mahars as it did for other castes.[152] A self-taught person, he showed unusual talent in writing letters and petitions, which he often used to create impact as exemplified by a passage from his petition:

> And it is most encouraging to know that the Honourable House of Commons... is composed, to some extent, of the representatives of the lower strata of English society, the working men, who, only a quarter of a century ago, were regarded as but Mahars and Pariahs by the more educated and affluent classes of their nation.[153]

With such perseverance, his efforts perhaps bore fruit when on 6 February 1917 at the height of World War I when the British Government took a decision not only to recruit Mahars in the army but to form two platoons of Mahars.[154]

Kamble founded an organization *Shri Shankar Prasadik Somvanshiya Hitchintak Mitra Samaj* on 1 August 1904 at Pune. The main aims of this organization were: to unite the Untouchables for their own development, to set up a school exclusively for the Untouchable students, to set up one library, and to arrange lectures and discourses for creating social awareness among the Untouchables. He started a school and a library but when plague struck Pune, he had to close them.[155] Through his paper *Somvanshiya Mitra*, he struggled against superstitions and bad customs such as Devadasi and Potraj that prevailed among the Mahars and Mangs in the Bombay Presidency. Acknowledging his reformist work, the Maharaja of Baroda, Sayajirao Gaekwad, had invited him to Baroda as his guest for two days on 11-13 September 1908 and felicitated him for his good work.[156] When V.R. Shinde formed the Depressed Classes Mission in 1906, Kamble requested him to open its branch in Pune cantonment. The branch was opened on 22 June 1908 and Kamble got associated with it.[157] In the conference of the Somvanshiya Mitra Samaj (founded by V.R. Shinde on 14 March 1907) held at Jejuri near Pune on 5 April 1910, he called upon the Dalits to fight against the social evils that prevailed among the Mahars. This conference was also addressed by Maharshi Shinde and Subhedar Bahadur Gangaram Krishnaji Ghatge.[158] He brought about a marriage of a Devadasi, Shivubai Laxman Jadhav, with one Ganpatrao

Hanmantrao Gaikwad. He also advised against the superstitious system of sacrificing animals to propitiate gods, eating beef and drinking.

Kamble founded a new organization called *The Depressed Classes Committee* on 16 April 1921.[159] This Committee appealed to the Education Minister to make education compulsory, to employ teachers from among the Untouchables, to give scholarships to the students, and to start at least one hostel in each district for the Untouchable students.[160] The then Education Minister had conceded them and promised to institute such scholarships and to open a hostel in Pune, which he did in 1922. In the wake of an International Congress at Geneva in 1925, the Government of India, in recognition of his social work, had sought his views on how to ensure the health of children. Kamble had provided a detailed account of the reasons for ill-health of the children and suggested the measures for improving the same. He attributed premature death and illness to superstitions, ignorance and poverty.[161] In a meeting called by G.R. Hingnekar, an editor of *Dnyan Prakash*, Kamble had appealed to the conscience of high caste people to treat the so called Untouchables on an equal footing and allow them entry into temples. He had attended the All India Depressed Classes Conference held in 1920 at Nagpur where he complained that the colonial government was not helping them in ameliorating their miseries and called upon the Dalits to abolish the caste system and bid for development on their own.

Kamble used an array of methods: forming organization for action, running a newspaper, writing pamphlets, organizing conferences, submitting petitions, opening schools and libraries, etc. to spread awareness of human rights among the Untouchables and organize them. He perseveringly represented to the British government through numerous letters and memorandums from 1904 to 1930 for providing education, employment to the Untouchables. When Dr. Ambedkar appeared on the horizon in 1920, Kamble welcomed him as a leader. Although, later dissociated with him because of difference of opinion on some issues, he never undermined his work.

Dalit Movement in Vidarbha

Geographically and geologically Vidarbha has been an important region of the country and, hence, Nagpur as its main city had assumed great importance. During the colonial period, it became a major supplier of cotton, coal, and forest produce. It became an industrial city with the establishment of the Empress Mill in 1877 and an important railway node with the completion of Bengal Nagpur railway in 1887. As a result, Mahars in large numbers migrated from villages to Nagpur. In the textile labour of Nagpur they constituted a majority. The Settlement Report by Sir R. Craddock on Nagpur published in 1899 had this to say about the state of Mahars in Vidarbha:

> The Mahar is of sturdier physique than the higher caste and he is ready to turn his head to anything from begging to banking, provided there is money in it. He got the opportunity when the cotton trade expanded and now many of the caste are petty cotton traders. ... A few have become landlords and quite a number substantial little capitalists ...[162]

Indeed, many Mahars made good progress and became malgujars (landlord), village patils, money lenders, contractors, shopkeepers, etc. The economically well-off Mahars naturally turned their attention to social reforms as they acutely sensed their handicap due to caste. There are examples like Janoji Kachruji Khandare, one of the first leaders of Dalits in Berar region, who started a free boarding in 1895 at Akola, which his family ran for years.[163] By the closing years of the 19th century, young people from amng the Mahar community started passing out from schools and colleges with English education. Irked by their bitter experience in society, they were impelled to take up reforms with the help of *Shetyes* (the chiefs of Mahar panchayats) and leaders of the old generation. The history of the Dalit movement as documented by Kosare (1984) of those days impressively reveals that there was a functional network of Mahars all over Vidarbha that was active in welfare and reform activities. Apart from this, it also aimed to sensitize others about the plight and the human rights of the Untouchables in a lawful manner and within the framework of the Hindu society.[164] While historically the *Sanmarg Bodhak Asprushya Samaj* (Society of Depressed Classes for Right Path), founded by Kisan Fagoji Bansode on 1 October 1901 appears to be the earliest formal organization of Mahars in Vidarbha, there is no information available on its activities.[165] One social activist who appears to have pioneered some kind of organized reforms and for the upliftment of Mahars was Vitthalraoji Moon Sant Pande, so known because of his old priestly conduct and saintly mode of preaching. He is credited with getting the Ambada tank in Ramtek, a place of pilgrimage, opened for bathing of Dalits in 1903 and building a ghat (bund) and a Siva temple there. He successfully organized a conclave of Mahars in 1904 that deliberated on reforms within the caste. He was also a noted labour leader in the region. Later in 1906, Moon Pande founded the *Antyaj Samaj Committee*, which mainly undertook reforms of religious nature like renouncing beef eating. He had informally founded the *Mahar Sabha* in 1908, which became a very important organization in pre-Ambedkar Dalit movement.[166] It organized a milestone conference in Town Hall, Nagpur from 13-15 April 1913[167], which was attended by community leaders from the entire Marathi speaking area. A vow was taken to do away with the practice of eating the meat of dead animals. This conference formalized the organization of the Sabha.

The Sabha not only comprised malgujars, moneylenders, contractors, brokers, traders in timber, patwaris, clerks, teachers, saints, priests, shetyes and other well-to-do Mahars, but also people like Shivram Janba Kamble of Pune, Dhondiba Narayan Gaikwad of Mumbai, Dharamdas Sant of Nashik, and Bapuji Pande of Pandharpur from Bombay province.[168] It appears from the composition of the committee that most social movements of the Untouchables in various parts of Maharashtra had communication between them. Mahar Sabha sought support and cooperation from the British officers, Christian missionaries, and Hindu sympathizers for the educational and social upliftment of Mahars. It was largely successful in uniting all sub- castes of Mahars in Vidarbha. The unity of Mahars of the Vidarbha region towards their civil rights could be considered the distinguishing factor in Vidarbha shouldering the future Ambedkarite Dalit movement. In the form of Mahar Sabha, a foundation was laid for the later developments of the Dalit movement in Maharashtra.[169]

Kisan Fagoji Bansode

Kisan Fagoji Bansode (1879-1946), a labour leader, newspaper editor, social worker, and poet began his activism around 1900, persisting with the approach of earlier generation that stressed 'Mahar claim to religious worth'.[170] He made great use of the fact that Mahars had produced a saint Chokhamela in trying to induce self-respect.[171] Born in Mohapa, a village 40 km away from Nagpur, Bansode was against caste, superstitions, and myths. As referred to earlier, he had founded the *Sanmarg Bodhak Asprushya Samaj* on 1 October 1901 and later the *Sanmarg Bodhak Nirashrit Samaj*, in 1903.[172] He wanted to spread education not only among Dalit boys but also among girls and established a school called the Chokhamela Girls School in Pachpawali area of Nagpur in 1907. Fiercely independent minded, he was influenced by the philosophy of Brahmo Samaj, which he embraced on 1 October 1909. He started a press for printing his newspapers, pamphlets, and booklets to promote reforms among the Untouchables. He started the journal *Nirashrit Hind Nagrik* in 1910, *Vital Vidhvansak* in 1913, *Majur Patrika* in 1918, and later *Chokhamela* during 1931-36. His wife Tulasabai shared the responsibility of press work with him. Besides he regularly wrote in the then popular newspapers. He used to go from house to house preaching self-respect and organizing people for his various activities. He was also a trade union leader in the Empress Mills, Nagpur, from 1918-1922. He established Chokhamela libraries, Chokhamela schools, and Chokhamela hostels. He believed in internal reforms of the Hindu society and, hence, worked with the caste Hindus for eradicating castes. He, therefore, urged the Mahars, Mangs, and Chambhars 'not to become Christians; to eradicate ignorance and superstitions; not to eat what is not to be eaten; not to drink liquor; to take education; to fight for civil rights; to uplift the economic condition; to organize; and to create a feeling among Hindus that the downtrodden should be raised up'. He wrote some tamashas (folk dramas) and wrote a play on the saint Chokhamela.[173]

Bansode is credited with founding of a few more organizations, *Mahar Sudharak Mandal* (Organization for Development of Mahars) in 1910 and *Antyaj Samaj* (Society of the Outcastes) in 1919. He had organized the *Varhad Mahar Parishad* (Berar Mahar Conference) in 1921 in which Mahars, Mangs, and Dhors took part and worked out a programme for political rights. While trying for all-out reforms of the Untouchable society, he was inclined to stay within the Hindu fold. When Babasaheb Ambedkar appeared on the scene, Bansode went almost all the way with him in social and political matters, but retained the belief that progress could be made only within Hinduism. When Ambedkar declared that he would renounce Hinduism in 1935, Bansode parted ways with him. An issue of *Chokhamela* of 27 February 1936 devoted much of its space to criticism of Ambedkar's intention to convert finding him 'too obsessed with reclaiming culture and not sufficiently concerned with analyzing conditions of material oppression.' He persisted with the approach of the Mahar claim to religious worth.[174] He associated himself with Shinde's Depressed Classes Mission, and wrote a biography of Chokhamela in 1941 and dedicated it to Vitthal Ramji Shinde.

Ganesh Akkaji Gawai

Ganesh Akkaji Gawai (1888-1973) was the son of a hereditary village Mahar servant at Thugaon in Amravati district. He had his school education at Akola, residing in a free boarding of Janoji Khandare. He came under the influence of Maharshi Shinde and believed that the Untouchables should fight against their oppression and discrimination without converting to any another religion. He, therefore, resisted the conversion of Dalits being done by the Roman Catholic missionaries in the Amravati district. In 1909, he became a member of Brahmo Samaj and started a library at his native place. In 1910 he formed *Mahar Sudharak Mandal*[175] at Amravati to reform and unite the Mahars, and started a fortnightly, named *Bahishkrut Bharat*[176] from Amravati in the year 1914.

Gawai participated in the Conference of Depressed Classes, presided over by Sir Narayanrao Chandavarkar, held in Bombay on 11 November 1917, convened to seek support for the Congress-League Scheme. He opposed it asking, 'if the Hindus demanded Swaraj, which meant the rule of Hindu bureaucrats, then what was the use of such a Swaraj to the Depressed Classes?' In order to unite all the Depressed Classes under one banner, he formed the *Depressed India Association* at Bombay on 12 January 1918. After noting his passion for the uplift of the Untouchables, the government nominated him to the CP & Berar Legislative Assembly in 1920. He was not well disposed towards Dr. Ambedkar and opposed him later on the issue of separate electorates as well as religious conversion.[177]

L.N. Hardas

L.N. Hardas alias Babu Hardas (1904-1939), as he was popularly known, was perhaps the youngest among the pre-Ambedkar leaders. A son of Laxmanrao Nagrare, a clerk in the Railways, he was born in Kamthi near Nagpur. He started a weekly *Maharatha* from Nagpur with a view to spreading social awareness among the Dalits; started a cooperative of beedi workers to obviate their exploitation; opened a *mahila ashram* (women's home) at Nagpur with a view to imparting training to Dalit women in household activities; and founded the *Mahar Samaj* organization in 1922 to rally his people under one banner. He formed one *Mahar Sevak Pathak,* a volunteer corps of youth to protect the Dalits from atrocities and to maintain discipline in the society. He sincerely endeavored to remove the sub-caste barrier from among the Mahars by organizing community dinners on the occasion of death anniversary of Chokhamela in the Chokhamela temple at Nagpur. In 1923, he had appealed to the Governor of CP & Berar to nominate members from among the Depressed Classes to the Legislative Council, district local boards, and municipalities. On behalf of the Mahar Samaj he started night schools at Bail Bazaar, Kamsari Bazaar, and Naya Bazaar Kamthi in the year 1924 and also a *Sant Chokhamela Library* at Kamthi. In order to arouse his people against irrational, immoral, and superstitious customs of the community, he wrote a book named *Mandal Mahatmya* in October 1924 and distributed it free of cost. It had significant impact insofar as people had stopped going to watch obscene mandals or Krishna Leela. He had written a play named *Veer Balak* for the similar purpose.

In a meeting of Mahars held at Ramtek near Nagpur in 1927, presided over by Kisan Fagoji Bansode, Babu Hardas exhorted them to stop worshipping at the steps of the temple and bathing in the dirty Ambada tank. Unlike the senior leaders like Bansode and Gawai, he went with Dr. Ambedkar, shouldering important responsibilities in his parties.[178]

Kalicharan Nandagawali

Kalicharan Ganoji Nandagawali (1860-1962), the son of a rich *Mahanubhav Panthi* Dalit landlord of a village in Balaghat district, was another prominent personality. He was active in the movement right from the days of Mahar Sabha, as one of the members of its Executive Committee.[179] He had settled in Gondia. He opened a school for girls in Gondia in 1910, which is said to be the first school for girls in Vidarbha.[180] He became a member of the Municipality of Gondia in 1914 and its chairman in 1916. In the same year, he founded the *Bharatiya Mahar Panchayat* to look into the problems of Mahars and convened a conference on the issue of untouchability. He appealed to the government to recruit Dalits in the army during the World War I. He gave evidence before the Southborough Franchise Committee and demanded representation for Dalits in the Legislature. He was nominated to the CP & Berar Legislative Assembly in 1920 for a period of three years along with Ganesh Akkaji Gawai.[181] He was the chairman of the reception committee of the Depressed Classes Conference held at Nagpur in 1920, presided over by Shahu Maharaj and Dr. Ambedkar as its chief guest. On 16 March 1921, he had proposed an important resolution in the Assembly for inquiring into the state of the Depressed Classes. The resolution was passed in the Assembly and a committee[182] was formed in June 1921 to look into their employment in the government services; their education; their rights as *kotwals*; boycotts in villages; and separate settlements for them.[183] The committee had completed its task within a year. In 1921 Nandgawali proposed a resolution to open all wells, dharmshalas, and other water sources which have been built and which would be built with public funds to all people irrespective of caste or communities and to the Untouchables.[184] Although the resolution failed by 10 versus 23 votes because of the government's attitude but it proved that many savarna Hindus had begun to support Dalits in their struggle for civil rights.[185] In this way both Nandagawali and Gawai actively struggled in the Assembly to get Dalits, farmers and workers their fair dues. In 1926, he formed the *Madhya Prant Tarun Mahar Sangh* (Middle Province Young Mahar Organization) with Patitpawan Das, Revaram Kawade, Dashrath Patil, G.T. Meshram, Hemchandra Khandekar, Tularam Sakhare, and L.N. Hardas, among its prominent members. The Sangh had supported the demand of separate electorates for the Depressed Classes made by Dr. Ambedkar, and had also appealed to the Simon Commission to grant this demand. Later, when he began leaning towards the Congress, people stopped supporting him.[186]

Other Important Personalities

The foregoing discussion sketches out the broad brush context for the Mahad struggle. It adequately shows that Dalit movement had already taken roots in the country in most urban centers where a section, howsoever miniscule, of the educated and economically well off Dalits, had emerged. Individuals from this section came forward to contribute to this new activism. One can easily mark Ayyankali's movement as the respectable exception to this general trend. The few prominent persons that we projected above were basically to understand the representative nature of this activism. There of course were numerous unnamed people besides and behind these prominent names who constituted the Dalit movement.

Ambedkar's Rise on the Dalit Horizon

The pre-Ambedkar movement of the Untouchables had certainly prepared a ground for the future leaders to take it to the higher plane. Their main focus was to awaken the Untouchable masses, and they were largely successful in that. In view of their meager resources, the methods they adopted, viz., calling upon occasional conventions; submitting memorandums and asking for some favour from the government; writing in local newspapers, pamphlets and booklets; starting newspapers/periodicals and establishing hostels and libraries, were commendable by any standard. This indeed prepared the people to come together and fight collectively against their social disabilities. However, much as these early movements tried to speak for all Untouchables in generic terms, they could not unite them across sub-castes. As seen from the foregoing account, although the tenor of the main movement of Mahars was all encompassing, the other Untouchable castes had not fully supported them and rather tried to start their own respective movements. All these movements note the injustice to the Untouchables but either they simply lament it or see it being undone through raising their status in terms of caste as well as material advancement. They did reflect the sense of deprivation of their civil rights and solutions through political processes, but the actual movement had to wait till the arrival of Dr. Bhimrao Ramji Ambedkar on the scene.

Dr. Ambedkar truly reflected the resonance of the historical development that befell the Dalits. He came from a family which had a history of more than one generation of military service.[187] He, thus, belonged to a typical military Mahar aristocracy that had come up in Konkan. These Mahar families were surely better off than the caste Hindu families in terms of education and cultural accomplishments but still could not escape the caste discrimination and humiliation. Ambedkar also had his fair share of such humiliating experiences in his growing up years.

When his father retired from the British Army at the rank of Subhedar in 1894, he settled like many others in Dapoli in the Ratnagiri district. He had to admit his two sons (Bhimrao and the elder Anandrao) in a local school which, being a government aided school, could not refuse admission on account of caste or creed. Even then, Ramji Ambedkar (Ambedkar's father) found it hard. Even after invoking his stature as an army officer, he had to agree with the condition that his sons and four other 'Untouchable' students would never come in contact with the caste children, and never take water from the school's pitchers. At the tender age of six years, the child Ambedkar had a brush with caste discrimination in this humiliating manner. The Hindu teacher at the school never entered the room in which the outcast children struggled with their lessons. He would look at their slates from a distance.[188]

When Ramji Ambedkar shifted his family to Satara for taking up a job there with the Public Works Department as a cashier, young Bhimrao was enrolled in a school at Satara. Even there he had bitter encounters with casteism. One of the incidents that left a deep scar on his psyche had taken place while he was in Satara. It was concerning a bullock cartman who threw him along with his elder brother and a nephew out on the road after he learnt of their caste. This incident happened when the brothers were on the way to Goregaon (in the Khatav taluka in Satara district) to meet their father who had called them to spend summer vacation with him as he could not get leave to go home.

They were put in such a miserable situation that he could never come to terms with it. When he returned from the United States laced with a doctoral degree from the prestigious Columbia University and had to take up a job in Baroda State as per the terms of his scholarship, he still suffered casteist humiliation at the hands of even the lowest rung of his own staff. They would throw files at him from a distance. Even outside the office his caste did not leave him away from the indignity of untouchability. No one would rent him a house in Baroda because of his caste and, therefore, he had to take shelter in a Parsi guest house, hiding his caste identity. But when they learnt about his caste, they literally threw him out on the road. Even in Bombay, as a professor in Sydenham College he faced insults and humiliation when some Gujarati professors who had objected to his drinking water from the pot reserved for the professorial staff. Ambedkar would recount all these humiliating experiences later in life. However, he could not let this bitterness come in the way of his rational analysis.

While in Columbia, he presented a paper *Castes in India: Their Mechanism, Genesis and Development* (in 1916), which stands testimony to his intellectual prowess as well as his courage. While observing inadequacy of the established theories, he provided his own profound insight. He had to return to India in June 1917 because of the expiry of the term of his scholarship. He gave evidence before the Southborough Committee that came to survey Indian opinion on the franchise in the light of the impending Montagu-Chelmsford reforms in 1918. In his evidence, he presented a strong case for the Depressed Classes demanding separate electorates with lowered franchise and a markup of seats in proportion to their population. Shortly thereafter he attended the All India Conference convened by the Untouchables in May 1920 at Nagpur, wherein he made a powerful speech attacking V. R. Shinde, who had considerable following among the Untouchables of Nagpur, for his evidence before the Southborough Committee that the representatives of the Untouchables must be elected by the Members of the Legislative Council rather than being nominated by the government or the institutions of the Untouchables themselves.[189]

It was the first time that his combative skills and ability as a prospective leader came before the people. He forcefully argued that howsoever hard the caste Hindus worked for their upliftment, they would not know their mind. At this conference he advanced an important principle, which was to become the cornerstone of his movement, emphasizing self-reliance in matters of organized action. He emphasized that '...The institution and individuals have no right to defend the interests of the Depressed Classes, if they are not run by Untouchables...' He, therefore, wanted the Untouchables to turn away from Shinde's Depressed Classes Mission and focus on strengthening their own organization. At the end of his speech, he exhorted the Mahar leaders to forget their sub-castes[190] and stay united.[191]

He had just entered public life with a launch of a Marathi fortnightly paper *Mooknayak* on 31 January 1920, with generous financial help from Shahu Maharaj of Kolhapur, to champion the cause of the Depressed Classes. Through *Mooknayak*, he put forth his famous viewpoint vis-à-vis India's independence, that it was not enough for India to be an independent country; she must rise to be a good state guaranteeing equality in matters religious, social, economic, and political to all classes, offering every man an opportunity to rise in life and creating conditions favorable to his/her advancement. Soon after the launch of the *Mooknayak* , he attended a Depressed Classes Conference at Mangaon on 21 March 1920, where he exhorted Dalits to rely on self-help for their emancipation. The conference was presided over by Shahu Maharaj himself who introduced him to the audience as their future leader. One of his first actions around this time was to get his sympathizers to organize the felicitation of P. Baloo (Baloo Babaji Palwankar) who belonged to Chambhar caste for his great achievements in cricket.[185] It indicated his anxiety to bring various Untouchable castes together under one banner.

He had left India for London in September 1920 and after completing his studies came back on 6 April 1923 with additional degrees of D.Sc. from the London School of Economics and Barrister-at-Law from Grey's Inn. The *Mooknayak* had stopped publishing while he was in London. He had to almost start everything again. He contemplated formation of a central organization devoted to the upliftment of the Untouchables. He began to participate in meetings and conferences of the Dalits and voiced his idea. It lent him enough confidence to found a central organization to launch a movement under its aegis. Accordingly, the *Bahishkrut Hitkarini Sabha* (Association for the Welfare of the Boycotted People) came into being on 20 July 1924 with a motto to 'educate, agitate, organize', the famous slogan of Fabian Society in England.[193] People of all Untouchable castes of Maharashtra, viz. Mangs, Chambhars, and Dheds, besides his own caste, started coming together under his leadership. The president of the Sabha was Sir Chimanlal Harilal Setalwad, LL. D., and its vice presidents were Meyer Nissim; J.P. Rustomji Jinwala, Solicitor; G.K. Nariman, Dr. R.P. Paranjpye; Dr. V.P. Chavan, and B.G. Kher,

Solicitor. The Chairman of the managing committee was Dr. Ambedkar, its secretary was S.N. Shivtarkar, and its treasurer was N.T. Jadhav.[194] The logic behind the composition of the Sabha as explicated in its first annual report was to keep the strings of the organization in the hands of the 'the majority of workers from the Depressed Classes', while not excluding 'the sympathy and support of the upper classes'. The Sabha was devoted to raising the Untouchables to a status of social and political equality with others and to promoting their economic interests.[195]

Inspiration from America

Dr. Ambedkar, while studying in Columbia University from 1913 to 1917, lived on the edge of Harlem, the vast African-American locality in Manhattan and so it is unlikely that he did not learn about the African Americans' protests against racial inequality. Between 1900 and 1906 Southern Blacks had developed boycott movements against Jim Crow.[185] They were perhaps more intense and remarkable than the 18 month boycotts in Montgomery and Alabama led by Martin Luther King Jr. half a century later.[186] It is unthinkable that the student Ambedkar had not known them during his stay at Columbia. The National Association for the Advancement of Colored People (NAACP) was founded in 1909-1910, just three years before he landed in the US. This was an important development because the NAACP was the first national protest organization formed specifically to attack the Jim Crow regime and racial inequality. It immediately began attacking the legal basis of racial subordination during the Jim Crow era.[198] The NAACP would win major legal cases against racial segregation throughout the first half of the 20th century especially with regards to segregated schools. All these developments had taken place during the years of his stay in New York.

Even after coming back to India, it is unlikely that he had not kept himself informed about the civil rights struggles of the African Americans in the US. Even a normal liberal person could not ignore them. Even without entering into the definitional controversy about race and caste, no one should deny that in their existential contours they are strikingly similar. From this perspective, Dr. Ambedkar could never have ignored it. He could not have missed the Garvey movement,[199] by far the largest mass movement of Black Americans of 1920s that challenged entrenched ideas of white supremacy and black inferiority. It spread the ideas that Black people, Black culture, Black history, and Africa were noble and that Black people had created great civilizations that rivaled the Western civilization on every front. Such was the receptivity of these ideas by the Black people that it soon developed into a major mass movement, shaking the very foundations of white supremacy. Then there was the Harlem Renaissance[200] around the same time. This was a major literary movement but essentially carryied the similar message. This movement produced what has come to be characterized as protest literature. It created a new consciousness of self esteem and self-worth among the Blacks. Suddenly they discarded the humiliating identity stuck to them by the whites and became proud of their Black heritage, which constituted the bedrock for their struggle for liberation.[201] Surprisingly, Dr. Ambedkar never spoke or wrote about these struggles, which were essentially for civil rights, when he was trying to secure the same for the Untouchables in India. His writings are replete with references to 'Negros'[202] but all of them are to stress that the plight of the Untouchables is no better, or rather worse than theirs. 'For most authors', writes Kapoor (2003), 'Ambedkar was not influenced by the Black American struggle, though his stay in America coincided with an efflorescence of Black protest literature. Instead he used his knowledge of American culture to analyze his own country's social situation.'[203] It may rather be more reasonably said that his American experience filtered through the Deweyan teachings of pragmatism.[204] Later in *What Congress and Gandhi have Done to the Untouchables*, published in 1945, Ambedkar quoted extensively from Herbert Aptheker's *The Negro in the Civil War* (1938) in chapter 7. Aptheker, a white American Marxist historian and political activist had devoted his life to studying black history. He had worked closely with W.E.B. Du Bois, the radical black intellectual, whom he took as one of his mentors.[205] The fact that Ambedkar read and made much of Aptheker suggests that he must have been fairly alert to important developments in the black movement. Surprisingly, Ambedkar never spoke of or cited anything from W.E.B. Du Bois, the premier black intellectual of Ambedkar's time and one of the most radical thinkers then living in the United States. Interestingly, Du Bois did not live far from Ambedkar's residence in Manhattan. Late in 1946, we find an exchange of letters between them. Dr. Ambedkar wrote:

> Dear Prof. Du Bois,
>
> Although I have not met you personally, I know you by name as everyone does who is working in the cause of securing liberty to the oppressed people. I belong to the Untouchables of India and perhaps you might have heard my name. I have been a student of the Negro problem and have read your writings throughout. There is so much similarity between the position of the Untouchables in India and of the position of the Negroes in America that the study of the latter is not only natural but necessary.
>
> I was very much interested to read that the Negroes of America have filed a petition to the U.N.O. The Untouchables of India are also thinking of following suit. Will you be so good as to secure for me two or three copies of this representation by the Negroes and send them to my address? I need hardly say how very grateful I shall be for your troubles in this behalf.

Du Bois's response, dated 31 July 1946:

> My dear Mr. Ambedkar,
>
> I have your letter concerning the case of the Negroes of America and the Untouchables in India before the United Nations. As you say a small organization of American Negroes, the National Negro Congress has already made a statement which I am enclosing. I think, however, that a much more comprehensive statement well documented will eventually be laid before the United Nations by the National Association for the Advancement of Colored People. If this is done I shall be glad to send you a copy.
>
> I have often heard of your name and work and of course have every sympathy with the Untouchables of India. I shall be glad to be of any service I can render if possible in the future.[206]

Kapoor (2004) who has written a book on the similarities between the African Americans and the Dalits felt that 'in his approach to the Dalit issue and strategies evolved for achieving their liberation, Ambedkar was influenced by W.E.B. Du Bois.'[207] There were striking similarities between these two towering personalities. As Dr. Ambedkar did in relation to the caste system, Du Bois also systematically examined the entire race question, the damage that racism had caused to their psyche and what should be done to come out of it. As Dr. Ambedkar emphasized higher education for Dalits expecting that a few of them would pull up the rest of the community, Du Bois in his famous *Talented Ten* essay, wanted at least ten percent of bright (Black) young men to be trained in the best manner possible so that they in their turn bring others up. In such an expectation both had imagined a kind of 'ethical role' being performed by the talented people of their respective communities; that they would subordinate their individual interests to larger interests of their community; be 'leaders of thought and missionaries of culture among their people.' And both were disappointed by the aftermath as their talented people turned elitist, abdicated their responsibility and imitated the standards and aspirations of the white middle class or the upper castes. Du Bois was forced to re-examine his thesis of the *Talented Ten* in a memorial address which he gave at the Grand Boule Conclave in 1948: 'I assumed that with knowledge, sacrifice would automatically follow. In my youth and idealism, I did not realize that selfishness is even more natural than sacrifice.'[208] Dr. Ambedkar publicly lamented in Agra on 18 March 1956 that those very people had cheated him. While one can find many such similarities between these towering personalities, as Kapoor presented in his book, one can note as many dissimilarities too. While the similarities may be taken as natural coincidences stemming from similarities of problems faced, the dissimilarities may be attributed to different situational contexts. The fact remains, as Kapoor himself notes, that Ambedkar did not mention Du Bois anywhere in his writings.[209]

Vaikom Satyagraha

While this build-up was taking place in Maharashtra for the launch of the civil rights struggle of the Untouchables, the national attention was attracted by a significant event in distant Kerala. It was the *Vaikom Satyagraha* against the Hindu orthodoxy to secure rights for the Depressed Classes to use the roads surrounding the Siva temple at Vaikom in central Travancore. For the first time in history, the agitation brought forward the question of civil rights of the low caste people into the forefront of Indian politics.

Way back in 1865 the Government of Travancore had published a notification that all public roads in the state were open to all castes of people and had reiterated the same in July 1884 with a fresh notification. Why it precipitated into a Satyagraha only in 1924 is explained by the activities of Arya Samajists in Kerala. In the wake of the Moplah revolt in 1921, the Arya Samajists had gone to Kerala and converted some low caste people. Initially the converts were allowed to use the roads around the Vaikom temple but later under pressure of orthodox Hindus, the authorities had announced that conversion to the Arya Samaj did not make a difference in the status of the low caste and closed the roads again.

In a judicial review of the notification, the High Court also favoured the orthodox opinion saying that the roads around Vaikom temple were the *grama veedhis*, barred to the avarnas and not the *Raja veedhis* covered by the notification. Interestingly, Muslims, Christians, and all animals could use it but not the avarnas. Enraged by this, Swami Shraddhanand and Pandit Rishiram issued a protest manifesto exhorting all Hindus, and in particular Pandit Madan Mohan Malviya as the head of the Hindu Mahasabha, to take action. Distressed by the condition of the Hindus of south India he wired Mahatma Gandhi to take some organizational action.[210] This is said to have prompted Gandhi to start the temple entry Satyagraha by the Travancore Congress.

The temple had a long history of notoriety, having humiliated Shree Narayana Guru, the founder of *Shree Narayana Dharma Paripalana Yogam* (SNDP) and Ayyankali, a noted Dalit leader and member of Pulayar caste. About two hundred years ago some two hundred bold and daring *Ezhava* young men, in and around Vaikom, had decided to enter the temple and worship the deity. Balarama Varma was the king of Travancore at that time and Kunchukutti Pillai was the Diwan (Dalawa). As protesters advanced towards the temple, they were attacked by the Diwan's swordsmen, killing most of them. All the dead bodies were collected and buried in the temple pond at the northeastern side of the temple, where now a bus station stands.[211] This memory was alive among Ezhavas who revived the issue in 1905, this time through their representatives in the Travancore Legislature. It was not entertained under the alibi of being a religious question. When T.K. Madhavan, a favorite disciple of Shree Narayan Guru and the organizing secretary of the SNDP, became a member of the Travancore Legislature he took up the matter. It is claimed that Madhavan met Gandhi at Tirunelveli on 23 September 1921 and secured his approval for starting the struggle. He later attended the Kakinada AICC meet (1923) and got the Congress to agree to include the eradication of untouchability in their constructive programmes and resolved to lend full support to the Vaikom movement, authorizing the Kerala Provincial Congress Committee (KPCC) to undertake the task.[212]

The KPCC met at Ernakulum on 24 January 1924, and formed an Untouchability Abolition Committee (UAC) consisting of K. Kelappan (convener), T.K. Madhavan, Kurur Nilakantan Namboothiri, T.R. Krishna Swami Iyer, and K. Velayudha Menon. The date for the Satyagraha was fixed as 30 March 1924, and in view of the prohibitory orders against the procession, it was decided to send only three volunteers every day to offer Satyagraha. All newspapers in India flashed headlines about the Satyagraha. Money flowed from different states to Vaikom. The Akalis of Punjab came to Vaikom to open a free kitchen for the Satyagrahis. E.V. Ramasami Naicker, who was active Congress activist came with his wife Nagamma and a group of followers and offered Satyagraha on April 14. As the head of the *Satyagraha*, Periyar was imprisoned twice.[213] Gandhi visited Vaikom along with his secretary Mahadev Desai, son Ramdas Gandhi, and Congressmen Alladi Krishnaswamy Iyer and C. Rajgopalachari. He spent time in fruitless discussions with temple priests on the problem concerning the

Untouchables and their *karma*—their status as the result of previous action.[214] He tried to strike a compromise with *the savarna* leader Idanthuruthil Devan Neelakandan Namboothiri but the latter would not budge. Eventually, Gandhi took assistance of W.H. Pitt, the then European Police Commissioner of Travancore and struck a compromise with the government. The government agreed to withdraw the prohibitory orders passed in February 1924, and Gandhi agreed to withdraw the Satyagraha. The government let the roads on three sides of the temple (north, south and west) open for public but the eastern approach road, and the two roads leading to it from the north and south remained reserved for the Savarnas only. Gates were to be put up at three places to be open only at the time of worship to admit those who had the right to enter the temple. It was also declared that the portion of the road enclosed by the three gates would remain closed to Christians and Muslims as well as avarna Hindus who had no right to enter the temple. Gandhi issued orders on 8 October 1925 to the Secretary of the *Satyagraha Ashram* to withdraw the Satyagraha.[215]

The Satyagraha thus ended only with a partial success for the Avarnas as they gained access only to the roads on three sides of the temple; the fourth and most important eastern road remaining inaccessible to them. It spelt a real blow to the Christians and Muslims as they lost their previously enjoyed freedom to have complete access on all the roads around the temple. The main gain accrued to the Congress through its tremendous expansion; it swelled from being a class party to a mass party.

In March 1926, one Murugesan, a Mala by caste, was tried before the Stationary Sub-Magistrate of Tirupathi for having ventured to enter a temple at Tiruchanur for the purpose of offering worship. The Lower Court regarded this entry as 'defilement with intent to insult the religion of a class' under section 295 of I.P.C. and fined the accused Rs. 75 or in default rigorous imprisonment for one month.[216] Dr. Ambedkar watched these developments carefully. By now he had earned a name for himself as a lawyer in the High Court and found himself nominated to the Bombay Legislative Council. It is at this stage that he had accepted an invitation to preside over the conference at Mahad, the aftermath of which would be hailed in history as one of the glorious struggles for civil rights waged by the ones who were not reckoned as humans for millennia. Indeed, as he himself observed, in its import it was comparable to the French Revolution, echoing its slogan of *'Liberté, égalité, fraternité'* (Liberty, Equality, Fraternity), albeit in symbolic sense.

NOTES AND REFERENCES

1. Although the better known civil rights movement of the African Americans happened during 1955 and 1968, it may be considered the culmination of a long series of campaigns, non-violent as well as violent, carried out by them as early as the 18th century. For instance, the famous New York Slave Revolt took place in 1712, wherein 23 enslaved Africans armed with guns, hatchets, and swords, revolted killing nine whites and injuring another six. "On the 300th anniversary of a slave revolt, we need to learn its lessons" http://progressive.org/300th_anniversary_of_slave_revolt.html. [Last accessed on 21 January2014].
2. Several theories are advanced for the origin of the caste system, which have little in common. The main theories are (1) Traditional or Indological theory, (2) Racial theory, (3) Racial/ Functional theory, (4) Occupational/ Functional theory, (5) Guild theory, (6) Religious theory, (7) Political theory, (8) *Mana* theory and (9) Multifactor theory. The Traditional or Indological theory is based on the Rigvedic proposition that the varnas, the precursor of the castes were originated by god. Castes and sub-castes were born later as a result of different types of marriages between varnas in ancient India. Although of little intellectual value, it underlies the popular belief in castes. Racial Theory propounded by Sir Herbert Risely [Herbert Risley, *The People of India*, Thacker, Spink & Co., London, 1915.] held that caste system was due to racial differences between Aryas and Anaryas (native people). G.S. Ghurye [G.S. Ghurye, *Caste and Race in India*. Alfred Knopf, New York, 1932.] and Westermarck [E. Westermarck, *History of Human Marriage*, Macmillan, London, 1901] appear to support this theory. Racial/Functional Theory, put forth by Slater [G. Slater, *The Dravidian Elements in Indian Culture*, London, 1924]; combines both the racial and functional origins, postulating that the caste system was created to safeguard the professional and

occupational secrets of different races. The Aryan invasions intensified and developed the existing structure making occupations hereditary and marriage only within the same occupation groups, sanctified later by ritual practices and religious ceremonies. Occupational/Functional theory, originally propounded by Nesfield [J.C. Nesfield, *Brief View of the Caste System of the North-Western Provinces and Oudh*, Government Press, Allahabad, 1885], held that occupation were the main base of caste-system. The notion of hierarchy of castes stemmed basically from the superiority or inferiority of occupations. The Guild theory put forth by Denzil Ibbeston [Denzil Ibbeston, *Panjab Castes*; Being a Reprint of the Chapter on "The Races, Castes and Tribes of the People" in the Report on the *Census of the Panjab* published in 1883, Nabu Press, 2010] holds that castes are the modified forms of guilds and the caste system was the product of three forces, (i) tribes, (ii) guilds, and (iii) religion. The guilds evolved into castes imitating the endogamy of the prestigious class of priests. The religious theory was advocated by Hocart [Arthur Maurice Hocart, *Caste: A Comparative Study* . University of Minnesota , 2010] and Senart [Emile Senart, *Caste in India: The Facts and the System*, Lawrence Verry Incorporated, 1975; E. Senart and A. Hegglin, *The Castes in India*, British India Press, 1912]. Hocart postulated that the caste system grew out of religious customs, traditions, sanskars, etc. The king recognised as the representative of the god and religion, allotted positions to different functional groups, the top position being given to priests as mediator to God. Senart tried to explain the caste system on the basis of prohibitions regarding sacramental food. The political theory held that caste system was the result of the political conspiracy of the Brahmans to secure control over the functions of the society. This theory was originally propounded by a French scholar Abbe Dubais and found tacit support in many people including S.G. Ghurye. *Mana* theory based on the views of J.H. Hutton [John Henry Hutton, *Castes in India*, Oxford University Press, New Delhi, 1963] accords the caste system pre-Aryan origin and suggests that the primitive belief in 'mana' among tribes accounted for the origin of the caste system. Mana was associated with magical and harmful powers and hence the ancient tribes evolved elaborate taboos or restrictions to protect themselves from other tribes' mana. Multifactor theory propounded by sociologists held that a complex phenomenon of the caste system could not be explained by a single factor and rather was a result of many factors such as beliefs in racial superiority, geographical isolation, metaphysical concepts, belief in *mana*, desire to maintain racial purity of blood and manipulation by Brahmans. In spite of a plethora of theories as above and numerous other books, essays and census reports dealing with the subject of Hindu castes, the problem of the origin of caste still remains one of the most difficult ethnological and sociological problems.

3. Book 10, Hymn 90, verses 11-12. *The Hymns of the Rigveda,* translated by Ralph Griffith, 2nd edition, Kotagiri (Nilgiri) 1896. Available: http://www.sanskritweb.net/rigveda/griffith.pdf. [Last Accessed on 16 June 2011].
4. "Atharva Veda (IV 6.1; XV. 8.1) mentions only three varnas. Even in the Rig Veda the Shudras have not been mentioned separately. But the later Vedic text mentions this word quite often. It shows that the concept of Shudra was originated during the later part of the Vedic period." See: A.R. Tripathi, *The Concept of Shudras in Manu Smriti: A Reappraisal.* The paper is available at www.indologica.com/volumes/vol30/23_Tripathi.pdf. [Last accessed on 21 Ianuary, 2014].
5. Patrick Olivelle, *Manu's Code of Law*, OUP India, New Delhi, 2006, p. 208.
6. Originally Vishnugupta, also known as Chanakya.
7. The authorship and period of the Arthashastra however is disputed among historians. While R. Sham Sastri, T. Gopinath Sastri, K.P. Jayaswal, D.R. Bhandarkar, R.K. Mukerji. K.A. Nilakantha Sastri, H.C. Ray, Kane, L.D. Benett, V.A. Smith, F.W. Thomas, Romila Thapar, D.D. Kosambi and others say that it was written towards the end of the fourth century BC, others like Julius Jolly, Keith and Winternitz are of the opinion that it was later produced in early centuries of the Christian era. Some others periodize it in the fourth century AD. See, K.S. Padhy, *Indian Political Thought*, PHI Learning, New Delhi, 2011, p. 33.
8. *The Laws of Manu*, translated by George Bühler, in *Sacred Books of the East*, Volume 25, I, 31. Dr Ambedkar had also used this translation.
9. Ibid., I, 87.
10. Ibid., I, 93.
11. Ibid., I, 91.
12. Ibid., VIII, 413.
13. Vivekanand Jha in *Subordinate and Marginal Groups in Early India*

edited by Parasher-Sen, Oxford Paperbacks, New Delhi, 2nd edition, 2007, pp. 157-158.

14. *The Laws of Manu*, translated by George Bühler, op. cit., X, 45.
15. Ibid., X, 46.
16. Ibid., X, 49.
17. Ibid., X, 55.
18. Ibid., X, 56.
19. Ibid., X, 50.
20. Ibid., X, 52.
21. Ibid., X, 53.
22. Ibid., X, 54.
23. Eleanor Zelliot, 'Untouchability' in *Encyclopedia of Asian History*, Scribner, New York, 1988, pp. 169-171.
24. This section draws on the Introduction to my earlier work, *The Persistence of Caste: The Khairlanji Murders & India's Hidden Apartheid*, Navayana, New Delhi and Zed Books, London, 2010.
25. The *shramanas* were wandering mendicant spiritual seekers. They came from castes other than the Brahmans and sought liberation by leaving society. They lived together in forests, with no caste differences, as a spiritual community (*sangha*), rather than as solitary ascetics. They organized their autonomous communities on the model of the republics, with decisions made by assemblies. Moreover, all of them rejected a supreme god, such as *Brahma*, or any other form of a creator. Although the *shramana* communities had no caste differences within them, the lay people who followed their teachings and supported them still lived with the structure of the caste system. Alexander Berzin, *The Berzin Archives*, March 1990, revised April 2007. Internet resource: http://www.berzinarchives.com/web/en/ archives/study/history_buddhism/buddhism_india/ indian_society_thought_time_buddha_.html. [Last accessed on 2 January 2014].
26. James G. Lochtefeld, *The Illustrated Encyclopedia of Hinduism: NZ*, Volume 2, The Rosen Publishing Group, 2002, p. 639.
27. At least five shramana schools are identified, viz., The Ajivika School, founded by Gosala, The Lokayata or Charvaka School, taught by Ajita, The Jain or Nirgrantha School, founded by Mahavira, The Ajnana School of Agnostics, led by Sanjayin, and Buddhism founded by Gautama Buddha. See Alexander Berzin, *Indian Society and Thought Before and at the Time of Buddha*, http://www.berzinarchives.com/web/en/archives/study/history_buddhism/buddhism_india/indian_society_thought_time_ buddha_.html. [Last accessed on 2 January, 2014].

28. Ibid.
29. Anand Teltumbde, *Introduction to Buddhavichar: Marxwadi Drushtikshep* (*Buddhism: A Marxist Persepctive*), Fourth Edition, Lokvangmay Gruh, Mumbai, 2011. (Marathi)
30. Edmund Weber, Buddhism: An Atheistic and Anti-Caste Religion? *Journal of Religious Culture/Journal für Religionskultur* No. 50 (2001).
31. Hans Wolfgang Schumann: Der historische Buddha, München 1992, cited in Weber, Edmund, op. cit.
32. Randall Collins, *The Sociology of Philosophies: A Global Theory of Intellectual Change*, Harvard University Press, 2000.
33. The main contributing factors to disappearance of Buddhism from the land of its origin are commonly cited as resurgence of Brahmanism led by Adi Sankara and the Muslim invasions. See, Padmanabh S. Jaini, "The Disappearance of Buddhism and the Survival of Jainism: A Study in Contrast", in A.K. Narain (ed.), *Studies in History of Buddhism*, B.R. Publishing Co., Delhi, 1980, pp. 181-91. While Muslim invasions destroyed physical marks of Buddhism, the resurgence of Brahmanism destroyed its ideological base. How could it be possible if the Buddhist ideology had taken root among common people? The plausible explanation is that Buddhism after getting patronage from Kings tended to become vihar-centric focused on abstract philosophising. The Buddhist monks generally ignored Buddha's exhortation to wander among people and got habituated with vihar comforts. See, Ankur Barua and M.A. Basilio, *Contributing Factors for the Disappearance of Buddhism from India*, Dissertation, University of Hong Kong (MBuddStud, 2009). Available at https://www.academia.edu/207076/CONTRIBUTING_FACTORS_FOR_THE_DISAPPEARANCE_OF_BUDDHISM_FROM_INDIA. [Last accessed on 16 June 2014].
34. Jerald D. Gort, Henry Jansen and Hendrik M. Vroom, *Religion, Conflict and Reconciliation*, Editions Rodopi, Amsterdam, 2002, p. 239.
35. Josef W. Meri and Jere L. Bacharach, *Medieval Islamic Civilization*, Routledge, New York, 2006, p. 120. It was Buddhism per se rather than Indian practices such as *bhakti* (devotionalism, in this context) that had some generalized impact on the early Sufi practitioners.
36. Ram Puniyani, *Religion, Power and Violence*, Sage, New Delhi, 2005, p. 210.
37. T.W. Arnold, Spread of Islam in the World, cited in A Ezzati,

The Spread of Islam: The Contributing Factors, Islamic College for Advanced Studies Press, London, 2002, p. 292.

38. Ibid.
39. Romila Thapar, *A History of India*, Penguin, New Delhi, 1996.
40. Shyama Charan Dube and Shyam Nandan Chaudhary, *Changing Status of Depressed Castes in Contemporary India: Essays*, Daya Publishing House, Delhi, 1988, p. 19.
41. Yoginder Sikand, *Caste in Indian Muslim Society*, http://stateless.freehosting.net/Caste%20in%20Indian%20Muslim%20Society.htm. [Last Accessed on 16 June 2014].
42. Bhagwat's website, http://pushti-marg.net/bhagwat/caste-2.htm; Hindu website, http://www.hinduwebsite.com/hinduism/h_caste.asp. [Last Accessed on 21 January, 2014].
43. Y.G. Bhave, (ed.), *Vinayak Damodar Savarkar: The Much-maligned and Misunderstood Revolutionary*, Northern Book Centre, New Delhi, 2009, p. 30.
44. Although the Bhakti movement did not exclusively spoke for the Dalits or proposed any agenda for radical changes in the social structure of Hindu society, through its spiritual idiom it established a pattern of questioning the Hindu social order. Many saints from among the Shudra and Untouchable castes such as Chokha Mela, Karma Mela, Banka and Nirmala, the courtesan Kanhopatra, as well as the non-Brahman saints Namdev (tailor), Gora Kumbhar (potter), Sawata Mali (gardner), Sena (barber), and Tukaram (kunbi—peasant) rose to prominence during the 13th and 14th century. Many of the *abhangas* of these poet saints (and especially those of the Untouchables) expressed in poignant terms the inequalities and injustices suffered by the lower castes as a result of the varna order. See: Jayashree B. Gokhale-Turner, Bhakti or Vidroha: Continuity and Change in Dalit Sahitya in Jayant Lele (ed.), *Tradition and Modernity in Bhakti Movements*, E.J. Brill, Leiden, 1981, p. 29.
45. Romila Thapar, op. cit.
46. The earliest Christian community in India is that of the Syrian Christians of Kerala (also known as Syrians, the Christians of St. Thomas or simply the Thomas Christians) who, according to their tradition are descendants of upper caste (Namboothiri Brahman) converted by St. Thomas, one of the twelve apostles of Jesus. A small group of endogamous Syrians (now Catholics and Jacobites) known as Knanaya Christians or 'Southerners' or 'Southists' claim to be directly descended from Syrian merchants ...consider themselves 'pure-blooded' and superior to the

'Northerners' or 'Northists'. They strictly enforce endogamy and do not accept converts from outside.' 'J. Tharamangalam, Caste among Christians in India' in M.N. Srinivas, *Caste: Its Twentieth Century Avatar*, Penguin Books, 1996, p. 266.

47. By 1534, there were 1503 Dominicans, 1542 Jesuits, and 1572 Augustinians working in India. *The Encyclopedia of Protestantism*, Vol. 2 [D–K].
48. Quoted in Nicholas B. Dirks, *Castes of Mind: Colonialism and the Making of Modern India*, Princeton University Press, Princeton, 2001, p. 25.
49. The ideals of humility and the rejection of worldly possession associated with Christianity appealed to the early Christians. Christianity was thought of as "the religion of the poor". Dick Kooiman, *Conversion and Social Equality in India*, South Asia Publications, New Delhi, 1983, p. 102.
50. Shekhar Bandyopadhyay, *Caste, Politics and the Raj: Bengal 1872-1937*, Department of History, University of Calcutta and K.P. Bagchi & Co., Calcutta, 1990, p. 22.
51. Richard Lovett, *The History of the London Missionary Society 1795-1895,* Henry Frowde, London, 1899, Vol. II, 4-6. The obstacles identified were: 'the institution of caste'; 'the absence of all religious and social liberty'; 'the utterly perverted standard of conduct'; the 'oppressive supremacy of the Brahman class'; 'polytheistic idolatry'; 'the fear of malignant demons'; 'the belief in religious merit'; 'pantheistic teaching'; 'the degradation of women'; 'the degradation of low caste'; and 'a whole jungle of superstitious beliefs and corrupt practices'.
52. Ibid.
53. Stephen Neill, *A History of Christian Missions,* Penguin, Harmondsworth, 2nd edn., 1986, p. 195.
54. Arthur Mayhew, *Christianity in India,* Gian Publishing House, Delhi, 1998, p. 161.
55. Schwartz, a German missionary established a Vestry school at Trichy in 1772 and at Tanjore, Vepery and Cuddalore soon thereafter. Later in 1787, he opened schools at Tanjore, Ramnad and Sivaganga and three years later at Kumbkonam. While schools at Ramnad and Sivaganga had closed because of the uncongenial attitude of the Indian ruler there, the other schools at Tanjore and Kimbakonam blossomed out into full-fledged colleges. In Bombay a school was established in 1719. In Bengal the first school was opened in 1731. See, Dev Raj Seth, *A History of Western Education in India,* A PhD thesis, prr.hec.gov.pk/

Thesis/1876.pdf. [Last Accessed on 2 January 2014].

56. William Carey to Jabez Carey, Serampore 20 August 1815. Cited in Brian Stanley, *The History of the Baptist Missionary Society 1792-1992,* T&T Clark, Edinburgh, 1992, p. 51; and Timothy George Steve Bishop 'Protestant Missionary Education in British India' *Evangelical Quarterly* 69:3 (1997), 245-266.
57. G. Smith, *Life of Alexander Duff,* 2 Vols., A.C. Armstrong, New York, 1879.
58. D.N. Thakur, *Education and Manpower Development*, Deep & Deep Publications, New Delhi, 2004, p. 528.
59. Joshua Kalapati, "The Early Educational Mission of the Scottish Missionaries in Madras Presidency: Its Social Implications" *Scottish Bulletin of Evangelical Theology*, Vol. 16, No. 2, Autumn 1998, pp. 140-155.
60. John Braidwood, True Yoke-fellows in the Mission Field; the life and Labours of the Rev. John Anderson and the Rev. Robert Johnson, traced in the *Rise and Development of the Madras Free Church Mission*, London, 1862, pp. 74-97; S.C. Neill, *A History of Christianity in India: 1707-1858*, Cambridge University Press, Cambridge, 1985, p. 320. Also cited in E.G.K. Hewat, *Vision and Achievement, 1796-1956*. Nelson, Edinburgh, 1960, p. 84.
61. S.C. Neill, *A History of Christianity in India: 1707-1858,* Cambridge University Press, Cambridge, 985, p. 324.
62. Govind P. Deshpande, *Selected Writings of Jotirao Phule,* LeftWord Books, New Delhi, 2002, p. 142.
63. In his evidence before Simon Commission on behalf of Bahishkrut Hitkarini Sabha on May 29, 1928, he states how the missionaries had been the only source of education for the Dalits. Moon, Vasant (ed.), *Dr. Babasaheb Ambedkar: Writings and Speeches*, Vol. 2, Government of Maharashtra, Mumbai, 1982, p. 419.
64. Adam Andrew and William Goudie had taken up the issue of reform in the land tenure system in Madras in the 1880s and 1990s. For that they did an economic survey during the late 1800s and submitted a memorandum to the British government to allot lands to the Pariahs to improve their socio-economic condition. See: G.A. Oddie, *Social Protest in India: British Protestant Missionaries and Social Reforms 1850-1900*, cited in Andrew Porter, *Religion Versus Empire?: British Protestant Missionaries and Overseas Expansion 1700-1914*, Manchester University Press, New York, 2004, p. 308. Also, see P.M. Gnanadurai, *William Goudie: Prince Amongst Missionaries*, The University of Michigan, 2002; and Lewis J., William Goudie, Wesleyan Methodist Missions in

Ceylon, India and Burma: Report of Secretarial Visit, 1920-21, *Wesleyan Methodist Missionary Society*, 1923, pp. 35-6, 39-40, 51, 57-9.

65. Franklyn J. Balasundaram, *Dalits and Christian Mission in the Tamil Country*, The University of Michigan, New York, p. 168.
66. This minute became the basis of education system and remained so in various forms right up till recent times. Parmatam Parkash Arya, *Higher Education and Global Challenges: Systems and Opportunities*, Deep & Deep, New Delhi, 2006, p. 124.
67. Narayan Mishra, *Scheduled Castes Education: Issues and Aspects*, Kalpaz Publications, New Delhi, 2001.
68. B.R. Ambedkar, Dr. Ambedkar with the Simon Commission: Statement "B" concerning the state of education of the Depressed Classes in the Bombay Presidency, in Moon, Vasant (ed.), *Dr. Babasaheb Ambedkar: Writings and Speeches*, Vol. 2, Government of Maharashtra, Mumbai, 1982, p. 419.
69. Richard B. White, *The Mahar Movement's Military Component*, op. cit.
70. B.R. Ambedkar, What Congress and Gandhi Have Done to the Untouchables, in Moon, Vasant (ed.), *Dr. Babasaheb Ambedkar: Writings and Speeches*, Vol. 2, Government of Maharashtra, Mumbai, 1991, p. 189.
71. Eleanor Zelliot, cited in Subodh Kapoor (ed.), *The Indian Encyclopaedia*, Cosmo, New Delhi, 2002, p. 4474.
72. Richard B. White, *The Mahar Movement's Military Component*, op. cit.
73. Morris David Morrios, *The Emergence of an Industrial Labour Force in India*, University of California Press, Berkeley and Los Angeles, 1965, p. 73n.
74. White, Richard B., op. cit.
75. Mamta Rajawat, et al. (eds.), *Encyclopaedia of Dalits in India*, Vol. 1, Anmol Publications, Delhi, 2004, p. 93.
76. Ibid., p. 93.
77. Ibid., p. 93.
78. Ibid., p. 93.
79. Ibid., p. 93.
80. Dhananjay Keer, *Mahatma Jotirao Phule: Father of the Indian Social Revolution*, Popular Prakashan, Mumbai, 1974, p. 14.
81. Rosalind O'Hanlond, *Caste, Conflict and Ideology: Mahatma Jotirao Phule and Low Caste Protest in Nineteenth-century Western India*, Cambridge University Press, New York, 2002, p. 111.
82. It happened to be the second such school in the entire country;

the first having been opened the previous year in Barsat, a suburb of Calcutta by Peary Charan Sarkar, a member of "Young Bengal".

83. Rosalind O'Hanlond, op. cit., p. 124.
84. Y.D. Phadke, *Biography of Mahatma Phule*, http://defeatpoverty.com/articles/Slavery%20Book/Bio%20of%20Phule.pdf. [Last Accessed on 16 June 2011].
85. Braj Ranjan Mani, and Pamela Sardar (eds.) *A Forgotten Leader: The Life and Struggle of Savitribai Phule*, Mountain Peak, 2008, pp. 7, 9.
86. C.H. Nikumbhe, *Aadya Asprushoddharak Gopalbaba Walangkar*, Sugawa Prakashan, Pune, 2006, p.8.
87. Kshîrasâgara, Râmacandra, *Dalit Movement in India and Its Leaders, 1857-1956*, MD Publications, New Delhi, 1994, p. 372.
88. Anupama Rao, *The Caste Question*, Permanent Black, 2011, pp. 47, 49.
89. Ambedkar referred to Phule as one of his three gurus, Kabir and Buddha being the other two.
90. Mikael Aktor and Robert Deliège (eds.), *From Stigma to Assertion: Untouchability, Identity and Politics in Early and Modern India*, Museum Tusculanum Press, Copenhagen, 2010, p. 104.
91. Sinha, Mrunalini, *Specters of Mother India: The Global Restructuring of an Empire*, Duke University Press, 2006, p. 29.
92. On April 13, 1919, British Indian Army soldiers opened fire on an unarmed gathering of men, women and children in Jallianwala Bagh in Amritsar, demanding the release of two popular leaders against whom deportation orders were issued. Official sources place the casualties at 379. According to private sources, the number was over 1000, with more than 1200 wounded. The Civil Surgeon Dr. Smith indicated that they were over 1800. The figures were never fully ascertained for political reasons. See, Raja Ram, *The Jallianwala Bagh Massacre: A Premeditated Plan*, Publication Bureau, Panjab University, 1978, p. 87.
93. See, Valerian Rodrigues (ed.), *The Essential Writings of B.R. Ambedkar*, OUP, New Delhi, 2008, p. 396.
94. In August 1917, Edwin Montagu, the Secretary of State for India, made the historic announcement in Parliament that the British policy for India was "increasing association of Indians in every branch of the administration and the gradual development of self-governing institutions with a view to the progressive realization of responsible government in India as an integral part

of the British Empire."

95. Eleanor Zelliot, Congress and the Untouchables: 1917-1950 in Sisson, Richard, *Congress and Indian Nationalism: The Pre-Independence Phase*, University of California, Los Angeles, 1988, p. 182; B.R. Ambedkar, What Congress and Gandhi Have Done to the Untouchables? in Moon, Vasant (ed.), *Dr. Babasaheb Ambedkar: Writings and Speeches*, Vol. 9, Government of Maharashtra, Mumbai,1991, p. 13.
96. Christophe Jaffrelot, *Religion, Caste, and Politics in India*, Primus Books, Delhi, 2010, p. 55.
97. Brahmo Samaj inspired many Brahman intellectuals to launch similar reform movements. When Keshavchandra Sen had lectured in Mumbai for the promotion of Brahmo Samaj, people like Dr. Bhandarkar, Justice Ranade, Atmaram Pandurang were immensely impressed and began thinking of starting similar movements in Maharahstra. Many such Samajs and Sabhas followed. 1. Paramhans Sabha was founded by Dadoba Pandurang in 1848. This Sabha operated secretly and was opened only for the educated people from Hindus and non-Hindus but not for the Untouchables. 2. Prarthana Sabha was founded by the members of Paramhans Sabha on 31 March 1867 at the house of Atmaram Pandurang, brother of Dadoba Pandurang. It attracted many progressive elements and had a wide range of programmes that included eradication of untouchability. Later, with the foundation of the Depresseed Classes Mission, V.R. Shinde speeded up the work for the Untouchables and attracted many people from the latter class. 3. Satyashodhak Samaj, was founded in September 1873 by Mahatma Phule, who had unleashed a social revolution by declaring the war against Shetji-Bhatji combine. 4. Arya Samaj was formed by Dayanand Saraswati, who had earler worked in Brahmo Samaj and Prarthana Samaj, on 10 April 1875 in Mumbai. It claimed to restore the Vedic basis to Hinduism and tried to negate birth-based varna distinctions. 5. Sarvajanik Sabha was founded on 2 April 1870, which worked as a general service organization and did not have much to do with the issues of Untouchables. See for concise discussion on these movements. See, B.R. Maske, *Vidabhatil Dalit Chalavalicha Itihas*, Nabha Prakashan, Amravati, 2012, pp. 47-54.
98. K.N. Panikkar, Was There A Renaissance? *Frontline*, Volume 28, Issue 05: February 26-March 11, 2011.
99. Full name, Krishnaji Keshav Damle, considered to be the father

of modern Marathi Poetry, denounced the revivalist hallucinatory trend in literature of his times, and wrote against differentiation between man and man on the basis of caste, creed or community and advocated liberty, equality and fraternity in his poems. See, Prabhakar Machwe, *Keshavsut, Indian Literature*, Sahitya Akademi, Vol. 9, No. 3 (July-September 1966).

100. Ramakrishna Gopal Bhandarkar, an Indian scholar, orientalist, and social reformer, he promoted liberal ideas and reforms like denunciation of the caste system, encouragement of widow remarriage, encouragement of female education, and abolition of child marriage. He contended that religious reforms were required as a basis for social reforms and helped found the Prarthana Samaj, a movement for religious and social reform. See, H.A. Phadke, *R.G. Bhandarkar* (National Biography series), National Book Trust, India, 1968.
101. A scholar, jurist, and author, Ranade was a founding member of the Indian National Congress and a founder of the Social Conference movement within the Congress. His reforms were directed against child marriage, maltreatment of widows, extravagant marriages, and caste discrimination. See, James Kellock, *Mahadev Govind Ranade: Patriot and Social Servant*, Association Press (Y.M.C.A.), 1926.
102. Gopal Ganesh Agarkar openly confronted conservativism of Tilak. Through his own periodical *Sudharak* he fiercely advocated reforms, campaigned against the injustices of untouchability and the caste system and abhorred blind adherence to and glorification of tradition. See, Aravind Ganachari, *Gopal Ganesh Agarkar: The Secular Rationalist Reformer*, Popular Prakashan, Mumbai, 2005.
103. Hari Narayan Apte was a Marathi writer who promoted social reform such as women's education. See, Ramchandra Bhikaji Joshi, *H.N. Apte*, Sahitya Akademi, New Delhi, 1978.
104. Also known as Maharshi or Karmveer Shinde.
105. They are discussed in his book in Marathi—*Bhartiya Asprushyatecha Prashna* (India's untouchability question), which was published in 1933.
106. Christophe Jaffrelot, *Dr. Ambedkar and Untouchabiliy: Analysing and Fighting Caste*, C. Hurst & Co. Publishers, London, 2000, pp. 44-45.
107. S.M. Dahiwale, *Emerging Entrepreneurship Among Scheduled Castes of Contemporary India*, Concept Publishing, New Delhi, 1989, p. 132.

108. Before the advent of Babasaheb Ambedkar, most socially-oriented educated Dalits were influenced by Shinde. His influence ranged far and wide. When he had organized *Asprushata Nivaran Parishad* (Untouchability Eradication Conference), which was presided over by Dr. Kurtkoti, many people from Vidarbha had gone to Pune to participate in it. Depressed Classes Mission had considerable influence in Vidarbha. Besides prominent community leaders like Kisan Fagoji Bansode and Ganesh Akkaji Gawai, educated person like P.N. Bhatkar, who was the first matriculate from Berar, had left his job to work for the Mission. Later, of course, this Bhatkar had worked as the editor of *Mooknayak*. See, B.R. Maske, op. cit., p. 66. Dahiwale notes that Dr. Ambedkar was also inspired by Shinde. S.M. Dahiwale, op. cit., p. 132.
109. Gail Omvedt, *Ambedkar: Towards an Enlightened India,* Penguin Books, New Delhi, 2008, p. 1921.
110. As Omvedt observed, Shinde and his Depressed Classes Mission antagonized Ambedkar by their apparently bland assumption that they could represent the interests of Untouchables; they made no efforts to take him or other Untouchable leaders into confidence when they were formulating demands. Moreover, their work appeared to him superficial as they did not make any effort to share food with Untouchables. See, Gail Omvedt, op. cit., pp. 1920-1.
111. Shivaprabha Ghugare, *Renaissance in Western India: Karmaveer V.R. Shinde, 1873-1944,* Himalaya Publishing House, Bombay, 1983, p. 113.
112. "Even the most reform-minded leadership agreed with Dadabhai Naoroji's statement at the second annual Congress meeting that Congress was a body "to represent to our rulers our political operations, not to discuss social reforms"" See, Eleanor Zelliot, Congress and the Untouchables: 1917-1950 in Richard Sisson, and Stanley A. Wolpert, (eds.), *Congress and Indian Nationalism: The Pre-independence Phase*, University of California Press, Berkeley, 1988, p. 182.
113. Sir Narayan Ganesh Chandavarkar was an early Indian National Congress politician and Hindu reformer. He was regarded by some as the "leading Hindu reformer of Western India" See, J.N. Farquhar, Modern Religious Movements in India, *Journal of the American Academy of Religion*, Vol. 43, No. 2, Book Review Supplement (June, 1975), pp. 349-351. Chandavarkar was a President of the Congress in 1900, General Secretary of the Indian

National Social Conference, and President of the Depressed Classes Mission Society. See, Eleanor Zelliot, Congress and the Untouchables: 1917-1950 in Richard Sisson, and Stanley A. Wolpert, (eds.), op. cit., p. 184.

114. Zelliot, Eleanor, Congreess and the Untouchables, 1917-1950 in Richard Sisson and Stanley A. Wolpert (eds.), op. cit., p. 184.
115. Ibid.
116. Quoted in G.P. Pradhan, and A.K. Bhagwat, *Lokamanya Tilak: A Biography*, Jaico Publishing House, Bombay, 1959, p. 306.
117. Gail Omvedt, op. cit., p. 1921.
118. The idea seems to have been born when Jotiba Phule demanded before the Hunter Commission in 1882 free and compulsory education for everyone along with proportionate representation in government jobs. In 1891, there was a demand for reservation of government jobs with an agitation against the recruitment of *non-natives* into public service overlooking qualified *native* people in the princely State of Travancore. See, Laskar, Mehbubul Hassan, "Rethinking Reservation in Higher Education in India" *ILI Law Review*, Vol. 1, No. 1, p. 25, 2010. Later, in 1921, Krishnaraja Wodeyar of Mysore state introduced reservations in the public positions and higher educational admissions in favour of non-Brahman communities including Muslims and the Untouchable. It was influenced by the Backward Classes movement in 1916 in the form of the Non-Brahman Conference, organized by the leaders of Justice Party. This movement had the objective of displacing Brahmans, who were in minority and yet dominated higher education, professions and bureaucracy. Harpreet Kaur and R.K. Suri, *Reservation in India: Recent Perspectives in Higher Education*, Pentagon Press, New Delhi, 2009, p. 42.
119. A.B. Latthe, *Memoirs of His Highness Shri Shahu Chhatrapati*, Times Press, Bombay, 1924, p. 454.
120. Mamta Rajawat, et al (eds.), op. cit., p. 94.
121. There were movements among the Dalits of Madras, Chamars of Chhattisgarh, the Depressed Classes of the Punjab, the Namashudras of Bengal, to name a few.
122. Mamta Rajawat, et al (eds.), op. cit., p. 93.
123. M. Nisar and Meena Kandasamy, *Ayyankali-Dalit Leader of Organic Protest*, Other Books, 2007, p. 67.
124. V.K. Ramachandran, "Kerala's Development Achievement and their Replicability", in Parayil, Govinda, *Kerala: the Development*

Experience: Reflections on Sustainability and Replicability, Zed Books, London, 2000, pp. 103-106.

125. Ghanashyam Shah, *Social Movements in India: A Review of Literature*, Sage Publications, New Delhi, 2004, p. 122.
126. M. Juergensmeyer, *Religion as Social Vision: The Movement against Untouchability in 20th-Century Punjab*, Berkeley, 1982, rev. ed. *Religious Rebels in the Punjab: The Ad Dharm Challenge to Caste*, New Delhi, 2009.
127. Om Prakash Singh, History of Depressed Classes Associations in United Provinces (1900-1950), *The Journal of Historical Research*, Vol. III, No. II, April 2014, pp. 1-16.
128. Mahendra Pratap Rana, *Swami Achhutanand Harihar (1869-1933): A Voice Against Social Exclusion, Economic And Political Marginalization*. Available at http://manukhsi.blogspot.in/2011/03/swami-achhutananda-and-his-adi-dharma.html. [Last accessed on 25 May 2015].
129. Gurpreet Singh, *Remembering an unsung Dalit hero of the Ghadar movement*. Available at http://www.vancouverdesi.com/news/nridiaspora/activist-remembering-an-unsung-dalit-hero-of-the-ghadar-movement/. [Last accessed on 25 May 2015].
130. The fourteenth century Mahar poet-saint in the Bhakti movement, who lived in Western Maharashtra, far from Vidarbha. See, Eleanor Zelliot, "Chokhamela, His Family and the Marathi Tradition" in Mikael Aktor and Robert Deliège, *From Stigma to Assertion: Untouchability, Identity and Politics in Early and Modern India*, Museum Tusculanum Press, Copenhagen, 2008, pp. 76–85.
131. K.N. Kadam, *Dr. Babasaheb Ambedkar and the Significance of His Movement: A Chronology*, Popular Prakashan, Bombay, 1991, pp. 66-67.
132. C.H. Nikumbhe, op. cit., p. 8.
133. Ibid., p. 11.
134. Ibid., p. 12.
135. Eleanor Zelliot, *Dr. Babasaheb Ambedkar and the Untouchable Movement*, Blumoon Books, New Delhi, 2004. pp. 42-44; Also, C.H. Nikumbhe, op. cit., p. 11.
136. C.H. Nikumbhe, op. cit., pp. 13-15.
137. Ibid., p. 13.
138. Ibid., p. 13.
139. Ibid., p. 13.
140. Dr. Ambedkar, following the death of his father, found a copy of the petition in his papers. Ambedkar "believed that his father

had obtained the assistance of Justice Ranade in preparing the petition."

141. Richard B. White, *The Mahar Movement's Military Component*, http://www.ambedkar.org/research/The%20Mahar%20Movement.htm. [Last Accessed on 16 June 2014]
142. C.H. Nikumbhe, op. cit., p. 20.
143. Ramacandra Kshirasagar, op. cit., p. 372.
144. A social reformer from Maharashtra whose original name was Gopal Hari Deshmukh (1823–1892). Lokhitwadi was the penname he adopted for his writings in the weekly *Prabhakar*, which were later published in Marathi as *Shatapatre*. He promoted emancipation (liberation) and education of women; wrote against arranged child marriages, dowry system, polygamy, the evils of the caste system, condemned harmful Hindu religious orthodoxy, and attacked the monopoly in religious matters and rituals which Brahman priests had through a long tradition.
145. H.N. Navalkar, *Shivram Janba Kamble ani Pune Parvati Satyagrahacha Sankshipt Itihas*, Sugawa Prakashan, Pune, 1997, p. 59.
146. Philip Constable, The Marginalization of a Buddhist Martial Race in Late Nineteenth and Early Twentieth Century Western India, *The Journal of Asian Studies*, Vol., 60, No. 2 (May 2001), pp. 439-478.
147. K.N. Kadam, op. cit, pp. 69-70.
148. H.N. Navalkar, op. cit. pp. 45, 62.
149. Raj Kumar, *Ambedkar and His Writings: A Book for the New Generation*, Kalpaz, Delhi, 2008, pp. 220-221.
150. H.N. Navalkar, op. cit., p. 46.
151. Raj Kumar, op. cit. pp. 220-221.
152. H.N. Navalkar, op. cit., p. 46.
153. Cited by Himansu Charan Sadangi, *Emancipation of Dalits and Freedom Struggle*, Isha Books, Delhi, 2008, p. 159.
154. C.B. Khairmode, *Dr Bhimrao Ramji Ambedkar Yanche Charitra*, Vol. VIII, Sugawa Prakashan, Pune, 1987, p. 251.
155. Ramchandra Kshirsagar, op. cit., p. 239.
156. H.N. Navalkar, op. cit., p. 60.
157. H.N. Navalkar, op. cit., p. 59.
158. H.N. Navalkar, op. cit., pp. 60-61.
159. H.N. Navalkar, op. cit., pp. 67-69.
160. H.N. Navalkar, op. cit., p. 69.
161. H.N. Navalkar, op. cit., p. 74.

162. H.L. Kosare, *Vidarbhatil Dalit Chalvalicha Itihas*, Dnyandeep Prakashan, Nagpur, 1984, p. 20.
163. Ibid., pp. 109-110.
164. B.R. Maske, op. cit., p. 60.
165. H.L. Kosare, op. cit., p. 22. However, Kshirsagar notes that it had become very popular in the Vidarbha region. Ramchandra Kshirsagar, op. cit., p. 176.
166. Vasant Moon, *Madhyaprant va Varhadatil Dr. Ambedkarpurv Dalit Chalval*, Sugawa Prakashan, Pune, 1987, p. 14.
167. H.L. Kosare, op. cit., pp. 25-29.
168. Vasant Moon, op. cit., p. 15.
169. It inspired people to form local organizations. A relatively better known such organization was *Mahar Sudharak Mandal*, which was formed in 1910 at Amravati by Vitthal Dasharath Makesar, Ganapat Naik and others. B.R. Maske, op. cit., p. 64.
170. Himansu Charan Sadangi, op. cit., p. 194.
171. Ibid., p. 149.
172. It is not clear whether these two organizations were the same but the dates of their establishment suggests renaming of the first after two years.
173. Sanjay Paswan, *Encyclopaedia of Dalits in India: Leaders*, Kalpaz, Delhi, 2004, p. 104.
174. Ibid., p. 104.
175. It is not clear whether it was the same organization as founded by Kisan Fagoji Bansode, the year of foundation being the same, 1910.
176. Dr. Ambedkar would start the organ of the Bahishkrut Hitkarini Sabha by the same name on 3 April 1927.
177. Ramacandra Kshirasagar, op. cit., p. 224.
178. Ibid.
179. H.L. Kosare, op. cit, 1984, p. 26.
180. See, Meenakshi Moon, 'We too have made history', *Communalism Combat*, May 2001. Similar schools were started in the Konkan region and at a few other places. Later, In 1924 in Nagpur the first woman to start a girls school was Jaibai Chaudhari, who herself secured an education against heavy odds and against the wishes of her husband.
181. Vasant Moon, *Madhyaprant va Varhadatil Dr. Ambedkarpurv Dalit Chalval*, Sugawa Prakashan, Pune, 1987, p. 48.
182. The committee comprised two European members, Deek and Kareb, Raobahadur M.G. Deshpande, a savarna Hindu; and Kalicharan Nandagawali and G.A. Gavai were the Dalit

members. The Secretary of the Committee was Mr. Nelson. Vasant Moon, op. cit., p. 51.

183. Vasant Moon, op. cit., p. 48.
184. Ibid., p. 57.
185. Ibid., pp. 59-60.
186. Sanjay Paswan, op. cit., p. 150.
187. Dr. Ambedkar's grandfather was in the military and his four sons were also in the military. Dr. Ambedkar's maternal side also had a similar military background. C.H. Nikumbhe, op. cit., p. 7.
188. Charles A. Selden, "Prince and Outcast at Dinner in London" *New York Times*, November 30, 1932; based on an interview with Dr. Ambedkar.
189. C.B. Khairmode, *Dr. Bhimrao Ramji Ambedkar*, Vol. I., Yashvant Bhimrao Ambedkar, Bombay, 1952, p. 267 (Marathi).
190. Mahar community had 18 sub-castes, which had salience in their every transaction.
191. Dhananjay Keer, *Dr. Ambedkar: Life and Mission*, (Second Edition), Popular Prakashan, Bombay, 1962, p. 43.
192. *Mooknayak*, 14 February, 1920.
193. The Fabian Society is the British socialist movement that began in 1884. It was a purely intellectual, anti-revolutionary, reformist movement which believed that socialism can be established by gradual reforms within the law and not a violent revolution. George Bernard Shaw, who was one of its prominent leaders had famously described the mission of the Fabian Society as to "educate, agitate, organise". See the web site of Fabians: http://www.fabians.org.uk/educate-agitate-organise/. Also Pugh, Patricia M., *Educate, Agitate, Organise: 100 Years of Fabian Socialism*, Law Book Co. of Australasia, 1984. The slogan was also used by Antonio Gramsci (1891-1937)), an Italian Marxist revolutionary and theoretician as a motto for the Italian communist newspaper *L'Ordine Nuovo* (The New Order), organized by him. He explained its meaning as follows: "Educate yourselves because we'll need all your intelligence. Agitate because we'll need all your enthusiasm. Organize yourselves because we'll need all your strength."
194. Dhananjay Keer, op. cit., p. 55.
195. Ibid., p. 55.
196. The Jim Crow laws were state and local laws in the United States enacted between 1876 and 1965. They mandated de jure racial segregation in all public facilities in the Southern states of the

former Confederacy, with, starting in 1890, a 'separate but equal' status for African Americans. See, A, Meier and E. Rudwick, *Along the Color Line: Explorations in the Black Experience,* University of Illinois Press, Urbana, 1976, pp. 267-289; For more information on Jim Crow and Struggle of Blacks, see W.E.B. Du Bois, *The Autobiography of W.E.B. Du Bois: A Soliloquy on Viewing My Life from the Last Decade of Its First Century,* International Publishers, New York, 1968; Grace Elizabeth Hale, *Making Whiteness: The Culture of Segregation in the South, 1890-1940,* Pantheon Books, New York, 1998.

197. Montgomery had witnessed a two-year boycott by its Negro citizens, when a city council enacted a trolley-car segregation bill. The streetcar boycott of 1900-1902 was part of a larger Negro protest against Jim Crow urban transit. There were boycotts in more than 20 southern cities between 1900 and 1906. August Mier and Elliot Rudwick, The Boycott Movement against Jim Crow Streetcar in the South 1900-1906, *The Journal of American History,* Vol. 65, Issue 4, May 1969, pp. 756-775.

198. G. McNeil, *Groundwork: Charles Hamilton Houston and the Struggle for Civil Rights,* University of Pennsylvania Press, Philadelphia, 1983; M. Tushnet, *The NAACP's Legal Strategy against Segregated Education, 1925-1950,* University of NC Press, Chapel Hill, 1987, p. 184. Marcus.

199. Mosiah Garvey, Jr., (1887 –1940), was a Jamaican political leader, publisher, journalist, entrepreneur, and orator who was a staunch proponent of the Black nationalism and Pan-Africanism movements, to which end he founded the Universal Negro Improvement Association and African Communities League (UNIA-ACL). The fundamental focus of Garveyism is the complete, total and never ending redemption of the continent of Africa by people of African ancestry, at home and abroad. It is rooted in one basic idea: "Whatsoever things common to man that man has done, man can do". Marcus Garvey and Amy Jacques-Garvey (eds.), *The Philosophy and Opinions of Marcus Garvey or Africa for the Africans,* Majority Press, Dover (Massachusetts), 1986, p. 163.

200. The Harlem Renaissance was a cultural movement that spanned the 1920s. It sought to break free of Victorian moral values and bourgeois shame about aspects of the lives of Black (African American) people that might, as seen by whites, reinforce racist beliefs. Never dominated by a particular school of thought but rather characterized by intense debate, the movement laid the

groundwork for all later African American literature and had an enormous impact on subsequent Black literature and consciousness worldwide. While the renaissance was not confined to the Harlem district of New York City, Harlem attracted a remarkable concentration of intellect and talent and served as the symbolic capital of this cultural awakening. See, Eric Foner, *Reconstruction: America's Unfinished Revolution*, HarperCollins, 1988.

201. Aldon D. Morris, A Retrospective on the Civil Rights Movement: Political and Intellectual Landmarks, *Annual Review of Sociology*, Vol. 25 (1999), pp. 517-539.
202. The term then in use but is taken as racial and hence objectionable. The Black people now prefer to be called "African Americans".
203. S.D. Kapoor, B.R. Ambedkar, W.E.B. DuBois and the Process of Liberation, *Economic & Political Weekly*, December 2, 2003.
204. Ambedkar was greatly influenced by John Dewey (1859-1952), his professor at Columbia University who was a very influential philosopher and public intellectual of those days. He professed a philosophy of pragmatism and was also known as an American Fabian. Ambedkar was so influenced by him that he would run after his classes and take copious notes. He would say, "The best friends I have had in my life were some of my classmates at Columbia and my great professors, John Dewey, James Shotwell, Edwin Seligman and James Harvey Robinson." See, Eleanor Zelliot, "Dr. Ambedkar and America", A talk at the Columbia University Ambedkar Centenary, 1991. http://www.columbia.edu/itc/mealac/pritchett/00ambedkar/timeline/graphics/txt_zelliot1991.html. [Last Accessed on 14 April 2015] He generously acknowledged his intellectual debt to Dewey saying in 1952, when he himself was considered great, "I owe my whole intellectual life to Prof. John Dewey." One of the prominent Ambedkar scholars, K.N. Kadam wrote, "I, for one, believe that unless we understand something of John Dewey, one of Dr. Babasaheb Ambedkar's teachers at Columbia University, it would be impossible to understand Dr. Ambedkar." For details see, an article on Dr. John Dewey at http://www.ambedkar.org/Babasaheb/JohnDewey.htm. [Last accessed on 21 January 2014]. Dr Ambedkar's Historical Speech at Agra. Available at http://drambedkarbooks.com/2015/03/26/dr-ambedkars-historical-speech-at-agra/.[Last accessed on 28 March, 2015].
205. Robin D.G. Kelley, 'But a Local Phase of a World Problem': Black

History's Global Vision, 1883-1950, *Journal of American History* 86 (1999): 1045-1074.

206. W.E.B. Du Bois, *The Papers Microform of W.E.B. Du Bois*, Microfilming Corporation of America, Sanford, N.C., 1980, reel 58, frame 000-467.
207. S.D. Kapoor, *Dalits and African American: A Study in Comparison*, Kalpaz, Delhi, 2004, p. 74.
208. Ibid., p. 76.
209. Ibid., p. 74.
210. *History of Arya Samaj Movement in Kerala*, http://www.aryasamajkerala.org/kerala-history.html. [Last Accessed on 28 August 2010].
211. Sathya Bai Sivadas and P. Prabhakara Rao, *Vaikkom Satyagraha*, http://www.sreenarayanaguru.in/content/vaikkom-satyagraha. [Last accessed on 21 January 2014].
212. Ibid.
213. For this, he came to be known as 'Vaikom Veerar' (Vaikom Hero)." K. Veeramani, *Periyar on Women's Rights*, Emerald Publishers, Madras, 1996, p. 14.
214. D.G. Tendulkar, *Mahatma: Life of Mohandas Karamchand Gandhi*, Vol. II, *1920-29*, Publications Division, Government of India, (Rev. Edn.), New Delhi, 1961, p. 182; Also, Mahadev Desai, *The Epic of Travancore*, Navjivan Publishing House, Ahmedabad, 1937 for detailed account of the Vaikom Satyagraha.
215. Sathya Bai Sivadas and P. Prabhakara Rao, op. cit.
216. *Young India*, March 11, 1926.

3

A Muted Manifesto: The Bahishkrut Conference: 19-20 March 1927

> *"Change does not roll in on the wheels of inevitability, but comes through continuous struggle"*
>
> –Martin Luther King, Jr

After forming the *Bahishkrut Hitkarini Sabha*[1] on 20 July 1924 as a vehicle to launch the movement, Babasaheb Ambedkar was in search for an appropriate issue. At this time a request came from Mahad for presiding over a conference of the Untouchables in Konkan. The person who approached him with this request was a young boy of 23-24 years, named Ramchandra Babaji More, who had personal acquaintance with Dr Ambedkar and his family. More would later join the Communist Party of India (CPI) in 1930 and become comrade R.B. More but without losing Dr Ambedkar's esteem and confidence. After the split of CPI, he became an important leader of the Communist Party of India (Marxist), contributing to its progress in various capacities, notably as the founder editor of *Jeevanmarg*, the Marathi weekly organ of its Maharashtra State Committee.

More had very bitter encounters with the monster of caste quite early in life. In 1885, at Dasgaon, where he lived, his grandfather Vithal Joshi-Hate, a Mahar, constructed a one-storey house, the first of its kind by an Untouchable, which created huge uproar among the Brahmans of the area. Construing it as defiance of the laws of the *sanatan dharma*, they ostracized the Brahman priest who performed the *bhoomipujan* ceremony and conspired to accuse More's father, Babaji More, of stealing wood from forest for the construction of the house, which resulted into his imprisonment for two years.[2] Ramchandra More was a brilliant student and had won a government scholarship on completing his primary education but was still denied admission in the Mahad High School since he was an Untouchable. At the tender age of 11, he had to struggle against the school authorities to get admission. The school admitted him only after he wrote an open letter to the government in a newspaper, mainly because of the fear of losing the government grant. But that did not end his travails; he had to sit outside the classroom due to his caste.[3] More was deeply angered by the inherent irrationality and injustice of the caste society and decided to rebel against it. After schooling, he naturally graduated towards social activism and quickly won confidence of the community as an intelligent, talented and an energetic activist. Within a short span of time he had successfully led several struggles in Mahad for the benefit of his people. Mahad was a prominent market place in the Konkan region, where people from the surrounding villages came for vending their ware as well as shopping for their needs. But those who belonged to the Untouchable castes faced a lot of hardships on account of casteism. They would not even get water to drink. More took the initiative and organized a drinking water facility for them. He organized a strike against the municipality for banning vending of vegetables and fish at public squares by Untouchables and succeeded in removing the ban. When the vehicle owners of Mahad had declared a boycott against the Untouchables and refused to carry their ware, More complained against them to the collector and got the boycott withdrawn. Since no hotel would serve Untouchables, one Mahar, Deu Joshi, had opened a tea shop in the old market area of Mahad, which came to be known as the Mahar Hotel. He had made this hotel a hub of his activism. This Mohoprekar's hotel served as the central office for organizing the Mahad conference.

More conceived the idea of organizing a conference of the Untouchables to awaken them to their rights and prepare them for struggles against their ongoing discrimination by the upper caste Hindus. He was basically inspired by the extraordinary scholastic achievement of Babasaheb Ambedkar, who had just returned from England with a D Sc from the London School of Economics and Bar at Law from the Gray's Inn in addition to his previous Ph D from Columbia University. He wanted to felicitate him such that the Untouchable students would get inspiration from him and it would shame the casteist savarnas who looked down upon them. In order to mobilize support for his idea, he held a meeting in May 1924[4] in Mahad's *Maharwada* (Mahar colony) with prominent chiefs of the caste pancahyats of the surrounding villages. Many prominent persons, whose names More recalled in his reminiscences, attended this meeting. (See chapter 5). More explained to them his idea of holding a conference at Mahad and inviting Dr Ambedkar to preside over it. The meeting unanimously approved the proposal and decided to start collecting funds from each village.

While felicitation of Dr Ambedkar was heavy on More's mind, the main inspiration behind this meeting was the Bole resolution. This resolution was so called because it was moved by Rao Bahadur S.K. Bole, the renowned social reformer, and was passed in the Bombay Legislative Council on 4 August, 1923. Bole was a remarkable personality of his times, who consistently worked against evil practices prevailing in the society. Notwithstanding the threats of ex-communication from his Bhandari community for having taken an active lead in organizing an inter-caste dinner with the Arya Samajists as early as 1906, he continued with his social work and consistently took a bold stand for promoting the interests of the Depressed Classes.[5] When young Ambedkar passed his matriculation examination in 1907, it was him in the chair of the felicitation function organized by the Mahar people.[6] While moving the subject resolution, Bole said that untouchability was an ugly blot on the name of India and added: "We resent the segregation policy of the South African Colonies and therefore we must set our house in order. It is in our interests and in the interests of the country that the Depressed Classes should be given better treatment." The resolution stated: "The Council recommends that the Untouchable classes be allowed to use all public water sources, wells and *dharmashalas* which are built and maintained out of public funds or administered by bodies appointed by the Government or created by statute, as well as public schools, courts, offices and dispensaries."[7] Though the Council adopted it, the Bombay Government was not enthusiastic in accepting it and reluctantly issued directions for its implementation with effect from 19 September 1923. Collectors were also requested to advise the local public bodies in their jurisdiction to consider the recommendation made in the resolution so far as it related to them. In 1926, the Bombay Legislative Council added a provision that municipalities depriving Depressed Classes of access to public amenities would suffer loss of government funds.

The meeting had assigned the responsibility of inviting Dr Ambedkar to More. More approached Dr Ambedkar along with Sambhaji Tukaram Gaikwad, an elderly social worker, who also belonged to the Kolaba district. Dr Ambedkar was happy at this proposition but said that he would decide the time of the conference later.[8] Bhai Anant Vinayak Chitre, who was sitting with Dr Ambedkar at that time, had enthusiastically queried More about the preparations for the conference and gave suggestions to mobilize money.[9] It was decided that 40 villages around Mahad could contribute Rs. 3 each and make a total contribution of Rs. 120. Chitre suggested organizing a charity show in Bombay for raising additional money and helped in getting a play—*Sant Tukaram* from G.B. Kadam, the chief of the *Sahakari Manoranjan Mandal* to be performed in charity.[10] This show took place in December 1924 in the Damodar Hall but could only get a paltry profit of Rs. 23.50.

More would visit Dr Ambedkar during Diwali and the summer vacation and reiterate his request, but Dr Ambedkar was not sure of the organizing capacity of a young boy. At last, he suggested that Chitre visits Mahad to take stock of the preparations. Accordingly, a preparatory meeting was organized in the Maharwada of Mahad in the early 1925, which was attended by all the Dalit activists of the region. At the last moment, Bhai Chitre had to drop out and send Kamlakant Chitre, as suggested by Dr Ambedkar to attend this meeting.[11] Kamlakant Chitre presided over the meeting in which Vishram Gangaram Savadkar, an energetic leader of the Untouchables from Veergaon in Kolaba district spoke, explaining the purpose of the meeting and assured that they would not fall short of funds for organizing the conference. Chitre spoke about the Bole resolution and informed how Surbanana Tipnis, who was the president of Mahad Municipality, got it adopted by the Municipality. After this meeting, More and Savadkar extensively toured the surrounding villages and held meetings there to mobilise support for the conference. Kamlakant Chitre came back to Bombay with a positive report on organizational progress in respect of the conference. Reassured by this report, Dr Ambedkar agreed to accept the invitation but was reluctant to preside over it. Eventually, he yielded to the persuasions from the organizers.[12] Thus, as Bhai Chitre commented, nearly three years had elapsed in getting him to agree to preside over the conference. With his consent, 19 and 20 March 1927 were declared to be the dates for this '*Kolaba District Bahishkrut Parishad*'. It was formally announced that Dr Ambedkar would be the president and Gangadhar Nilkanth alias Bapusaheb Sahasrabuddhe, an activist of the Social Service League[13], who would remain Dr Ambedkar's associate for many years, the main speaker. Sambhaji Gaikwad was made the president of the reception committee.

Once it was decided, Dr Ambedkar involved himself in oversseing preparations for the conference, particularly its propaganda among the Untouchables in Mumbai. He organized a meeting of over hundred activists including Sambhaji Tukaram Gaikwad, Subhedar Sawadkar, Keshavrao Govind Adrekar, and Ramchandra More in his office and explained to them the importance of having the conference in Konkan. He said that there were lakhs of Untouchables from Konkan settled in Mumbai in whom a wave of awakening should be created first. Only then could they take up bigger struggles. People had assured him that they would hold propaganda meetings for the conference in their respective *mohallas*, and literally began having 15-20 meetings every week in different parts of the city. It galvanized people into action, who would constantly pour into his office all the time in connection with some or the other task of the conference. Dr Ambedkar had begun dictating his presidential speech to C.B. Khairmode, a young graduate who would be the first to write his 12-volume biography, the first volume of which had been seen by Babasaheb Ambedkar. Ambedkar would take a pause to speak to people and resume the dictation. The process to prepare the speech took about a week. Even in the Khairmode's clean copy, Dr Ambedkar would continue to make additions and deletions till the date of his departure.[14]

There was a challenge to decide on the venue for the conference. The temple premises, where such congregations usually took place, were unthinkable for the Untouchables. After trying out many options, the activists decided on Vireshwar theatre hall/premises as the venue, near the Mahad bus depot. It was made up of bamboo and twig impregnated mud walls and could accommodate a sizable number. Since this venue often had *tamasha* shows by Mahar atistes, the activist hoped to get it on rent. Moreover, since the theatre hall was not occupied during the day time when the conference was to take place, the rentals would be pure profit for the contractor. Expectedly, the contractor easily agreed and rented it out for two days. The issue of arrangement for lodging and boarding for the delegates was resolved by hiring land around the bus depot to put up pandals which would cater to both the needs. The material required for pandals as well for cooking were collected from people either as contribution or at nominal cost. Although Mahad Municipality, under the influence of its young president —Surbanana Tipnis[15], had adopted the Bole resolution to open all public water sources within its jurisdiction to the Untouchables, it remained just on paper. The ground realities stood unchanged. The area was so deeply tradition bound that nobody, neither the Untouchables nor the Touchables, would come forward to violate its writ. As such the arrangement had to be made to buy drinking water and store it.

More does it at Dasgaon

While the preparation for the Mahad conference were on, another organization by name *Bahishkrut Aikya—Samvardhak Mahar Samaj Seva Sangh* (The Mahar Service League for

Conservation of the unity of the Depressed Classes) was founded under the leadership of Dadasaheb alias Sambhaji Tukaram Gaikwad, a senior leader of the Untouchables in Konkan region, on 10 August 1926. The object of this organization was to prepare the Untouchable youth in Bombay-Thane area to work for eradication of untouchability, carrying out social reforms and spread awareness amongst Untouchables about concomitant social and political developments. Later, in October the same year, it was rechristened as *Kokanastha Mahar Seva Sangh* (The Kokanastha Mahar Service League), shortening its lengthy name. The founders were apologetic about naming it by a particular caste as they aimed at forging unity among all the Untouchable castes. The chairman of this organization was Bhikaji Sambhaji Gaikwad, the son of Dadasaheb Gaikwad.[16] Ramchandra Babaji More and Keshavrao Govind Adrekar were the secretary and the treasurer, respectively. Soon many branches of this organization came into being in various parts of the Bombay city. The *Sangh* started nearly a dozen schools and also some night schools for the boys and girls belonging to the Untouchable castes. The activists of the *Sangh* had made significant contribution in mobilizing and canvassing for the Mahad conference by holding meetings at Ratnagiri, Dabhol, Khed, Dapoli, Mahad, Mangaon, Rohe, and Pen. Many of them had taken a month's leave from their jobs and camped in Konkan for the purpose. Much of the credit for the success of the Mahad conference was due to the untiring efforts put in by the activists of this organization.[17]

The Bole resolution inspired many progressive elements in Maharashtra to carry out anti-caste reforms. A successful attempt took place at Goregaon, a prominent market place in Mangaon taluka of the Kolaba district. A noted working class leader, N.M. Joshi, belonged to this village. He influenced many Kayastha and Brahman people into progressive thinking. These upper caste people took a lead in calling the Untouchables in the village to explain the Bole resolution and asked them to make use of the public tank and the well in the village. Goregaon being a prominent village, there was significant spread of education amongst the Untouchables. They soon organized under a Chambhar leader named Ramchandra Chandorkar, and along with him, jumped into the village tank. It infuriated the Touchables people who collectively attacked them. The police just came and went away. All the victims along with Chandorkar went to Mumbai and informed the *Mumbai Mahar Sewa Sangh* about this incident. The Sangha organized meetings all over Mumbai to condemn the incident and collected funds to help the victims of Goregaon. More went to distribute this fund on behalf of the Sangh and later took Chandorkar to his own village Dasgaon to lead a similar action.

In Dasgaon, there was a public tank well known as 'Crawford' well. More decided to implement the Bole resolution there under the aegis of the *Sangh* and called for a public meeting on 4 December 1926 on the grounds of the Dasgaon Dharmashala. This meeting was presided over by one Shri Adarkar, a progressive upper caste person from the area, and was attended by 200-300 persons from Vir, Goregaon, Wahur, Dasgaon, Sape, etc. Apprehending trouble, Mahad Mamlatdar and police officials also were personally present at the spot. More spoke to the people explaining the Bole resolution and led the march to the tank and the well. They collectively drew water from the tank and the well and drank it. There was no resistance from the upper caste Hindus. On the contrary, a progressive teacher and a friend of More, Ramji Babaji Potdar, participated in the Untouchables' march and drank water along with them. Later, he suffered social boycott from the caste Hindus for three months. This perhaps was the first instance; the previous one in Goregaon having gone unnoticed, of public implementation of the Bole resolution in Maharashtra, which significantly inspired the Untouchables from Ratnagiri and Kolaba district to go to the forthcoming Mahad conference. It may have even reassured Dr. Ambedkar about the success of the conference at Mahad.[18]

March to Mahad

There was a deliberate attempt to get some progressive people from the non-Dalit communities to the Mahad conference but eventually only two names materialized. One was Bapusaheb

Sahasrabuddhe, who belonged to Agarkari Brahman caste and the other was Bhai Chitre, belonging to a caste called *Chandraseniya Kayastha Prabhu* (CKP). Both were named as public speakers in the pamphlet for the conference. This pamphlet was sent out to many newspapers for publicizing the conference but none took any cognizance of it.[19]

More was assigned the responsibility of bringing the leaders including Dr. Ambedkar to Mahad. People from Bombay had left by boat on 16 March and taking halts en route reached Mahad Dak Bungalow by 12 noon on 19 March. They were Sitaram Namdeo Shivtarkar, Bapusaheb Sahasrabuddhe, Bhai Chitre, Balaram Ramji Ambedkar (elder brother of Dr Ambedkar), Ganpat Mahadeo Jadhav alias Madkebuwa, Wakharikar Gaikwad, Devji Dagduji Dolas, Sitaram Kalu Hate, Dattatray Mahadeo Chitre and Dr Ambedkar. From Pune, Shantaram Tipnis, Pandurang Nathuji Rajbhoj and some others reached Mahad. Majority of the delegates, of course were from Konkan. Mahad Municipality president, Surbanana Tipnis was actively putting in efforts to make the conference a big success. Some people had reached Mahad the previous evening. On 19 March, people continued pouring into Mahad and by noon time they crossed a figure of 3000.[20] Everyone except people from Bombay carried a *lathi*, considered to be a caste identity of the Mahars. Those days every caste had its identity in Maharashtra: Kunabi (cultivator caste) had a plough, Bhoyees (fishermen) had a palanquin, Chambhar (shoe makers) had a *rapi* (a leather cutting implement), and so had Mahar, their lathi. Therefore, the delegates to this conference proudly brought their lathis with them, symbolizing their caste power.

The Conference Begins (19 March 1927)

By 4 pm, the Vireshwar theatre, the venue of the conference, was filled to the brim with people. As they sat with their lathis, their faces shone with grim determination. At about 5 pm[21] as Dr Ambedkar, along with Chitre, Sahasrabuddhe and some other prominent leaders, were conducted into the theatre, 3,000 lathis[22] went up greeting him. Soon thereafter the conference began. At the beginning, the chairman of the reception committee, Sambhaji Tukaram Gaikwad, welcomed the delegates to the conference and explained the purpose behind organizing it. More introduced all the prominent delegates. Thereafter, the president of the conference Dr Ambedkar read out his Presidential speech.

Speech of Dr Ambedkar[23]

> Gentlemen, I am very much grateful to you for bestowing me with this honour. When it was proposed that I should accept the presidentship of this conference, I tried to avoid it as per my nature. But only after realizing that it would not be possible to avoid it and if done, it would cause a great deal of annoyance to people, initially with some hesitation, but eventually with immense pleasure I accepted this responsibility and accordingly I am standing before you.
>
> Gentlemen, in a way I am extremely happy to come here. Everyone, even though he may not be particularly proud of his place of origin, bears definite love for it. After becoming a pensioner, my father had come to Dapoli with the intention of settling there permanently. I had taken my first lessons in a school at Dapoli. But under the pressure of the circumstances, when I was about 5-6 years of age, I had to leave the base and go to live on the *ghat* (elevated region). Today, after 25 years, I am coming down the *ghat* which is so richly embellished by Mother Nature. Anyone would be delighted stepping into this beautiful region. There is no surprise if this delight is multiplied for the one who considers this region as his motherland. But I cannot resist telling you that I experience as much sorrow as I feel happy. At one time, this region had gone far ahead in terms of the progress of Untouchables. It was fraught with well-to-do retired army officials, belonging to the Untouchable castes. Similarly, excepting the white-collared people, the Untouchable class was far ahead of other classes in education.
>
> The military profession of the Untouchables was one of the important factors responsible for this progress. One cannot say for sure what kind of space was available for the Untouchables to realize their destiny before the advent of the British rule. But, those days the notions of touchability and untouchability were so strong that the Untouchables had to take long diversions in order to avoid their shadow falling on touchable people. They had to walk with an earthen pot tied round their neck to contain their spit lest it

should pollute roads and had to tie a black thread round their wrist to identify themselves as Untouchables so as to alert others from getting polluted. If at all there had been any scope [for progress], it must have been certainly very little. Only after the British stepped into this country, the Untouchables of this region got an opportunity to raise their head. Taking advantage of this opportunity, they had demonstrated to the world how brave and bright they were and the level of intellect they possessed.[24]

If one needed a testimony, one may just take a glance through the old army records. If I wanted to provide you details of how many people belonging to the Untouchable class rose to become subhedars, jamadars, hawaldars in army; how many reached the designations of headmasters after passing through the schools like Normal School, how many demonstrated their competence in responsible posts like adjutant clerks and quarter master clerks, this speech would extend beyond its permissible limits. It should suffice here to say that the Untouchable class that lived as a class of servants once upon a time had become so powerful through military employment as to rule over other classes. Without hesitation one can say that the recruitment of Untouchables in the military had brought about a revolution in the structure of the Hindu Society.[25]

The sepoys belonging to Maratha and such other castes who considered Mahars and Chambhars in villages as Untouchables and who took it as an insult if they did not pay obeisance to them with a Johar or a Ram Ram, had to salute Mahar and Chambhar subhedars and could not dare to raise their head even if they were humiliatingly questioned by their Untouchable bosses. This kind of authority had never been available to the people of Untouchable castes in any other province of this country earlier. The Untouchables in this region had not only raised their living standard but also accomplished significant progress in education. They had 90 per cent literacy, 50 per cent of them being well educated to higher standards. The most noteworthy aspect of this spread of education is that the educational progress was not confined only to menfolk but it had reached their womenfolk too. Some women had acquired such proficiency that they interpreted scriptures in the meetings that their menfolk held. This progress in education was largely attributable to the military profession.

Those who express unhappiness over the fact that even after 150 years of the British rule, they have not started free and compulsory primary education and therefore make a demand for it however, do not seem to know the reality. The education loving people always blamed the East India Company for being self-centered in its governance and for not paying any attention to the interests of the people. It is however not quite true. At least, as far as its military department is concerned, it is completely untrue. Those who have served the military for generations can easily vouch that during the company's rule, primary education was free and compulsory. Primary education was provided to both boys and girls. For boys, besides primary education, even the lower rung of secondary education was made compulsory. The method of compulsion however, was not simple and easy. If a child did not go to school, the parents could not escape just by paying the fine. It is significant to note that this compulsion was not confined only to children; even the new recruits to the army also were compulsorily sent to the night schools.[26]

When the company rule had ended and the rule of the British crown begun after the defeat of the mutiny of 1857, the British government had constituted a commission to enquire into the army in India. Some of the witnesses had complained in their testimonies to the Commission that the spread of education in the army would lead to disastrous consequences. Scared of this consequence, education in the army began to be slowly ignored and eventually it was completely abandoned. Whatever it may be, so long as education was available, the Untouchable classes had greatly benefited from it. They made such an excellent use of it that anyone could only feel proud. It may not be an exaggeration to observe that due to this spread of education the collection of books amongst the Untouchables was disproportionately large compared to their population.

The manuscripts of Sridhar Swamy's book[27] are available in plenty. But I have seen rare manuscripts of our great saint poets such as Mukundraj[28], Dnyaneshwar[29] and Mukteshwar[30] in possession of many Untouchables. Not only this, I am confident that copies of other rare books may also be found in the homes of Untouchables. It is not commonly known that Dnyaneshwar Maharaj had written a book called *Panchikaran*.[31] I have seen this book in the house of a one of my friends who is no more today. Some years ago, a certain Mr Pagarkar had printed an advertisement in *Kesari* that if anyone had a book titled *Dnyansudha* written by the poet Raghav Chittadhan, he should be intimated. If he has not yet got a copy of this book already, he will get it to see in the collection of one of my Untouchable friends. One can only imagine the kind of effort and expenditure of resources that might have been entailed for such a collection of books by the Untouchable in such times when all the doors of knowledge were formally closed to them.[32]

There cannot be two opinions about this commendable thirst for knowledge in those days. Looking at it from the other side, it appears that people in those times had made appropriate use of their knowledge. If one categorized people in public life, one would note that some people indulge in public life just for name sake but some people plunge into it genuinely for doing some service. The majority belongs to the former category, i.e., the category of the 'name sakes'. There is no dearth of these 'name sakes' even among the leaders of Untouchables. People from Pune claim that they alone are the original creators of awakening among the Untouchables. There are people in Mumbai too who stake claim to this honour. Some leaders of the Depressed Classes Mission Society state that the awakening among the Untouchables had begun only by them. One must say that the people who make such boastful claims, do not know the true history of the movement for emancipation of the Untouchables.[33]

It would be observed through research that the *Anarya Dosh Pariharak Mandali* (People for removal of blemishes from non-Aryans) is the first organization that had come up in the Bombay region for doing service to the Untouchable community. In 1893, when a ban was imposed on recruitment of Untouchables in the army, it was this organization which had made a forceful representation to the government against it with the help of Mahadev Govind Ranade. This clearly shows that this organization had consultative relations with great people of those times. In 1897, it is this very organization which had prepared a questionnaire addressed to the Congress. In that questionnaire it had posed one serious question about the moral authority of the Congress in demanding political reforms without bringing about social reforms. This shows the enthusiasm of this organization in pursuing its mission. In 1898, when Sir Herbert Risley had begun the work of collecting and compiling information on the traditions and the customs of the Indian people, he had sent his questionnaire even to this organization. This also clearly establishes the fact that this organization was important enough for even the government to make enquiries.[34]

I say all this with testimonial evidence, since all the documents of this organization are currently in my possession. This organization was established in Dapoli in Ratnagiri district. It is therefore clear that if the honour of starting the movement for emancipation of the Untouchables is to be accorded to someone; it is bound to go to this organization and in turn to this region. The leaders of this organization have not only done the work of solving problems of the Untouchables but also carried out remarkable amount of work towards creating awakening in them through their writings. There were some true comrades of Jotiba Phule, the founder of the Satyashodhak Samaj and also his passionate disciples among the leaders of this organization. I cannot resist the temptation of mentioning the name of one such important leader. That leader is the late Gopalbuwa Walangkar. The awakening he created among the Untouchables through his writings is just incomparable. Those who want to see it will have to read the old files of *Deenbandhu*.

The people who were so advanced once, have fallen today to such a pathetic state! Objectively speaking, I do not have any hesitation in saying that the condition of the Untouchable class in this region is so miserable today that there are no people even among the Untouchables in any other province who are as poor, as illiterate and as ignorant as they are. It is indeed perplexing how such a painful and worrisome change has befallen the conditions of Untouchables of this region. The usual answer to this question is that this change has befallen because of the ban on their recruitment to army imposed by the British Government. I do not have any doubt in my mind about this answer being largely true. It is unjust to ban any section of people in recruitment for the government service from political, moral or economic standpoint. One is compelled to say that the proscription of people of the Untouchable class from military recruitment not only exhibits partiality but also exemplifies betrayal and worse, treachery against friends. Without the cooperation of the Untouchables, the British Government could never have been able to enter this country.[35]

Many reasons are proffered by historians for how the British vanquished the Marathadom (Maratha kingdom). Some explain it by casteism that had reached extreme levels during the Maratha rule; some give reasons of increased factionalism and internecine conflicts among the Marathas. But according to my humble intellect none of these reasons is true. If the Marathas were weakened because of casteism or conflicts among them; were the British powerful? As a matter of fact, when the British captured this country, Napoleon was harassing England, their own country to her wits end. So much so that it was impossible for them to extend any help either through money or soldiers to the East India Company that was ruling in India. On the contrary, in order to save the country from Napoleon's assault, they had sought economic and military help from the East India Company. Even though the British in India were in such a pathetic condition, they had managed to capture this country. This cannot be explained just by saying that the Marathas were ridden with factionalism and internecine conflicts.[36]

I feel there is only one satisfactory explanation which is that if after entering this country, the British had not raised an army of native people they could have never conquered this country. At this stage, I would suggest to our compassionate and justice loving British Government that it should ask itself a question as to who amongst the natives constituted the majority in its army. If it peruses its own old records, it would realize that they were none other than the Untouchables. Now it becomes quite clear that if the Untouchables had not backed the British, they would never have been able to conquer this country. One is compelled to make a sad observation on this interesting method of doing justice by the British in banishing the very people from their army who won them this country.[37]

You all may have heard about the incident that took place recently, which again illustrates how selfish the British people are. In 1917, at the time when the World War I broke out in Europe, our government again remembered the Untouchable classes. The desire to enter the army has always been overflowing in the Untouchables. The demand was just for one platoon but people willingly offered themselves in such numbers that two platoons would easily be formed. The government raised one platoon. Everybody was happy that the ban on their military recruitment was now lifted. One hoped that the process of actualizing their destinies had restarted. But soon after the war had ended, their platoon was disbanded with an alibi of cost cutting. One does not understand what to call this conduct of the government.[38]

Gentlemen, I feel that since we have been friendly with the government, it always took us for granted and ignored us. The attitude of taking whatever the government gives us, of hearing whatever it tells us, of living howsoever it keeps us, is the main reason behind this government's indifference towards us. We bear all injustice heaped upon us quietly. If someone slapped us on our right cheek, we offer him our left. But our hand never goes up to resist the assaulter. Even if the sky collapsed, we would sit helplessly taking it as our destiny. The earliest we give up this self-destructive attitude, the better it would be for us. Therefore, I would like to tell you that we must strive to get the ban on our recruitment to the army lifted at the earliest.

However, I am going to pose a question to you: if we are recruited to the army, shall we consider that our mission is accomplished? Many of us think that once the recruitment to the army is opened up, everything is done. We do not need to do anything more. I feel it is wrong. First of all, it is not possible that all our people will get entry into the army. When people of other classes were not prepared to work in the army, our people had ample scope to enter it. But now it is no more so. We will get whatever is there along with the others. To expect more is futile. Hence, we must ponder over the measures that need to be taken besides military employment for our advancement. There are very few people among the Untouchables who are engaged in any profession. Chambhars are the only people who have a profession. But even they have more or less given up that. As a result there is a huge majority among the Untouchables that does not have any profession. When there is a custom of a particular caste monopolizing certain profession, it would be senseless to ask people to take up a profession just because they are capable of managing it. If you want to plunge into a profession, that profession should be available for all the castes. It should not be a monopoly of a particular caste. Such professions, as I see, are only two; one is the white-collared profession and the second is farming.

I know that people from the upper classes do not like the idea of Untouchables taking up white collared professions. They feel that people belonging to the Untouchable classes should become carpenters, blacksmiths or weavers, etc. In no case should they accept whitecollared jobs. I state with all emphasis at my command that this advice is of no use to us. In my opinion, two things are very necessary for the advancement of the Untouchables: One, the rust of the old foolish, irrational and evil thoughts formed on their mind needs to be totally removed. Until the decontamination of their conduct, thought and articulation is accomplished, the seeds of awakening and advancement will never germinate in the Untouchable community. In the present circumstances, nothing new will sprout in their rocky minds. In order that their minds become cultured, they must adopt white-collared professions.[39]

There is another reason also for why I say that the Untouchables should adopt white-collared professions. The government is the most important and powerful institution. The manner in which the government thinks, makes things happen. However, we must not forget that what the government wants, depends entirely on the government employees. The mind of the government is basically the mind of its employees. One thing clearly follows from this, which is that if we want to get something of our interest through the government, we must get ourselves into the government service. Otherwise, the kind of neglect we suffer today will continue forever. If we intend to stop this, the people of the Untouchable class should make sure they enter the government service in maximum numbers. Without that they will never attain their state of vigor. And without adopting white-collared profession, there is no entry into government service.[40]

The importance of this fact is realized by the Musalmans and the Maratha caste and they have begun agitating for it. We also must wake up in time and get ourselves into the government service. Brahmans look down upon such a movement and canvass around that there is nothing left in the government service. But there is neither truth nor honesty in their statements. It is not true simply because if the Brahmans of this region had no power of government employment, they would have been either water-fetchers or cooks like their counterparts in other regions. If the superiority of Brahmans here had been based merely on the scriptures, it would have collapsed long time ago as it did in other places. It is sustained because it is backed by the authority of the government. The argument of Brahmans therefore is as misleading as it is untrue. The fact remains that the Brahmans have not renounced their liking for the government service. On the contrary, their perseverance for government service is as strong as it ever was. Therefore, we must not fall prey to their fallacious and dishonest propaganda.

Gentlemen, at this occasion, I am compelled to make a painful observation. I have already told you that this region was fraught with subhedars and jamadars, and that these people had done many good things. However, they have not done one thing. If they had done that, it would have been very useful to all of us. That one thing is educating their own children. Gentlemen, these people were not poor. Going by their times, they were getting quite a fat pension. If they had decided, they could have easily educated their children up to B.A. and M.A. One can well imagine the impact of this single thing. If these educated boys and girls had reached the ranks of mamlatdar, collector, and magistrate today, they would have constituted an armoured shelter over the entire Untouchable community. Under its protective cover, all of us would have made progress. But in its absence, we are living under the hot sun and getting scorched. I am fully convinced that unless we create this protective cover over ourselves, we will not achieve our development. This protective cover is not possible without our adopting white-collared jobs and entering the government service. Therefore I am making a suggestion to all of you that we should first pay attention to higher education. The kind of support a boy educated up to B.A. can provide to the Untouchable community is not possible by even a thousand boys passing the fourth standard. I am not saying that you should ignore primary education. What I am saying is that in view of our peculiar condition today, it would be better for us to push our students who are getting higher education to the peak as early as possible. For that it is essential to have a boarding in this region. I have planned a boarding at Panvel for the students coming from Thane and Kolaba districts. It is hoped that all of you will extend help by donating whatever money is possible for you.

The second profession that I suggested to you is farming. My purpose in suggesting this profession is that our Untouchable people should make arrangements for their economic independence. I do not have any hesitation in saying that today, among all the Untouchable castes the Mahars are nothing but a bunch of beggars. This caste is completely habituated to collecting crumbs of stale bread from door to door every day with a weird sense of right, to live off them. Because of this custom this caste does not enjoy any dignity or respect in the village. It has completely destroyed its self-respect. Call me anything, treat me as your footwear if you like, but throw some scraps of your stale food at me! This has been the attitude of this caste. Because of this custom, it is not possible for this caste to chart out a path of progress independently. For, if we decide today to enter temples, to draw water from public water-sources, or decide not to carry carcasses, the next day people will stop giving us food in the villages and deaden our nerves. It is utterly shameful to sell your humanness for the stale remains of food. Would it not be better, if you give up begging for this food and earn your livelihood through farming as other people in villages do? It may perhaps be difficult for the Untouchables to purchase farm lands. But there are many fallow pieces of land belonging to the forest department. They may be available if they make a request for them.

But how would these things be accomplished? I feel that until we get to eat these pieces of stale bread, our condition may stay the same. So long as the old path exists, nobody will take the new path. By clinging to the old path we have been deprived of our dignity. You ought to think how far you are going to walk that path. Gentlemen, for every reform, the people of this region invoke 'custom of forefathers' as a big mantra and chant it against all kinds of new plans irrespective of whether they are good or bad. That means if the forefathers have started some custom out of ignorance, their descendents must continue it, howsoever it may be harmful to them. If we just sit tight by adhering to the adage of 'old is gold' everywhere, no new reform will ever be possible. By the way, will it not be a normal desire of any parent to see their offspring living in better condition than what they had? I for one would not understand the difference between animals and such parents who would not have such a natural desire. Gentlemen, you must pay attention to what I say at least for the sake of your children, if not for yourselves. Today, we get bread. That is enough. We do not want any conflict. You will raise a wise question: why give up the half in hand and run after the full? But I am warning you here that if you do not make efforts in the direction I am showing, you may not get even the quarter of bread tomorrow that you get today.

I am not putting forth these thoughts only before you. Wherever I had an occasion to speak, I have presented the same thoughts. I want to particularly emphasize that all of us have to speed up our work of creating awakening among our people. With the generation of military pensioners having gone from here, the people of this region appear almost lifeless. There is no movement whatsoever. There have been many conferences on the *ghat*. Here, this conference is happening only now. You should never let the fire of awakening douse. For the work of awakening, you will need a team of local leaders. It is difficult to walk a new path without one showing it. It is the duty of the pensioners amongst you to involve themselves in this task. I conclude my speech with a hope that they will take a lead in this work of emancipating their own people.

After the presidential address by Dr Ambedkar, the people from the touchable communities in attendance delivered their speeches. The theme of their speeches was that the Untouchables should exercise due care not to create antagonism or a sense of hatred in other communities while agitating for their emancipation. One of the speakers[41] emphasized that the Untouchables should get their civil rights as all others. He informed that the Mahad Municipality had passed a resolution to open the Chavadar tank to all, including the Untouchables, which needed to be implemented immediately. Thereafter Bhanudas Kamble, a local person from the Chambhar community spoke on how the society perpetrated oppression on the Untouchables and why it was important to spread the ideology of Satyashodhak Samaj. At the end, Gangadhar Sahasrabuddhe, the designated main speaker rose to speak. He said that if the touchable people desired the Untouchables to love them, then they should first love the Untouchables, since it is a rule of nature that love grows out of love. The only way to make the Untouchables realize that the touchable people love them, is to strive to remove hurdles in their path of progress. With these speeches the programme for the day had come to an end.

March to Chavadar Tank (20 March 1927)

In the morning some prominent persons met at the house of Surbanana Tipnis. Among them were Dr Ambedkar, Bapusaheb Sahasrabuddhe, Bapu Tipnis (i.e., Ganesh Narayan Tipnis alias Gampu Master), S.N. Shivtarkar and Bhai Chitre. They discussed the speeches that the touchable people made the previous day. They also decided that after the day's proceeding, they would collectively march to the Chavadar tank and give effect to the municipality resolution[42]. The conference was to begin at 9 am and hence all people rushed to the venue. As regards the proposal to march to the Chavadar tank, since it was not a part of the original agenda, the modalities of handling it— who would propose it, how and when it would be proposed and which way to march to the tank—remained, as a result, undecided.

On the second day, various resolutions were taken up. One of the resolutions related to the condemnation of the murder of Swami Shraddhanand,[43] the leader of the Arya Samaj, who was assassinated on 23 December 1926 by a Muslim fanatic named Abdul Rashid at his home at Naya Bazaar, Delhi. The conference passed a resolution expressing grief over his death. Another resolution[44] dealt with what the upper castes should do for the Depressed Classes. The President requested Purushottam Prabhakar Joshi and Govind Narayan Dhariya, as the representatives of the upper classes to speak on this resolution. With the exception of one clause in the resolution dealing with inter caste marriages, they both accepted the resolution.[45] In all, thirty three resolutions were passed in the conference, most of which related to the measures to be taken by the government, caste Hindus, as well as the Untouchables for bringing about social, educational and economic progress of the Untouchables. For instance, in relation to the implementation of the Bole resolution, it pointed out that whenever the Untouchables tried to assert their civil rights to use public places and water sources, the upper caste people resorted to observing boycott against them. They were advised not do so and rather actively help the Untouchables in their endeavours. It suggested to the government to put up boards at such places to facilitate implementation of the Bole resolution and if required, impose section 144 of the IPC to thwart resistance from the orthodox elements and to lend protection to the Untouchables.[46] Many people made speeches on these resolutions until 12 in the afternoon. These resolutions have been provided in the **Appendix 1.**

After the president delivered his concluding speech, Shivram Gopal Jadhav rose to propose vote of thanks and thereafter Bhai Chitre to second it. After completing this formality, Chitre addressed the conference: "I feel that the conference should not be concluded without accomplishing an important task. The Untouchable people in Mahad face a lot of inconvenience in respect to drinking water. Even we had to buy water for this conference worth Rs 40 at the price of one paisa per pitcher. In order to do away this inconvenience, the Mahad Municipality has already declared all of its tanks to be open for the people of all castes by adopting a resolution to that effect. However, the practice of taking water from these tanks is yet not established by the Untouchable people. If this conference helps them to do this today, we would be able to say that it has accomplished a very important task. Therefore, I propose that all of us along with the President should march to the Chavadar tank to drink its water."[47]

These few words from Bhai Chitre electrified the gathering. This single step was to give revolutionary turn to their lives. The entire hall became tumultuous with enthusiasm. Under the guidance from leaders, soon the delegates began filing themselves behind Dr Ambedkar. They began marching in a long procession through the market place of Mahad with utmost discipline, shouting slogans of *mahatma gandhi ki jai* (victory to mahatma Gandhi), *shivaji maharaj ki jai* (victory to Shivaji the great)[48], and victory to equality. They stopped at the Chavadar Tank and followed Dr Ambedkar, who entered it and picked up its water with his cupped hands. They all shouted *'har har mahadev'* (victory to Lord Mahadev)[49] and drank its water.[50] After this the conference was declared as concluded.

Attack by the Upper Castes

After the conclusion of the conference, president and the guests from Mumbai returned to the Government Dak Bungalow, where they were put up and the other people went to the conference kitchen for eating their lunch before proceeding to their respective villages. Around 2 pm a *Gurav* (priest) of the Vireshwar temple ran around the town shouting that the Untouchable people were entering the temple and called upon people to protect it. In addition, they sent people to the nearby villages to incite the Kunbis by telling them that the Mahars had defiled the Chavadar tank and were planning to enter their temples.[51] Soon people began collecting at the Vireshwar temple with their lathis and started hurling abuses at the Untouchables. Seeing this commotion, the police superintendent of Mahad went to the Dak Bungalow and asked Dr Ambedkar, "The people of Mahad have collected near the temple because your people are planning to enter the temple. What should I tell them?" Dr Ambedkar told him, "Neither have we any desire nor necessity to enter the temple. You should talk to them and calm them down." After the SP left, he sent some people to the conference kitchen to warn the people there about this matter. People were preparing to leave for their homes after taking their lunch. As some of them were passing through market on the way to their homes, they were suddenly attacked by the hooligans. Some of them had gone to the conference kitchen and attacked the people who were still eating their lunch. They broke water containers and destroyed food.[52] In all, 20 people were seriously injured and 60-70 people, including 3 to 4 women were wounded in the attack. Important Untouchable leaders from Pune, P.N. Rajbhoj and Bhanudas Gundojirao Kamble were publicly humiliated and badly thrashed on the main road. When Kamble's wife along with her infant child went to rescue her husband, the attackers did not spare her and even her child. Had some Muslims not come to their rescue at that point, there would have been some fatality. When the Untouchables ran for shelter to nearby houses, some upper caste people sheltered them but most drove them out. Muslims and Kayasthas of Mahad generally had been helpful. When the people returned to the conference pandal, they were attacked by the stone pelting mob.[53] A correspondent of *Dnyanprakash* in his report, dated 21 March, wrote that when the delegates had returned to the pandal carrying the wounded people under police protection, they faced a volley of stone pelting again. That angered them, but Dr Ambedkar and Tipnis calmed them down and requested them to maintain peace at any cost. Instead of taking action against the culprits the police had reached the people gathered at the temple. The entire episode was enacted in such a way that the Untouchables would be scared to even attempt approaching the Chavadar tank in future. It reported that the meeting of all Brahman priests was called in a Vishnu temple and shuddhi of the polluted tank was done according to the scriptural process by emptying out one thousand pitchers from it.[54]

The local administration was well aware of this build up, but it did not take any action to dissipate it. They could easily disburse people collected at the Vireshvar Temple and prevent subsequent violence. Instead, at around 4 pm, the Mamlatdar along with the police sub-inspector came to the Dak Bungalow and requested Dr Ambedkar to go with them. They said large groups of agitated people, from both touchable and

Untouchable communities have gathered in the town and they did not have adequate force to control them. They said that the touchable community leaders were ready to talk but they insisted that he went to them. They asked him to control his people and they would control theirs. As a matter of fact, there was absolutely no question of controlling the Untouchables. They had done nothing to disturb the peace of the town and rather were being beaten as these talks happened. Still, in the interest of maintaining peace, Dr Ambedkar along with some other people who were with him at the Dak Bungalow, went with the mamlatdar to the town. On the way, the people who had gathered at the Vireshwar temple stopped them. On their behalf, Dingankar and Chunilal, brother of Tuljaram Seth, began bombarding them with a volley of questions about the plan to enter the temple. In response, Dr Ambedkar gave them similar reply as he had given the police superintendent some time before. However, they began to argue in the way which would provoke the crowd instead of calming it down. Raising the issue of the Municipality resolution, they argued that it was not the resolution by the people and asked why the Untouchables did not intimate them before going to the Chavadar tank. Sensing there was no point in getting into those arguments, Dr Ambedkar and the people with him started walking ahead. On the way, they found people were running helter skelter, shouting that the Untouchables had entered the temple. The magistrate was seeing this with his own eyes but he did not make any movement to arrest those people. On the contrary, he laughed it away.[55]

At last, not finding any Untouchable around there to control, Dr Ambedkar and people with him, returned to the Dak Bungalow. They found about hundred Untouchable people waiting for them, some of them with wounds.[56] Until then, nobody had any inkling that the rioting had culminated into such bloodshed. The leaders of the Untouchables were astonished that although the magistrate was in town, he did not prevent caste Hindus from rioting. People began collecting there infuriated by the information of attack. The goons had attempted to attack the base camp of the conference but were scared off by two young activists, Shivram Gopal Jadhav and Sambhaji Tukaram Gaikwad, who stood at the doors with an axe and iron bar in their hands. The people in rage broke the pandal and pulled out the sticks and bomboos to avenge the cowardly attack. They just wanted a approving nod from their leader. But Dr Ambedkar calmed them down and asked them to maintain peace.[57]

Leaving everything aside, arrangements were made to reach the wounded people to the hospital for treatment. Only the CKP people from the town came forward to help. From there they were carried to the police station to file complaints. It was extremely difficult to collect evidence. None of the upper caste people would come forward to tell the truth as they were all together in the conspiracy. The local Untouchable people were so terrified that they would not dare to take names. Those who were beaten would not know who the attackers were. In such circumstances, the people from Bombay stayed on for two more days just to collect whatever evidence there was possible. The local police did not appear enthusiastic about incriminating the guilty. In view of this, telegrams with details of the incident were sent to the Governor as well as the collector of Kolaba, requesting them to issue proper instructions to the local police.

It appeared that the fire of this rioting had spread beyond the Mahad town. After the passions were cooled off in Mahad, some mischievous people belonging to the upper castes sent messages to the Marathas of the neighbouring villages that they should thrash Mahars when they pass through their villages. These people had provokingly written to even the distant villages that Mahars had polluted their Chavadar tank; they should at least protect their wells. Thus the fire had spread all over the region. The Untouchables being in minority everywhere, were at the receiving end in many villages. At some places, they were seriously hurt.[58]

In order to protect people, a village-wise list was prepared by the team that stayed behind providing details of atrocities, along with names of victims as well as criminals and sent to the district police superintendent of Kolaba. Having completed this work, the people from Bombay returned as they had exhausted their leave of absence from work. Dr Ambedkar and Chitre stayed back. They met with the district superintendent again and gave him all the details and explained to him what the police should be doing to protect the Untouchables. On Tuesday (22 March) evening a private meeting of the non-Brahman leaders was called. It was meant to discuss how to avoid recurrence of such incidents in future in the light of the fact that it was mostly the non-Brahmans who had taken special lead in the attack on the Untouchables. Unfortunately, barring a couple of individuals all people cast off the responsibility of preventing such behaviour of their caste-men. Having put in these sorts of efforts, Chitre and Dr Ambedkar returned to Bombay on Wednesday. There was no doubt that this conference had caused considerable upheaval in the region. For many months its ripples would be seen in the media.

Reflection in the Media

There were passionate reactions in the Marathi press over the Chavadar Tank episode in Mahad. Dr Ambedkar had responded to them in *Bahishkrut Bharat* of 6 May 1927 in 11 columns called 'Current Issues'. These columns not only contained important information but also reflected argumentative prowess as well as the journalistic skills of Dr Ambedkar.

Kolaba Samachar of 16 April 1927 had written that the number of Mahar people who got beaten that day as reported in various papers was grossly exaggerated. It wrote that even Dr Ambedkar did not give such a bombastic figure in his *Bahishkrut Bharat*. It was written that the people who went to him after being assaulted numbered approximately hundred and amongst them a few were wounded. *Kolaba Samachar* contended that the news carried by many papers that the people from the upper castes had attacked the Mahars while they were having food and destroyed their food was not true as it has not been mentioned in the *Bahishkrut Bharat* account. Dr Ambedkar demolished the logic of *Kolaba Samachar* by saying that since a particular account did not contain specific information, the information does not become false. He cited the instance of what was carried by the *Bahishkrut Bharat* was not carried by other papers, which by the logic of *Kolaba Samachar* would be construed to be false. He stated that to accept what suits one's prejudices and discard the rest is not the logic but pure idiocy. He explained that the narration of the incident that was carried by papers like *Vijayi Maratha, Dyanprakash,* and *Navakaal* were based on eye witnesses of their respective correspondents and hence could not be taken as doubtful. The difference between the accounts of the incident in the *Bahishkrut Bharat* and other papers could only be explained by the fact that there might not be a single person who has noted all aspects of the incident. It was possible that he could have integrated all these accounts in the *Bahishkrut Bharat* but after coming back from Mahad he did not get an opportunity to meet with these correspondents. He finally stated that the readers should therefore take many such accounts as complimentary to what appeared in the *Bahishkrut Bharat*.

Dr Ambedkar had also rejoined the issue with *Kolaba Samachar* doubting his statement that the team of Mamlatdar and Fauzdar of Mahad had not shown any sense of anxiety in quelling the clash. *Kolaba Samachar* had contended that if the Mamlatdar and Fauzdar had opened fire to please some of the Untouchable leaders, there would have been a massacre in Mahad. Dr Ambedkar answered this argument by saying that it would have been reasonable if it was spoken in respect of the uncompromising and courageous community like Muslims. But to expect timid Hindus to react violently to police action was ridiculous. The issue was however not the speculation about what would have happened, if the administration had taken steps to quell the clash. The issue was whether it had taken any of those steps at all. And the answer to this question doubtlessly is in negative. He said that he had ample proof for it, which is already presented to the government which could also be made public if the mamlatdar does not have any objection.[59]

Mr Kolhatkar of *Chabukswar* of Mumbai had published on 16 April, 1927 a narration of the incident which would create an impression that the version published in the *Bahishkrut Bharat* was untrue and therefore Dr Ambedkar dealt with it in his column. The editor of *Chabukswar*, claimed to have himself visited Mahad and had written that the attack on the Untouchables at Mahad was not due to their taking water from the Chavadar Tank but because of the rumors that they intended to enter the Vireshwar Temple. Dr Ambedkar stressed that the attack was only because the Untouchables had polluted the Chavadar Tank. He argued that although the rumours were spread that the Untouchables would enter the Vireshwar Temple, they could not be believed by any reasonable person. If the Untouchables intended to enter the Vireshwar Temple they would not have returned from the Chavadar Tank to the venue of the conference as the temple was just adjacent to the Chavadar Tank. When the Fauzdar learnt that the people of upper castes had collected at the temple, why did he not disperse them instead of bringing the news to Dr Ambedkar? Of course, their intention was not to protect the temple but to avenge the pollution of the tank by the Untouchables. When Dr Ambedkar was led to the temple, leaders of the caste Hindus gathered there had not asked him whether he and his people would enter the temple. Instead they asked why they had gone to the tank. It showed that people were irked by the Untouchables polluting the tank. The temple was just an alibi as they did not want to violate the resolution of the Mahad municipality and the support of a section of the touchable class. Moreover, if the touchable people were not angered by the pollution of the tank, why had they done *shuddhi* (purification) of the tank? It was also reported that the Untouchable people had pounced upon a basket of watermelons in the market or teased girls of the touchable class, which resulted in their being assaulted by the touchables. This was utterly mischievous. The Untouchables have displayed such exemplary patience that the opponents did not have any option other than sullying their character.

It was also published that if the leaders of the Untouchables including Dr Ambedkar were not kept under police protection their lives would have been at stake that day. Such statements were not only misleading, but also untrue. Where did they get the news that the people who were leading, did not get caught by the rioters that day? The delegates that came to the conference had stayed in two camps Dr Ambedkar along with some other leading people who came from Mumbai was accommodated in the government bungalow, situated about 200 yards away from the Vireshwar Temple. This place was at least one and a half miles away from the main camp where the majority of the delegates stayed. It shows that Dr Ambedkar and other leaders were quite within the reach of the touchable people gathered at the Temple. If they attacked them, there was no possibility of any help coming from the other camp. Even then these 'brave' people could not muster courage to turn their evil eye towards the Dak Bungalow. Not only were these leading people well within their reach, but, at one time also within their jaws. Dr Ambedkar along with his colleagues had gone to the temple and had arguments with the mob. Thus it is untrue that they were kept in police protection and had not exposed themselves to the mob. The fact was that the government Dak Bungalow was available for them only for two days, i.e., 19 and 20 March. Since the police superintendent of the Kolaba district was to come the next day, the delegates had to vacate the bungalow and take a room in the police station before going to Mumbai.

It was evident from the above explanation that the details of the incident carried by the *Chabukswar* were a pure distortion of the reality.

Doublespeak of the Upper Castes

The decision to go to the Chavadar Tank was basically taken on the basis of the suggestions made by the touchable speakers who enthusiastically spoke on the evening of 19 March. It was discussed on the morning of 20 March at the residence of Surbanana Tipnis. But all the touchable leaders retracted their statements when it came to implementing the decision with various excuses. For instance, Prabhakar Joshi had written a letter on the 1 April 1927 to *Dnyanprakash* and tried to escape his responsibility. He wrote, "I did not even make a mention of the Chavadar tank in my speech, therefore the statement that the Untouchable people were encouraged to go to the Chavadar Tank by my speech is totally a lie." Dr Ambedkar refuted their contention as follows:

The decision of marching to the Chavadar tank was obviously not taken just on the basis of the suggestion from Joshi or Dharia but with the consent of all, the Untouchables as well as touchable delegates. The resolutions that were passed in the meeting were shown to all of them and they had approved them except for the one related to the inter-caste marriage. Since it was not possible for all of them to speak, they had delegated this task to Joshi and Dharia, their two friends. It is clear therefore that the support of Joshi and Dharia to the resolution was not only merely on their personal behalf but was also on the behalf of all. Keeping all this aside, when Joshi argues for himself that the Untouchable people had not marched to the Chavadar tank with his encouragement, it is not factually correct. The concerned resolution was presented in a general form and it was couched in a language which implied that the touchable people should help the Untouchable people in drawing water from the public water resources. What is the objection in taking the person who lends support to such a resolution as among those who encouraged the Untouchables to march to the Chavadar tank to assert their human rights? The alibi of Joshi for his doublespeak therefore is dishonest.[60]

Joshi wrote with great pride that he had told not only the leaders of the Untouchables that he would not come with them but had also warned the Untouchable brothers that they would lose sympathy of the upper caste people with their daredevilry. If just to save his skin Joshi feels that such kind of statements are necessary, he is free to make them. We do not care for that. Joshi's language still resounds into our ears. On asking to come, Joshi had said, "We do not come. Your thoughts are not our thoughts." To this, the Untouchable leaders said, "Your conduct is not as per your thoughts. As our conduct is as per our thoughts, if you are not coming with us, we go." This conversation is almost verbatim. But still if Joshi insists that our version is untrue and his version is true, we do not feel any necessity for getting into argument with him. For if the Untouchables had complained against Joshi that he had not stopped them even though he had an idea that if they had gone to the Chavadar tank they would be beaten, there would have been a dispute about whether Joshi had given them this advice or not. But the complaint against Joshi is entirely of a different type. It is that as Joshi supported the resolution, he should have gone with the Untouchables to the Chavadar tank, whether that entailed life or death. If he had come, it is not that the Untouchable would have escaped beating. But why did Joshi not act as he spoke? He should have got beaten along with the Untouchables. If he had done so it would have proved that Joshi would not eat mud for his caste but will bury the caste for his principles.

We do not wish to persist with our grudge against Joshi and Dharia. The news that they are being oppressed by their caste people has already been published in newspapers. Joshi's caste fellows had tried to socially boycott Joshi. It was averted by his consent to do the shuddhi of the Tank. And still, it is said that he had to take their reprimand.[61]

Joshi's friend Dharia also was fined Rs 1.25 by his caste fellows for having committed a crime of participating in the conference[62]. Both these gentlemen must be cursing themselves for having gone to the conference. It is natural for them to feel so. Because, more than the Untouchables, they were the targets of rioters' wrath. If they had been caught by the rioters that day, they would have really felt the heat of it. We would say that if it had happened, it would not have been bad. It would have been just the repentance for their sin. How will those who are not prepared to give up their caste protect people of other castes from the oppression of their own caste? The current times are critical. We feel that not to show courage of acting as one speaks is a great sin. Those who are convinced of the importance of some reform should act in accordance with it. It is vital for the progress of the nation in these times.[63]

Dr Ambedkar thus exposed the doublespeak of the so called upper caste people. He perceptibly commented,

> We do not feel that there is significant difference between the regressive people who openly reject reforms and the so called progressive people who say that they want reforms but would like to relegate it to the congenial time and not to do anything beyond speaking about it. On the contrary the people of second category are the thorns in the path of reforms. And therefore it is impossible that anybody can benefit from them. They however, can mislead people with their deceitful speeches. It rather dims the flame of awareness in people as they think that these great people incarnate are struggling to bring about reforms, they do not need to do anything special.[64]
>
> On the one hand these people would get into wordy debate with their own caste, but when challenged, they would be prepared to bury reforms and lick dust for their caste, on the other.

It is our clear opinion that dabbling of such people into these matters leads to loss rather than profit. We consider such betrayers sinners. It is proper that such people are humiliated in this manner for their betrayal of both the parties. We are aware that the people of the touchable castes, who have sympathy for the Untouchable classes, may be surprised by this kind of our thinking. But we are not afraid of it because there is no value to us of any wordy sympathy in the current warfare.[65]

In the current battle of reforms it is not possible to rely on the so called reformists who cling to their caste. Since the dispute between the reformist and the orthodox is of principles, the reformist is basically an enemy of his own caste. Unless he gives up his caste and unites with the people of similar thinking from the other caste in a team, he would never see the fruit of victory of his principles. Those who think that they cannot survive without their caste should not indulge into matter of reforms.[66]

Confronting Orthodoxy

Dr Ambedkar stated that he would prefer rabid orthodox people to the fake reformers. Because the former could be relied upon as an enemy and could be dealt with as such but the latter cannot just be trusted. He has dealt with one such orthodox editor of a paper called *Bhala* (a spear). In reference to the assault on the Untouchables at Mahad, *Bhala* had arrogantly warned the Untouchables to stop polluting temples and water-sources of the caste Hindus and threatened to beat them up if they did not stop. Dr Ambedkar responded through his *Bahishkrut Bharat* in a tit for tat manner saying that they would never stop their struggle and would be prepared to break the heads of those who dared to oppose them. He warned the editor of *Bhala*:

> We do not need any sympathy from intellectuals or phony patriots... We don't care for your worthless advice. If you do not want to promote our rights, just get aside. But if you come in our way and incite others, we will not spare you. We are on the side of justice and therefore we shall fight till last. The Depressed Class is not made of dung and wax. It has shown its prowess on battlefields. We do know how people like the editor of *Bhala*, who relish issuing threats, get scared to their bones in front of Musalmans and Europeans. If the occasion comes we will not hesitate in breaking the skulls of those who threaten us, whatever be the consequence.[67]

This response immediately brought *Bhala* to its senses. From the next issue itself it began writing in a reconciliatory tone."[68]

Such a gist of the confrontation does not however convey the kinds of arguments that used to be raised by the orthodox elements those days and at what level of polemics they had to be dealt with, by the reformists. For the younger generation of today it is impossible to imagine this social context. Since it is in this context that the Mahad struggle has taken place, it is imperative that this social context is understood adequately. The confrontation of Dr Ambedkar with the orthodox editor of *Bhala* probably serves as a representative component of this context and hence it may be profitably read in full. Besides the content, the combatant manners, the argumentative style and the rustic Marathi Dr Ambedkar employs, provides a glimpse of his journalistic prowess, which still remains unappreciated by the mainstream. Although, some parts of it might be lost in translation, it is still hoped, the following extract from *Bahishkrut Bharat* of 6 May 1927 may serve the substantive purpose.

Dr Ambedkar continues his response to the *Bhala* of 28 March 1927:

> Soon after our response reached him, this Kaiser got so terrified merely with fire of words that he began pleading right from the next issue in a pitiful and apologetic manner. With just one attack this Kaiser came out in his real form of a eunuch. It can be seen by anyone that he was originally a eunuch and his posturing in the first issue was like a dancer borrowing her costumes. This eunuch has given up the language of street fight and has entered the intellectual debate. Therefore we would also leave our weapons aside and adopt the language of intellectual debate.

The editor of *Bhala* has argued in his issue dated 11 April 1927:

> Many of those Mahars and Mangs, who went to drink water from Chavadar tank, would have begged for cooked food the previous day and even on that day. A person who on his own goes to others' door and gets food in alms, which may only be worth eating by animals, and enjoys it, never deserves to be considered as a touchable. An Untouchable after converting to Islam and becoming a Muslim gives up begging. Likewise, if Mahars and Mangs also gave up begging at the doors of touchables, they could

> well be rid of their untouchability within a generation. But the Untouchables would like to have ready cooked food in alms to eat and on the other hand would like to enter the tank also. Both things cannot happen at the same time.[69]
>
> Mahars and Mangs are the only two castes among the Untouchables which can be considered unclean. Dhor and Chambhars do not beg. Do they die of hunger? The Bhangis do not accept the leftover food (*ushte*). Why should the Mahars and Mangs only relish leftovers? Therefore we would suggest Mr Ambedkar that he should endeavour to remove these vices from the people of his own caste instead of hurling abuses at us.

The Mahad episode brought in a real crisis for the editor of *Bhala*. Actually it is his strong desire that the Untouchables should permanently stay as Untouchables. He was thinking of ways of how to make it happen. He tried with threat. But soon he realized that it would not work. Therefore, he has devised a new definition of untouchability with which to confine the Untouchables to their untouchability.[70] Ambedkar further writes:

> The editor of *Bhala* has posed a challenge to the Untouchables, "if you give up begging for the cooked food, we would treat you as touchables". We are perplexed at such a simple definition of untouchability by the editor who actually wishes them to remain permanently Untouchables. One does not know why he does not feel scared about his beloved Hindu religion if all the Untouchables become touchables by giving up begging for cooked food. Probably he must be self assured that the Mahar and Mangs would never give up their habit of begging as it has become an integral part of their living. Had it not been so, he would not have conceived of such a condition. Actually he is projecting that the Untouchables would not do such a thing despite the fact that they have already passed such a resolution in the Mahad conference. This is because *Bhala*-kar (editor of *Bhala*) is so engrossed with his prejudices that he imagines Mahars and Mangs would never implement such a resolution. Therefore before blurting out such a ridiculous proposition, he does not feel a need to verify whether such a resolution is passed or not. Firstly, we do not understand why one who eats cooked food from a Brahman's house should be treated as Untouchable. Is the Brahman caste so unholy that the one who ate their food be degraded to the level that he is

considered polluting? We are hearing such a thing for the first time from the editor of *Bhala*. Untill now, the Untouchables did not hesitate in eating cooked food from a Brahman house because they considered Brahmans pure. But now if the editor of *Bhala* himself says that his caste is impure, he should be rest assured that the Untouchables would give up their practice at once.

Seen from the other side, eating the begged cooked food is not the caste vocation of the Mahars and Mangs. It is true that in villages, Mahars and Mangs demand bread but not as alms. They demand it as their right. Even if one grants that they beg for the cooked food, there are many castes like them which also consume cooked food from many houses. We have to regretfully point out the fact that the Marathas also take cooked food from Brahman houses. In Pune many women of Maratha caste go for cleaning utensils in Brahman houses and run eateries at their own homes. They however, do not cook fresh food themselves for their eateries but get the leftover cooked food from Brahman houses and serve it to their clients, who eat it with relish, without any objection as it tastes of ghee. If there is untouchability in consuming cooked food from other's house, will the editor of *Bhala* treat Marathas as Untouchables? What do the students from his own caste who live off *madhukari* (a tradition of poor students belonging to Brahman caste eating at different houses as per predetermined schedule) do? Do they not beg for cooked food? The editor of *Bhala* who enjoys humiliating Mahars and Mangs does not seem to know such a practice in his own caste. But we may remind him that there is a custom among Brahman families in Punjab to live off the cooked food taken from other castes. Will the editor of *Bhala* become the leader of the Poona goons to thrash these Punjabi Brahmans if they come to the water tank in Sadashiv Peth? We feel glad that at least the editor agrees with us that untouchability should not be permanent and rather should be transitional.

However, we feel sorry because the editor of *Bhala* does not seem ready to judge everyone with the same yardstick of law. If one were to judge, then as per his definition, the Chambhars and Bhangis will have to be adjudged among the touchables because he himself has admitted that they do not beg for cooked food. On the other hand, the Brahman students asking *madhukari*, or the begging Brahmans from Punjab or the Marathas from Pune eating leftover food, will have to be counted among the Untouchables along with the Mahars and the Mangs. Is the editor of *Bhala* ready to bring about this new classification? He does not appear to be aware of the crisis that would befall the entire Brahman folks if he insisted on implementation of his definition of untouchability. It is widely known that like Mahars and Mangs the Brahman women also eat the leftover of their men in Brahman houses.

If such a rule is applied that one who eats leftover food is Untouchable than all the Brahman women will have to be driven out of the house by declaring them as Untouchable. Therefore, we would make a friendly suggestion to the editor of *Bhala* that he should take back his definition of untouchability and rather try some other ideas to make untouchability permanent. He should not commit foolishness of cutting his own nose just to make a bad omen for the Untouchables. But we do not feel the editor of *Bhala* will realize it. It is difficult to be sure about the goddess of brahmanic justice being resolute. It is her usual habit to undermine rules by making an exception for her own caste. The editor of *Bhala* who thinks, "Brahman may be amoral, but still he is superior in the entire universe", would easily dismiss law and maintain that the Brahman woman continues to be touchable even after eating the leftover of her husband.

The editor of *Bhala* is so intoxicated with the discovery of this new definition of untouchability that he has again put the same dish to reboil in his issue of 25 April 1927. But we do not find it necessary to spoil our mouth by tasting it as we know it is bad. There is only one thing in this issue that deserves consideration. The editor writes: "The four subcastes of the Untouchables, viz., Chambhar, Dhor, Mahars and Mangs, should unify their temples and water sources before putting up their demand for such a thing before the touchables." Whatever one says, the Untouchable castes are uneducated. It would not be prudent to pose such a difficult question to them. If it is a test, then even that could also be accomplished. But we feel sorry that a superior caste like Brahman should beseech the most inferior caste such as the Untouchables, saying, "Oh lords! Please put up a lesson of right path before our backward Brahman caste!" What a degeneration of the Brahman caste! Is it not better to be extinct than suffer such degeneration?[71]

In this way he battled out the reactionary observations of most Marathi newspapers of those days on the Mahad episode.

Hindu Sabha of Pune had sent Shripad Mahadeo Mate[72] to Mahad on a fact finding mission. *Kesari* (Tilak's paper, while being very vocal and militant on political issues was equally conservative on social and religious things) in its issue of 3 May

1927 had published Mate's observation. Mate also delivered a lecture on 4 May 1927 in Shivaji Mandir, Pune in which he contradicted certain details of the incident in Mahad. The main point was that in the attack on Dalits at Mahad, the Brahmans had not participated and rather they (shetjis *and bhatjis)* helped the Dalits in their programme and sheltered them during the attack. Dr Ambedkar ruthlessly refuted every such insinuation with counter evidence in his fortnightly *Bahishkrut Bharat*.

Post-Conference Reflections

The Mahad conference created a wave of awakening among the Untouchables and lent them strength and confidence to work for their emancipation. The notions of inferiority instilled in them by the Hindu religious scriptures, which had shackled their existence for millennia suddenly began cracking, freeing their self confidence. Although, the timorous attack by the caste Hindus at the end of the conference created a bitter taste in the mouth and pushed Dr Ambedkar into a long drawn litigation. He was extremely happy with its outcome. He felt that the Untouchables, if they won the war against the decadent custom of caste, could claim veritable credit for freeing all Hindus from the bondage of irrationality of their religion. In order to reach this goal he felt that the Untouchables should keep the torch of struggle for their civil rights burning. Being acutely aware of their [lack of] strength, he wanted to prepare the terrain that might make their struggle a bit easy. With this objective, he had written three articles in *Bahishkrut Bharat* explaining the standpoint of the Untouchables in their struggle for civil rights to the upper caste Hindus and to the government. He addressed the last one to the Untouchables exhorting them to fight this battle without fear for their emancipation. These articles were titled as the *Crusade of Mahad and the Responsibilities of the Touchables* (22 April 1927), *Crusade of Mahad and the Responsibilities of the Government* (6 May 1927), and *Crusade of Mahad and the Responsibilities of the Untouchables* (20 May 1927). In his first article addressed to the Touchables Ambedkar argued:

Addressing the Touchables

What happened in Mahad could be belittled as a simple issue of water facility, which as the editor of *Bhala* suggested, could perhaps be resolved by putting up pipelines or with other such sanitized solutions. But from the other viewpoint, it becomes very important as it is concerned with a bigger social issue. The real character of the issue is not revealed by saying that the riot broke out because the Untouchables went to Chavadar tank. In fact what happened there cannot be called a riot. In our opinion, it may be more appropriately called a crusade. Because, at the root of it lay the issue of whether the Untouchables, as the constituents and followers of Hinduism, had rights equal to those of others. By now the entire world knows that the answer to this question has been given in negative by the upper castes of Mahad by attacking the crusaders. We are astonished at the wicked behavior of the upper caste Hindus. It is not that such crusades have not happened in other countries. They did but they took place as a result of difference of opinions. Religious quarrels between the followers of *Vaidik* Dharma and Buddhism took place in this country and between Heathens and Christians and Christians and Muslims in Europe several times but they were all due to the differences in principles of those religions. But the quarrel at Mahad cannot be said to be due to any religious tenets because both the parties belonged to the same religion. Therefore, undoubtedly any outsider will feel surprised to see people resorting to physical fight against their own co-religionists just to prove that they were socially inferior.

In western countries, social equality is a well entrenched principle. By instituting rights to vote, they have established even political equality, which has abolished the notion that someone is ruling over us without our consent. Following social and political equality, they have rather began to discuss why there should be inequality in the economic sphere. The signs of establishing economic equality there are becoming visible. As a matter of fact the scriptures of Christianity and Islam are not known to promote equality. Their philosophies are quite constricted. "All humans are the children of god and they are equal in his view", is all that they would say about equality. They have not reached the level where they would explicitly hold that human beings are inherently equal. The tenets of Hinduism are relatively more congenial to promoting equality than those of Christianity and Islam. Hinduism does not stop at saying that all human beings are children of God;

it fearlessly propounds that they are all forms of god. There cannot be any such thing as someone being superior or inferior to the other. Such is the lofty principle of Hinduism. It is difficult to find better basis for establishing the empire of equality than Hinduism. Despite this, one does not find even a trace of social equality in the Hindu society of the kind one finds in Christian or Muslim nations. On the contrary, the people who try to establish equality are violently obstructed by those who call themselves Hindus. It only shows how little Hindus know about their own religion.

While endorsing the behavior of the people who treated their coreligionists differentially, like people sans religion, the proud Hindus project two aspects of Hinduism: one philosophy and the other practice. They argue that although the Untouchables are equal in philosophy, from the viewpoint of practice they are not only unequal but also impure. That makes transacting with them violation of religion. If it is proper to discard philosophy and continue with practice, taking the tradition as sacrosanct, then why not apply the same principle to politics. Is it not shamelessness that the people who get angry and do not hesitate in creating chaos, question the use of sterile principles. This is when even a passionate imperialist like Curzon pleaded that it was impossible to implement the principles in the queen's manifesto, should accord supremacy to the practice-based religion and say that Vedant or the philosophical religion is not useful for practice? Even if one agreed that there are two aspects of religion, one cannot forget that the practical aspect of religion has to be based on its philosophy. The society, in which religious practice is not anchored to its religious ideology, is like a ship floating in sea without a navigating system. One cannot say when it will dash against rocks and get destroyed. If Vedant had principles of ethics and religion, and if ethics and religion are needed in practice, then instead of arguing that Vedant is not useful for practice, these meek people lack the courage to make it practical.

We do not say that ideology and practice of religion always go together. We do find a difference in them. But in that event, it is necessary to amend the practice to make it cohere with religious ideology. Tilak himself said it at one place, "the scriptural scholars of Hinduism have accepted other principles based on *dharanatdharmah yatohbhyuday nihshreyas-siddhi sa dharmah*, distinct from the characteristics of the practice-based religion. The scholars have given religious elite the authority to amend the practice based on religion. When the elite bring about changes in customary practice by exercising their authority and by becoming role models themselves, people also accept it and that then becomes a part of the traditional religion." We have cited Tilak because the brahmanized people take moral support in his opinions. As a matter of fact, this rationale does not need any support. If it had not been so, clinging to the ancient practice itself will be the religion and the customs which are not desirable would never die. Abominable customs like untouchability will then continue forever.[73]

But who should come forward in establishing new religious practice? In our opinion and also in Tilaks's, the elite have to do that. In light of this, the question naturally arises what the elite have done in Mahad. We feel that the elite should have made efforts to remove accusation of hypocrisy leveled against Hindus on account of their mouthing that all humans are forms of god, but treating some of them as impure, just because they are born in a particular caste. It was their duty to deflect religious fanatics who habitually maltreat Untouchables, bringing a blot to their great religion. While looking with open eyes at the declining state of Hinduism, these people should have arrested the evil attempts of some who oppressed their own co-religionists. They should have become the role models by consolidating Hindus by treating the Untouchables with justice and equality. But these people calling themselves elite have done nothing like this. On the contrary, when the time came for discharging their duty, they feigned ignorance and rather became accomplices of a criminal lot. If they had stopped with the clash over the Untouchables' taking water from the Chavadar tank, we would not have felt as bad as we have when these very people displayed reactionary attitude by performing purifying rites for the tank. The elite have committed a heinous crime thereby, by approving the orthodox notion that Untouchables are impure and contact with them pollutes. There is no doubt that the people who did and supported this purification function have insulted the Untouchables. It also leads to the question as to why a legal action should not be taken against them.

Even if one kept this matter aside, the people who conducted the purification of the tank have proved that if the Untouchables become Muslims, the question of pollution would not arise. Because their current practice amply proves that if Musalmans draw water, it does not pollute their tank. We do not know what to call such an act other than treason against one's own religion.

Making endeavors to get back people who have migrated to other religions by performing *shuddhi* on one hand and harassing and annoying your own coreligionists, is surely not the symptom of sensible behavior. We feel that it is not the commemoration of the noble mission of Swamy Shraddhanand; it is a distortion of the work that he had begun. About the movement of *shuddhi-sanghatan* (purification and organization), it is our considered opinion that what the Hindus need today is *sanghatan*, more than *shuddhi*. It is true that with *shuddhi* your numbers may go up. But, wherever the Hindus are getting beaten by Muslims today, the reason is not that Hindus are in minority. Strength does not always dependent on population. The real strength lies in determination, not in numbers.

People who are determined, will not shake even if they are in small numbers. If one examines the source of strength of the Muslims, one would find that it lies in their determination and not in number. If this observation is correct then it is beyond doubt that what Hindus today need is not *shuddhi* but *sanghatan*. If the aim of the *sanghatan* is to achieve determination of the Hindus, it will not be accomplished through the external physical methods like gymnastics, training, etc. Without destroying casteism and untouchability, which has sapped the organized strength of the Hindu society, destroyed the feeling of oneness in its constituents, and pitched the interests of one caste against those of others, the task of achieving determination and consolidation of strength cannot be accomplished. But what is seen in Mahad is exactly the opposite of this dictum.

In times of emergency for Hinduism, the grossly condemnable and irresponsible manner in which the elite have behaved, and that in such riots, it is essentially the non-Brahmans who participate. We got to experience it at Mahad. Not only did they attack the Untouchables at Mahad, but as per the news reaching us, their caste fellows have also been harassing the Untouchables in far flung villages. These people are so adamant that they do not feel anything in assaulting people or outraging the modesty of women. I am of the firm opinion that the condemnable behavior of these people, who claim to be a part of the non-Brahman party, which imagines itself as an incarnation of god for eradicating inequality and reconstructing the Hindu sociality on the foundation of equality, is surely bringing bad name to the lofty principles of that party. I am going to express my thoughts separately about the non-Brahman party. At that time I would

> certainly write in relation to its responsibility. But a strange thing we got to see in Mahad is that the *shetjis* and *bhatjis*, the persons in Gandhi caps and Tilak shirts, not only rushed for the defence of Brahmanism but also spread misinformation to the surrounding villages: "they polluted our tank, you protect your wells" and incited the majority of non-Brahman population against the Untouchables. While we congratulate the *shetjis* and *bhatjis*, who rushed in defence of Brahmanism, on their prowess, we must remind them that the castes comprising non-Brahman group are like monkeys in present times. These *shetjis* and *bhatjis* should bear in mind that giving a torch in these monkeys' hand may prove to be suicidal for them. It is known to history that these very non-Brahman castes at one time had devastated the *shetjis* on the *ghat*. Who can say, what happened on the *ghat* will not happen on the lower parts? They should remember that the people, who hold the batons in their hand today, can easily turn against them tomorrow. Recently, *Kesari* of 29 March 1927 published a news about how these monkeys have used their torches to burn Brahman houses. The story was related to the harassment of the Brahman minority by the Marathas, purportedly belonging to the Satyashodhak Samaj, who constitute a majority in the villages.

He further writes:

> The Untouchables also are a minority in every village and suffer atrocities by the non-Brahmans. They should normally feel bad about the hapless Brahmans as their co-sufferers. But they do not feel that way. One runs to the help of those who come to one's rescue in the times of crisis. But these *bhatjis* haven't yet fully realized the difficult future in store for them. If they had realized it, they would not have behaved with the Untouchables in this manner. This issue however relates to their defence and has to be resolved by them. We wish to say that until today, like Mahatma Gandhi, we also consider that untouchability is the biggest blot on the Hindu religion. But now we have changed our opinion; now we consider it to be a blot on our own body. When we thought it to be the blot on Hindu religion, we had relegated the task of its eradication upon you. Now that we have realized that it is a blot on ourselves, we have accepted the task of washing it off ourselves. We would not hesitate even if some of us had to sacrifice our lives for accomplishing this task. You may try again, if you so wish, the kind of detestable attempts to prove our impurity by performing

purification rites at the Chavadar tank. But we would not sit quiet until we make you say that we are pure.

If it is our destiny to wash off the blot you brought on to the Hindu religion with our blood, we would consider ourselves very fortunate. We have become fearless with the notion that we are the agents to accomplish this noble work. We do not feel bad at all for the Untouchables having got wounded in the Mahad riots. If we feel bad, it is because the Untouchables have lost an opportunity there. If they had decided, it was a great opportunity to teach the attackers a lesson. But we have never looked at this issue as a riot. We consider it as the first battle in the war for establishing equality. Whosoever gets victory or defeat in its course, we do not have slightest doubt that eventually victory shall be ours. It is our ardent desire that there should be no bloodshed in this noble battle for emancipation of our community as well as the people of our religion. But if the people infected with Brahmanism bring in bloodshed, we will not retreat and then the responsibility for whatever happens will not be ours, this should be kept in mind positively by them.

Addressing the Government

The second article, addressed to the British government, appeared in the Bahishkrut Bharat of 6 May 1927, in which he presented the case of the Untouchables that they had civil rights to enjoy public places including temples like anybody else and hence nobody should obstruct their exercise of those rights. He cited a case between Hindus and Muslims on the issue of prohibiting playing of drums in front of a mosque in the Madras Province. The lower court had ruled in favour of the Muslims on the basis of religious feelings and age old customs. When the case went to High Court, the judge Turner overruled the lower court saying: "As per my understanding, never before the support of tradition was cited in the courts to establish caste specific rights. Since the Madras province was never entirely under the Muslim rule, it would be baseless to assume establishment of such a custom all over. It may be that wherever the Muslims had dominance, they might have imposed certain customs ordained by their religion on the Hindus as the vanquished community."

He used this judgment to drive his argument that the validity of rights, based on customs and traditions is dependent on whether those customs and traditions are just or not. Applying this inference to the dispute between the caste Hindus and the Untouchables, one will have to assess whether the custom of untouchability is legally valid or not. He cited some additional cases in support of this inference, particularly a case of a custom that demanded of an Untouchable to walk in such a way that his shadow does not pollute a Nair. The high court did not accept this. When the case was taken in appeal, even the Privy Council upheld verdict of the high court. He contended, the law which applied to the public roads should be equally applicable to other public places such as temples and water sources. He cited the judgement of Justice Harrison which upheld the right of the Chamars in Ludhiana district of Punjab to take water from the public well along with the others. He also cited a case from the Madras High Court where the judgement of a lower court punishing people considered as Untouchables, for having entered a temple on the basis of a custom was reversed. The court had observed that although it was true that as per the tradition these people had never entered the temple, they could not be complained against for having polluted the temple if they decided to enter it.[74]

After citing such judgments, Dr Ambedkar proved that the contention of the Untouchables in Mahad was correct and that of the touchables wrong. He emphasized:

> The custom of untouchability is not lawful. This custom has neither granted any rights to the touchable community against the Untouchable community nor has it abolished any rights of the Untouchables. Human rights in public life cannot be established by issuing an ordinance by someone. It is inherent in every human being. Just because it was not used or there was a gap in its usage, it does not cease to exist. It is as foolish to forbid a person from using a water source just because he had not used it before, as it is to say that a person cannot walk on a particular road because he had not done it before. Therefore, the Untouchable people have committed no crime by going to the Chavadar tank. Nobody can accuse them of committing an unlawful act even if they had entered the Vireshwar temple. The crime is committed by the

touchable people. They have opposed the Untouchable people unlawfully while they were exercising their rights.

After systematically establishing what is lawful and what is unlawful, Dr Ambedkar points out the duty of the government to protect law. He points out that to protect and help the people exercising their lawful rights from the unlawful opposition by others is the prime duty of the government. The omnipotent institution of government is created to ensure all people exercise and enjoy their rights equally and no one obstructs anyone doing so, by force. If the government fails in this fundamental duty, the very existence of the society would be threatened. By sensitizing the government about its duty in this way, he comes back to the point and hopes that the rioters of Mahad will be duly punished. He also stresses that the government should administer law in an impartial, fearless, equitable and a stern manner. If the rioters realized that the government would act in this manner, the kind of crime that took place in Mahad would never recur.

He advocated that the government should not wake up only after the crime is committed. Nobody can dispute the general principle of administration that the prevention of crime is better than punishing the criminal. If the government uses the weapon of law in face of the probability of crime taking place, it can prevent consequent damage to the lives of the victims. He then points out that section 144 of the Indian Penal Code (IPC) is a tool in the hands of the administration for preventing the likely crime by miscreants and explains its objects citing the authority of justice Turner. Turner had emphasized that magistrates should use this section for protection and not prevention of the exercise of rights. Instead of obstructing the lawful act, he should prohibit the unlawful act. While observing law, if the Magistrate sensed the likely violation of peace, it is unlikely that he would not know the people by whom the violation is likely. Therefore, in such events, it was his duty to obtain surety from them.

This section, according to Turner, was basically meant to help in lawful exercise of rights. Preservation of peace was secondary to its purpose. In view of this, Dr Ambedkar argued that the government should make use of this section in future to help the Untouchables exercise their rights without fear of resistance from the touchable people.

Dr Ambedkar detailed out the manner in which the touchable people variously harass the Untouchables. They would humiliate them for doing their customary tasks like dragging dead animals and begging for food, but when the latter decided to give them up, they would take it as an insult and punish them by imposing various boycotts. They would not stop at that and would go on to create scuffles with some alibi. In this way, they make hideous attempts to obstruct the Untouchables from trying out old or new ways for their emancipation and make them behave. He argued that if the government wanted to help the Untouchables in the exercise of their rights, it may have to use section 144 to the extent which would prevent such unlawful attempts of the touchables:

> If it is decided to adopt this measure, a general notice as per the above section should be put up at the public water sources and temples. It will serve to alert the public about the position of law. Along with it, the government will also have to obtain surety from the orthodox leaders. This is very important. Because, it is usually experienced that some orthodox elements incite gullible people in the society by exploiting their religious sentiments and keep themselves aloof. In order to thwart this roguery, the option of taking surety from such elements will be easy, extremely necessary and at the same time an effective measure. It will also be necessary to especially warn the business people who would not deal with the Untouchables.
>
> The order issued under this section is usually valid for a limited period of only two months. We feel that it will not be sufficient. The notion of untouchability is very old. It will take a long time to destroy this notion and to make the touchable people behave with the Untouchables amicably. Therefore the prohibitory order should be of perennial nature. The local government has authority under section 144 to issue such perennial orders. We suggest that they should invoke this authority.

While he made a strong case for the government to act, he expressed apprehension that the government would accept all his suggestions. He wrote, "We have little doubt about whether the government will accept our suggestion and implement it without delay. Although our British government is not reactionary, it is extremely slow. It has developed an attitude of marking time instead of marching on. And when a social issue is involved, it gets invariably paralytic."

He explained the reason behind his apprehension that like some touchable people, some English officials in the government also advise the Untouchables for conducting themselves with etiquette. He insisted that the government should observe the same principles in the dispute between touchables and Untouchables, as for instance advocated by Tilak in the dispute between Hindus and Musalmans. Tilak had written in this context, "It is not the duty of the government to implement etiquette with force. Rather people are themselves prepared to observe etiquette and courtesy so long as they believe that when they approach the government, only the law would prevail." He warned that the government should not bring in the issue of etiquette or forbearance when the Untouchables wanted to exercise their rights. Because, if the Untouchables had to confirm their conduct to the expectations of the touchables, which is what etiquettes mean, there would be no need for for the British government. He declared to the government the resolve of the Untouchables to exercise their human rights and to fight against anyone who comes in their way. It was necessary for the government to treat both the parties impartially and lawfully. The Untouchables had decided to discard the old religious notions that made them servile to the touchable people. They were determined to transcend their rung and stand at par with any other people. He warned the government that the Untouchables had not retaliated the attack by the touchables in Mahad because they believed in law and hoped that the government would do its duty by punishing the culprits. But if their hope was belied, they would have to pick up their sticks in response in the future. If this happened, he cautioned, it would prove far costlier for the government to control. He warned:

> The Untouchables had tolerated the outrage, highhandedness and the injustice of the touchables in Mahad only with a hope that the government will provide them due protection. If that hope is

> belied, it will not be possible for them to maintain the peace that they maintained at Mahad at other occasions. They will be compelled to pick up their sticks in self defence.

Dr Ambedkar expressed surprise over the government's decision to delegate the responsibility of implementation of the Bole Resolution to the local Boards and municipalities although it was accepted by it. The government ought to have known that the local boards and municipalities were generally fraught with orthodox elements. To expect them to open up public facilities in their jurisdiction to the Untouchables was to ask the latter to wait for hundreds of years for the change in their attitude to materialize. He pointed out that over the six years since the resolution was passed, few such institutions might have really implemented it. He hoped that the government would realize and undertake the responsibility of implementing the resolution on itself.

He also pointed out the confusion about the word 'public' and explained that public was not only determined by the funding from the government but with the intention of use by people at large. Even if someone built a temple for people other them his family to pray, it should be construed as a public place. He stressed that the government ought to take this meaning of 'public' and protect people's right to use them. If the government took a conciliatory stand in these matters, people could lose faith in it and resort to doing what they think fit. It would be total anarchy, and disastrous for everybody. He ended his editorial by quoting Justice Turner,

> If the government, instead of protecting the lawful rights, tries to put obstacles, people will think that the government officers are helpless in front of the rioters. Hence, instead of going to the courts for establishing their rights, pretending to riot will prove more fruitful. When the majority of society (Bahujan) will start thinking in this way, it will be more dangerous for the government to say that they can't provide protection for those who want to establish their lawful rights than to seek protection.

Addressing the Untouchables

In the third article, published in the Bahishkrut Bharat of 20

May 1927, Dr Ambedkar elaborated on the responsibilities of the Untouchables in the Mahad episode. It throws light on his approach to their problems at that time.

He asked the Untouchables to think why the touchable Hindus reacted so harshly to their mere taking water from the Chavadar tank. It was because they were considered impure in the Hindu religion. Even their shadow was considered polluting by the touchables. There was no rational basis for this notion except for the custom. There was a section of people who thought that the government should not interfere in any manner with customs and should wait for the people to change their attitude. He pointed out that the behavior of the government appeared to be receptive to such a retrograde view. He explained it on the basis of the decision of the government that had taken to partition Bengal from the administrative viewpoint, but later retracted it under the force of public opinion. He exposed the doublespeak of the people who advocated public opinion vis-à-vis the government, but did not pay any heed when it came to the opinion of the Untouchables, as though the latter were not public. When the Untouchables were unanimously saying that they were not prepared to accept Hindu customs, the people who pretended to respect public opinion should have taken steps to abolish these customs. But it did not happen. As the Bengali public opinion opposed the partition of Bengal, the Untouchable public opinion was against untouchability. He asked the Untouchables to understand that the public opinion of the touchable Hindus was against the abolition of untouchability. Hence, they were faced with the formidable problem of how to make these people congenial to their cause. He advised a twofold solution to the Untouchables (i) Resistance protest by starting movements like Mahad everywhere and to make the touchables think of the consequences if they resort to high handedness, as they did in Mahad, and be prepared to fight them back if attacked. (ii) Boycott protest: instead of keeping their inherent strength dormant, they should not hesitate using the same for boycott of the touchable Hindu society. He then presented his analysis:

> Why the touchable Hindus have developed such a hardened attitude towards the Untouchables is to be found in their religious tradition as well as in their self interest. Most of them have been blindly following this tradition and not thinking on their own, whether they are right or wrong. The challenge therefore becomes how to force them to think for themselves. Since the Untouchables have not objected to their being treated as Untouchables, the touchable people never felt the need to rethink about their customs. But once the Untouchables come out and forcefully oppose the customs, the touchables will also be forced to introspect about their conduct. If the Untouchables had resisted their being called Untouchables, the others would not have called them so. The importance of the Mahad conference precisely lies in the fact that it communicated the objection of the Untouchables to being treated as such. It has brought the touchables face to face with their evil customs. Until now, they have, just followed it because it did not cost them anything, but now they realize that it could cost them their life. Although, the Untouchables have not raised their hands on the touchables at Mahad, but they have amply communicated that in the future they may not take their beating lying low.

He advised them saying:

> Therefore we suggest to all our Untouchable brothers that they should start taking similar actions everywhere as they did in Mahad. Things will not happen without such resistance. Otherwise the thoughtless touchable people will not be pushed to think about the custom of untouchability, whether it is good or bad. And this custom of thousands of years will go on for the next thousands of years. The second aspect of the programme of eradication of untouchability is to make the thinking people behave as per their own thoughts. The method of achieving this will always be different from that of making the thoughtless people think.
>
> There is a big difference between bringing about change in public opinion and in the behavior of powerful people. Where there is no connection between opinion and self interest, the change in the former can be brought about through peaceful means like debates, discussions, negotiations, etc. But where such connection exists, the change in opinion cannot be brought about merely through amicable means, without denting self-interest. This principle can be seen by anyone in practice. Without applying this principle to the thinking people of the touchable Hindus, they will never be prepared to behave in conformity with their own thoughts.

From this perspective, the Untouchables should ponder over the ways in which they can make a dent in the interests of the touchable people. It is only then that we would succeed in bringing about the desired change in their opinion. The Touchables are wealthy, whereas the Untouchables are poor; the Touchables are a majority and the Untouchables are a minority; the touchables are powerful whereas the Untouchables are powerless. As such, one may think that while the touchables can do without the Untouchables, the Untouchables cannot do without the touchables. In view of this, it will be utterly preposterous if the Untouchables indulged in thinking of making a dent in the interests of the touchables. It may appear even suicidal not only to the ridiculing critics but also to the Untouchables themselves. But the Untouchables must understand that this comparison between power and powerlessness is superficial.

Those who look at things in worldly terms will never realize the true strength of the Untouchable community. While it is generally true that they are weak compared to the touchables in some aspects, we wish to warn our Untouchable brothers as well as the touchable Hindus that they should not cherish a misunderstanding that the Untouchables are absolutely weak in all respects. The touchable Hindus must think over what would happen to the Hindu society if the Untouchables boycott Hinduism and convert to Islam.

What is wrong if the Untouchables decide to convert? We do know that many orthodox religious people think that at least they would get self-rule with dominion status if not the pure swaraj. But we do not feel that such people have considered this issue in depth. These people do not understand that the current dispute is not about self-rule (swaraj) but it is the cultural battle between Hindus and Musalmans. The importance of Untouchables in this dispute is far greater than what their numbers would indicate. If the Untouchables continued as Untouchables within the Hindu fold, the culture of the Arya dhrama would be protected in this country. But if they decided to become Muslims, it will establish the dominance of Islamic culture by defeating the Aryan culture. None other than the Untouchables possess the strength of bringing about this momentous change. There should be no doubt about it.

If our Untouchable brothers gain a simple understanding that the Musalmans cannot win without them and the Hindus cannot progress without them, they will realize what enormous strength they possess. If at this critical juncture they used this strength they will be able to easily bring the bigheaded touchables to their senses. This is not a mean strength. It is our firm understanding that if this strength is realized and used in this manner, it may not take any time to make the touchables behave. Therefore, our passionate advice to our Untouchable brothers is that they should not keep this strength locked up their inaction and make use of it in this boycott. They should not have any hesitation doing it.

We are fully aware that some touchable people will call me crazy for suggesting such options to the Untouchables. But I would ask them a counter question: What else should the Untouchables do if they do not consider such options? It is the tradition of the moderates that they expect the Untouchables to put forth their unanimous demand before the touchables. But today, what has been achieved from the history of the movement of the last 25-30 years is that howsoever the opinion of the Untouchables may be rational, their complaints well-founded, demands just, and howsoever they may have been moderately presented, the touchable Hindus have always ignored them with haughtiness. In such a context, I do not know what to say to those who advise the Untouchables not to consider such options of resistance or boycott.

They argue that the custom of untouchability has come through thousands of years; what if it survived for the next hundred years or so. We would like to tell these people that injustice has no tradition. It is the mentality of forest people to allow injustice to continue just because it has come through the past. But for people like us who have woken up to their rights, would never think like that. On the contrary they would be furious at this injustice having survived for so long and for that very reason would want it be stopped at once.

Untouchability is such a grave sin and such an enormous injustice that we demand its immediate eradication. This is our ideology. We might consider an alternative suggestion to accomplish it from those who agree with us. But we are confident that there may not be a better option than what we suggested if our aim is to eradicate untouchability soon. There is no point in making big speeches, or passing elaborate resolutions by organizing huge conferences. These methods may work with people who are sensitive to public opinion. But the people who have become insensate by enjoying unbridled power need such shocks to bring them to their senses.

No amount of paper game will throw light into their heads and create any impact on them. When their skulls would start breaking because of untouchability, only then will they begin to think what it means to observe such customs. This important objective of bringing about awareness will never be achieved through any other means other than through resistance.

We are aware that some touchable people are angry at our suggestion of boycott. But we do not give a damn about it. We do not care for Hinduism; we care for humanity. If we could get this humanity by remaining in Hinduism, we would not have suggested the boycott of the Hindu society. The tenets of Hinduism are great. But we are not fools like school boys to get engrossed in the psychological comfort of great tenets and forget practical things. We do know that if the entire Hindu society recognized our humanity; it would not be because we inherently possessed it, but because of situational compulsion.

Whether it is the Hindu society or any other, it is natural to be a slave of the existing conditions. The society would not normally alter its established conduct unless it begins to experience intense pinch. With this understanding of the natural tendency of the society, Tilak used to say, "The reforms do not happen just like that. The society needs to know what comes in the way of its progress. Once it realised it, the society will automatically come forward to remove those obstructions." What other means other than boycott does the Untouchable class have for making the Hindu society realize that the custom of untouchability is coming in the way of its progress? If they cannot make use of even what is in their hand, then should the Untouchables just rely on the whims and fancies of the touchables? This suggestion of ours rather confirms Tilak's thinking. The only difference is that he conceived it for politics, whereas we mean it for a social situation. It is amazing to see all the people nodding in approval when Tilak thinks of declaring boycott of state power which might not be affecting even a hundredth of the population, but we are condemned for suggesting the same boycott against the religious power that has destroyed the humanness of every Untouchable.

We would like to tell these friends that howsoever they are our well-wishers, in the present context they being the adherents, props and the authority of orthodox religion, they are disqualified for advising us. Because, the issue relates with authority, caste, and selfishness and not with education, knowledge or intellect. Understanding that this blemish in you is a natural product of your situation, we would advise that you should not indulge in offering advices. If you do, instead of asking us not to transcend the moderate limits, advise your touchable brothers: "The Untouchables are becoming serious. Therefore, adopt the ways that reflect your sympathy in practice".

We do know that some touchable people ridicule seeing the Untouchables coming forward to destroy the ancient custom of untouchability in a flash. But we do not care for their ridicule, because, the solutions that we have proposed are so intense and powerful that not only would they disturb their minds, but will also endanger their lives. Who will not surrender with such potent means? We feel that there is no need of even using both of them. The enemy is really so weak that even with one option of resistance, keeping the other option of boycott in reserve, we may accomplish our objective. Even that may not need to be used for long.

... As the two pieces of red hot steel do not take time to join, the action met with its reaction will result in an agreement between two parties in no time. The question is whether this potent option will be accomplished by the Untouchables.

At this stage, it is necessary for us to remind our Untouchable brothers of one story. In the *van parva* [of *Mahabharata*] Bhim had told Dharmaraj that the lost kingdom cannot be got back by entreaties like "give me alms". Begging is the *dharma* of Brahmans; not of Kshatriyas. Therefore give up begging. Have confidence. You will meet your goals. Nothing will come through making mere moral appeals. In our opinion, the time has come to tell the Untouchables about this policy. You cannot get back your lost human essence by crying or begging, or by relying upon the moral sense of the robbers. Everyone must secure it with his own prowess.

It is true that the option of resistance that we suggested is difficult. We also know that when you resist there will be response from the touchables too. That does not mean the Untouchables should get scared of that. They should rather be prepared to fight back if they attack. It will not work without that. The Untouchables have to show their prowess. If they abide by this advice, they can be rest assured about the success of the option we suggested.

Before I conclude this series of articles on the water issue at Mahad, I would like to say to our Untouchable brothers that demons only follow the timid. You do not make offering of violent animals like tigers to the almighty gods; you make an offering of a poor chicken or a goat!

We do not feel, our Untouchable brothers belong to a *mesh rashi* (corresponds to Aries sign in Zodiac), so as to be sacrificed in offering like chickens or goats. At least history testifies that the *rashi* of their ancestors was *sinha*.[75] If that had not been so, how would Nagnak Mahar of Nagewadi get the power to perform the valorous feat of reclaiming *patilki* (village headmanship) for his family and win the Vairatgarh fort from the Mughals for the Marathas, would materialize?[76] And there is this Shidnak Mahar! The Brahman sardars who insisted on observation of casteism on the battlefield as being observed in the matters of meals, had complained that his troupe (*got*) should be taken out. But he managed to get a sardar like Hiroji Patankar to rule by the maxim "one whose sword is firm, he is the soldier" and preserved his honour by holding his troupe in the midst of all. He showed extraordinary prowess in the battle of Kharda, in saving the life of Parashurambhau from the Pathans and made many sardars who humiliated him as a Mahar to lower their heads. Who would say that Shidnak Mahar was not of the *sinha rashi*? Was Rainak Mahar, who, fell at the end of fifteen days of fierce battle against the British army while holding on the Raigadh fort quite like Baji Prabhu Deshpande, devastating the huge Islamic army of Vijapur at the mouth of the *Pawankhind*,[77] with the help of a handful of *Mavlas* (peasant soldiers of Marathas) before embracing martyrdom, of a *mesh rashi*? Likewise, to which *rashi* other than *sinha*, would those ancestors have belonged when they fell in the battle that would bury the *Peshvai* (kingdom of Peshawas) and for that brave act, whose names are engraved on the *jaistambh* (victory pillar) of Koregaon? Is the option of resistance going to be so difficult for the people whose ancestors have achieved such great feats with their bravery and prowess, undermining the severe constraint of untouchability? We do not at all feel so. They do have bravery; what they do not have is consciousness. Therefore, those amongst the Untouchables, who have realized their self identity, should come forward for the crusade that has just begun to wash off the blot on their clan and be the role model for their other castemen.

Ripples in Administration

The preparation for the Mahad conference continued over three years as per R.B. More's account. The decision to hold the conference was taken in 1924, following the adoption of the S.K. Bole resolution by the Bombay Legislative Council on

4 August 1923, opening all schools, courts, offices, dispensaries, public water sources, wells and *dharmashalas* built and maintained by public funds or managed by government appointed bodies to the Untouchables. However, the conference took place after three years in 1927. The state had no inkling about this conference. If the delegates to the conference had not decided to march to the Chavadar tank and exercised their right, thereby provoking the caste Hindus to brutally attack them, the conference perhaps would have passed off without much notice by the state. It would have taken a definitive turn if the delegates, who had easily outnumbered the orthodox elements, were not restrained by Dr Ambedkar from avenging the cowardly attack. Most delegates gathered were with military background and were already charged with the anger of being wronged. As some subsequent commentators poetically remarked, if they had decided to retaliate, Mahad would have seen streams of blood on its streets. Dr Ambedkar maintained his cool in the face of belligerence of the orthodox Hindus and ensured his followers returned safely to their villages. Dr Ambedkar had expected that the conference would shake the orthodox Hindus out of a state of inebriation with their traditions, into introspection and prepare them for reforms. But instead, he had to face vicious reactions from them in the form of physical attack on his followers, litigation over defiling their tank and a volley of vitriolic comments in their press. He decided to persist with his battle by organizing a much bigger conference at Mahad with exclusive focus on satyagraha at the Chavadar tank with renewed vigour at the earliest. These developments attracted the attention of the state which began following them closely as reflected in the documents available in the Maharashtra Government Archives.

A report on the first conference from J.R. Hood, District Magistrate, Kolaba (Alibag) vide his letter No. P.O.L.S.R. III-94 dated 20 April 1927, addressed to the Secretary to the Government, Home Department (Political), Bombay, gives a number of attendees of the conference in the range of 2,500 to 3,000, who "consisted almost entirely of the Depressed Classes with a sprinkling of Mohammedans, Gujars, Brahmans,

Prabhus, Marathas, etc." It reported what Dr Ambedkar spoke in the conference:

> The President said that the British conquered India mainly with the help of sepoys and officers from the depressed classes who at that time had good social and educational standing, but went down gradually when the army was closed to them as a career in favour of the other classes. He blamed the government for opening military service to the depressed classes when recruits were wanted for the Great War, but closing it immediately after the war was over. He advised his listeners to effect their betterment by acquiring education, seeking government service and taking to independent vocations as government service cannot provide an opening for all.

The report states that the next day the conference met again and a resolution was passed relating to the use of public wells and tanks by the Untouchables. It was pointed out that in 1924 the Mahad Municipality had passed a resolution to throw them open to all people. It described the historic incidence of the Dalits marching to the Chavadar tank following Dr Ambedkar and exercising their right by drinking its water:

> When the Conference was closed at about 1 p.m. the Mahars and other Untouchables, led by Ambedkar, went to the Chaudar tank in the heart of the Brahman quarter and took water. The news spread among the other castes and left them rather bewildered but no actual objection was taken. It may be noted that the municipality's resolution of January 1924 was apparently a mere gesture, resulting from a resolution in the Legislative Council and subsequent orders of the Government, and had never been given effect to. But soon after the taking of water from the Chaudar tank the priest or *Gurav* of the Vireshwar Temple went around the town crying out that the Mahars were defiling the temple and its tank (not the Chaudar Tank but another tank near the temple). The rumour spread quickly and a crowd from all parts of the town collected and began to assault the Mahars. The mamlatdar, the police inspector and the sub-inspector soon came and kept the two mobs apart, and Dr Ambedkar was sent for. He told the crowd that the depressed classes had no intention of even entering the temple much less defiling it. He also appealed to the depressed classes, who greatly outnumbered the other party not to retaliate or use any violence, and they showed commendable restraint in

> following his advice. Thus peace was restored after nine or ten Mahars had received slight injuries.

The district superintendent of police and the sub divisional magistrate visited the Mahad next day, but by that time all was quiet. Enquiry was made into cases of assault and the police had filed cases against some nine persons. There was no disturbance thereafter. The caste Hindus (shopkeepers and others), who had threatened to boycott the Depressed Classes, had also abandoned their plans.

While the District Magistrate (DM) underscores the resolve of the Depressed Classes to break the barriers that prevented them from enjoying their rights conferred by the legislation, in a typical bureaucratic manner he observes that this movement was not of 'local origin but had its inspiration in Bombay in bodies such as the *Rohidas dnyanodaya samaj*.' He accused Dr Ambedkar of instigating the local people:

> These people, like Dr. Ambedkar ..., instigate the local depressed classes to enforce their claims by direct action and appeal to me to save them from the resulting retaliation of the higher castes. Signs of this have appeared not only in Mahad but also in Mangaon taluka, notably at Goregaon where I found very similar trouble in progress when I took charge in December.

The DM reported that he had warned the outside instigators that there action would certainly cause suffering, either by boycott or by actual violence, to their ignorant followers. He also claims to have advised them that "their proper course is not "direct action but education of public opinion." He himself however expresses doubt whether the Untouchables would ever consider it because it would take a long time. Therefore, apprehending the outbreak of disturbance, he proposes "to maintain a neutral attitude and to take such precautions as may be possible against any breach of peace".

In response to the above, J. Monteath, the Secretary, Home Department (Political), Mahabaleshwar reacted in his reply vide his confidential memo [Confidential No. S.D. 428 dated 4th may 1927], against Hood's 'neutral stand':

> The governor in council does not think that you are in order in adopting a 'neutral' attitude, by which you apparently mean,

> judging from your advice to outside instigators, not impartiality, but rather a definite discouragement of the depressed classes in their efforts to exercise rights which in this case had been granted to them by the local municipality. It is of course essential that you must do all you can to keep the peace, but to throw cold water on the aspirations of the depressed classes amounts in effect to assisting the more bigoted members of the advanced classes to maintain their domination.

This sharp reaction from a top bureaucrat in favour of the Dalits, may be cynically seen in consonance with the colonial policy of 'divide and rule', as it would add to the existing communal cleavage, the ensuing caste cleavage, and thereby weaken the resistance against their rule. It may also be read as the counsel of justice, inherent in the Western liberal ethos. Monteath's rebuttal of Hood's advice for educating public opinion certainly sounds impressive:

> While it is true that 'public opinion' is only too often satisfied with what you call 'a mere gesture', it is on the other hand, useless for the depressed classes to educate public opinion of that type. The only public opinion which is of any real value is that which approves of the depressed classes using the rights which have been secured to them on paper.

Not only he did not confine his advice to Hood, who confronted with a unique case of Dalit defiance, but also made it universal in his domain by issuing a confidential circular to all commissioners on 10 May 1927 [No. S.D. 461] requesting them to instruct the DMs in their respective divisions on the lines suggested by his letter to Hood. He considered that in the event of a similar situation arising in any district, the DM should at least endeavor to encourage public opinion of that type which approves of the Depressed Classes using the rights, secured to them on paper. He wrote,

> The Governor in Council (G. in C) does not, however, think, judging from the DM's advice to the leaders, that the DM was in order in adopting a neutral attitude by which he meant not impartiality but a definite discouragement of the depressed classes in their efforts to exercise their rights which, in this particular case,

> had been granted to them by their municipality in 1924, though not exercised till now.
>
> While it is essential that DMs must do all they can to preserve peace, to throw cold water on the just aspirations of the Depressed Classes amounts in effect to assisting the more bigoted members of the advanced classes to maintain their domination. The G. in C therefore, considered that in the event of a similar situation arising in any district, the DM should at least endeavour to encourage public opinion of that type which approves of the Depressed Classes using the rights secured to them on paper, though he admits that it might at times be difficult for a DM to adopt such a course without seeming to encourage inter-communal strife. It is, of course, useless to educate opinion of the type which is satisfied with a mere gesture, such as the passing of a resolution by a municipality or the other body which, it knows, will not be brought into effect.

He acknowledged that "[T]the question was of a delicate kind; but when rights have been accorded by the authority to a certain class of the community, the use of violence or even the pressure to prevent the exercise of those rights should also be discouraged by authority".

The caste Hindu attack on Dalits in Mahad had its reverberations in the form of protest meetings in Maharashtra. The police commissioners' note of 4 July 1927 about one such meeting held in Bombay reveals the momentum of the agitation created by the Mahad conference. It was titled the 'Bombay Untouchables' Protest against "Atrocities" at Mahad'. It reported:

> Under the auspices of the Bahishkrut Hitkarini Sabha, a public meeting of the depressed classes was held under at the Cowasji Jehangir Hall on the evening of July 3rd to protest against the hardships inflicted on the Untouchables of Mahad in Kolaba District. Dr. Bhimrao Ramji Ambedkar, Bar-at-Law, presided over an audience of about 1,000 people.
>
> Speeches were made by the president, Raghoba Narayan Vanmali, Mahadeo Abaji Kamli, Sitaram Namdeo Shivtarkar, Nirmal Limbaji Gangawane, Gitanand Brahmachari and Samant Nanji Marwari condemning the treatment meted out to their brothers in Mahad by the higher classes. They decided in order to carry on a peaceful agitation against this treatment to enlist

> volunteers and collect funds. They would first have a conference at Mahad after the Diwali holidays and then it would be decided to start satyagraha in order to enforce their rights as citizens. A resolution to this effect was passed.
>
> Another resolution was passed requesting the Government to establish a separate department to deal with the grievances of the depressed classes as was done in Madras.

In response to an appeal for funds made by the speakers, the note says, about Rs. 350 were collected and a dozen people consented to become volunteers for the forthcoming Satyagraha movement.

A report in *Bombay Chronicle,* dated 5 July 1927 on the above meeting reveals the mood of the people. One of the speakers, Gitanand Brahmachari, who had come from Malabar, had made a strong speech exhorting the Untouchables to assert themselves. He said, "If the Brahmans prevented you from drinking tank water, you should have caught hold of their leaders and given them a good ducking there and then."

The District Magistrate Mr Hood had reported that the situation was quiet after 20 March. The threats of boycott by the caste Hindus were also abandoned. Wherever the Dalits sought to give up their traditional caste functions in accordance with the resolutions passed in the conference, the caste Hindus had reacted with threats of driving them out of the villages. The extract of the confidential diary of the district superintendent of police, Kolaba for the week ending 23 July, 1927 cites the *Kolaba Samachar*, "at the village of Irumbhe, Pale, Vodgaon and Asanpur, in Mahad taluka, the Marathas threatened the Mahars that they will be driven out of the villages if they do not remove carcasses, salute them and beg for bread". There appears to be a sustained campaign amongst the Untouchables to abandon their caste functions. The weekly letter of the District Magistrate, Kolaba, dated 27 August 1927 reports that Dr Ambedkar was advising the Mahars of Mangaon taluka to refuse to skin dead animals and to refuse to accept bread from villagers. A similar agitation was in progress in Roha taluka.

NOTES AND REFERENCES

1. It means the Conference for the Wellbeing of the Excluded. After his return from England, Dr Ambedkar began thinking about the upliftment of the Untouchables. He convened a meeting on March 9, 1924, at the Damodar Hall, Bombay, to consider the establishing a central institution for the purpose. As decided in that meeting, the 'Bahishkirt Hitkarini Sabha' was formed and was registered under Act XXI of 1860. The aims and objects of the Sabha were: (a) To promote the spread of education among the Depressed Classes by opening hostels or by employing such other means as may seem necessary or desirable; (b) To promote the spread of culture among the Depressed Classes by opening libraries, social centers, classes or study circles; (c) To advance and improve the economic condition of the Depressed Classes by starting Industrial and Agricultural schools, and (d) To represent the grievances of the Depressed Classes. The President of the Bahishkrut Hitkarini Sabha was Sir Chimanlal Harilal Setalvad, LLD; and its Vice-Presidents were Meyer Nissim, J.P. and Rustomji Jinwala, Solicitor; G.K. Nariman, Solicitor; Dr. R.P. Paranjpye, Dr. V.P. Chavan and B. G. Kher, Solicitor, who would become the Prime Minister of the Bombay Province 15 years later. The Chairman of the Managing Committee was Dr Ambedkar; Secretary S N Shivtarkar and Treasurer N T Jadhav. See, Dhananjay Keer, *Dr. Ambedkar: Life and Mission*, Popular Prakashan, Mumbai, 1971, p. 55.
2. Subodh More, Dasgaon Town Honours Com. R.B. More's Memory, *People's Democracy*, Vol. XXXI, No. 15, April 15, 2007. Another account says that Vithal Joshi was Babaji More's maternal uncle. See, Anupama Rao, *The Caste Question: Dalits and the Politics of Modern India*, University of California Press, 2009, p. 312 nn 157.
3. R.B. More narrates these incidents in his own words in Chapter 5.
4. S.A. Chitre, *Vegalya Vatecha Vatsaru* (Anant Vinayak alias Bhai Chitre), Akshar Prakashan, Mumbai, 1994. p. 26.
5. Dhananjay Keer, op. cit., p. 53.
6. It is at this meeting that Dr Ambedkar was first introduced to Buddha, who would be one of his three Gurus, through a book – *Life of Gautam Buddha*, written by Krishnaji Arjun Keluskar, which was presented to him in felicitation. Ibid., p. 19.
7. B.R. Ambedkar, Dr Ambedkar in the Bombay Legislature in Vasant Moon, (ed), *Babasaheb Ambedkar; Writings and Speeches*,

Vol. 2, Government of Maharashtra, Mumbai, 1982, p. 279.

8. It is stated by S.V. Chitre, son of Bhai Chitre that Dr Ambedkar had initially declined it by saying that he did not want to enter the public life and just wanted to become a district judge. See, S.V. Chitre, op. cit. It contradicts R. B. More's account which is obviously more authentic.
9. Chitre is supposed to have said that Dr Ambedkar delayed accepting More's invitation for almost two years as he was reluctant to get into active public life. Chitre records him saying that he wanted to become a district judge. See, *Vegalya Vatecha Vatsaru*, p. 26. This part of the story appears unlikely in the light of More's version as well as the fact that Ambedkar was already in public life having participated in a number of important conferences and having especially established Bahishkrut Hitkarini Sabha for carrying out social work among the Untouchables. He had also opened a hostel for the Untouchable students at Barshi in 1926. Khairmode blanks out this entire background including the initiative of More in his literary narrative. See C.B. Khairmode, *Dr Bhimrao Ramji Ambedkar yanche Charitra*, Vol. 3, Pratap Prakashan, Mumbai, 1964. It can only be reconciled by the fact that unlike his earlier activities, this conference probably proposed some direct action, which he wanted to avoid.
10. Chitre was one of the founders of this Mandal and carried influence with Kadam.
11. R.B. More's narrative indicates that Bhai Chitre proactively wanted to ensure the arrangements for the conference and sent Kamalakant Chitre for the purpose.
12. Bhai Anant Chitre, Athavanichi Mohanmal, *Janata*, Special Issue, 1934.
13. Social Services League, a unique charitable institution, was founded on 19 March 1911 by a group of social workers like Sir Narayan Chandawarkar, Sir Jamsetji Jijibhai, Sir Henry Proctor, Shri Gagan Biharilal Mehta and some other prominent personalities of Bombay. N.M. Joshi, famous socialist, was its secretary. The objective of the League was to improve the living standards of the mill workers. Accordingly, the League had undertaken multifarious activities like setting up a free mobile library, night schools, adult-education, and Industrial School for Women (ISW), etc. KNOW...LOVE...SERVE was its credo.
14. C.B. Khairmode, op. cit., p.18.
15. Who was just 25 years old then!

16. Not the Bhaurao Gaikwad of Nashik, who would become most important lieutenant of Dr Ambedkar as Dadasaheb Gaikwad.
17. Satyendra More, *Dalit va Communist Chalvalicha Sashakta Duva Comrade R.B. More*, Paryaya Prakashan, Mumbai, 2003, pp. 121-122.
18. Satyendra More, op. cit., pp. 123-125.
19. Satyendra More, op. cit., p. 126.
20. R.B. More gives a figure of 5,000. See p. 265; *Bahishkrut Bharat* and Khairmode give a figure of 3,000, which is used here. *Atmavrutta* – Kolaba District Bahishkrut Parishad First Conference at Mahad. (*Bahishkrut Bharat*, 3 April 1927, pp. 5-8 and C.B. Khairmode, op. cit., p. 18.
21. More says it was 2 pm, which appears more plausible. See Chapter 5.
22. R.B. More's account gives the figure of 5,000. See Chapter 5, but the Home Department's figure is 2,500 to 3,000. DSP, Kolaba mentions 3,000. Also see note 20.
23. Translated from *Bahishkrut Bharat* – Atmavrutta – Kolabo District Bahishkrut Parishad First Conference at Mahad. (Bahishkrut Bharat, 3 April 1927, pp. 5-8).
24. No para break here in the original *Bahishkrut Bharat* or Khairmode's account.
25. No para break here in the original *Bahishkrut Bharat* or Khairmode's account.
26. No para break here in the original *Bahishkrut Bharat* or Khairmode's account.
27. Shridharswami (1678-1729), was a great classical Marathi poet. The reference here may be to his book *The Shivalilamrit*, which is an epic narrative, the recitation of which occupies an important place in the daily worship ritual of many *Shaiva* devotees in Maharashtra. Written in 1718 CE, it consists of 14 chapters and contains a total of 2453 *ovis* (verses).
28. Mukundraj's *Vivek Sindhu*, published in the year 1188, was the first Marathi book to be published. Before, all classical and scholarly discourses were written in Sanskrit, and were not accessible to common Marathi populace.
29. Dnyaneshwar was a 13th century Maharashtrian Hindu saint, poet, philosopher and yogi of the Nath tradition, whose works *Bhavartha Deepika Teeka* (a commentary on *Bhagavad Gita*, popularly known as *Dnyaneshwari*, and *Amrutanubhav* are considered to be milestones in Marathi literature.
30. Mukteshwar (1574-1645) wrote *Bharati Parv*, a rendering of five

parvas of the Mahabharata with 14,687 *ovis* or verses. It is considered the best example of a great narrative poem in Marathi.

31. There are many works like the *Yoga-vasishtha, Bhaktiraja, Panchikaran, Shukashtaka, Gayatri-tika, Uttargita, Prakritgita* and *Samas* which are ascribed to Dnyaneshwar but scholars dispute it to be the works of the author of *Dnyaneshwari*.
32. No para break here in the original *Bahishkrut Bharat* or Khairmode's account.
33. No para break here in the original *Bahishkrut Bharat* or Khairmode's account.
34. No para break here in the original *Bahishkrut Bharat* or Khairmode's account.
35. No para break here in the original *Bahishkrut Bharat* or Khairmode's account.
36. No para break here in the original *Bahishkrut Bharat* or Khairmode's account.
37. No para break here in the original *Bahishkrut Bharat* or Khairmode's account.
38. No para break here in the original *Bahishkrut Bharat* or Khairmode's account.
39. No para break here in the original *Bahishkrut Bharat* or Khairmode's account.
40. No para break here in the original *Bahishkrut Bharat* or Khairmode's account.
41. He is named as some Shet in Chitre's biography; see S.A. Chitre, op. cit., p. 28.
42. There is no evidence that the implementation of the Bole resolution by collective marching to the Chavadar tank was pre-planned and included in the agenda. If it had been so, it is unlikely that *Bahishkrut Bharat*'s account of the conference will miss it. It is consequential because it would lend a different character to the conference from others.
43. Swami Shraddhanand (1856–1926) was an educationist and a missionary of the Arya Samaj founded by Swami Dayanand Saraswati. He became an active member of the Hindu reform movements playing a key role on the *Sangathan* (consolidation) and the *Shuddhi* (re-conversion). In late 1923, he became the president of *Bhartiya Hindu Shuddhi Sabha*, created with an aim to reconvert Muslims, specifically 'Malkana Rajputs' in western United Province, which antagonized the Muslims and brought him into direct confrontation with Muslim clerics and leaders of the time. This led to his assassination by a Muslim fanatic. See,

G.R. Thursby, *Hindu-Muslim Relations in British India: A Study of Controversy, Conflict, and Communal Movements in Northern India 1923-1928*, Brill, 1975, p. 15; Chetan Bhatt, *Hindu Nationalism: Origins, Ideologies and Modern Myths*, Berg Publishers, 2001, p. 62.

44. See the Appendix 1.
45. *Bombay Chronicle.*
46. *Bahishkrut Bharat*, 3.4.27.
47. C.B. Khairmode, op. cit., p. 28; *Bahishkrut Bharat*, first issue dated 04.04.27.
48. C.B. Khairmode, op. cit., p. 35.
49. A report by a correspondent printed in Gandhi's *Young India* cited in Harold Coward, Gandhi, Ambedkar and Untouchability, in Harold Coward, *Indian Critiques of Gandhi*, State University of New York Press, New York, 2003, p. 45.
50. This assertion of human rights by the Untouchables however embarrassed two local leaders, who had declared in their speeches just the previous day that the Untouchables wanting to wash off their sins of untouchability must assert their human rights. These two leaders were Purushottam Pant Joshi and Tulajram Bhai Metha. Anant Chitre chided their double speak in his memories. Not only that they both escaped the venue of the conference soon after Bhai Chitre's exhortation but also had written later disassociating with the march of the Untouchables to the Chavadar tank to draw its water.
51. See, Chapter 5 for R.B. More's account.
52. *Dnyanprakash*, 27 March 1927.
53. Ibid.
54. Ibid.
55. See, R.B. More's account in Chapter 5, p. 267.
56. While Chitre was with Dr Ambedkar, a mob of the caste Hindus had gone to Surbanana Tipnis's house and was asking for Chitre. They were speaking of killing Chitre. When in response, Tipnis took out his gun and threatened the attackers, they disbursed. See, S.A. Chitre, op. cit., p. 32.
57. For additional details, see Chapter 5.
58. Khairmode, op. cit., p. 31.
59. Ibid., p. 45; *Bahishkrut Bharat*, May 6, 1927.
60. Khairmode, op. cit., p. 52.
61. Ibid.
62. Ibid., p. 53.
63. Ibid., pp. 53-54.
64. Ibid., p. 54.

65. Ibid., p. 54.
66. Ibid., p. 54.
67. Ibid., p. 45.
68. Ibid., p. 55.
69. Ibid., p. 55.
70. Ibid., p. 56; *Bahishkrut Bharat*, 06.05.27.
71. Khairmode, op. cit., pp. 55-58.
72. Shripad Mahadeo Mate (1886-1957), a Brahman, headed an *Asprusya Niwarak Mandal* (Committee for Emancipation of Untouchables) aimed at abolishing untouchability in traditional Hindu culture of his times. Known as Mate Master, he wrote extensively on the lives of the downtrodden people belonging to tribal communities and other socially neglected castes like Katkari and Ramoshi. The lives of these people were never presented so authentically and effectively in Marathi literature before Mate. After working continually for twenty years, he published a book entitled *Asprushyaancha Prashna* in 1933. Mate looked upon himself as a traditional but compromising reformist. The Untouchables, for whom Mate worked, found his compromising stance inadequate. As a result, when he found both the sides opposing him tooth and nail, he withdrew from the cause he had been involved in. See, *Sripad Amrit Mate*, Unique Features. http://uniquefeatures.in/e-sammelan-13/ Shreepad-Mahadev-Mate. [Last accessed on 21 January 2014].
73. No para in original, either in *Bahishkrut Bharat* or C.B. Khairmode, op. cit.
74. Khairmode, op. cit., p. 82.
75. Lion; in the Zodiac system, it corresponds with Leo and is associated with the people who like to "rule".
76. Nagnak, a Mahar of Nagewadi in Wai *paragana*, enjoyed the *patilki watan* of that village for a long time. Nagnak Patil's father brought two Guravs from outside the village to perform the daily rituals in the temple of the village deity, *Nagvad Sidha*. The Guravs, however, proved to be traitors in the course of time and usurped the *patilki watan* of Nagewadi. Nagnak, therefore, lodged a complaint against the Guravs with Parashram Pant Pratinidhi, who decided the case in favour of Nagnak, because the defendant Guravs did not appear before him, and also because the Patils of the neighbouring villages, on enquiry, confirmed that the *patilki watan* originally belonged to the Mahar family. The Guravs, however, rejected the decision of the Pratinidhi and appealed to Chhatrapati Rajaram, who, being surrounded by the Mughals,

was going through a critical period of his life. He asked the Mahar to perform an ordeal called *dhardivya*. This required the Mahar to recapture a fort called Vairatgad from the Mughals and restore it to the Maratha swaraj. The Mahar accepted the challenge and won back the fort for the Marathas. Pleased with this *dhardivya* of the Mahar, the Pratinidhi, for the second time, gave the verdict that the Mahar proved to be the right claimant to the *patilki watan* and the Gurav a false one. The Guravs raised the issue again after half a century (1753), but failed for the third time. See, A. R. Kulkarni, "The Mahar Watan: A Historical Perspective" in Meera Kosambi (ed.), *Intersections: Socio-Cultural Trends in Maharashtra*, Orient Longman, Hyderabad, 2000, p. 122.

77. Battle of Pävankhind is a much celebrated battle that took place on July 13, 1660 at a mountain pass at the fort of Vishalgad, near Kolhapur, Maharashtra, between the Maratha sardar Baji Prabhu Deshpande and Siddi Masud of Adilshah. The Marathas held the Adilshahi forces till Shivaji reached Vishalgad. The Adilshahi forces were 15,000 strong against 300 Maratha light infantry.
78. C. B. Khairmode, op. cit., p. 135.

4

The Silenced Salvos: Satyagraha Conference, 25-27 December, 1927

We, who are the living, possess the past. Tomorrow is for our martyrs.

–James Farmer, *Lay Bare The Heart: An Autobiography of the Civil Rights Movement*

The Mahad conference had an electrifying impact on the Untouchables of the Konkan region. The people who lived on alms received from Kunbis and Brahmans in villages for centuries started refusing to drag dead animals and beg for food. Consequently, it gave rise to clashes between them and others in villages. The vested interests in the form of Patil, Kulkarni, and other criminal elements fanned them further to extract money from both sides. Although, the Untouchables were generally poor, many of them fell prey to their intrigues and paid them money selling whatever little they had only to realise at the end that they were cheated. A majority of them, however, struggled against the dominant castes. They were guided and supported by activists such as Sambhaji Tukaram Gaikwad, Ramchandra Babaji More, Jamadar Kudwalkar, Jamadar Vishram Gangaram Savadkar, Subhedar Raghoram Ghatge, Adrekar Baba, Shivram Gopal Jadhav, Hate Master, etc., who were vigorously touring the interiors of Konkan.

Babasaheb Ambedkar had realized that if the Mahad struggle succeeded, it would have a good impact not only in Konkan, but also all over the Marathi speaking area and even beyond. But if it failed, it could be disastrous, demoralizing the movement at the inception itself. It was therefore imperative to persist with it until the conclusive win. The march to Chavadar tank by the delegates to the first conference for exercising their civil rights had met with harsh reaction from the caste Hindus, which clearly showed that the Hindus would not easily accept any reforms and therefore indicated the need to intensify the struggle. If it was left at that it might have been misconstrued as a failure and demoralized the Untouchables, neutralizing the gains of the conference. It was imperative therefore to demonstrate the resolve of the Untouchables to persist with the struggle until their objective was achieved. It was also strategically important to relaunch the agitation without much gap, and on a larger scale.

Accordingly, Babasaheb Ambedkar decided to hold another conference associated with Satyagraha at the Chavadar tank with full preparation. He explained his plan to all his leading activists and kicked off preparations soon after his return from Mahad. The news of the first conference had reached far and wide, encouraging Untouchables to rise in revolt and alarming the caste Hindus about the incipient danger to their caste culture. The attack on the delegates by the caste Hindus served as a blessing in disguise in imparting it news value as well as creating controversy, which would linger on for months on the pages of newspapers. Soon after the conference, on 3 April, 1927, Babasaheb Ambedkar launched *Bahishkrut Bharat*, as the organ of the Bahishkrut Hitkarini Sabha, which would play a big role in mobilizing support for the second conference. Soon the activists began conducting meetings every day in Dalit *bastis* (localities) of Mumbai. Massive propaganda was launched through public meetings, handbills, wall paintings, and pamphlets in Mumbai and all over the Marathi speaking provinces. People began donating money generously to the Satyagraha funds. This was the first such extensively planned event of the Untouchables ever in history.

With the experience of the conference and sharp reactions it provoked among the caste Hindus, Dr Ambedkar imagined a need for a separate teams of volunteers not only to make and maintain arrangements at Mahad but also to look after the security. The first unit of volunteers was established by the people in his own chawl. They just numbered 15 to start with. The number of volunteers rose everyday as more and more units started coming up in other localities. This volunteer corps became the harbinger of the *Samata Sainik Dal* (Equality Army Corps), which would be formalized later.

Both, the Untouchables as well as the Touchables began reacting to the propaganda. Keshavrao Jedhe and Dinkarrao Jawalkar, the prominent non-Brahman leaders published two letters in newspapers declaring their support to the proposed Satyagraha. Their second letter however voiced a condition that it should not include any Brahman person. Dr Ambedkar took note of some of the reactions and commented in his editorials in *Bahishkrut Bharat*. In the issue dated 29 July 1927, he commented on the condition of Jedhe and Jawalkar that it was not acceptable to him:

> We do not believe that no one born in the Brahman caste can be liberal in his mind. ... We do need all people who are sympathetic to our cause, whether they are Brahmans or non-Brahmans. To exclude Brahmans will not only be wrong in principles but also in strategy. ... One of our Brahman sisters from Pune, with due permission from her husband, conveyed her desire to us by a letter to participate in the Satyagraha as a volunteer. Mr Jawalkar also would not be able to say that we should discourage such persons. If we have a fear that participation of Brahmans will jeopardize the mission, then we may have to have such a fear in respect of not only many non-Brahmans but also of the boycotted class people themselves. We do not want to do anything in a surreptitious manner. We are going to act very openly. Therefore we do not need to fear either Brahmans or anybody else. Some orthodox Brahmans and even non-Brahmans may consider our touch as polluting. But we would not consider cooperation from those Brahmans and non-Brahmans who are inspired by good intention. We will only be grateful to all those who come forward with moral commitment to help us in our noble work. Many other people also have expressed their desire to participate in the Satyagraha by writing letters to us. Hundreds of those belonging to the Untouchable class are just waiting for the announcement of the dates for the satyagraha.

He further explained,

> ... we feel that it is appropriate to confine the Satyagraha movement only to the eradication of untouchability. There should not be any objection to the participation of all such people along with the Untouchables, who genuinely believe that eradication of untouchability is extremely necessary from the viewpoint of reforms, justice, human compassion and national unity. For example, those whose opinions are like Mahatma Gandhi might perhaps feel difficult to sign on the undertaking suggested by Mr Ghorpade. But, it will not be appropriate to discard their sympathies and assistance only for that reason. Their thoughts may be wrong in principle. But just for that to declare proscription against them will be wrong.
>
> The movement like satyagraha is required to be focused on specific issues. It is necessary not to entangle it with many issues. And it is advantageous to all to cooperate with people of varied opinions and attitudes without compromising the principles.

Volte Face of Mahad Municipality

Following the Bole resolution, Mahad municipality had passed a resolution throwing open all the public amenities to the Untouchables in January 1924. It had remained dormant till the Untouchables exercised their right after the conference at Mahad on 20 March 1927, which angered the caste Hindus. The caste Hindus of Mahad began thinking about how the problem posed by the Untouchables could be thwarted. It was possible for them to do it by showing the tank was not a public property and rather it belonged to that private person. But they could not collect enough evidence to effectuate this argument. Therefore the only thing that was possible for them was to argue that the government should not insist on the implementation of the Bole resolution, for all the water tanks and public places belonging to the municipality, if it wants to preserve peace in Konkan and in Mumbai province. It is precisely this kind of a resolution that the Mahad municipality passed in its meeting of 4 August 1927 and send to the government.[1]

The Administration had become quite alert to these matters after the incident in Mahad. It appeared to be following it closely. This resolution of the Mahad municipality therefore created a good deal of reactions in the government. The confidential diary of the district superintendent of police, Kolaba, for the week ending August 13th 1927, reported on the move of the Mahad municipality to retract its earlier resolution as follows:

> On August 4 in a general meeting of the Mahad municipality it was resolved that the resolution (no. 67 of January 5 1924) regarding the free use of water of the tanks in the municipal area by Untouchables, passed then, should be withheld till the public were prepared to remove Untouchability. Because, owing to the present public opinion it was impossible to bring the aforesaid resolution into force. It was however, resolved that the municipality should remove, as soon as possible, the inconvenience in connection with the supply of drinking water to Untouchables.

The District Magistrate (DM) was not happy with these developments. He remarked on the diary:

> The Mahad municipality's retrogressive resolution is unfortunate, though undoubtedly representative of public opinion. It is likely to complicate matters, if the depressed classes presently make a further active assertion of their claim to take water from the municipal tank as I am told they intent to do.

The Home Department (Political)[2] took a correct stand calling both passing of the first resolution as well as its later retraction by the Mahad Municipality as superfluous. It makes an exception of only such tanks which were specifically built for the caste Hindus and were later taken over by the municipality with that restriction. However, it puts the onus of proving that this exception applied to a particular tank onto the claimant and advised the Commissioner and the DM to be guided by it. It emphasized that "the DM cannot assist the municipality or the high caste people in any attempt to prevent the low caste people from exercising their rights." The memo wrote:

> There is no law allowing the imposition of caste or class distinction in the enjoyment of public property. If the 'caste' Hindus had a right to exclude an Untouchable from a municipal tank, such right could only have been a custom not enforceable at law. From a legal point of view, therefore, the resolution of January 1924 and that of August last, were both superfluous in as much as the former

gave the Untouchables no new rights and the latter took away none. In short, there appears to be no legal grounds on which the Untouchables, as such, can be excluded from the free use of water from the municipal tanks of Mahad.

It may, however, be the case that certain tanks were specially built for 'caste' Hindus and were taken over by the municipality with that restriction. Such tanks cannot legally be thrown open to the Untouchables by a resolution by the municipality. It is presumed however, that there are no such tanks in Mahad, but if any such claim should be made in respect of a particular tank, it will of course be for those claiming to prove it right.

The Commissioner, Southern Division, Belgaum, wrote to the Secretary to Government, Home Department, Bombay, forwarding the letter from Hood, District Collector and Magistrate, Kolaba on the subject of the Chavadar tank at Mahad and the intention of the Untouchables to make an organized attempt in December next, to assert their right to use. It said,

> "in the absence of any ground for suppressing that the tank was taken over by the municipality for use only by the caste section of the public in general", and also to the fact that the collector's report showed no ground for such a supposition, the only possible attitude for government to take up is that the 'Untouchables' were entitled to use it. In view of the probability that resistance would be offered to such use, he recommended that the district magistrate should be directed to protect the 'Untouchables' in using the tank and to resist any attempt at interference with their so doing by force.[3]

With regard to the ownership of the Chavadar tank, DM, Kolaba confirmed to the Commissioner, Southern Division, Belgaum[4], that there was no documentary evidence as to the ownership of the tank. It was in Gaothan (village ownership) and had no separate entry in the survey papers. There was no record as to who constructed it or when. The municipal records were destroyed by fire in 1905 and therefore did not have any information on it. The tank had apparently been regarded as vested in municipality as the result of the Government Order No. GRRD 6111 of 9.9.1887. There was also no evidence that the tank was built by, or for caste Hindus or that the municipality took it over with any restriction as to its use by particular classes. Hood then writes about the possible arguments likely to be put forward for excluding the Untouchables from the tank as, "(1) the situation of the tank is in midst of the caste Hindu quarters. (2) the custom of 'Untouchables' not taking water from it hitherto. (3) the existence of a separate well maintained by the municipality for the 'Untouchables' of Mahad town at about a quarter of a mile from the tank. (4) the existence of private ghats of the surrounding caste Hindu residents on all sides of the tank; there are about 20 such private ghats and 3 built or maintained by the municipality. The municipality seems to be managing the tank under section 50(2)(b) of the district municipal act though that section does not define the term 'public'.

Hood, in his communication indicated that 'the towns people' were trying to find evidence to show that the tank was private property. While he could advise them the position of the government vide the DO letter No. SD1041 of 15.9.1927, it would not help him in preserving the peace if the 'Untouchables' tried to enter the tank en masse in December. He apprehended a serious riot and wanted orders to use force to prevent the 'Untouchables' from making an attempt or to prevent the caste Hindus from obstructing or retaliating as per his previous letter No. MSC 192 of 27.8.1927.

There were reactions to this new resolution from the public too. Bahishkrut Bharat reproduced a letter from one S.G. Deshpande, obviously a Brahman, who had commented upon the double speak of one Mr Virkar, who often claimed himself to be pro-reform liberal but was instrumental in bringing about the *volte face* of the municipality with regard to the implementation of the Bole resolution. It revealed how public posturing of people could not be taken in the face value in the matters of caste. Virkar seemed to have argued that the municipality needed to exercise that kind of caution as the illiterate people had not accepted the reform. When it was pointed out by another member, Tuljarambhai Seth, that the demand for it had not come from the illiterate people but from the well educated or semi-educated people belonging to the Brahman, Gurav and other such castes, Virkar fumbled expressing the doubt whether the tank was a public place at all. What the letter had revealed was that the so called liberal Hindus generally mouthed reformist slogans but made a quick retreat when it came to the putting it into action. However, there were some people like Tuljarambhai and Deshpande who held on to their sanity in the face of odds.

Dr Ambedkar commented on these developments in the Bahishkrut Bharat of 12 August 1927:

> The orthodox people have not kept quite with just the *shuddhikaran* (purification) of the Chavadar tank at Mahad, which created such an uproar in the entire country. This tank was opened up for the people of all the castes with an earlier resolution of the Mahad municipality and only after that the boycotted people had a conference and exercised their right by taking its water. We understand that the municipality has now annulled the resolution by a majority vote. Since Mahad municipality is fraught with reactionary members, we are not at all surprised by this 'reform' that the Chavadar tank will be open only for the Hindus of the high *varna*. The Mahad municipality has changed its previous resolution and has banned the Untouchables from accessing the Chavadar tank. We hope it will attract attention of the district collector of Kolaba who will take appropriate action against the municipality. It is an illusion if the orthodox Hindus think that they have permanently blocked the Untouchables with this municipality resolution. This issue cannot be settled with such a flimsy resolution. On the contrary, the illiberal members of the Mahad municipality must bear in mind that the real movement for the *shuddhikaran* of the Chavadar tank from the viewpoint of the boycotted will pick up more momentum. The khadi-wearing elitist lot wanted to escape the responsibility of the assault at Mahad by blaming it on the illiterate people of the touchable castes. But this resolution tears off their mask and exposes their true colour to the world. Needless to say, if they had been conscious of the lawful rights of the excluded and if the attack of the illiterate goons on the Untouchables had been really unacceptable to them, they would not have indulged in the intrigue of retracting the previous resolution.[5]

As indicated before, the government took a serious note of the new retrogressive resolution of the municipality. It[6] threatened that "in the event of the Mahad municipality taking any steps to put into effect its resolution of the 4 August 1927,.... against the declared policy of the government", no discretionary grants would be made to the municipality. It required the commissioner to inform the Mahad municipality accordingly and directed the collector of Kolaba "to report to government at once if any attempt is made by the municipality to put its resolution into force." General Department also asked the DM Kolaba whether he considered the issue of a warning to both parties, as suggested by the Under Secretary, would be political and to report whether the communication of the above orders from the government had any effect on the public.[7] The DM, Kolaba sent a detailed reply to the Commissioner SD, Belgaon, describing the situation of the Chavadar tank as follows:

> Tank is enclosed on all sides, partly by wooden fencing and mostly by private plots containing ghats, gardens, temples, and other buildings. Beyond this is a public street running around the tank on all sides, the houses of the plot owners stand beyond and along the streets. But there are three municipal ghats, two on the west and one on the east side, leading direct from the street into the tank. Thus there is ample access to the tank without using the private property. The owners of all the private plots and ghats are orthodox caste Hindus of reactionary views and none of them are likely to allow the Untouchables the use of their ghat.[8]

Hood was obviously not in favour of taking any precipitate action as suggested by the Secretary to the Government. He opined in the same memo as follows:

> I am of the opinion that it will not be politic to issue a warning to both parties that if neither party makes an effort to obtain a clear decision of their civil rights in the court of law, I shall be constrained to close the tank to all parties to prevent disturbance of peace. To put such a warning into effect would involve immense hardship to the town as a whole, as the tank is the chief source of drinking water, and on grounds of public health it would be impossible to continue such an embargo for any length of time. In fact we should be taking up a position from which we should have to withdraw before long, for which reason I should prefer not to take up that position at all. Further, closing of the tank to all parties would involve the closing of all private ghats (about 20 in number) and would be very difficult to enforce, and might easily

> involve government in a number of civil suits. My third reason for regarding such a course as impolitic is that such closing of the tank would stultify the much advertised "satyagraha" of the Untouchables and would certainly be hailed by that party as an unsympathetic act out of keeping with the expressed policy of the government.
>
> The threat of stopping discretionary grants to the municipality does not seem to have had any appreciable effect on the public. It is said that the dispensary grant is the only discretionary grant received from the government at present.
>
> I understand that some of the caste Hindus are at last beginning to talk of seeking an injunction to prevent the Untouchables from entering the tank. I think that the surest way of assuring that they shall translate this talk into action is to adopt the course previously recommended by me and supported by you in your letter dated 19.10.1927. I do not think my closing the tank will do it, because, while that will have the excellent effect (from the Touchables point of view) of bringing to naught the Untouchables' satyagraha campaign, the Touchables are clever enough to realize that I cannot possibly keep the tank close for long, against those who live on its banks, though it may be a long time before the Untouchables' leaders in Bombay may be able to organize and lead another campaign on the tank. In fact such closing of the tank by the DM though apparently impartial, would work against the Untouchables.

The above report from the Collector, Kolaba appears to have gone well with the government as the Under Secretary's note dated 21.11.1927 almost approvingly restates the points therein. The majority of the entrances to the tank being in private ownership, anybody forcing entry through them would mean an invasion of private rights. Only three ghats were under the municipality and could be held out of bounds of any private ownership. The Under Secretary hopes that either party could obtain an injunction from the civil court and ease the matter for administration. Secretary's endorsement dated 22 November 1927 on the above envisages the possibility of riot if the tank is closed. It therefore advises the DM "to see that an adequate police force is provided to prevent any breach of peace, which will naturally involve preventing the Untouchables from using the private ghats and keeping the municipal ghats open for any member of the public to obtain access to the tank." Accordingly a memo was issued on 29 November 1927 advising the district magistrate Kolaba to ensure the municipal ghats were kept open for the public to obtain access to the tank and to instruct the police to see that the Untouchables are not prevented from using these ghats.[9]

A confidential letter (No. SD 1432) from the Home Department (Political) to Hood, DM, Kolaba dated 3 December 1927 explains the attitude of the government and advises the line of action for him that "...would help the depressed classes in their aspiration rather than assist the more bigoted members of the advanced classes to maintain their domination. ..... presuming the tanks in question were the property of the municipality, the Mahad municipality's resolution of January 1924, which threw open tanks to the Untouchables and that of August last which rescinded that resolution." It called the action of the Mahad municipality in passing these resolutions as 'superfluous', "as the tanks being public property were, subject to certain restrictions were open to every member of the public." In addition "to seeing that the Untouchables should not be prevented from access to the tank", it also advises the DM to "endevour to induce those of the touchables who are strongly opposed, to modify their attitude or at least to do nothing that is likely to endanger the peace." Making reference to the weekly report from the DM (dated 20 November 1927) it expects him to have little difficulty "in view of the division and wavering in their ranks". In consonance with the policy of the colonial government, it advises to shun "any public declaration of government support to the Untouchables" and let the government steps "percolate through any of the leaders on either side you may interview".

One thing that comes out clear from these documents is that the Government did not have much option other than supporting the Untouchables, if they wanted to exercise their right at the Chavadar tank. The intrigues of the caste Hindus in rescinding the earlier resolution of the municipality, it knew did not hold much water. The preferred development from its viewpoint was that either party obtains a court injunction, which would make its task simpler. As there was no possibility of the Untouchables getting such an injunction, only the caste Hindus could manage it somehow, projecting the Chavadar tank to be a private property. As the subsequent developments unfolded, this is what precisely happened. It is quite possible that the local government, faced with this problem, had prompted the caste Hindus to get such an injunction.

Clouds of Apprehensions

By November, the preparations for the Satyagraha conference at Mahad were in full swing. The extracts from the confidential diary of DSP, Kolaba dated 5 November 1927 confirms that handbills for them were being distributed all over Mahad and the Mangaon talukas. The handbill duly highlighted that the nine persons who had attacked the Untouchables during the previous conference were convicted to show that they had legitimate right to draw water from the tank. It called upon the people to attend the meeting at Mahad on 25 December to establish that right. The *Kolaba Samachar* of 5 November carried the news on the proposed Satyagraha and pleaded with Dr Ambedkar "to think the matter coolly and not to be over hasty." It also issued an advice to the inhabitants of Mahad "to allow the Untouchables to use the tank on the condition of cleanliness." Such ripples of the news about the conference were thus seen all over.

DSP Kolaba's note of 19 November reports Mahars having meetings at various places in the Mangaon taluka for collecting subscriptions and canvassing for participating in the Satyagraha. It also reported on a meeting held in the Vireshwar temple on 17 November to discuss the steps to be taken if Mahars carried out their proposed Satyagraha. Some 200 Brahmans, Gujars, Marathas, etc., supposedly opposing the Satyagraha were present but some of them turned out to be in favour of the Satyagraha. No one wanted to preside over the meeting. Eight or nine names were proposed but all declined and the meeting had to be dissolved without any decision being taken.[10] The note contains the DM, Kolaba's remarks: "I have every hope that as it begins to be realized that the Untouchables have the sympathy and support of the authorities, the opposition will fade away, at least so far as any open violence is concerned." The diary dated 3rd December of the DSP, Kolaba noted the meeting of the Mahad municipality, which was held on November 23 to discuss the question of the Satyagraha. Eight members were present, viz., the first class magistrate, Mahad Surendranath Govind Tipnis, Mahadev Ramchandra Oak, Sunder Vallabh Mehta, Vishnu Narayan Khandke, Balkrishna Balal alias Bandopant Joshi and Pitamber Gokul Mehta. S.G. Tipnis (the president), said that the Mahars should be allowed to take water from the tank. He was supported by M.B. Virkar, M.R. Oak and V.N. Khandke. It was then decided that the opinion of the municipal voters should also be taken.

The declaration of Satyagraha had influenced even some caste Hindus from outside to come forward in support. *The Times of India* dated 8 December reported that Mr D.V. Gokhale and Mr J.S. Karandikar, assistant editors of the *Maratha* and the *Kesari* respectively had a public meeting in the Vireshwar temple on 30 November and advised the audience of caste Hindus not to alienate the Untouchables any more, and rather get them with them so as to strengthen their demand for swaraj. They exhorted them to admit the claim of the Untouchables to take water from the Chavadar tank like all other people including Mohamadans.[11]

As there were sympathetic reactions to the civil rights struggle by the Untouchables from a small section of the touchable community, there were angry reactions from its majority that spoke of punishing them for their defiance. The diary of the DSP, Kolaba notes one such instance: "On 27 November about 200 Marathas from some 28 villages assembled at Deopur (Poladhpur police station) and decided that the practice of giving a bundle of straw with paddy, which the Mahars used to get from each house, should be stopped. No bread or any animal carcasses were to be given in future. They decided to review the situation after the Satyagraha." On 28 November J.R. Hood, DM, Kolaba reported the developments in the DSP's note to the Secretary to Government, Home Department (Special). After the fiasco in which the meeting of

17 November at the Vireshwar temple had ended, some municipal councillors requisitioned the president of the Mahad municipality to call a meeting of the municipality. But this meeting on 26 November also had to be adjourned for the want of quorum, the president having deliberately absented himself. The DM observed that the Touchables were 'somewhat' divided on the issue'. The DM was inclined to make a definite declaration that "opposition to the Untouchable's entering the tank will not be permitted", which would "lead to bloodless victory for the Untouchables", and hoped the government would authorize him "to make that declaration as soon as possible before the divided and wavering counsels of the Touchables are welded into a united plan for opposition." This was quite a bold proposition that reveals inter alia anxiety in the administration to avoid the complexity of the law and order problem arising during the Satyagraha. There were indications that with every passing day the opposition to the Satyagraha was dwindling. DSP, Kolaba's note of 26 November says, [although] "the Brahmans had continued their efforts to oppose the Satyagraha even after the failure of their meeting on 17 November", "[T]there seems to be a growing feeling of brotherliness among the Touchables towards the Untouchables. In other words there are now more Touchables in favour of better treatment of the depressed classes."

Mr Hood, the DM, Kolaba wrote a letter on 9 December 1927 to Mr Monteath, Secretary to the Government, Home Department (Political) reporting the developments at Mahad. He had visited Mahad on 7 December and interviewed about 15 of the leading people of the caste Hindu camp. Some of them, including the president of the municipality, appeared to be in favour of allowing the Untouchables to take water from the municipal tanks. However, the majority of the Touchables were still strongly opposed to it. He had argued over an hour with them but in vain; he could not convince the orthodox elements about the Untouchables' legal right to use water from the Chavadar tank. He made it clear to them that the government had been unable to find the municipality or anyone who had legal rights to forbid the Untouchables from drawing water from the tank. He said that they must first get an injunction from the civil courts. Until they did so, the government would be on the side of the Untouchables. They should at once approach the court for an injunction, but he apprehended they would not do so. They were afraid; the legal decision might go against them. Although much of the talk did not bear fruit, he gathered an impression that the Touchables would not attempt any violence against the Untouchables, there will be no organized obstruction by force. At the same time the situation would be tense and result in violence. The DM therefore wrote that he had asked the DSP to have not less than 40 armed policemen in Mahad on 24 November and that he intended to camp at or near Mahad during Christmas.

Around this time, the government issued a transfer order for J.R. Hood, DM, Kolaba. Hood was to hand over to one Mr Kriplani and go to Sukkur. Painter, Commissioner, Southern Division sent a telegram on 9 December to Home Secretary requesting postponement of the sudden transfer of Hood in view of the Mahad Satyagraha on 25 December. Painter persisted with his efforts to get the transfer postponed. Hood had also indicated his displeasure over his transfer order. He wrote:

> I feel I ought to be in Mahad using such influence as I can, not only to avert any danger of a breach of peace, but also to try and induce the Touchables generally to take a different attitude as suggested in your letter. But unfortunately the orders of transfers have tied my hands and compel to leave it to my successor. .... I should like to be allowed to say in conclusion that I believe I could have camped at Mahad as I had intended. I would have carried ... the wishes of the government successfully and without any outbreak ... and I had hoped to get a sufficient number of influential .... on my side to avert any undesirable aftermath such as boycott ...., etc. As it is I feel that any successor will start with a difficult situation.

Not getting unnerved by the failure of the meeting of the Mahad municipality on 26 November, the opposition camp of the Touchables could eventually accomplish the voters' meeting on 3 December. How the orthodox section of the touchable camp conspired to isolate the Untouchables is commented by the DM, Kolaba himself:

> I received yesterday the copies of the resolutions passed at the meeting of some 280 municipal voters on the 3rd instant calling on the municipality to close the Chavadar tank and two other tanks to the Untouchables. One of these is in the Mohammedan quarter and the idea clearly is to enlist the Mohammedans on the side of the caste Hindus. I have replied that if the tanks are public, the municipality had no legal power to exclude members of the public, and if the ... the municipality is not concerned, thus in either case it has no power to take the action suggested in the resolution. I sent a copy of my reply to the president of the municipality.[12]

The representations against Hood's transfer were immediately heeded and he was allowed to stay on till 6th January 1928.[13] As Hood learnt of the Touchables' ingenuous plan to get the Mohammedans on to their side by "including the *Habus* tank in the Mohomedan quarter among the tanks now proposed to be forbidden to the Untouchables, he heard about the Untouchable leaders adopting equally ingenuous and curious method for securing the attendance of Mahars from outside the Mahad taluka at the Satyagraha. They were propagating that the government wanted all Untouchables to attend this meeting. Hood wrote,

> I am now informed that in the Mangaon Taluka, the Mahars are under the impression that a big meeting is to be held at Mahad on 25th instant, and that the government wants all Mahars to attend. Some Mahars actually asked a circle inspector in Mangaon why the government was going to hold a big meeting of the Mahars at Mahad.[14]

As the dates of the Satyagraha neared, his apprehensions about violence also evaporated. Nevertheless, with 'an enormous mass of ignorant people invading a town of some 6,000 inhabitants in a state of tension', he could not fully eliminate the possibilities of disorder.

Fraudulent Injunction

The Touchables were planning to counter the impending Satyagraha of the Untouchables by various methods. They appeared to have taken Hood's advice seriously to obtain an interim injunction against the invasion of the Chavadar tank by the Untouchables. His weekly letter, dated 12 December 1927 alludes to these possibilities. It says, "The Mamladdar of Mahad reports that (presumably as the result of my talk with them on 7th instant) the touchables are moving the civil court for an injunction restraining the Untouchables from the Chavadar tank. I do not know yet which court, whether they are likely to get any decision before the 25th instant." The Touchables were also planning a petition against the Satyagraha to be signed by all for presentation to the collector and higher authorities. A rumour was also afloat in Mahad and surrounding areas that Marathas and other caste Hindus from Poladpur were coming to Mahad in large numbers to strike terror among the Untouchables so that they do not carry out their plan of entering the Chavadar tank.

Dr Ambedkar has provided information on the movement opposing the Satyagraha in the *Bahishkrut Bharat* dated 23 December 1927. The orthodox people of Mahad had appealed to the collector against it. In order to create an impression amongst the people as well as in the collector that there is support of the members of the Mahad municipality. The orthodox members had called a meeting and passed a resolution therein that the Chavadar tank should not be open to the Untouchables. 261 members had voted for the resolution, 7 opposed it and 13 were non-committal. The collector had told the people of Mahad during his visit that the government will not stop the Untouchables from marching to the tank. However, if someone filed a case with the government or a court claiming that the tank was a private property, the government would verify it and only after validation, the government would be able to stop the Untouchables from going to the tank.[15]

The information on the massive preparations for the Satyagraha was sending jitters in the caste Hindu community of Mahad. One Pandurang Raghunath Dharap and other eight touchable residents of Mahad[16] came forward and filed a suit No. 405 of 1927 on 12 December 1927, barely 13 days before the Satyagraha, against Dr Ambedkar and other four

Untouchables[17] in the court of second sub judge, Mahad. They had complained that the subject tank at Mahad was known as Chowdhary tank and was privately owned. As per the prevailing custom, the Untouchables had no right to draw water from it. Therefore the Satyagraha that the Untouchables were to perform at the tank under the leadership of Dr Ambedkar from 25 December was illegal and so the court should issue appropriate orders to Dr Ambedkar and his comrades to stop it. Based on this complaint, the second sub judge G.V. Vaidya issued an injunction on the same day that Dr Ambedkar and other respondents should not go to the tank or touch its water. If they did so, it will amount to a criminal act for which they will be legally proceeded against. The said order is given in the **Appendix 2**.

The confidential diary of the district superintendent of police, Kolaba, for the week ending 17 December, 1927 notes that the leaders of the Touchables at Mahad had filed a suit in the civil court to restrain the Untouchables from drinking in the Chavadar tank and they also had obtained an injunction *ex parte*. It expresses doubt whether the Satyagraha would still be carried out by the Untouchables. The district magistrate remarked on 24 December 1927,

> The injunction granted ex parte by the local sub judge is of course temporary pending hearing of the regular suit. The Untouchables are at present pouring in by hundreds. It is hoped to turn the Satyagraha into an ordinary peaceful conference, but much depends upon the attitude taken by the Untouchable leaders and in particular Dr. Ambedkar, who is expected tomorrow. I am informed that his present intention is to disregard the court's injunction and carry out the proposed entry into the Chavadar Tank. I have arranged to see him immediately on his arrival, and hope to induce him to accept wiser counsels.

The diary of DSP, Kolaba, dated 24 December 1927 noted the following:

> On 18 December Dr. Ambedkar held a meeting at Panvel, which was attended by some 75 people, both Touchables and Untouchables. He explained the circumstance which, he said, had compelled him to offer Satyagraha at Mahad. On 22 December

> Marathas held a meeting at Mahad during which they declared that they would remain neutral and would not come in the way of the Untouchables. On 23 December about 35 persons met at Mahad to discuss the Satyagraha. They were addressed by Purshottam Prabhakar Joshi and P.B. Pujare, both of whom were in favour of allowing the Mahars to use the Chavadar tank. Pujare said that the *Kshatriya* community was not against the Satyagraha. On 24 December, by evening over 3000 Untouchables had collected at Mahad, coming from all parts. Dr Ambedkar and over 2000 more were expected on 25 December in the morning. The town was very quiet.

The injunction was always favoured by DM, Kolaba, but the government appeared skeptical about it. When the DM wrote[18] to the Secretary to Government, seeking government approval for prohibiting the Untouchables from entering the Chavadar tank, the Home Department was not happy with the injunction itself. It commented that "the issue of an ex parte injunction in a matter of this sort was a scandalous abuse of legal process" and that they might have "to consider whether any action on this point was necessary."[19] Another endorsement on the note dated 23 December by an official expresses astonishment at these developments. It reads, "I must however, confess that I am mystified by an injunction issued against the Untouchables in the world. The plaintiff must have cast his net very wide to obtain such an injunction even temporarily." However, in view of the circumstances described by the DM, it felt that there was no other option other than approving the action plan. A confidential letter from Hood, DM, Kolaba to the Secretary to Government, General Department dated 1 December 1927 provides his views on the interim injunctions and the likely developments at Mahad. It said,

> My personal opinion on the propriety of the temporary injunction issued by the subjudge of Mahad on 14th December is of little value. It will no doubt be attacked in due course. It is certainly open to attack on several very strong grounds, e.g., the touchables were granted their injunction ex-parte on the ground of urgency, ignoring the fact that they had let several months go by without taking any action and on contrary to a well established maxim of equity, allowing them profit by their own laches. The immediate

> result, of course was, that the Untouchables, who had been preparing for their satyagraha, i.e., entry into the tank, for several months, had to be persuaded or if necessary, compelled to abandon their cherished place with consequent great disappointment to themselves.

Notwithstanding DM's comments, the Secretary to Government, Home Department (Political) Bombay called for certain documents from DM, Kolaba in order to enable the Government to consider whether any action was necessary in respect of the grant of ex-parte injunction by the sub-judge's court at Mahad. The legal opinion on the same, however, validated it. It explained that the temporary injunction was granted on a consideration of balance of convenience, and with a view to preserve the status quo if no special hardship was involved to the parties in that. It said that the merits of the dispute are hardly ever taken into consideration in deciding question of temporary injunction. In the subject case it was not unfair to preserve the status quo. If the injunction had not been granted and the suite was decided in favour of the Touchables they would be put to considerable expense and inconvenience for purifying the tank. On the other hand, if the Untouchables won the suit the only effect would be to prolong the oppression that has gone on for centuries by a year or so. Most judges would have granted the injunction in the given circumstances. While the RLA (Regional Legal Advisor) thus saw the grant of injunction as fair, he also commented that it was 'more or less a farce'. "Because it was not binding on anyone except the few defaults even though the defaults are sued in a representative capacity. If any other Mahar bathed in the tank the court could not punish him. Nor were the proceedings binding on every 'touchable'. If a Brahman of Mahad tells the court that he is not willing to be represented by the plaintiff, the suit would fail."

Tragi-Comic Instances

Even the illiterate Untouchables also were conscious of the importance of the Satyagraha. The old hands who suffered the oppression of untouchability were convinced in their mind that it was the struggle to break the chains of their slavery. As such, they prayed every day for the success of the Satyagraha. The *sadhus* (mendicants) of various sects that existed among Mahars of those days, viz., *Kabirpanth, Ramanandpanth, Nathpanth, Bhagwat (varkari) panth,* had begun to perform *pujas,* say prayers and observe fasts according to their respective rituals for the success of the Satyagraha. Sambhaji Tukaram Gaikwad had organized a meeting of the *sadhus* living in Kamathipura, Colaba, Naigaon, Kurla, Bandra, etc. in the Cement Chawl at Clark Road. The purpose of the meeting was to impress upon them that they should do some social work, and not just live off, begging from the community. The collectivity of *sadhus* agreed to work for creating awareness among the Untouchables about the Mahad Satyagraha. But nothing much came out of it. On the contrary, they gave rise to futile controversies. Some *sadhus* created controversy that if God had taken an *avatar* in the form of Bhimrao (Ambedkar) for emancipating the Untouchables, which God was it. There was a big debate among the *sadhus* over this issue. At the end, one *sadhu* (his name was Shambhubuwa More who lived in the same Poyabawadi chawl where Dr Ambedkar then lived) suggested that it was *Rudra,* who had similar demeanor as Dr Ambedkar. Another *sadhu* however disagreed and argued that Rudra avatar could not come in full form in the Untouchable community; it could only come in half form. Therefore all the *sadhus* decided that Dr Ambedkar was the incarnation of half Rudra. Some opposed even that. On this issue there was a division among the *sadhus.* Instead of preparing people for the Mahad Satyagraha, they indulged in futile debate of making Ambedkar an *avatar* of half Rudra. When Sambhaji Gaikwad told Dr Ambedkar about it, he had a big laugh over it. After some time he became serious and said to the people seated around him, that precisely with these notions, the Brahmans have ruined the society. He advised them not to let such notions spread in the community any more.[20]

Khairmode cites another episode of a *sadhu,* Atmaram Kamble, from Mayani village, taluka Khatao in Satara district. He had come in contact with Dr Ambedkar's father, Subhedar Ramji, when he was working as a cashier in Satara. Atmaram *sadhu* had left his son, Swarupa, at Ramji's house as a domestic aid. Swarupa became *varkari*, running the legacy of his father. He came in July 1927 to Mumbai and met Dr Ambedkar in his office. He told Dr Ambedkar that when he went to Pandhari, he warned Lord Vitthal to make the Mahad Satyagraha a success or else he would smash his (Vitthal's) head like an onion. Dr Ambedkar kept quiet for a few seconds and then asked Swarupa what food he had carried while going to Pandhari. Buwa replied, "stale bread, onion and chutney". Ambedkar asked him whether he carried *puran poli*[21] any time. Buwa responded by saying yes, that he carried stale *puran poli* in torn pieces. Then Dr Ambedkar asked him why he had not told Vitthal so far that he should give him enough money for eating *puran polis* like Brahmans did, or else he would smash his head like an onion. When Buwa said that he had no desire for such food, Dr Ambedkar angrily retorted that it was this slavish mentality that had kept them shackled in poverty. They should give up this mentality as well as their Gods, and rather learn to live with self respect. Swarupa buwa felt ashamed, but he could not give up a custom that had been followed for years and would invariably exclaim in the name of Vitthal that he would grant success to *Bhimdeva*! [22]

Dr Ambedkar had planned to mobilize money for the Mahad Satyagraha. He personally met many lawyers and barristers in the high court and requested them for contribution, but majority of the Hindus among them, did not pay. Musalmans and Jews did contribute, but their cumulative contribution did not exceed Rs 100 as against an estimated expense of over Rs 2,000. He was worried about how to mobilize such a huge sum. One day while sitting in the high court library, he happened to voice his worry to Motiram Talapade, who took him to the office of *Vividhvrutta*[23] in Thakurdwar. He discussed the problem with Ramchandra Kashinath Tatnis and his colleagues seated in his office. Tatnis phoned up many prominent Hindus and asked them to make some contribution for the Satyagraha. While many declined outright, some promised to contribute. However, nothing materialized out of this exercise too. Tatnis then suggested a charity show of a play and sent Dr Ambedkar to Bapurao Pendharkar of *Lalitkaladarsh.*[24] Although his company was not financially well off, Pendharkar agreed to help, but with a condition that it should not be declared in support of the Satyagraha, and should rather be advertised as in support of the schools or the students' boardings run by the Bahishkrut Hitkarini Sabha. Ambedkar agreed. The play was performed at the Elphinston Theatre at Grant Road and got about Rs 200; the money for many tickets sold on credit having not been realized. Later it was followed by Sakharam Narayan Kajrolkar who performed a charity play of *Bhaktimargdarshak Natak Mandali* and contributed around Rs 100. Nirmal Limbaji Gangawane had also performed a play with his amateur theatre group and contributed about Rs 150.

A word spread around about these charity shows and the Satyagraha. It reached the famous *tamasha*[25] artist Patthe Baburao, a remarkable person who was born a Brahman, as Shridhar Krushna Kulkarni, but took up liking for the *tamasha*, which was considered the art form of the lower castes. Since he had had many performing girls like Pawalabai belonging to Mahar caste in his troupe, which earned him name, fame and money, he helped many Mahar *tamasha* artists to set up their own troupes. He usually stayed in a Mahar locality and was very affectionate and respectful to the Mahars in general. He decided to help the movement launched by Dr Ambedkar and came to meet him along with two of his Mahar lady artists on 10 September 1927. He offered Ambedkar four performances in charity. However, Ambedkar angrily rejected it. On being asked for the reason for rejecting him, Ambedkar had said, "don't you feel ashamed? This Brahman earns money by making the Mahar women dance in *tamasha* and you ask me to accept that money! You don't know the meaning of 'self respect'!"[26]

For the preparation of the Mahad Satyagraha, the Untouchables held hundreds of meetings in Mumbai and outside. A meeting of select leaders was held in Damodar Hall on 11 September 1927 under the presidentship of Ganpatrao Chandorkar Hawaldar, to make an official announcement of the Satyagraha committee and also the drive for fund collection. The names of the committees were announced. People gathered there collected Rs 26.50 for the Satyagraha fund. On 15 September 1927, another meeting of some select people was held in Dr Ambedkar's office in which the dates for the Satyagraha were decided as 25 and 26 December 1927.[27] A public meeting was organized on 17 September 1927 in the compound of David Mill Chawl on Elphinston Road at 9 pm under the chairmanship of Dr Ambedkar. This was termed as the first public meeting for the preparation for the Satyagraha in the *Bahishkrut Bharat* of 30 September 1927.[28]

The next mammoth meeting took place on 20 October 1927 in Cowasjee Jahangir hall at 4 pm under the chairmanship of Dr Ambedkar. Until then, this hall had seen only the meetings of the elite classes, and that too, under the presidentship of some prominent capitalist or political leader. With a mere sense that their meeting was taking place in the Cowsajee Jehangir Hall, the enthusiasm of the Untouchables knew no bounds. The hall overflowed with people. This meeting convincingly communicated to the political parties and the Bombay Government that Dr Ambedkar had lit the fire in the souls of the Untouchables. The meeting passed a resolution, "This meeting lends its wholehearted support to the Mahad Satyagraha and requests the Untouchable class to contribute money as per their capacity and register their names for the Satyagraha in the office of the Bahishkrut Hitkarini Sabha." In the meeting a sum of Rs 517, annas 9 and paise 3 was collected, which was handed over to Dr Ambedkar. The major donors' names were declared in the *Bahishkrut Bharat* dated 4 November 1927, p. 16. The Untouchable employees of the Saint George Hospital held a meeting in the compound of the hospital on 3 December 1927 under the chairmanship of Dr Ambedkar and donated Rs 134 for the Satyagraha fund.[29]

Non-Brahman Lip Service

The pamphlets declaring support to the Satyagraha on behalf of the non-Brahman party and the *Satyashodhak Samaj* were issued by the non-Brahman leaders. The letters of Jedhe and Jawalkars, referred to earlier, were amongst the first. The non-Brahman leaders had not done much beyond issuing these letters of support. Some of the savarna leaders continued their efforts to incite the orthodox elements against the Untouchables while outwardly declaring support to the Satyagraha. The non-Brahmans and the Untouchables are the co-sufferers of the caste system. However, inexplicably the non-Brahmans opposed the Untouchables' movement for annihilation of Brahmanism. In this connection, Dr Ambedkar had written a comment in *Bahishkrut Bharat* of 23 December 1927:

> ... It is the prime duty of the Touchable leaders to make those of their people who are opposed to Untouchables congenial to their (Untouchables') cause. It appears that this duty is being performed by the leaders of the Brahmans to some extent. The Brahman leaders from Pune, Mr Baburao Gokhale and the sub-editor of Kesari, Mr J S Karandikar had purposefully gone to Mahad from Pune a few days ago. On 30 November, they organized a meeting of the people from Mahad and conveyed the message of the Hindu Mahasabha that they should not oppose the Satyagraha of the Untouchables. It will surely have a good impact on the Brahmans of Mahad. At least they would be able to say that the Brahmans had made efforts to discharge their responsibility. The non-Brahman leaders however have done nothing in this respect. We hear that the Marathas from the surrounding villages are preparing for a strong opposition to the Untouchables' Satyagraha. In such a situation, it was necessary for the responsible Maratha non-Brahman leaders to visit the Kolaba district and dissuade their castemen from doing so. If it was not possible for them to physically visit these places, they should have immediately arranged to publish a letter explaining their stand on the proposed Satyagraha in every village. If the non-Brahman party ignored this duty, not only the responsibility of the future consequences will be on their head but also it would also have spoiled the Untouchables' opinion about them.
>
> The non-Brahmans of Cheul have faced a similar crisis as the Untouchables of Mahad are facing today. The way the Untouchables are forbidden to drink water from the Chavadar tank at Mahad, the non-Brahman people belonging to Koli, Bhandari, Aagri, Maratha, etc. were banned from entering the sanctum sanctorum of the Rameshwar temple at Cheul by the Brahman trustees. The local non-Brahman people have been agitating against it. In such a situation, it is a matter of extreme

> shame that the non-Brahmans who have been trampled upon by the *Brahmanya* should oppose the Untouchables who are struggling against the *Brahmanya* (meaning essence of Brahmanism) in the same district. But, what would these poor people do? There is no one around to show them the right path since all their leaders are busy celebrating the birth centenary of Mahatma Jotiba Phule.
>
> During the Mahad Satyagraha, the non-Brahman leaders would celebrate Brahmanism being annihilated in Mahad by hailing "victory to Mahatma Phule" while sitting at home. However, their disciples would come to Mahad and rush to the defence of Brahmanism shouting *"Har Har Mahadev"*!![30] One has to say with a heavy heart that the people coming to Mahad may get to see a big fun in the non-Brahman party. May God, save this party from such humiliation!

While the clash between the viewpoints of the Brahmans, non-Brahmans, Untouchables and the government was manifesting all over, registration of the volunteers for the Satyagraha was continuing with full speed. Dr Ambedkar issued a communication exhorting the Untouchables to be fully prepared for the Satyagraha. He explained the reasons for the conference and asked people to participate in large numbers and also contribute in cash and kind. This communication is given as **Appendix 3**. The Satyagraha Committee also took out pamphlets which were widely distributed all over the Marathi speaking areas. It exhorted people to participate in the Satyagraha in large numbers and notified them how to do it. A copy of the original pamphlet and its translation are provided in **Appendix 4**.

This way the propaganda for the Satyagraha was carried out in Mumbai and outside. It created considerable curiosity, anxiety, and excitement in the general public. In the Untouchable community itself, it generated a mix of fear, self-respect, confidence, and courage. The old people reflected fear of oppression, whereas the younger lot appeared charged with self-respect and a battling spirit, unmindful of the consequences. The orthodox Hindus considered the movement of the Satyagraha as irreligious and they were also working to create an atmosphere for opposing it by touring the surrounding villages.

The Mahars faced the consequence of this poisonous propaganda with exemplary courage and displayed their preparedness to sacrifice their lives in the battle for their rights. This new face of the Mahars in Konkan created a terror in the minds of the opponents, who feared for their lives in an ensuing civil war in Konkan if the Mahars really came out to fight. The Brahmans would normally incite the non-Brahmans against the Untouchables and see them fighting from a distance. Since many of the non-Brahman people slowly realized this fact, the intensity of their opposition to the Satyagraha had been decreasing. Still, the opposition had not completely vanished.

Organizational Aspects

Dr Ambedkar was deeply involved in all the preparatory matters for the Satyagraha, which had totally affected his daily routine. Right from early morning till late into the night, he was busy with its myriad tasks and would often skip his bath and lunch. His lunch used to be brought from home in a tiffin box. That box would remain unopened in a corner and ultimately carried back. Poor Ramabai (his wife) would start crying, looking at the unopened tiffin box. She would think that he did not like her cooking. He would rarely go home for lunch except on full moon days. He had to observe certain customs started by his father and perform certain rites at home on the full moon day. Only after this, he would take lunch and then return to the office. Sometimes he would return even without having lunch if he had left something unfinished.

After fixing up the date of travel to Mahad, he went home and slept after lunch. He felt relaxed for the first time after two months' of hectic activity. When he got up in the evening after enjoying a good sleep, he looked unusually fresh. Otherwise, he used to be irascible and would often lose his temper at people around him. That evening, he went to his neighbours for a relaxed chat after months. The discussions naturally turned to Satyagraha. People learnt with surprise that many women were also going to participate in it. When he went home, Ramabai queried about it. In a lighter vein, he told her that many women from Mumbai would be going to Mahad and she could take up their leadership. Poor Ramabai blushed and said, leadership was not her cup of tea and she would rather come there to look after the arrangement of food for the participants. She and Lakshmibai, her co-sister[31] were under the impression that Dr Ambedkar will really take them to Mahad. But on 24 December, they suddenly learnt that he had already left for Mahad. They were both deeply disappointed.

The preparation for the Satyagraha Conference at Mahad was assigned to Anant Vinayak Chitre. The manner in which he discharged his responsibilities was exemplary. Indeed, Chitre deserved the epitaph 'vanguard soldier' given to him by Dr Ambedkar in the *Bahishkrut Bharat* of 3 February 1928. Considering his physical built, anybody would doubt whether this small skinny soul would really accomplish such a complex task. But the Satyagraha committee that nominated Chitre for the job was well aware what a treasure of energy Chitre was. And whosoever had seen his performance in respect of this conference was convinced of it. The *Bahishkrut Bharat* gratefully acknowledged that if the conference was a success, the entire credit went to Chitre.

Chitre had reached Mahad 15 days before the conference. He sensed that except for some young people, all the touchable people of Mahad were against the Satyagraha. They had conspired to create all possible hurdles for the Satyagraha. In these circumstances, he had decided to accomplish the task with the help of a few young people from his Kayastha community. He received tremendous support from people like Shantaram Potnis, Keshavrao Deshpande, Wamanrao Patki and Kamlakar Tipnis. If these people had not helped him, the conference would not have been able to manage procurement of required things.

Due to the conspiracy of the Mahad's savarna people, it was difficult to find a place to put up a pandal for the conference. As all the lands surrounding Mahad belonged to the Gujar Brahmans, they were resting in glee that they controlled the levers of the conference. However, the organizers found a land belonging to a Muslim named Fatehkhan. He gave this land for the conference with great pleasure. As the news reached the

Gujar Brahmans, they were not too pleased. However, since they had decided not to allow the conference to take place in Mahad, they approached Fatehkhan and requested him not to give his land for the conference. But it did not work. Fatehkhan replied that he would not take his words back. The organizers put up a huge pandal enough to seat seven to eight thousand people. It was duly decorated with *torans* (decorative hanging) and flags. There were big hangings with inspiring verses from Marathi saint poets put up all over.

As the local merchants refused to have any dealings with the men connected with the conference, the Reception Committee had to purchase grocery and other materials from outside, sufficient to last 10 days. The conference could have borrowed many things and managed with a small expenditure. But as the local opinion was not congenial, it had to purchase even the minute things, including the ones meant for temporary purpose. As a result, it became quite expensive. In the circumstances where tons of gold also would not buy a small thing, it was indeed an astonishing feat that Chitre accomplished in making excellent arrangement for the conference. Subhedar Ghatge was entrusted with the food arrangements and the maintenance of order and discipline.

He could not be thanked enough for this. Subhedar Ghatge was joined by Thorat from Pune and Bhanagarkar Jamadar from Bhanagar on 24 December at Mahad. Subhedar was assigned a difficult task like maintaining discipline among the delegates and arranging for their meals. The kind of efficiency and enthusiasm with which he accomplished this responsibility, stunned everyone. Realizing the importance of the conference, government officials like the collector, the district police superintendent, etc. had reached Mahad and camped there since 19 December itself. The delegates started reaching Mahad right from 23 December. Their number had gone beyond 10,000. The collector was stunned to note the general discipline with which the delegates conducted themselves and adopted a reconciliatory approach towards the conference. However, he made concerted efforts to advice people for staying away from the Satyagraha right from 23 December itself by meeting them every morning and evening. But whenever he asked the delegates whether they would listen to him or Dr Ambedkar, he was surprised to receive the answer in unison that they would listen to Dr Ambedkar.[32]

Departure to Mahad

On 24 December morning, Dr Ambedkar along with 200 to 250 people started off from Bombay for Mahad by Padmavati boat. His entourage included leading people like S.N. Shivtarkar, Dhondi Narayan Gaikwad, Kamble, Gangawane, Vanmali from Bombay; Rajbhoj from Pune and Bhaurao Gaikwad from Nashik. Shri Sahasrabuddhe of *Social Service League*, and Pradhan brothers of the *Samata Sangh*, also travelled with Ambedkar. Devrao Naik, the editor of the *Brahman-Brahmanetar* could not come because of illness. Before this group of satyagrahis reached the pier a big crowd of people was there to bid them adieu. They felicitated the leaders with bouquets and garlands. The entire pier reverberated with their slogans—victory to the Satyagraha. Padmavati set sails at 9 in the morning and reached the *Hareshvar Bandar* (pier) at 5.30 in the evening. At every *Bandar* on the way large number of people had gathered to greet the leaders with slogans — victory to the Satyagraha!

It was easier to go to Mahad from Dharamtar. But since it involved uncertainty of getting transport for such a large contingent of people to travel some 50 to 55 km to Mahad, they planned to go to Dasgaon. People even had apprehensions that the transporters being caste Hindus, might go on a strike and make it impossible for them to reach Mahad. As they set off, on the way to Dasgaon, they were accorded a big reception by people at a small village called Kolmandla. They had formed a special reception committee for the purpose and made excellent arrangement for the stay of all *satyagrahis* (participants in Satyagraha). People were all praise for Pandurang Babaji Mandlekar, the president of the reception committee. The *satyagrahis* spent the night at this place and after taking light refreshment the next morning, they started off at 8 am for Dasgaon by 'Amba' boat. They reached Dasgaon at 12.30 pm.

There were about 3,000 people waiting to join Dr Ambedkar and others to go to Mahad. Also, the district police superintendent of Kolaba, Mr Farrent, police inspector, Fauzdar, and other police officials were also waiting for Dr Ambedkar. After exchanging greetings, the police superintendent handed over a letter from Mr Hood, District Collector, Kolaba to Dr Ambedkar for inviting him for the talks. Accordingly, Dr Ambedkar and Sahasrabuddhe went to Mahad in Mr Farrent's car. Before starting he had directed the people to reach Mahad in peaceful and disciplined manner.

Mahad is just about five miles away from Dasgaon. After Dr Ambedkar and Sahasrabuddhe left, Shivtarkar and Pradhan brothers requested the satyagrahis to make a column of five people and march off in a procession shouting slogans like *har har mahadeo* and *mahad satyagrah ki jai*. They had about 25 placards with pertinent quotations and also flags. Headed by the volunteer corps of the Bahishkrut Hitkarini Sabha that played the band accompanied by the Satyagraha songs sung in chorus by the people behind, the procession entered the Mahad town. The police took continuous rounds of the procession. Marching along the prescribed route, as the procession reached the Satyagraha camp, Anantrao Chitre came forward to welcome it. Pointing at the Raigadh fort, which was clearly visible from there, he asked the crowd to shout the slogans of victory to Shivaji and Jeejamata (Sivaji's mother) so as to get their blessings for the success of the conference. These slogans from the euphoric crowd had filled up entire atmosphere. Energized in such an inspiring ambience, people entered the Satyagraha camp.

The Conference Begins

The Satyagraha Committee had published a formal programme for the conference as given in **Appendix 5.**

The venue of the conference was decorated with many banners that bore the *abhangas* of the *Bhakti saints* condemning caste discrimination and upholding equality. The approximate English translation of a sample of them may be read as follows:

- Whether I am a Brahman or a Mahar, I would not consider anyone inferior
- The brilliance in this nature is only the humanness
- Have no arrogance, we shall all rise together
- The mines of eggs and sperms, we all come through the same womb
- The religion of *vaishnavas* is filled with god, the notion of discrimination is unholy
- Such is this religious battle that if you do not fight now, you will sink the fame of your religion and will go to hell

There was only one picture in the pandal, and that was of Mahatma Gandhi. At the entrance of the pandal a nicely decorated *vedi* (platform) was constructed for the celebratory burning of the *Manusmruti*. People gripped with Brahmanism were incensed by the thought of burning *Manusmruti*. Hence, they spread a canard that since it was not possible to go ahead with the Satyagraha, Ambedkar had come out with a fantastic idea of burning *Manusmruti* to hoodwink people. The fact that while putting up the pandal itself, the burning *vedi* (a place prepare to perform a ritual fire) was constructed, exposed their lie. The plan of burning *Manusmruti* was not an afterthought, and was rather included in the conference programme, well before the injunction was granted. It is a different matter that the conference did not start as per the programme at 10 am. Many delegates from Bombay could not reach in time, for which the programme had to be postponed to afternoon. The conference eventually began at 4 pm. After the prayer sung by a group of children, the secretary of the Satyagraha Committee, Sitaram Shivtarkar, read out solidarity messages received from Sridhar Balwant Tilak (son of Lokmanya B.G. Tilak), Dr Purushottam Solanki, MLC, and others. Thereafter, he called upon the President of the Satyagraha Committee to deliver his address. In the midst of a thunderous applause, Dr Ambedkar rose to read out his presidential speech.

Speech of the President, Dr B.R. Ambedkar[33]

The following is the full text of the presidential address of Dr

Ambedkar:

Gentlemen! I thank you all as the President of the Conference for having come here in deference to the invitation of the Satyagraha Committee.

Many of you may remember that we all had collectively marched to the Chavadar tank here last on the 20th March.[34] Although the savarna people of Mahad had not objected to our going to the Chavadar tank, later by physically assaulting us they made us realize that they had serious objection to it. The end of that conflict came about the way it was expected. The touchable people who attacked us were convicted with four months rigorous imprisonment. They are in jail today. If on 20th March we had not faced resistance, it would have been established that the Touchables had accepted our right to draw water from the Chavadar tank and we might not have to resort to do all this today. But unfortunately, it has not happened that way. And therefore we had to call this conference today.

This tank of Mahad is a public tank. The people of Mahad are so considerate that not only they themselves take water from it, but they have also granted liberty to people from other religions to do so. Accordingly, people of other religions like Islam freely take water from the tank. They do not even object to birds, animals, etc., considered inferior to humans, drinking water of this tank. Not only that, the animals belonging to the Untouchables are also allowed to happily drink the water of the tank. The touchable people are really the epitome of love and compassion! They do not commit violence and never oppress others. They are not the class of misers and selfish people who would not drive a crow away with a hand smeared with food.[35] The mushrooming of mendicants and beggars in this country is the live testimony of their spirit of charity and benefaction. Their conduct reflects that doing good to others is a merit, and hurting others is a sin. Not only that, their nature reflects the dictum: *didhale dukkha parane usane fedu nayechi sosave*! (Even if others have given you sorrow, you should not think of giving it back and rather should bear it quietly.) That is why they protect dangerous reptiles like serpent with the same compassion as they treat a benign animal like cow. The noble maxims like *sarva bhuti ek atma* (A single soul resides in all bodies) guide their character!

This touchable lot however forbids people of their own religion from taking water from the same Chavadar tank. The question that naturally arises therefore is why they should do so. Why should they prohibit only us from taking the water? It is extremely important that all of us fully understand the answer to this question. Without that I do not think you will realize the importance of today's meeting. Hindus, according to their scriptures have four *varna*s and according to their customs, five *varnas*—brahman, kshatriya, vaishya, shudra and atishudra. *Varna* order depicts the first rule in the set of rules Hinduism prescribes. The second rule of this religion is that these *varnas* are unequal. One is lesser than the other in the descending order. These rules have not only established the hierarchical status of each *varna*, but they have also fixed the boundaries of each *varna* in order to distinguish them.

In this regard, there appears to be a commonplace notion that there are limits only on transactions between these *varnas* such as the ban on intermarriage, inter-dining (dining together), use of common water source — pitcher or tumbler— and inter-meeting (meeting together).[36] But this notion is obviously inadequate. All these proscriptions of course put limits on the mutual transactions between *varnas* but they are basically meant to indicate the unequal status of unequal people belonging to these *varnas*. As one who wears a crown over his head is considered king, one who bears a bow is a *kshatriya*. The ones who are not bound by any of these proscriptions are considered the most superior and the ones who are bound by all of them are considered the lowest. So much effort is invested in preserving these proscriptions just to maintain this iniquitous order intact. If it is not done, the inequality established by the religion would go away and equality might get established in its place. The touchable people of Mahad do not let the Untouchables drink water from the Chavadar tank not because the water would get putrid or dirty or evaporate away with their touch. The reason for not letting them drink it is that they do not want to admit that these castes (Untouchables), which have been established as inferior in the *Dharmashastra* (scriptures), are equal to theirs.

Gentlemen, from this you will understand the meaning of the struggle that we have begun. Do not have any misunderstanding that you have been invited by the Satyagraha Committee for drinking the water of the Chavadar tank. It is not that you and I will become immortal by drinking the water of this tank. We are not dead because we have not drunk water of the Chavadar tank till today. Therefore, if we march to the Chavadar tank, it is not merely to drink the water of the tank. We go there to establish that we are also human beings like others. That should make it clear that this conference has been called to make a beginning towards establishing equality. If one conceives this conference in this manner, I am quite confident; no one would have any doubt that it is unprecedented. I do not think that this day will have any parallel in the history of India. If you want to see a comparable meeting in the past, you may have to enter the history of France in the European continent.

Some 138 years ago, on 24 January 1789, Louis XVI, the king of France had issued an ordinance and called a similar meeting of the representatives of the people of his kingdom. Some historians shower curses on this national assembly, as it was called. This assembly had sent the king and the queen to the gallows; made the upper classes run for their lives and slaughtered them and devastated those who escaped death. It confiscated the wealth of the rich and pushed the entire European continent into a civil war for more than 15 years. Such is the complaint they (historians) make against this natural assembly! In my opinion this complaint is totally misfounded. Rather one is compelled to say that these historians have not understood the real import of its accomplishment. The accomplishment of this assembly has not only benefited France, but the entire European continent. Today, if the European nations enjoy happiness and prosperity it is only because of this accomplishment. The principles of social organisation proclaimed by the revolutionary national assembly in 1789 were presented and rather forcefully imposed on the fragmented and the debauched French nation of those times, and they were also accepted and implemented by the entire European continent later.

In order to comprehend the importance of this national assembly and the greatness of the principles it articulated and proclaimed, we have to take into consideration the condition of the French society of that time. We all know that our Hindu society is based on the *varnashram dharma* (a religion of *varna* order). Similar order of *varnashram* existed in France in 1789. The only difference is that the French society comprised only three *varnas*. Like the Hindu Society, the French society had a *brahman varna*. It had a *kshatriya varna* too. But instead of having three separate *varnas* of *vaishyas, shudras and atishudra*, the French society had combined them into a single *varna*—the third *varna*.

This difference is quite unimportant. The important thing is that both the Hindu as well as French societies had very similar *varnashram* order. Difference in their societies arising out of their respective *varnavyavastha* (varna system) is not only to be considered while equating them but also the fact that inequality due to *varnavyavastha* was also a part of the French society. In France, the nature of inequality was a little different. The inequality there was of economic nature, although it was as severe as existing anywhere. In sum, the thing worth bearing in mind is that **there is a great similarity between our meeting today and the revolutionary national assembly that took place on 5 May 1789 at Versailles in France.** (bold in original)[37]

Similarity is seen not only in their respective conditions but also in most of their objectives. The assembly of the French people was called for the purpose of reorganizing the French society. This conference of ours is called with the same purpose of reorganizing[38] the Hindu Society. Before discussing the principles for this reorganization, we must have some idea about the principles and strategies that the assembly of the French people adopted for reorganizing their country. The scope of the French assembly was far more extensive than that of today's conference. The French people's assembly wanted to reorganize it in a threesome way—political, social and religious. To us, it is necessary to consider how to achieve only the social and the religious reorganization. Since we do not have to bother about political organization right now, we have to only see what the French assembly did about religious and social organization.

The kind of strategies the French assembly adopted regarding social and religious organization can be clearly seen from the three important manifestoes issued by their Assembly. The first manifesto was announced on 17 June, 1789. This manifesto was concerning the *varnashram* system in France. As said before, the French society was based on three *varnas*. This manifesto not only demolished the structure of three *varnas* and made a single *varna* of the entire society but also ended the separate reservations given to these three *varnas* in the political arena. The second manifesto was concerned with the priests. According to tradition, the nomination or removal of the priests was not vested in the nation but was a monopoly of a religious authority like Pope from another country. Whosoever was nominated by the Pope became a priest. Notwithstanding whether he deserved the post or not in the perception of those whom he was going to preach, he became one. In this manifesto, the self grandeur of the religious authority was abolished and the rights of decision on who should become a priest, whether one is capable or not, whether one is to be given a salary or not and so on, were transferred to the French nation. The third manifesto did not concern the political, the economic or the religious order—it was general; it was about the principles on which any kind of social order should be based. From the structural perspective, this manifesto is most important of all the three manifestoes. Rather, it will not be an exaggeration if one calls it a king of all the manifestoes. This manifesto is becoming famous all over the world as the manifesto of the fundamental human rights. This manifesto is unprecedented not only in the history of France, but also in the histories of all the advanced nations. Because, following this assembly, every nation in Europe has adopted it for its self governance. Thus, it would not be an exaggeration to claim that it has brought about a revolution not only in France, but also in the entire world. There are in all 17 articles in this manifesto. The important ones of these are:

1. All human beings in birth are of equal status and they will continue to be of equal status until their death. They could be differentiated only for the reason of welfare of people. Their equal status otherwise must be permanent.
2. The purpose of politics must be to ensure the above fundamental human right stays permanent.
3. The people are the source of all authorities; they are sovereign. Any authority of an individual, collective or class, if they are not granted by the people will not be accepted on any other basis, be it politics or religion.
4. Every person has full liberty to conduct according to its fundamental human rights. They are only limited by the consideration that other person also must have scope to enjoy his/her fundamental human rights. This limit will be determined by the law. It will not be decided by the authority of either religious scriptures or anything else.
5. Law will only prohibit things that are injurious to society. Everybody will have liberty to do things which are not prohibited by law. Likewise, no one would be forced to do things which are not considered necessary by law.
6. The law is not a set of rules framed by a particular class. The right of deciding how the law ought to be shall be vested in people or in their representatives. The law, whether it is protective or administrative, must be equal to all. All persons are equally entitled for any kind of respect or honour, authority

> and profession because any kind of order is justified only if it is based on the principle of equality of all. If at all any discrimination had to be done, it could only be on the basis of the difference in merit of a person; not because her/his birth.

I feel that this conference of ours should keep the ideal of this French national assembly before us. It should adopt the same path for conservation of the Hindu society as was discovered by it for the French society and which was accepted by all the advanced nations of the world. It should remove the nails of this framework of *varnashram* that has established proscriptions from intermarriage to inter-community meetings, and make a single *varna* of the entire Hindu society. Without that untouchability will not go away and equality will never be established.

Now, some of us may feel that we are Untouchables and therefore it would be enough if the bans on our transactions with others such as use of common vessels for drinking water etc. (*loti bandi*) and inter-community meeting (*bheti bandi*) are abolished. What do we have to do with the *varna* order? But this understanding in my opinion is absolutely wrong. If we have a strategy of just abolishing untouchability, while preserving the *varnashram*, people would think that our goal is trivial and mean. The human emancipation requires ambition as it requires external efforts. Rather, it is doubtful whether human efforts would ever materialize without ambition. Therefore, if we want to attempt a big thing, we must have a commensurately big enough ambition. At the time of having ambitions we need not have any shame or fear about whether it would be fulfilled or not. If at all, we should feel shame for having a petty ambition. There is no shame in failure if we had big ambition. By abolishing untouchability we might become a *shudra* from our present status of *atishudra*. But just by becoming *shudra* from *atishudra*, can we say that the untouchability is completely rooted out? I would not suggest you to insist upon the abolition of the *varnashram* order, if it was possible to abolish untouchability with small ambition such as ending of the *bheti bandi* (ban on inter-community meeting) and *loti bandi* (ban on use of common vessels for drinking water, etc.). Gentlemen, you very well know that if you want to kill a snake, just striking on its tail will not work; you will have to hammer on its mouth. If you have to destroy any harmful cause, you must discover where its roots are and strike at them. One has to strike only after knowing where exactly the roots are.

Duryodhan died because Bhim had struck his *gada*[39] (club) at his thigh. If he had struck it on his head, Duryodhan would have never died because his death lay in his thigh, not in his head. As we encounter numerous examples of fruitless efforts of a village doctor in curing a disease, just because he could not diagnose exactly where the root of the disease is, we do not get to see or read about similar cases of failures to cure social disease because of imprecise diagnosis. Such examples of failures are not documented in history. Nevertheless, I would like to introduce to you one such example of failure that I came across in my reading. In the ancient times in Europe, a nation called *Rome* had two classes, viz., Patricians and Plebeians. Patricians were considered a superior *varna* and Plebeians, the inferior *varna*. All the powers were in the hands of Patricians and because of it they used to treat the Plebeians very badly. In order to liberate themselves from this harassment, the Plebeians organized themselves and with the strength of this organizational unity raised a demand to end the prevailing disorder, which was basically due to Patricians' whims becoming the law. Therefore they demanded documentation of laws for the information of all and convenience of justice. Their adversary, the Patricians had to accept this demand, as a result of which a list of 12 laws were prepared. But just with documentation of the laws alone, the harassment of the oppressed Plebeians did not end. Because not only all the implementers of laws belonged to the Patrician class but also the highest authority called tribune of the Roman nation also comprised of the people from the same class. As a result, even if laws were the same for all, their implementation could not be impartial. Therefore, as a last resort, the Plebeians put forth their demand that the administration of the Roman nation should be in the hands of two tribunes instead of a single tribune. One of these tribunes should be elected by Patricians and the other by Plebeians. This demand also was conceded by the Patrician people. Plebeians became happy thinking that their trials would now come to an end. But their happiness did not last long. There was a custom among the Romans that without the approval of their village goddess – Delphi, they would not do anything. As per this custom, even if a tribune is elected, if it is not accepted by Delphi, it would have to be annulled and such tribunal would have to be re-elected until it would be acceptable to Delphi. According to the scriptures, the priest who performed the ritual for knowing what is liked or disliked by Delphi had to be born of parents who were married with *Conferacio* custom of wedding, one of the many customs prevalent among the Romans of those times. This custom of conferacio marriage existed only among the Patrician people. Therefore the priest of this Delphi goddess always came from the Patrician class. Because of the intrigues of this Patrician priest, if the Plebeians had elected a strong and spirited person as tribune, Delphi would never grant her approval. Only when Plebeians elected such a person as their tribune, who would be completely subservient to Patricians, Delphi would accept him and he would get to sit on the position of power. What did the Plebeians achieve in securing the right of electing their own tribune? One has to answer it as 'nothing'. All the efforts of Plebeians proved meaningless because they had not fully understood where exactly the death of all their woes lay. If they had, they would have also demanded the resolution of who the priest should be alongside their demand to have their own tribune. The death of the disease did not lie merely in the demand for tribune. It lay in grabbing the priesthood. They failed to comprehend this precise point. While searching for a remedy for the abolition of untouchability, we also must make a full enquiry into where exactly the death of this disease lies. Otherwise, there will be a strong probability of our committing a mistake. Do not commit foolishness of taking untouchability as eradicated, just because the *bheti bandi* (ban on inter-community meeting) and *loti bandi* (ban on use of common vessels for drinking) are abolished.

In this regard, one should understand that merely by abolishing *loti bandi* and *bheti bandi,* untouchability does not get eradicated. With the abolition of these two bans, untouchability outside the home may go, but untouchability within the home would not be shaken. If we want to abolish untouchability within, as well as outside home, we must abolish *betibandi,* the ban on intercaste marriage. There is no other option. Thinking even from the other side, the abolition of the ban on intercaste marriages only becomes the way of establishing true equality. Anybody will have to admit that once the main difference is abolished, the other differences would automatically collapse. But if the subordinate differences are abolished, they do not necessarily lead to the abolition of the main difference. *Roti bandi* (ban on interdining), *loti bandi* (ban on use of common vessels for drinking water, etc.) and *bheti bandi* (ban on intercaste meeting) have all emerged out of a single *beti bandi* (ban on the intercaste marriages). If this ban is lifted, no special efforts may be needed to lift others; they will be lifted automatically. In my opinion the eradication of untouchability lies in the demolition of *beti bandi*. Only then will the real equality be established. If you have to eradicate untouchability, you must realise that its roots lie in the ban on intercaste marriages. If our attack today is directed on *loti bandi*, its strike must eventually be on *beti bandi*, the ban on the intercaste marriages. Without that, untouchability will never be rooted out.

Who will accomplish this mission? No one needs to be explained that the Brahman class is not going to perform this mission. As long as the *varna* order lasts, the superiority of the Brahman class will also last. No one gives up existing power in hand voluntarily. The Brahman class has enjoyed its sovereignty over other classes since many centuries. There is absolutely no probability that it would give it up and be prepared to live with others as equals. Our Brahman class does not have love for nation as the Samurai class in Japan has. The Samurai class once upon a time gave up its special social rights to secure unity of the nation on the basis of equality. There is no hope that our Brahman class would ever perform that kind of sacrifice. It is not possible that even the non-Brahman class would perform it. Non-Brahman class means the Marathas and other castes of their ilk. This class typically constitutes the middle band between the classes with power and without power. There is always a possibility that a class endowed with power would show compassion and make a little bit of sacrifice. The class devoid of any power always possesses transformative objective. At least for its own selfish end, this class wants to bring about a social revolution. Therefore, this class internalizes love for principles more than the love for its selfish interests. The non-Brahman class, being in between these two classes, can neither show the kind of compassion that is possible for the class endowed with power nor can it have the internalized love for principles which characterises the class sans power. And therefore, instead of aiming at claiming equal power with Brahmans it is engrossed in preserving its special privileges over the Untouchables.

For the mission of social revolution, this class proves to be utterly incapable. If we expect help from it, our plight will be the same as that of the farmer who depended upon neighbours for harvesting his crop in the lesson on *Lavi bird and her Children*. The responsibility of establishing equality by abolishing untouchability that we have taken upon our heads must be discharged only by ourselves. It will not be possible for others to do it. The fulfillment of our life lies in our sincere efforts in its discharge, as though, our birth is only to accomplish this single mission. Let us collect this merit that is coming to our share by default. Certainly, this mission is the mission of our own emancipation. In order to remove obstacles from the path of our progress, we must take this responsibility on our head. You can very well imagine how untouchability has mixed *soil in our food*.[40]

You are all aware that at one time we had surfeit of our people in the army. Working in the army job was a kind of monopoly of our people and because of it, none of us had to worry about our livelihood. People belonging to other classes have entered the army, police and the government service in a big way and are living happily. But we will not get our man, even for the sake of a sample in these departments. It is not that we are debarred there by law. Under the law, things are open to all. But since other people consider us Untouchables and treat us as inferior, the government succumbs to this pressure, and does not let us enter the government service. We cannot even do any business with our heads high. It is only partly true that we cannot do business because we lack capital. Our real obstacle in business is that nobody will buy things from us because of our untouchability. In summary, our untouchability is not a simple matter; it is the mother of our poverty and inferiority. It is only because of untouchability our condition has been so miserable today. If we wish to rise up from this miserable condition, we must undertake this mission. Without that there is really no future.

As this mission is for our own interest, in the same way it is also in the national interest. The Hindu society does not have any option for survival unless it abolishes untouchability within the *chaturvarna* system. Among the resources, necessary for any society for survival, social morality constitutes a prominent place. Anyone will have to admit that the society with such morality that favours things which would disunite it and prohibit things that could unite it, has got to face defeat in the struggle for survival. On the other hand, the society with the type of morality that condemns things that splinter it and upholds things that binds it together, cannot but be successful. The same criterion has to be applied to the social order. *Chaturvarna* is a disintegrative order and the single *varna* is integrative of people. There is nothing surprising if the society, which even after seeing this with open eyes, sings praises to the system that leads to its own disintegration, has faced repeated defeats in history. If this plight is to be overcome, the framework of the *chaturvarna* system must be smashed to make the Hindu society a single varna.

This may not, however, be sufficient. Along with it, the inequality within *chaturvarna* also should be abolished. Many people ridicule the principle of equality. From the perspective of nature, no man is equal to another. Some are endowed with huge body whereas some are dwarfs; some are intelligent by birth, whereas some are stupid. These people think it imprudent when the protagonists of equality ask for equal treatment for all people who are actually born unequal. One is compelled to say that such reactionary people have not understood the full meaning of the principle of equality. They ask a counter question: if the meaning of the principle of equality is to treat the possession of rights as dependent on the attributes of a person and not on his/her birth or wealth or any such other thing, how could one demand that one who is talented, clean, and with character should treat a person who is untalented, unclean and characterless, with equality. It is appropriate to apply the definition of equality while granting rights that a person who is equal in merit should be treated equal. But to treat all people equally, howsoever, unequal they may be before they become capable of rights through the process of development of their inherent qualities, is only justice. According to sociologists, the social order is the most important causal factor in the full development of the inherent qualities of a person. If slaves are always treated unequally there may not be any quality developed in them except for the one suited to their slavery and therefore they will not be eligible for any other rights. Likewise, if a clean person always distances him/herself from and stops all his/her transactions with an unclean person, the unclean person will never develop the desire to live with cleanliness. If the ethical castes have not helped the unethical castes, the latter will never receive the education of ethics.

The above example proves that although the treatment of equality may not be able to generate qualities in a person who did not already have them but it is clear enough that without it, there is no possibility of development of natural qualities. Also, there is no possibility of fruition of those qualities without the ambiance of equality.

On one hand the inequality in the Hindu society thwarts the development of a person and dwarfs the society; on the other, it does not let the society utilize the energy accumulated in a person appropriately. From both sides this inequality is incapacitating the Hindu society, which is already disoriented because of the *chaturvarna*.

Therefore, if we want to make the Hindu society strong, we will have to completely destroy the *chaturvarna* and inequality. We will have to reconstruct the Hindu society on the basis of two principles, one *varna* and equality. The path of eradication of untouchability is not different from the path of strengthening the Hindu society. Therefore, there should not be any doubt that the mission we have undertaken is as much in the interest of the nation as it is in our self-interest.

This mission has been initiated for bringing about true social revolution. Nobody should have any misconceptions that it is just a gimmick devised to console our minds which are habituated to getting enthralled with sweet words and melodic voices. This mission has a basis of emotions. These emotions being the motive force behind this mission, it is not possible for anyone to break its speed. I pray to the almighty God that the social revolution that has begun here may come through peaceful means.

The responsibility of bringing about this social revolution through peaceful means is more on our adversary party than it is on us. Nobody can have any doubt about it. Whether this social revolution will be violent or non-violent is entirely dependent on the behaviour of the touchable people. Those who blame the national assembly of the French people in 1789 for violence, forget the fact that if the French state had not treated the national assembly with treachery, if the French elites had not opposed it, and had not committed the sin of suppressing it with the help of outsiders, the national assembly would not have had to resort to violence. It could have brought about the social revolution in a peaceful manner.

We would like to tell our adversary party not to oppose us. Discard your scriptures and adopt the path of justice. We assure you that we would accomplish this mission in a peaceful manner.

Manifesto of Birthright of the Hindu People

After the presidential speech, four resolutions were passed in the conference. These resolutions were drafted by Dr Ambedkar in English, taking into account the French revolution in which the French people had ended the monarchy and established their republic based on the principles of liberty, equality and fraternity and the salient developments in the world in the recent past, such as the Bolshevik revolution in Russia that established the rule of equality by destroying the totalitarian rule of the priests, landlords and the Tsar. He had also taken into account the ongoing movement in England for the socialist government. The ethos of these revolutionary changes is clearly reflected in these resolutions, which sought to have direction for the reconstruction of the Hindu society. These resolutions were translated into Marathi by Anantrao Chitre and Dr Ambedkar himself just before their proposal to the conference. These resolutions are given in **Appendix 6.**

After many important and thought provoking speeches on the above resolutions, the cremation rites were performed on the *Manusmruti*. These rites were done by the saints and monks belonging to the Untouchable class.

With this, the agenda for the first day came to an end.[42]

Second Day of the Conference: Satyagraha or No Satyagraha

When the work of the conference on the first day ended by 7.30 pm, people were hungry. They anxiously waited for dinner. People coming from distant places had brought *bhakari* (Indian bread made of sorghum, wheat or rice) with them as per the prior suggestion of the Satyagraha Committee. But since many of them had reached two days before the start of the conference, they had already exhausted them. People coming from Mumbai, having reached late, were already without food for the entire day and they were feeling very hungry. But since the cooking utensils from Mumbai had not yet reached Mahad, despite the availability of all provisions, dinner could not be cooked. Therefore everybody felt disappointed. The Satyagraha Committee was aware of such a possibility and hence it had purchased *chana* (gram) along with rice, lentils, etc., as a contingency measure. That night, everybody had to be satisfied with *chana* in place of dinner. People did not appear particularly pleased with having to do with *chana*. However, when Dr Ambedkar took his share of *chana* and began enjoying it, people followed him.

The next day, the work of the conference began at 9 am. Since the conference had to decide on important issues of the Satyagraha, it was given a form of a regulatory committee.

Accordingly, Dr Ambedkar instructed the volunteers standing in guard for the conference not to allow any outsider inside the pandal of the conference. Thereafter, Dr Ambedkar proposed a resolution before the conference for performing the Satyagraha. While putting forth this proposal, Dr Ambedkar said:

> I was called by the collector for an interview. He told me that he was not against the Satyagraha. But the touchable people have filed a case in the civil court and they have obtained an injunction from the court that until the result of this case, the Untouchable people should not go to the Chavadar tank. He has to intervene in the matter just to ensure there is no contempt of the court. I responded to him that I myself have come determined to do a Satyagraha. I will not let my determination falter and I will also suggest that all the people who have come for the conference to do the same. However, I will not impose my own opinion on them. But at the same time, because of the injunction, I will not even dissuade them from doing the Satyagraha. On that the collector expressed his desire that if the majority decided to go ahead with the satyagraha, he should be given an opportunity of addressing the delegates so as to tell them some words of good counsel. I have promised the collector the grant of that concession. Beyond that, I have not committed myself to anything. Therefore, you can decide whatever you wish to decide.
>
> In this episode one thing needs to be borne in mind, which is that if you want to secure your permanent interests, you have to bear trouble and pain. There is no evidence in any *purana*s or history of any boon having materialized without penance. Happiness always comes at the end of sorrows. Therefore, we should not hesitate to go to jail if required, for violating the court injunction. The injunction has been granted on the basis of the custom. It needs to be seen whether this custom is just or unjust. Otherwise, in the delusion of obeying the court injunction, there is a possibility of accepting the very injustice against which we are fighting. Satyagraha is a hard penance. The satyagrahis will have to exercise control on their mind and bear suffering. We have to put our neck in the hands of others on our own accord. You cannot go with your *lathis* (staff) to a Satyagraha. You cannot disobey any order of an officer. On the way to Satyagraha, if you are caught by an official and put into jail, you should not beg pardon. We have to maintain that whatever we have done is right till end. In summary, you must strictly follow the following

> conditions: (i) not to keep *lathis* with you, (ii) obey the government order, (iii) be prepared to go to jail, and (iv) not to beg pardon from the government. Only then there would be some use of participating in the Satyagraha. There is no use of your coming to the Satyagraha just because I say. If you are convinced that our path is just and if you are prepared to endure all troubles and suffering, then only can you perform the Satyagraha.

After speaking in this manner on the resolution, Dr Ambedkar asked the audience to listen carefully to the speeches both for and against the resolution and then decide whatever they felt right. Thereafter, by maintaining an alternating order of 'for Satyagraha' and 'against Satyagraha' arguments, the following twelve persons spoke for the Satyagraha:

1. Padmanath Rajaram Hate
2. Pandurang Babaji Mandlekar
3. Dhondiram Gaikwad
4. Pandurang Nathuji Rajbhoj
5. Bhikaji Mahadu Pensioner
6. Bhambu Ganu Shenvalikar
7. Sonu Devji Khambolikar
8. Hiru Barku Shelar
9. Govindbuwa Malkhedkar
10. Bhivba Bhowadkar
11. Girja Shankar Shivdas
12. Ganu Dharma Ambolikar

The following eight persons spoke against the Satyagraha:

1. Shivram Sakharam Hate
2. Krishna Yesu
3. Gadgebuwa Saheb
4. Govind Hawalkar
5. Raghu Ananda Shivtarkar
6. Ragho Narayan Vanmali
7. Punjaji Navsaji Jadhav
8. N.T. Jadhav

It may be noted that Vithoba Mahadeo Wadval, a resident of Kolvali was the only Maratha person who had come for the

Satyagraha despite his old age. After these 'for' and 'against' speeches, he rose up and said, "I am a Maratha. In my village, the Mahar brothers are upset and are not coming into the village. The village is thus orphaned.[43] It is of no use to us. Our Mahar brothers are insisting on getting water. We must fulfill it. Therefore, I have come here to offer Satyagraha."

There was no doubt in anyone's mind about the impact of these speakers. Those who had such doubt initially did not take much time to dispel it. The audience was apparently supportive to the 'for' speakers and disruptive to the 'against' speakers, so much so that Dr Ambedkar had to intervene requesting the audience to listen to the latter. At the end of the speeches, Dr Ambedkar said, "One is compelled to conclude that the opinion of the house is for the Satyagraha. I am happy about it. But I do not want to have an army of blindmen behind me. I do not want people to land up in prisons just because I say or some others say so. I want a man who says that I will go to jail in order to overcome my untouchability. Before deciding whether to go for Satyagraha or not, it is important to determine how many of you are ready for such a sacrifice. This is not a simple matter to be decided by the sound of claps or raising hands. It has to be decided by actual count. Therefore, I am asking to get the count of people who are prepared to go to jail. On the basis of this count, if the majority is found to be in favour of the Satyagraha, I will inform the collector accordingly and invite him to speak before you in the evening. Even after hearing him, if you still remained firm on your opinion, then we will go for the Satyagraha". It was 12.30 pm and as the meeting was being declared adjourned for lunch, Keshavrao Jedhe and Dinkarrao Jawalkar of the non-Brahman Party, who travelled from Mumbai by a special car, entered the pandal. President invited them to speak. Jawalkar spoke as below:

> It is alright that you have come here to fight a religious battle. Unfortunately, some Marathas are opposing you. Since I am a Maratha, I feel ashamed of that. We Marathas and Brahmans are sinners for having harassed you for this long. You should discard the broom that we have put in your hand. You are equal owners of things that we claim to own. The movement launched by your

> leader, Barrister Ambedkar is for the establishment of your rights. I have gone to jail twice. There is no need to fear jail. There is no caste discrimination in jails of the British government. It is much better to live in jail than living in the hell of discrimination of the outside world. I and Shri Jedhe have come here to express sympathy of the *Satyashodhak Samaj* for you. The Marathas extract more work from the Mahars. Their sweat does not create compassion in Kulkarni's heart. God should make Marathas Untouchables in their next birth. There is none as knowledgeable and capable as Dr Ambedkar even among the Touchables. He is struggling for you. You should follow him. India's God is uninterested; he is not going to end your sufferings. They are going to end only through a man like Barrister Ambedkar. If I had been a Mahar, I would have been happy today to go to jail along with you. You should establish your rights by breaking the law. This day will be counted among the most important days in the history of Hindus. There is no reason for you to fear jail. The Brahmans who eat *ghee* and *roti* should have that fear. To make the touchable people behave is in your hands. You are the sons of Hindus. You capture the tank saying *'har har Mahadev'* and follow the advice of your leader Dr Ambedkar *Saheb*. This is my own position. The position of the non-Brahman party is however different from this and I have come to explain it. The message from the non-Brahman party is that you should suspend your Satyagraha until the conclusion of the civil case. According to the Party, it is not in the interest of the Untouchables to oppose the government.[44]

After him Keshavrao Jedhe rose to speak:

> The people, who oppressed you, have to be subjected to brutal dissection. This battle is for establishing humanity. It is a shame that you should be prohibited to take water from the tank where dogs and donkeys freely drink it. It is absolutely right that you have burned down *Bhala, Sangram* [45] and the *Manusmruti*. It is better to go to jail after performing the Satyagraha. Do not listen to those who oppose it.

After this, the meeting was adjourned at 1.30 pm for lunch.

Mediation of the Collector

In order to have a count of people who were prepared to go to jail, Dr Ambedkar nominated 10-12 people to make a list of them with their name, address, etc. Within an hour, 3,884 people registered their names. "We have already told our families that we are going to jail; now how could we go back?", everyone was using such an argument. Ultimately, the people who were preparing this list got bored and declared that there was no point in taking down names when everybody seemed ready to go to jail. Therefore, the registration of names was stopped at 3.30 pm. Dr Ambedkar informed the collector with a letter saying, "The people are determined to offer Satyagraha. You said that you would come to the meeting to put forth your views. If you wish, you may come at 5 pm when the meeting resumes." Accordingly, the collector along with police superintendent Mr Farrent, Police inspector, Fauzdar [46], etc., came to the meeting. Dr Ambedkar spoke to the audience, "I had told you in the morning that the collector desired to say a few words to you. Accordingly, he has come to the meeting. Therefore, I request him to say whatever he wants to say." The collector addressed the delegates in Marathi as follows:

> The president has already told you what purpose I have come here for. I am sorry that I do not know proper Marathi. We have been hearing that you were preparing for this satyagraha for the last 3-4 months. You will feel bad to hear that you cannot do this satyagraha. Because of that I wish to advise you. As per the resolution of the Bombay Legislative Council, it is necessary to give access to schools and public water sources to all. Accordingly, the Bombay government issued orders and instructed Municipalities and local boards that they should not object to the Untouchables using these places. Therefore, you have decided to go to the Chavadar tank as per the government orders. If there was no objection [from some people], we would have [easily] granted you permission to go to the tank. However, 10-12 touchable people have filed a case in the civil court claiming that the [Chavadar] tank is a private property. I cannot say whether it is really private or public. We will decide after seeing the documents and hearing the lawyers. If it is private, then the ban of the touchable people would be valid. But if it is not private then there is no objection to your going there. But it will be opened when the court gives its verdict that the tank is a public property. The second issue is—they have obtained an injunction from the court that until the decision of the court, you cannot go there. My advice to you today therefore is that you should respect the court

order. I do not think you will benefit by rejecting the court order. I am aware that you have prepared for this struggle for the last 2-3 months and are very excited about going to the tank. But the wise man always behaves according to law. You are aware that the people who violated law, opposing you have been punished.[47] Likewise, if you do not behave as per law you will also face trouble and punishment; you will not benefit. Your aim is to go to the tank, but we will have to stop you. You know that I am a district collector. I am informing you that there are two parties here. One is the touchables, and the other, Untouchables. Which side is the government? It is on the side of the Untouchables. If you do not listen to my advice and insult the government, then it will be a different matter. You should remember that I am your friend. And the government is your *ma-bap* (literally parents, saviour). I am hearing emotional voices that you should perform the satyagraha with all determination, and must go to the tank even at the cost of insulting the government. The people who say these things are not your true friends; they are bogus friends. All this work should be done peacefully, and as per the law. For this, you should have patience. There is a legal case in the court. If the decision comes in your favour, the tank will be freed for you. If it comes against you, you file an appeal in the court. Until then, do satyagrahas for other tanks. In sum, do not go against the law and undermine the government. It will not benefit you. In this respect, I may tell you a story. Assume there are two brothers. One is Hari and the other is Bhau. Hari said to Bhau, "After the summer, we will plant rice." To this, Bhau said, "Only after all preparation are made, we should plant rice." Hari did not agree and soon after the summer, planted rice. As for Bhau, he prepared his land and then planted rice. You can guess who got better crop. Likewise, you will get a result depending on your behaviour. Today, if you behave in haste against the government, the result will be bad as indicated by the above example. You may ask what you should do when you have already gathered here for the satyagraha. I would say that you resolve to start [your struggle] now and work until you get victory and until all the public tanks are opened for the Untouchables. Your president is a barrister and he knows legal work. As per his advice, you prepare the evidence with witnesses. It requires money and you should plan for that. (This is not my work). I will tell you one more thing, and then stop. I know Mahar people of this area since 12 years. I know they are good people. They do government service. There are many people who have worked as *subhedars, hawaldars, jamadars, sepoys* in military. I do not think that they will insult the government. My advice to you is that until the result of the court case, give up the tank as your target. What benefit will you get if you do not follow this advice? On the contrary, your interests will be certainly damaged. You are aware that we have made police *bandobast* (security arrangement) that there will not be any way to approach the tank. If you still try to go there, you will not only be opposed by the touchable people but also by the government. There is surely no benefit in going there. You have wise people among you who understand court work. You should work with them. The result will be in your favour. There will be no hurdle then. This is my advice to you. I hope you will consider it as coming from your friend.

Thereafter, with the permission of the president, Jawalkar spoke,

After coming here in the morning, we have met with all the Maratha leaders. Each of them has promised us that they will not go against the Untouchables. In testimony of it, they have given me a written manifesto which reads as follows:

To

Shri Keshavrao Jedhe and Dinkarrao Jawalkar,
Mahad, 16. 12. 1927.
Please present the following opinion of the Maratha Samaj of Mahad before the Untouchable Samaj.

Some irresponsible people of other castes have been spreading rumours that the Maratha people are against the Untouchables who are trying to agitate for their self emancipation and are coming for Satyagraha at the Chavadar tank. They are all baseless. We, the Maratha people of Mahad as also the leaders of Maratha Samaj declare that the Maratha Samaj is not prepared to come in the way of the Untouchables striving to establish their human rights. On the contrary, we feel we have all sympathies with them and with their agitation. However, we feel that if the Untouchable class agitates in a legal manner they will succeed immediately.

On 21.12.1927 a resolution was passed that in respect of the Satyagraha, we [the Marathas] shall remain impartial.

Presently, there is one Maratha man among the nine people, who have filed a case in the court against the Untouchables. He has not taken the consent of the Maratha Samaj and his action do (sic) not have the approval of this Samaj.

> Signatures
> Narayan Mama Mangde, Painter
> Kondiraam Pandurang Shinde
> Kisan Baba Dhumal
> Tukaram Savlaram Pansare
> Krishnaji Gyanuba Pawar
> Babajirao Madhavrao Dalvi
> Sitaram Gopal Chaudhary
>
> From the above manifesto it will be clear that Maratha class is not against you. Nonetheless, the advice of the non-Brahman party is that suspension of the Satyagraha would be desirable until the result of the case is out. The opinion of the collector is also the same. I feel that it would be better if you listen to both these opinions."[48]

Thereafter Subhedar Ghatge said,

> I also feel the same. I am a pensioner Subhedar. If I participate in the Satyagraha, I am sure that my pension will be affected. Still, I have come here from Pune with the determination of performing the Satyagraha. But I must tell you one thing—I have come to participate in the Satyagraha against the touchables. However these people are hiding behind the government and pushing us into a conflict with the latter. We should do proper thinking before playing out this conflict. If the government had been prejudiced [against us], it would have been necessary for us to accept this conflict. But it doesn't appear so, going by the speech of the collector. He had complete sympathy with us. Then why should we get into a conflict with the government unnecessarily? The enthusiasm that you showed today is unprecedented. I congratulate you for that. With this kind of enthusiasm, we are bound to get victory. However, I would request that we should exercise patience, taking into consideration the changing circumstances.

The collector had to leave the venue and therefore Dr Ambedkar thanked him and saw him off at the gate. The collector's speech did not seem to have had any impact on the audience. Because when the people began to speak after the collector had gone, it seemed people were still not in the mood to listen to speeches against the Satyagraha. At the same time speakers like Krishnaji Davane and Kumari Shantabai Shinde who were for the

Satyagraha received huge applause. This discussion went on until 7 pm. Dr Ambedkar opined, "there shall be discussion on this issue again at night and we will take a decision tomorrow morning." With this he declared the adjournment of the meeting.

Third Day of the Conference

As decided, a meeting of the select people was organized the previous night to discuss whether to go in for Satyagraha or not. After a lot of debate, it was decided by a majority opinion to suspend the Satyagraha and to take a procession through the town. It was accordingly communicated to the collector. But the issue arose about who would propose the resolution in the conference the next day. There was a possibility of its being passed only if it was proposed by Dr Ambedkar. For, if the conference would listen to some one, it was only him. Hence all insisted that Dr Ambedkar puts it forth. Dr Ambedkar accepted this responsibility. Next day, when the conference resumed in the morning, he put the following resolution before it:

> **Resolution:** This conference was called basically to offer a Satyagraha against those people of the touchable class who were not letting Untouchable people take water from the Chavadar tank. These touchable people have managed an injunction from the civil court at the eleventh hour against the Untouchable people going to the Chavadar tank and thus created circumstance wherein the satyagraha to be offered by this conference against them will automatically be the satyagraha against the government. In view of this fact and the explanation offered by the District Collector that the government is not prejudiced against the Untouchables and rather it has all sympathies with them in their struggle for equal rights, this conference decides to suspend the satyagraha until the court pronounces its verdict in the civil case.

While proposing the resolution, Dr Ambedkar said,

> In view of the fact that it was I who proposed the resolution yesterday for doing the Satyagraha and today it is I again who is proposing its suspension, you would think that I am a featherheaded person. But it is not so. Both the things are done with due thinking. Yesterday, I wanted to estimate the degree of

determination in you. I have had my assessment of it. Nobody has any doubt about your determination. I am satisfied with it. It was a big lacuna in us that we did not have the strength of determination. You have overcome that lacuna. When I am saying that you should not do the Satyagraha, it is after taking into consideration all these things. It is not necessary to use the strength immediately, just after you realized you have it. Strength has to be used after assessing the appropriateness of time. After serious thinking, I have also realized that we should not use our new found strength today. If we do the Satyagraha today, it would be against the government. Had the government been prejudiced against us, there would not be any objection to do a Satyagraha even against the government. But is the government prejudiced against us? Think of it; the government has sympathy for us. Then why should we put the government in dilemma unnecessarily? Next, you see that the touchable people do not have any sympathy for our Satyagraha. The touchable people have been openly uncooperative with us. The business people have stopped their business with us. *Khots* (landlords in Konakan Area) have started to take back lands. *Kunbis* (peasant castes) have started to put our cattle into the cattle houses (*kondwada*). We have to survive through this trap of injustice and oppression. For this kind of survival, we need cooperation from the government. There is nothing wrong if someone says, doing Satyagraha against the government is not proper while the government is giving assurance of such cooperation. Therefore, at this occasion you please listen to me and accord your approval to this proposal. People cannot laugh at you. The Collector himself was beseeching your favour; therefore nobody can say that you have suspended the Satyagraha because you are timid. At the most they might tease that your leaders have gone back on their resolve. But you need not feel hurt with it. At least I do not feel it. As I know, if I am retreating, it is for the sake of your interests. I consider it as the matter of not only great pleasure but also great pride for me that my followers have gone four steps ahead of me. While I ask you to suspend the Satyagraha today, I am as determined as you are that we should not give up our struggle without capturing the Chavadar tank. Please keep in mind that I will not sit quite without accomplishing this task."[49]

The delegates became disappointed listening to this kind of speech. Nonetheless, in deference to the advice of Dr Ambedkar, all accorded their approval to the resolution with silence.

Procession in lieu of the Satyagraha

A procession of the delegates to the conference was taken through the town. In the front were 50 volunteers from Mumbai. They were followed by 50 women. Then the rest of the people followed in four person in a row formation. Intermittently, people held banners with slogans/quotations written on them. During the last conference in March, in response to Untouchables' polluting the Chavadar tank, the touchable people of Mahad had become soldiers of religion!! They did a gory dance here, and some of them have gone to jail. Now, they should have walked with their head high as they had got an injunction from the court. Surprisingly, they had all shut their doors behind them. Not only women and children, but also the men folk had disappeared from roads. The leaders had left the town as though running for their life. Not a single soul was to be found in the town. Everybody was surprised to see this miserable condition of the touchable folks of Mahad despite the government being temporarily on their side because of the injunction of the court. It was a riddle how the cubs of lions had become the kittens. Entire Mahad town, already its people bewildered with the conference, was bemused with this procession moving through the marketplace. It was the first time that Mahad witnessed such a procession. Slogans like 'Victory to the King George V, Victory to Mahad Satyagraha, Victory to Gandhi, Victory to Agarkar, Victory to Lokhitwadi, Victory to Eknath Maharaj' were echoing from all over the Mahad town. The procession passed through the marketplace and reached a corner of the Chavadar tank. There it divided into two parts. One part was directed to move in one direction around the Chavadar tank and the other in a reverse direction so that they would meet at the opposite corner. The unified procession then returned to the conference pandal. Thus effectively the Chavadar tank was encircled by the delegates from all the four sides. After seeing this, the local people nervously wondered, whether anything had remained in capturing the Chavadar tank. It was a natural reaction. The show of this procession with participants walking with their *lathis* on their shoulder was reminding of the march of the army of dark *mavla*s (peasants in Pune region) of Shivaji. The procession was so huge that when the leading people reached back to the pandal, the rear end of the procession was yet to move from the pandal. The procession was not moving slowly. One could imagine the hugeness of the procession from the fact that it had started at 10.30 and ended at 12.

After the people came back from the procession, the conference had resumed again. Shivtarkar put forward the following resolution:

> This conference expresses its thanks with a sense of gratitude to those gentlemen from the non-Untouchable communities, especially the following gentlemen, who have helped in making this conference successful:
> 1. A.V. Chitre
> 2. Surendranath Tipnis
> 3. Fatehkhansaheb Mutholikar
> 4. Shantaram Raghunath Potnis
> 5. Keshavrao Deshpande
> 6. G.N. Sahastrabuddhe

On this resolution, Pandurang Nathuji Rajbhoj, More, Vanmali, etc. made autobiographical speeches. This resolution for proposing vote of thanks was concluded with thunderous clapping. Thereafter, Anantrao Chitre and Sahasrabuddhe spoke in reply. Dr Ambedkar then said, "Though the agenda of the conference has ended, some other important issues have remained undiscussed. As those issues are extremely important, without their consideration I will not be able to say that this conference has reached its conclusion. Today, since it is quite late, I have to push this discussion to night. Therefore I would like to request you all not to go home and attend this important meeting of this conference." After this speech by the president, the meeting was adjourned at 1 pm.

Women Visitors for Dr Ambedkar

After the meeting the delegates went to the dining pandal and Dr Ambedkar went to the office of the conference, where the arrangement of his stay was made. As he reached there, a crowd of women had collected there to see him. They had come from far away villages, walking some 9-10 miles, just to have a glimpse of their leader. Their desire to see him was so intense that many of them had left their breast-fed babies back home. By evening the crowd became really huge. An old woman came out of the crowd and after seeing Dr Ambedkar, began crying aloud. Seeing her condition, the people gathered there thought that some goons of the touchable community must have beaten her. Therefore, they asked her why she was crying, and who beat her. She replied that some scoundrel had told her on her way to Mahad, "Your king has been murdered." Only then the people realized the cause of her crying and also why so many women had collected there. Taking advantage of the fact that such a large gathering of women, charged with emotions of love and affection, had come to see him, Dr Ambedkar told them that he had a couple of things of social importance to tell them. For that, he had requested all of them to attend the night session of the conference. Accordingly, all the women stayed on.

Night Meeting in Chambharwada

The *Chambhar* community of Mahad was also woken up by the programme of the Satyagraha Conference. They decided to hold a meeting in the Chambharwada and requested Dr Ambedkar to attend it. In deference to their request, Dr Ambedkar, along with his friends, went to the meeting at 7.30 pm. Chambhar population in Mahad was quite large. As such sizable crowd of *Chambhar* men and women had collected there. At the beginning, R.N. Vanmali, Girjashankar Shivdas, L.R. Chandorkar, Govind Zipru Jadhav delivered inspiring speeches on social issues. After that Dr Ambedkar rose to speak and said,

> It was a matter of great surprise that barring 2-4 *Chambhars*, the rest of the *Chambhar* people do not take part in the important work like Satyagraha. I do not understand the reason for it. I do not understand why you hesitate to cooperate with Mahars. If you think of organizing a big programme like a Satyagraha on your own, I do not think it will be possible for you. Your population is

much smaller. Therefore, you do not have an option than cooperating with majority population like Mahars from the sheer view point of efficiency. Likewise, there is no reason to feel that your caste will be polluted if the Mahars cooperated with you.

As a matter of fact, the band of satyagrahis is a band of brave people and as even the Brahman kingdom like Peshawai admitted, there is no scope for caste like thing entering the band of braves. If that had not been the case, the tent of Shidnak Mahar would not have been allowed in the camp of Maratha sardars (chieftains). Yet, nobody is insisting that you should break with your caste. Actually speaking, you are business people, well off and accustomed to happy living. You should rather help us. You could perform a Satyagraha of not giving shoes. Despite your community possessing such strength, you are not making use of it. I do not understand whether to call it your disinterest or astounding laziness. Please decide whether you want happiness or human dignity. Without human dignity, your splendor is useless. Happy and free people like you should enthusiastically participate in the work of restoring human dignity to the Untouchables. Try to earn little of this merit. If you participate in these tasks, your name also will become immortal in history along with Mahars'. Otherwise your next generation will curse you for having been impotent.

Thereafter, S.N. Shivtarkar spoke:

Since you are not participating in the work of emancipation of the Untouchables, you are being considered as timid. You are not performing your historical duties. This work is not only of the Untouchable castes but is also of all human beings. But despite being Untouchable yourself, you do not participate in this work. This is utterly shameful. Do not become brahmanized and try to cooperate with and help us in this work.

Thereafter, P.N. Rajbhoj spoke:

I feel very bad seeing the *Chambhars* becoming brahmanized and feel worse about some people from the Matang caste. *Chambhar* people are better off compared to other Untouchable people but since they do not have education, they have become inactive. Today, a crisis has descended upon the Untouchable leaders. At this time, you should give up feelings of jealousy and hatred. Casteism is a dangerous disease. Forget it and cooperate with the Mahar community; become satyagrahis. There lies benefit to all.

Thereafter, Sahasrabuddhe Spoke:

> Barrister sahib (Dr Ambedkar) is born in your clan but after returning from Europe, he is a bigger intellectual than any Brahman. It is therefore that despite being a Brahman, I have accepted to be his disciple. You also get similar education to abolish caste discrimination, and help the work of emancipation of the Untouchables. Nothing has gone wrong with me because I took food with Dr Ambedkar. Please do not give unnecessary importance to distinction in eating, or drinking.

Thereafter, Vanmali said, "I feel very bad that you have not taken part in the Satyagraha. Do not forego this opportunity to brighten up your life. If you do your historical duty, your names will be immortal in history." After these kinds of speeches, snacks and tea were served. The meeting ended at about 9 pm after due vote of thanks.[50]

Concluding Session

After returning from the above meeting in Chambharwada, the Satyagraha Conference restarted its work at 10 pm. It was decided to have a lecture of Shri Deo, who was the founder promoter of the *Khadi Prasar Mandal* of Dhule. Since his arrival got delayed, Ganpatbuwa Jadhav and Kamble performed their satirical *Kirtans* on the issue of 'God and the devotee' for 15 minutes each. They had a very significant impact on the people. After the speech of Deo, the original agenda of the conference was taken up. Firstly, a resolution was proposed to thank Wamanrao Patki and Kamlakar Tipnis, the two youth belonging to the Kayastha (CKP) caste and presented them with a gold ring each, presented as a reward for their contribution to the success of the conference on behalf of the Satyagraha Committee. Sambhaji Gaikwad, Govind Ramji Adrekar, Hawaldar and More spoke on this resolution. On the same resolution, Dr Ambedkar said that the performance of these two youth is certainly becoming of their clan and caste. Brahman class has tried several times to put a stamp of inferiority on the Kayastha caste, to treat it lowly. However, the Kayasthas have faced the challenge every time and resisted these evil intrigues of the Brahman caste. It is natural for the Kayastha caste, which itself has fought the battle for equality, to feel sympathy for the Untouchable class fighting for equality and strive for their emancipation. Thereafter, Kamlakar Tipnis and Patki spoke in reply. Surendranath Tipnis, President, Mahad Municipality then rose to speak. He explained how necessary the Untouchable class was for the protection of the Hindu religion. Following him Shantaram Potnis said that even if the entire Gujar and the Brahman communities opposed, he and his friends in his community would continue to support the Untouchables physically, mentally and financially and would not give any value to the old people among the *Kayasthas* who were also against the Untouchables. Until the Untouchables get the permission to go to the Chavadar tank, he himself would not drink its water, he added.

The next resolution, put forward by Dr Ambedkar himself, was as follows: "This conference records its thanks to the propagators nominated for the Satyagraha Conference, namely, Shivram Gopal Jadhav, Sambhaji Tukaram Gaikwad, Bhau Balu Warangkar, Pandharinath Ramchandra Asudkar, Bhaviknath Buwa Phanalkar and Pandurang Mahadeo Vourkar for having discharged their responsibility in an excellent manner and taking into consideration the fact that Sakharam Vourkar, Gopal Achlolkar and Mahadeo Achlolkar, who have voluntarily dedicates themselves to the conference work, presents each of them with a silver token as reward."

By this time, the work of the conference had come to an end. As such, it was announced by the president as concluded.[51]

Address to Women

After the formal conclusion of the Conference, Dr Ambedkar started a very important programme. According to him, it was so important that it should have been given the top most priority in the agenda of the conference. The serious manner in which it was dealt with by him made all the delegates realize its importance. Moreover, it made them conscious of many of their duties, which were not touched upon hitherto. The first task in this agenda was the address to the women. As decided, all the women who had collected in the afternoon to see Dr Ambedkar had come to the conference pandal. A space in the middle was especially reserved for them. Addressing them Dr Ambedkar said,

> I am extremely happy that you have come to this conference. The way the problems of the households are solved jointly, the problems of the social households should also be solved by men and women collectively. There is no doubt that it would take a long time if only men took upon them the responsibility of solving this problem. I am sure, if the women take up the same responsibility, they would accomplish it in much lesser time. However, although it may not be possible for them to undertake this work on their own, they should not keep away from their menfolk working on the problem and should rather cooperate with them. Therefore, I ask you that you must attend all the conferences in future. As a matter of fact, the issue of eradication of untouchability relates more with you than with the menfolk. You have given birth to us men. You are well aware that other people consider us less than even animals. They do not tolerate even our shadow at some places. Other people get positions of prestige in the courts and government offices. But the children borne by you do not get even a job of sepoy in a police department. Such is our low status. While you are aware of all this, if someone asks you why you have given us birth, what would be your answer? What is the difference between the children of the Kayastha and the Brahman women, seated in this pandal, and the children borne by you? You must consider that you too possess as much character as the Brahman women do. You too possess as much fidelity as the Brahman women do. Rather the amount of mental courage, determination and dash that you possess cannot be claimed by the Brahman women. Despite this, why should a child borne by a Brahman woman be respected all over, whereas a child borne by you is despised everywhere? Have you ever considered why they should not even have a simple right as a human being? I think that you have never thought about it. If you had thought over this issue, you would have come forward to do a Satyagraha much before your menfolk. The only sin that we committed is to get birth from you and we are condemned to endure the punishment of untouchability only for this sin. Therefore, you must think why getting birth from your womb should become a sin whereas getting it from other women's womb should be a merit. If you think over this issue, either you will

have to stop bearing children or will have to wash away the stigma of low birth on your children, which is due to you. You may have to do one of these two things. You take a vow that you will not live in such a stigmatized condition in future. The way your menfolk have decided to work for social emancipation, you too should decide to work for the same objective.

The second thing I wish to tell you about is that you all should give up old decadent dirty customs and traditions. As a matter of fact, there is no stamp of identity on the forehead of an Untouchable person that he is Untouchable. But the touchable people immediately recognize the Untouchables based on the kind of customs and traditions the Untouchables observe. It is my opinion that these customs and traditions were forced upon us at one time. But such a compulsion is not possible in the rule of the British Government. Therefore, you must give up the things with which the people recognize you as Untouchables. The way you wear your *lugadi*[52] is a mark of your untouchability. That mark should be removed by you. You must establish the practice of wearing the *lugadi* in the manner in which the upper class women wear them. There is no expense in doing this. Likewise, bunch of *galsuris*[53] on your neck and armful of *goth patlya*[54] made of tin or silver are also the marker of recognizing you as Untouchables. There is no necessity of wearing more than one *galsuri*. It does not add to the lifespan of your husband or contribute to your beauty. The clothes contribute more to appearance than the ornaments do. Therefore, instead of wasting money over tin or sliver ornaments, expend it over good clothes. If at all an ornament is to be worn, get it made of gold. Otherwise do not wear it. Likewise take the responsibility of observing cleanliness. You are the *lakshmi*[55] of a household; you must exercise care not to allow any inauspicious or unclean things to take place in your household. It is a matter of pleasure that since last March, all people have given up eating meat of dead animals. But if you find any household, which is still not observing it, you must undertake the responsibility of making it fall in line. If your husband brings in meat of a dead animal, you tell him clearly that such things would not be tolerated in your house. I am sure, if you take this upon your mind, these practices will be totally stopped. Likewise, you should educate your daughters. Knowledge and learning are not for only men; they are necessary also for women. This was even recognized by our forefathers. If it was not so, the people in military would not have educated their girls. Considering the

> maxim—as the mine, so the clay, if you wish to improve your next generation, you should not keep your girls without education. I hope, you will not take this advice of mine lightly. You should not delay its implementation. Therefore, before you leave for your homes tomorrow morning, you should show me the change in wearing your clothes. It is only then that I would consider that my advice has not gone waste.

One Vithabai got up and assured on behalf of all women that they would behave as advised.

Address to the Caste Leaders

After explaining to the women, their responsibilities, Dr Ambedkar collected the leaders and officials of the caste panchayats and addressed them:

> Do not feel angry with what I am going to tell you. I am a child of the *panchas*.[56] If I am erring, you should pardon me. I am of the opinion that the arrangement of *panchas* made by our forefathers is a very good thing. The customs and traditions of each community are fixed. Everyone has to behave according to those customs and traditions. If someone violated the community customs and traditions, the community punishes him with social boycott or a fine to make him behave. This right is given to you people by the caste. It will show you what prestige you enjoy in our caste. You are the judicial as well as the religious authority for the community. The community will have a good or a bad orientation according to the way you lay down the religion, and exercise justice. But people have a serious complaint against you that you behave as per the policy of *'beli tikade boli'*[57] and make truth out of lie and vice a versa. As a result, the immorality has been on increase in the community and for this you are solely responsible. Therefore what I have to tell you is—you should understand your duty. Understand that times have changed. Realize the need of what we have to do to change circumstances. You should adopt new customs and practices and discard the old ones. Not only that, wherever people are not inclined to adopt these new customs and practices, a dose of social boycott could be used to make them fall in line. If you are prepared to do this, we will accept your traditional authority coming from generations. And if you are not prepared to do this, we will have to nominate new *panchs* with new policies and new orientation and take away

> your authority. I am going to call a meeting of all the caste leaders to consider which rules should be appropriately made applicable to our caste in the changing circumstances. I hope that you will ensure that the rules decided unanimously in that meeting are implemented.[58]

Thereafter, Shivtarkar placed the last resolution before the conference. It proposed to thank all people who have come from the Marathi speaking districts of the Bombay Province for the Mahad Satyagraha on behalf of the Satyagraha Committee. The unprecedented aspect of the Mahad conference was that the issue of Chavadar tank was not taken as belonging only to the Untouchable people of Mahad but was considered as belonging to the entire Untouchable community. There was not a single Marathi speaking district from which people had not come for the Satyagraha. If the Untouchable people show such a spirit of unity, the task of eradication of untouchability would become much easier. After Shivtarkar's speech along these lines, and Sambhaji Gaikwad seconding him, the resolution was passed in a clamour of clapping. It was 1.30 am when the conference concluded its work.[59]

Fourth Day

There was an immediate and visible impact of Dr Ambedkar's speech on the women present in the conference. They literally followed his advice and changed their style of wearing clothes before starting off to their villages in the morning. To commend their determination, each woman was given eight annas [50 paise today] each as a present. Likewise, there was a visible impact on the menfolk too. They also discarded some of their customary ornaments, worn in hand and ears, which were indicative of their backwardness, immediately. Even the Mahars who were employed in the Mahad Municipality as sweepers had resigned from their jobs.

After the conclusion of the conference, and even the extended progrmame at the instance of Dr Ambedkar, people returned to their homes. However, Dr Ambedkar, Shivtarkar and 10-12 people who came from Mumbai stayed back to visit the Raigadh fort. Among them were Sahasrabuddhe, Chitre,

Pradhan brothers from Mumbai, Kholwadikar, Gangawane, Gaikwad, Ganpatbuwa Jadhav, Subhedar Ghatge, and Rajbhoj. In the morning around 10 am, they went to see the rock carvings in the Mahad caves. They had decided to speak about reforms to whosoever among the touchable class met them on the way. Accordingly, when they met with Marathas at Pachpale village, they called them near and asked for their opinion about the Chavadar tank Satyagraha. They replied hesitatingly in a vague sense that they basically follow the old customs without understanding their meaning; just because Brahmans do it; they simply follow. While returning, the Untouchable women came to meet them. They had brought about a kind of revolution in the way of their dressing and appearance. They just wanted to demonstrate how Dr Ambedkar's speech had impacted them. Ambedkar and others returned to the Conference office around 1 PM after seeing the caves.

After lunch and some rest, Dr Ambedkar, Shivtarkar and others set off for Raigadh at 5 pm by a motor vehicle.

Reflections in Administration

As seen earlier, the state administration was seized of the developments after the first conference ended up with an ugly incident of caste Hindus attacking the Untouchable delegates for having defiled the Chavadar tank. It followed the developments, very closely particularly when it knew that Dr Ambedkar had planned the second conference and an indefinite Satyagraha at the Chavadar tank till it was opened up for the Untouchables. To diffuse the impending law and order situation, the DM had invoked the court injunction in the course of ideating possible alternatives. As it happened, it appears that this was used by the orthodox elements of Mahad to prevent the Satyagraha. The collector thereafter had ensured that the Satyagraha does not take place, personally pleading with Dr Ambedkar and going out of way in personally speaking at the conference.

After the Satyagraha, the DM, Kolaba wrote a note to the Secretary to Government, dated 31 December 1927, giving a brief on the conference as follows:

I camped at Mahad from 19th to 29th instant. The Untouchables began to pour in on the 24th and by the evening there were some three thousand of them, from all districts. I went and talked to them and found that they had little or no knowledge or understanding of the injunction and no intention of abandoning their entry into the tank. About 3000 more, including there [sic] leaders arrived on 25th. I arranged to see Dr. Ambedkar immediately. He arrived and he said that he proposed to ignore injunction and risk the consequences. He did not expect very serious consequences because he held that the injunction was illegal. The obvious risk of a breach of the peace he left out of account, considering that [it was] my affair. .... However [after] considerable discussion he began to see the difficulties and possible injury to his cause which might result from maintaining such an attitude. To cut a long story short, after two days [of] constant discussions, the Untouchables' conference accepted my view and decided almost unanimously to abandon the Satyagraha until after the decision of the civil suite. Some two thousand or so left on the night of the 26th and the rest of them on the 27th. There was no breach of peace or any untoward incident whatsoever. For this I think the greatest credit is due to the Untouchables and particularly to Dr. Ambedkar. Their disappointment was great, and their peaceful acceptance of the situation and their loyalty to government were quite remarkable and deserving of appreciation.

Bombay Chronicle of 27.12.1927 had published the following account of the conference:

Presiding over the Mahad Satyagraha Conference on Sunday, at which about ten thousand people were present, Dr B.R. Ambedkar, MLC of Bombay said that the Untouchables had met in that conference not solely for the purpose of drinking water from a particular tank but for the purpose of establishing human rights. Dr Solanki, MLC and Mr. S.B. Tilak, son of the late Lokmanya Tilak, sent messages expressing sympathy with the objects of the conference.

During the course of his presidential address, Dr Ambedkar said that the removal of untouchability would benefit not a particular community, but the whole Indian nation. The ideal of the movement was a noble one, namely the abolition of the *Varnashram* system and the enunciation of the principle of equality. He said that human rights, services, and position were to be determined not by the accident of birth but by merit alone.

> Mr G.N. Sahasrabuddhe, a Brahman, read a few extracts from *Manusmruti* to show what kind of treatment was to be meted out to others than Brahmans. Resolutions were then passed. The first resolution considered *Manusmruti* and certain other books contained vulgar passages and went against human rights. It was resolved to burn such books. Other resolutions declaring the rights of man were passed unanimously. This resolution declared that all the Hindus should be regarded as of one *varna* and should be recognized as such and that it should be laid down by law that to call oneself a Brahman or a *Kshatriya* and so on should be prohibited. Another resolution laid down the necessity for holding of competitive examinations for admission to priesthood. Towards the end of the day's session, the ceremony of the burning of *Manusmruti* took place.

Mr Hood, DM, Kolaba received a lot of acclaim for his deft handling of the situation. A note of C.W.A.T. dated 12.01.28 said, "Mr Hood has handled this affair very creditably. I think a DO letter might be sent to him expressing appreciation of care and tact in dealing with the affair." The note also extended the government's appreciation to the DSP, Kolaba, Mr Ferrant of the good work done by him and the police. It also praised Dr Ambedkar and hoped that "His Excellency will at some convenient opportunity express his appreciation of his judicious action." The misgiving about the appropriateness of the grant of interim injunction by the sub-judge of Mahad had not yet disappeared. This note still puts a caveat about the action of the sub judge. It says, "We have not yet sufficient material to judge finally whether he was right or wrong. And if in the end it is decided to take notice of his conduct it will have to be done in a very different way."

The abandonment of the Satyagraha must have come as a great relief and created a sense of victory among the Touchables. While the proposed Satyagraha at the Chavadar tank did not happen, the conference succeeded in burning the *Manusmruti*, symbolically negating the very ideological basis of the caste system. It had naturally infuriated the orthodox Hindus everywhere. It was reflected in some protest meetings that took place around Mahad after the conference. The confidential weekly letter from DM, Kolaba dated 31 January 1928, notes one such meeting of Marathas, which was "held at Nigampur on 19 January 1928 to protest against the 'sacrileges' of Dr Ambedkar at Mahad and Raigadh through the Satyagraha movement of the Untouchables. It was attended by about 500 persons. Captain Jagtap was to preside over but he could not attend due to an illness. The Police Patel therefore presided. The Mahars were called upon not to transgress their customary social limits. The Patel was later ordered by the Mamlatdar to desist from doing anything against the Mahars in caste matters."

Those who sympathized with the Untouchables and favoured their struggle to establish their human rights were excommunicated by the orthodox establishment. It is interesting to see the amount of indignation among the people for such progressive Hindus. DM's weekly letter provides us a glimpse of one such incident. It was a meeting of Mamlatdar that was held at Kinjoliin in Mahad taluka on the 22 January to consider the question of readmission into the caste of about seven or eight persons of Mahad who had been outcasted for their sympathy with the Mahars during their Satyagraha. Messers Jedhe and Javalkar of Poona had specially come down to attend the meeting. Mr S.G. Tipnis, President of the Mahad Municipality was also present. He was a Kayastha Prabhu and had taken a leading part on behalf of the Mahars during the troubled times of Mahad, incurring a good deal of unpopularity among the caste Hindus. After four or five persons had addressed the meeting, Mr Tipnis rose to speak. This was a signal for the meeting to break up without coming to any decision.

The struggle of the Untouchables may have induced even other communities to sense their deprivation and inspired them to assert their rights. While the trouble at Mahad continued, another Satyagraha was brewing in Alibag *taluka*, over the exclusion of Kolis, Agris and Bhandaris from the inner sanctum of the local Rameshwar Temple. The trouble came to a head a few months ago when the Sarpanch of the Temple Committee wired to the District Magistrate that he apprehended a breach of the peace if the Kolis forced an entry as they were thinking of doing. No action was however then taken as no breach of peace seemed imminent. DM's above weekly letter stated that some people on behalf of the excluded communities asked him to take action under section 43 of the District Police Act. As there was no likelihood of any imminent breach of the peace, the DM had declined to use the emergency provision of the law and rather advised them to follow the precedent at Mahad and have recourse to the civil court to establish their rights. A meeting of the Bhandaris was called for at Cheol where it was decided, as a retaliatory measure, not to have the Brahmans in their (Bhandaris') religious functions. The meeting approved this, only 4 or 5 dissenting. It also decided to boycott the dissenters.

On the 23 February 1928, the sub-judge at Mahad after hearing arguments dissolved the interim injunction prohibiting the Mahars from touching the Chavadar tank. Dr Ambedkar had argued the case for the Untouchables. The confidential weekly letter of the DM, Kolaba, dated 25 February significantly noted it. The RLA's noting dated 28.2.1928 stated that the injunction granted was valid only up to the date that the defendants showed cause against it, and not (as I thought of first) up to the date of the decision of the suit. The sub judge was right in granting such an injunction for a few days reserving the authority to cancel it if Dr Ambedkar showed good cause. *Bombay chronicle* of 3rd march 1928 carried the news with a sub head "Magistrate regrets grant of injunction" and reported the sub judge saying, "I cannot conclude this order without expressing my regret at the inconvenience and the hardship caused to the defendants by the injunction granted by me. Temporary though it was, at having been instrumental in keeping one more wrong upon a community already labouring under the most cruel and unjust social wrongs, dissolve the injunction issued by me".

Bombay Chronicle dated 02 March 1928 published a long story under the head "Mahad Tank Opened to Untouchables" giving salient details on the struggle:

> When in March, last, Dr. Ambedkar led the Untouchables to the Chavadar tank at Mahad, the orthodox section of the caste Hindus lost their sleep, appetite and all over the 'sacrilege' and mercilessly

belaboured the poor unsupported Untouchables while they were returning from the tank. Soon after the criminal proceedings were taken against the rowdies and they were punished for disturbing the public peace. Every effort was made by the so called 'protesters' of the religion to oppose the Untouchables from coming near the tank and they were encouraged in their action by the orthodox press. It was to assert their right of ordinary human privileges; the Untouchables launched the Satyagraha movement, and in December last a Conference of about 10,000 assembled and unanimously resolved to march on to the tank. But the orthodox caste Hindus who smelt this resolve by their nose got a temporary injunction from the sub-judge of Mahad against the Untouchables using the tank on the ground that it was the private property of one Mr. Chowdhari and the touchable classes. Having secured this respite from the authorities, the Touchables thought that they had gained the upper hand at the expense of the Government and the Untouchables. Dr. Ambedkar at once saw through the game, but decided to postpone the *Satyagraha* till the civil suit was disposed off. The suit came for hearing on 23rd February 1928 before Mr. Vaidya, the sub-judge of Mahad, and Dr. Ambedkar by his lucid exposition not only got the injunction cancelled but also convinced the judge about the bona fide of their right to use the public tank. Since the ban has been removed the tank is now to be open for public use as per the resolution of the Bombay Legislative Council.

Bombay Chronicle reported about a public meeting held on Sunday, the 26 February, in Bombay, attended by about 2,000 people, which resolved to relaunch the Satyagraha at Mahad. The exact date was to be decided by the Satyagraha Committee. Observing that this movement under the leadership of Dr Ambedkar was cosmopolitan in character, the said report indicated that its scope extended beyond the opening of the tank for the public use; it was directly paving the way for the evolution of the national movement for asserting ordinary privileges of citizenship by majority of people.

The diary of DSP, Kolaba dated 3 March 1928 refers to the above story in *The Bombay Chronicle* of 2 March and notes that "a meeting was held on Sunday, February 26 in Bombay attended by about 2000 people. It was resolved to relaunch the Satyagraha at Mahad. The Satyagraha committee is meeting shortly and the exact date will be announced shortly." A weekly letter of the Special Branch of the Bombay City Police dated 2 March also noted this public meeting of the depressed classes. It was held at Damodar Thackersey Hall on February 26 and was presided over by G.N. Sahasrabuddhe. The meeting was attended by an audience of about 500 people. Dr B.R. Ambedkar, who was the principal speaker, said that as the sub judge of the Mahad court had dissolved the interim injunction against him and the satyagrahis, he would leave the question of resuming Satyagraha to the discretion of the Satyagraha committee of Bombay.

The dissolution of the interim injunction however was short lived. The orthodox Hindus appealed against the decision of Mr Vaidya, subordinate judge, Mahad, dissolving an interim injunction granted by him previously against the Mahad Untouchables forbidding them from using the Chavadar tank in the district court, Thane. Mr D.N. Sanjana, district judge, Thane heard the appeal filed by Pandurang Waman Dharap and others at Mahad on 28 March 1928 and passed order granting an interim injunction to restrain the respondents from using the Chavadar tank pending the decision of the declaratory suit filed by the Touchables in the Mahad Civil Court. On the same day, i.e., 28 March 1928, the Home Department (Political) asked Mr Kriplani, DM, Kolaba to obtain and forward to the government a copy of the proceedings in the court of the District Judge at Thana leading up to and including a copy of this order granting the interim injunction. The papers were sent to Mr McDonell, assistant secretary home department (political) Bombay.

A note of the Home Department (Special) dated 24 April 1928 explains the 'rationale' of the decision of the District Magistrate:

> The District Judge states that the first injunction was granted (by the sub judge) on grounds which appear to be beyond exception. That injunction was granted principally on the grounds that the past history of the tank showed that it had been used exclusively by the touchables and that, therefore, no great inconvenience would be caused to the Untouchables if the status quo were

> maintained a little longer, i.e., till the civil suit filed by the Touchables for a declaration that the tank is a private property and that they alone have the exclusive right to use, was decided. The DJ considers that the facts related to the past history of the tank make out an 'unanswerable case' for the grant of a temporary injunction. He also observes incidentally that it certainly could not have been the case, as declared in a manifesto by the Untouchables, that the decision in the riot case of last year (in which a few touchables were convicted) had put their rights beyond dispute.
>
> As regards the withdrawal by the sub judge of the injunction previously granted by him, the DJ observes that the former was induced to do so on the strength of some extracts from revenue records and municipal papers, in which the tank was described as a public tank vested in the municipality. He considers that the sub judge was not justified in coming to the conclusion—solely from these documents—that a section of the public cannot have exclusive rights to use the tank, for it would appear from certain sections of the District Municipal Act that the municipality can have control over the source of water supply though it belonged to a section of the public and can limit a particular source of water supply to a particular section of the public committed to its care. In the view of the above considerations that the DJ has set aside the sub judge's order and issued a temporary injunction. In regard to the grant of temporary injunction, please see the RLA's opinion on pages 221-222 of file 355 (65) II put up. In the circumstances we can perhaps do nothing but await the result of the civil suit filed by the touchables for a declaration of the rise. It will be seen from page 5 ante that Dr Ambedkar has promised to give a fortnights notice before re launching *satyagraha*. It is, however, unlikely that he will organize any mass demonstration at Mahad before the civil suit is decided.

Thus the decision of the District Judge was mainly based on the grounds (1) that the tank is situated in a locality occupied wholly by superior classes; (2) that it is the principal, if not the only source of water supply for all purposes; (3) that a touch by a member of the depressed class is considered to be sufficient to make water unfit for use by the orthodox Touchables; (4) that in the whole past history of the tank, its water was exclusively used by the 'touchables' and not by 'Untouchables'; (5) that the tank was entered in municipal and revenue records as a public tank was not sufficient evidence to dissolve the first order of temporary injunction; and (6) that from certain sections of the District Municipal Act the municipality can have control over a source of water supply though it belonged to a section of the public and can limit its use to a particular section of the public.

Mahad episode had antagonized the caste Hindus against Dr Ambedkar but had given a momentum to the movement he launched. With the accelerated pace of the movement, aggressiveness of *Bahishkrut Bharat* to sustain the same and his decision to submit the case of the Untouchables to the Simon Commission, which was boycotted by the national parties, was adding to the annoyance of the Hindus. The upper caste advocates, solicitors and barristers, who monopolized cases in the High Court, had turned against him and stopped giving him cases. The Brahman servant who served him tea in a cup in the court canteen began serving it in a glass keeping it at a distance. These humiliating developments so infuriated him that he stopped going to the court. The resultant physical and psychological stress began telling upon his health. His wife Ramabai was already indisposed with a long drawn illness. His only source of income was Rs 200 he earned from taking classes in Batliboy College, which job also was coming to an end on 31 March 1928.[60] He therefore sought a job of professor in the Government Law College, Bombay and luckily got it, easing his financial woes to some degree.[61]

Although the caste Hindus of Mahad had filed the complaint, they were not seriously following the case. As such the ruling came in the favour of the Untouchables on 13 June 1929 opening the 'Choudhar' tank for Untouchables. The order of the sub-judge V.V. Pandit was mainly based on the complainants being absent in the court, their advocate not having any instructions from them to proceed with the matter and their questionable *locus standi* in the case as the representatives of the upper castes.[62] The *Bahishkrut Bharat* jubilantly announced the win in a special supplement to its issue of 13-14 June but this victory also remained short-lived. The complainants filed an appeal in the upper court against this judgment. It was clear that they wanted to drag the case as long as possible to divert the energy of the Untouchables. But they did not realize how determined Dr Ambedkar was to win the case.

He began preparations for the case with renewed vigor. It was vital for him to win the case lest it should embolden the Hindus and conversely demoralize the Untouchables. He wanted to marshal massive evidence from the Hindu scriptures to break the backbone of the case. In this context, he thought the personal evidence of some of the prominent Hindu scholars would strengthen his case. As such, he spoke out his mind to Palaye Shastri, a Brahman pundit with whom he had some acquaintance[63] Shastri readily agreed and further suggested Dr Ambedkar to approach N.C. Kelkar and Dr Kurtkoti, Hindu Shankaracharya for the same. Kelkar obliged and provided him a lot of literature that could be useful for the case but he did not turn up for evidence in the court.[64] He was quite hopeful about Dr Kurtkoti too and therefore followed up with him through B.K. Gaikwad as he was then at Nashik. Unlike Kelkar, Dr Kurtkoti did not even show his willingness to give his witness.[65]

The result on this appeal again came in favour of the Untouchables on 8 June 1931. The sub judge V.R. Saraf said in his ruling that the complainant had failed to establish their case. The complainants then appealed to the District Court, Thana against this verdict. The second Assistant judge, S.M. Konkani dismissed this appeal on 30 January 1933. The complainants then went to the Bombay High Court in appeal. The case dragged for four years in the High Court. Besides massive evidence presented to the court, some reformist savarna Hindus like Palaye Shashtri, Dr N.D. Savarkar, and Bal Gangadhar Kher gave witness in the favour of the Untouchables. Eventually, Justice Wadia dismissed the appeal of the complainants by his order of 17 March 1937. He held that since the complainants had failed to prove that the land of the Chavadar tank belonged to them, the Chavadar tank becomes a public property and the custom that the Untouchables did not have the right to take water from the tank could not be held fully legal. This order is provided in the **Appendix 7**. The case was thus dragged for nearly a decade and when the victory came, the context had changed to such an extent that it proved totally inconsequential.

NOTES AND REFERENCES

1. C.B. Khairmode, *Dr Bhimrao Ramji Ambedkar Yanche Charitra*, Vol. 3, Pratap Prakashan, Pune, 1964, p. 135.
2. The Home Department (Political) confidential memo No. S.D.1041 dated 15 September 1927 to H.L. Painter, Commissioner and copied to DM, Kolaba.
3. A letter from H.L. Painter, Commissioner, Southern Division, Belgaum, No. P.O.L. 411 dated October 19, 1927.
4. J.R. Hood, DM, Kolaba's letter No. MSC 192 dated October 14, 1927 to H.L. Painter, Commissioner, Southern Division, Belgaum.
5. Also reproduced in C.B. Khairmode, op. cit., pp. 137-8.
6. A memo from the Secretary to Government No. 4770/13055 dated 7 October 1927.
7. Vide its memo dated October 18, 1927.
8. A confidential letter from J.R. Hood, No. MSC192 dated 9 November 1927.
9. Secretary to the government of Bombay order No. 4770/316A general department, Bombay Castle, November 29, 1927.
10. Khairmode writes about this meeting as follows: "They had called a meeting of Mahad on November 17, 1927 in Vireshwar temple with the intention to discuss the proposed Satyagraha of the Untouchables on the Chavadar tank. But when the people collected for the meeting, some people turned the agenda to pass a resolution opposing the proposed Satyagraha, big quarrel ensued and the meeting was called off after two hours without being able to elect even the chairman." C.B. Khairmode, op. cit., p. 146.
11. Paraphrased extract from the confidential weekly letter from the District Magistrate, Kolaba, dated December 10, 1927.
12. J.R. Hood's confidential letter to Monteath (Secretary to the Government, Home Department (Political), Bombay) dated 9 December 1927.
13. A letter No. S.D.1455 dated 12th December 1927 from Asstt. Secretary to the Government of Bombay, Home Department (Political). The order for postponement of his transfer came on 11 December vide a telegram.
14. Extract from the confidential weekly letter of the District Magistrate, Kolaba, dated the December 10, 1927.
15. C. B. Khairmode, op. cit., p. 146.
16. The details of the Appellant were: 1. Pandurang Raghunath Dharap, Caste Brahman, Profession Business, Age approximately

62 years, Residence Mahad, 2. Narahari Damodar Vaidya, Caste Brahman, Profession Vaidik Brahman, Age approximately 75 years, Residence Mahad, 3. Ramnarayan Giridhari Marwadi, Profession Business, Age approximately 65 years, 4. Ganapat Bhiku Gandhi Gujar, Caste Gujar, Profession Business, Age approximately 55 years, Residence Mahad, 5. Balkrushna Narayan Bagade, Caste Shimpi, Profession Business, Age approximately 45 years, Residence Mahad, 6. Narayan Anandrao Deshpande, Caste Kayasth, Profession Writing applications, Age approximately 70, Residence Mahad, 7. Ramchandra Dharmaji Jadhav, Caste Maratha, Profession Business, Age approximately.

17. The details of the respondents were: 1. Dr Bhimrao Ramji Ambedkar, M.A., Ph.D., D. Sc., Bar at Law, M.L.C., Caste Mirashi, Profession Lawyer, Age approximately 40, 2. Sitaram Namdeo Shivtarkar, Caste Mirashi, Profession Service, Age approximately. 40. No. 1 and 2 Respondents: Damodar Hall, Parel, Mumbai. 3. Kutannak alias Krushna Sayanak Mahar, Caste Mirashi, Profession Military Pensioner, Age approximately 50, Residence Kinjloli, Tq Mahad, 4. Ganya Malu Chambhar, Profession Business, Age approximately 65, Residence Mahad, 5. Kanu Vitthal Mahar, Caste Mirashi, Profession Farming, Age approx. 65, Residence Mahad.
18. A letter from DM, Kolaba No. MSC 192 on 17 December 1927.
19. A note from HM, HD on the letter from the DM, Kolaba's above referred letter forwarded by GD and C.W.A. Turner confidential note No. 4770/337-A, General Department, Bombay Castle, December 22, 1927.
20. C.B. Khairmode, op. cit., p. 138.
21. A classical Marathi dish, which is a dessert served during auspicious occasions and during important festivals such as *Holi*, *Padwa* in Maharashtra. It resembles a roti (a poli) with stuffing of *puran* made of chickpea lentils with a pinch of turmeric for colour.
22. It means 'God Bhima'; Bhima refers to Dr Bhimrao Ambedkar.
23. A popular Marathi periodical.
24. Vyanktesh Balwant Pendharkar (December 10, 1892-March 15, 1937), popularly known as 'Bapurao' Pendharkar, was a legendary theatre personality, who performed in Keshavrao Bhosale's theatre 'Lalitkaladarsha'.
25. A traditional Marathi folk art form, often with singing and dancing, widely performed by local or travelling theatre groups within the state of Maharashtra, India.

26. C.B. Khairmode, op. cit., p 142.
27. *Bahishkrut Bharat*, 16 September 1927, p. 9.
28. *Bahishkrut Bharat*, 30 September 1927, p. 8.
29. *Bahishkrut Bharat*, 23 December 1927.
30. A battle cry of Hindus, literally meaning praise to lord Shiva.
31. Wife of Anandrao Ambedkar, who lived together with Dr Ambedkar, after her husband's demise, along with her children.
32. C.B. Khairmode, op. cit., pp. 155-7.
33. Supplement of *Bahishkrut Bharat*. February 3, 1928, pp. 181(1) to 185 (5).
34. In the *Bahishkrut Bharat* it is given as nineteenth, and the same is reproduced by Khairmode. But the actual date is twentieth, the second day of the first conference. It is corrected here.
35. "*ushtya hatane kawla na haknarya*"—it is a Marathi phrase, which depicts extremely miserly characters.
36. Ambedkar used Marathi phrases in common usage of the Untouchables to depict these transactions. They were *betibandi, rotibandi, lotibandi and bhetibandi*, respectively.
37. No paragraph break in original.
38. Ambedkar used *sanghatana*, which would translate to 'organise' but the sense in which he used it is 'reorganise'.
39. A weapon usually used by people in mythology, resembling a metallic bulb at the end of a handle for striking at the enemy.
40. A Marathi phrase, *'annat mati kalavane'*, meaning, spoiling our life-chances.
41. Nowhere is his full name given.
42. The entire account is also given in C.B. Khairmode, op. cit., pp. 174-7.
43. He said it in a metaphorical way, *gawachi ves randki jhali,* which translates: the village boundary has thus been widowed. In English, there is no equivalent phrase than what is translated. It means the village lost its prestige.
44. C.B. Khairmode, op. cit., pp. 180-1.
45. These two are Marathi magazines, which were against the Mahad struggle. There are no other references for their being burnt in the Mahad conference, however.
46. A police designation above constable and below subinspector, called sometimes head constable.
47. Touchable people who were held guilty of assaulting the Untouchable people during the first conference were sentenced to a jail term.
48. C.B. Khairmode, op. cit., pp. 183-4.

49. Ibid., pp. 186-7.
50. Ibid., pp. 190-2.
51. Ibid., pp. 192-3.
52. A six yard sari that was worn by women in Maharashtra.
53. A kind of necklace made of beads as a mark of a married woman. While all Hindu women wear it, the lower caste women wore them in multiples.
54. Ornaments to be worn on the arm.
55. Goddess of wealth.
56. Jury of the caste body.
57. The meaning of which is similar to "He *who pays the piper* calls the tune."
58. C.B. Khairmode, op. cit. pp. 196-7.
59. Ibid.
60. C.B. Khairmode, Vol. 2, op. cit., p. 65.
61. C.B. Khairmode, Vol. 3, op. cit., pp. 264-5.
62. C.B. Khairmode, op. cit., p. 266.
63. Just after the first conference, he was invited to preside over a meeting at Badlapur in Colaba District for celebrating 300th birth anniversary of Shivaji Maharaj. Palaye Shastri was the host of the meeting, who had extended this unique invitation in consultation with the people in the neighboring villages. See, Gail Omvedt, *Ambedkar: Towards An Enlightened India*, Penguin, New Delhi, 2008.
64. C.B. Khairmode, op. cit., p. 263.
65. Ibid., p. 270.

चवदार तळ्याचा सत्याग्रह

डॉ. आंबेडकरांच्या नेतृत्वाखालील
दलितवर्गाच्या चळवळीचा मानदंड–

महाडच्या
दोन ऐतिहासिक परिषदा

लेखक
आर. बी. मोरे
(प्रमुख संघटक : महाड सत्याग्रह)

१ रु. ५० पैसे

5.

The Satyagraha of Chavadar Tank[1]

R.B. More

Chief Organizer, Mahad Satyagraha

(Translated into English by Shailendra Mehta, Shridhar Pawar, Sanober Keshwar and Niranjani Shetty)

I saw Babasaheb Ambedkar for the first time when he came for a meeting of the caste panchayat at a *chawl* known as 'Family Lines', which was inhabited largely by military pensioners. He had acquired his M.A. and Ph.D. degrees from Columbia University and had recently come back from America. It was 1917, when I was a teenager of 13-14 years, studying in the third standard in an English medium school. I had come to Bombay from my village during Diwali. When I learnt that subhedar Ambedkar's son, who had acquired a degree from abroad and his brother were coming for the meeting of the brigade panchayat, I became curious and with an intention to have a closer look at them, I perched closer to one of my relatives at the meeting spot. After a while when they arrived at the venue, people flocked to see them. The duo cut through the crowd and occupied their seats. I was gazing at Bhimrao. I almost got lost into his resolute, serious and radiant persona. Later Balaram dada (as his elder brother was known) introduced some people to Bhimrao. 'He is the *subhedar* of this particular platoon'; 'he is *hawaldar-jamadar* of that platoon'; 'he is this one's son, that one's brother...', the introduction session went on for some time. While this programme was on, Bhimrao was recounting several memories of his childhood with those people and was sharing laughter over some funny recollections. People also responded with jovial remarks and laughed and so did I. Observing me laughing, someone asked me a pointed question, 'why are you laughing?' My relative answered for me and made him quiet. However, because of this conversation, Balaramdada's attention was drawn towards me and he asked my relative about me. My relative told him that I was a grandson of *Madiwala* [person owning one storyed house; those days a distinction of sorts.] Vithal Joshi from Dasgaon, studying in third standard English medium at Mahad. Balaramdada said something to Bhimrao pointing at me. Soon thereafter, the meeting began. For about an hour several people spoke. However, Bhimrao did not utter a word until the meeting was over. As if he was present there as an observer. This was my first chance to see Doctorsaheb from such close quarters.

About two to three years later, with one of his friend's reference, I met Ambedkar in person at his residence at Poybawadi cement chawl and narrated him some of the difficulties in my educational career. He treated me with great affection and guided me with due concern. He presented me with an atlas and encouraged me to study. Until then, I was proud of him as one of the intelligent persons amongst my relatives. I was not grown up enough to comprehend his real achievements. When he left for London for the second time, to complete his D.Sc. and Bar at Law, I was staying at his brother, Balaramdada Ambedkar's house for about six months. I would work the entire day, have my meals at his place, and sleep in the office of *Mooknayak*. This was my daily routine. I got an opportunity not only to reside with the Ambedkar family, but also the inspiration to involve in social work. I would like to make special mention that, by the time Dr Babasaheb came back to India after completing his studies abroad; I was active as a student and a social activist.

A Little about Myself

If I have to recollect about my social life, I will have to go back, half a century ago. After I passed my high school scholarship examination in 1913-14 from Alibag in the Kolaba district, I was offered a scholarship of Rs. 5 per month and was asked to be admitted to an English medium school. Any student above the age of 11 years belonging to any caste was eligible to take this examination. There were no special concessions for the students from the Untouchable castes. I was sent for this examination as a primary school student from Dasgaon. Those days, even the shadow of an Untouchable was considered sacrilegious by the upper castes in the Konkan region, and Alibaug was known as the stronghold of rabid fundamentalists. It would be beyond the imagination of the current generation to think of the treatment from these orthodox elements that I had to endure. Nonetheless, I was successful in that particular examination and therefore went to the Mahad English High School for admission. The school was located in Dharap's house near the old post office of Mahad. I was told by the school authorities that if I was admitted to the school, the house would no more be rented to the school. Under such circumstances, they would have no option other than closing down the school. Since it would entail a huge loss to the other students, they (school authorities) would not like to close down the school. The barrier of untouchability rose up between me and my education. The next one year was spent grazing cattle at Ladawli in my uncle's village. One day while I was bathing in the river near the farm of a noted Tipnis family, Bhikoba Narayan Tipnis, who had a high reputation as an agriculturist, artist and a dedicated social reformer, belonging to this family, asked me as to why I was not attending the school. I told him about how I was denied admission in the Mahad English School. After some two to three months, he sent a message for me to go to Wada of Gondal. There I was introduced to a famous dramatist Yeshvant Narayan Tipnis along with Anant Vinayak Chitre alias Bhai Chitre, a friend and close associate of Dr Babasaheb Ambedkar, who was also an activist of the Social Service League of Bombay during its initial days. They were surprised to learn that a student who had acquired government scholarship [through competitive examination] was denied admission by the management of the school merely on account of his caste. They advised me to write an open letter to the government through a newspaper, demanding cancellation of grants to the school on the basis that I was denied admission.

Accordingly, I sent the letter to *Prabodhan*, which was duly published in my name. It created a lot of turmoil [in the management of the school]. Consequently, the school management called me and enrolled me in the school. Though I was admitted to the school, I was made to sit in a corner outside the classroom on a stool, segregated from the rest of the students. As a result of the published letter signed by me, many people became angry and muttered, "this small kid talking of cancelling the grant of the school; it is due to this attitude that these people are kept away from the society". This small incident marks the beginning of my social activism. In short, I began my social life at the age of 11, when I wrote that letter, protesting against the school management for the injustice and the discrimination it had done to me. Since this event had taken place in Mahad and since Dr Babasaheb had flagged off the movement of the Dalit liberation in Mahad itself, albeit after a decade, I have written about it in so much detail. Another significance attached to this incident came from my own need as well as the need of my class. It is with this spirit that I participated in the movement and spent my later years in social life.

Before Preparing for the Satyagraha Conference 1924

As mentioned earlier, I began the movement against untouchability at a very young age, since I was born in a family belonging to the Untouchable caste. Since then, until 1924, I was active in various social struggles like providing drinking water facility to the Untouchable villagers who came to Mahad from long distances to sell wood; organizing strike against municipality to restore the rights of Untouchable vendors to sell their products; writing a petition to the collector against the ban imposed by vehicle owners on Untouchables for travel, which was also won. However, my real social activism began in 1924. In the month of May that year, I convened a meeting of the prominent members from the Untouchable castes, which decided to hold a conference at Mahad under the presidentship of Dr Ambedkar. The head of the Mahad caste panchayat, Babu More, and community leaders like Raya More, Krisnabua Kinjloliker, Jamadar Kapdekar, Ramji Asgikar, Vargherkar,

Ramji Shirgaonker were present at that meeting. A slipper shop owner from Satara, Maruti Agwane, was also present. During those days the cobbler brethren from Khandesh region used to migrate and set up shops in Konkan region during the eight months of summer. During the rains, they would go back to their own region. People from all the Untouchable castes overwhelmingly welcomed the decision of this meeting. When we used to inform others about how learned Dr Ambedkar was by citing his degrees such as M.A., Ph.D., D.Sc., Bar at Law, etc., the educated Touchables would remark with disdain, "it cannot be. It is impossible for a Mahar to be so learned". We would respond, "he will be present in person at the conference." You can personally meet him and confirm the facts." Soon I went to Bombay and met Babasaheb along with Sambhaji Tukaram Gaikwad, a veteran social worker and the executive member of the Bahishkrut Hitkarini Sabha founded by Babasaheb. I requested Babasaheb to preside over the proposed conference at Mahad. He was very happy to know about the conference but said that we could decide upon the time of the conference later.

Another significant event that occurred during this trip of mine to Bombay was a meeting with Anantrao alias Bhai Chitre of Poladpur, the person who helped and guided me in getting admission in the Mahad English School. When I met Babasaheb, he was sitting close to him and after I finished my conversation with Babasaheb, he led me to his room and very affectionately enquired about the conference and noted the amount of effort we had put in. I provided him all the details about the preparatory work and said that altogether a sum of Rs. 120 is estimated to be collected from the surrounding villages of Mahad, each village contributing Rs. 3. He was happy listening to me and assured me of all possible help from his side. He suggested to me to organize a charity show of *Sahakari Manoranjan Natak Mandal*, which was formed by Shri Kadam to supplement the fund collection for the conference. Accordingly, a play "Sant Tukaram" was staged in Bombay at the Damodar Hall towards the end of the year. We were responsible for the sale of tickets but since we did not know many people in

Bombay, we managed to collect only Rs. 23.50 from this show. That day another memorable incident occurred. I approached Dr Ambedkar and requested him to ask either Balaramdada or someone else to propose a vote of thanks to Chitresaheb and the Drama Company that staged the play. He retorted,"why someone else? You speak". I tried to convince him by pleading that I had never spoken before the city audience. He advised me and insisted that I should speak. In deference to his advice, before the final act of the play started, I stood on the stage of the Damodar Hall and made a speech like school children cite composition in class as dictated by their teachers. This was the first public speech that I gave in my life and interestingly it was with the motivation from none other than the great icon to be of the Dalits. I always cherished it as one of the landmarks of my public life.

During the following years, I would regularly visit Babasaheb during Diwali and May vacations and discuss about the conference. It had become my routine programme. For each of these meetings, Bhai Chitre usually accompanied me. Some times Balaramdada Ambedkar and Subhedar Sawadkar were also around. They had shouldered the responsibility of finalizing the dates for the conference. I requested Bhai Chitre to come for one of the meetings at Mahad in order to convince him about the support for the conference at the local level. But since he couldn't leave important tasks at hand in Bombay, he sent Kamlakant Chitre, who was to became Babasaheb's assistant later and also the first secretary and registrar of the People's Education Society. The meeting presided over by Kamlakant Chitre at Maharwada of Mahad in 1925 was very significant from the point of view of preparations for the historic conference. Subhedar Sawadkar was working with the Jat regiment at that time and had a good influence over the Mahar soldiers in his platoon. He explained the importance of the conference to them and this strengthened the financial side of the conference.

First Glimpse of the Satyagraha 1925

Another noteworthy incident happened in 1923. Shri C.K. Bole, the noted social reformer from the earlier generation who was to become one of the founder members of the People's Education Society and a member of its governing body had tabled a resolution in the Bombay Legislative Council for opening up all the public wells, tanks, *dharmashalas*, other water sources as well as government schools, courts offices and hospitals for the Untouchables. This resolution was passed. Shri Bole had earlier presided over a function where Bhimrao was publicly felicitated after passing the Matriculate examination in 1907. For the Untouchable masses, suppressed under the insults and injustice at every step of life, this resolution naturally came as a ray of hope. They began to think of ways and means to bring this resolution into practice. It would not be an exaggeration to state that this very resolution acted as our main inspiration to hold the grand conference at Mahad under Babasaheb's presidentship. We wanted to achieve two things through this conference. One was that people from this area belonging to our own class of Untouchables as well as the learned people from upper class would come to know about a very highly learned person like Dr Ambedkar and would benefit from his guidance. At the same time, certain hypocritical orthodox elements from the upper castes who considered themselves superior to others and prided over their intelligence and knowledge would get humiliated. The second was to create awareness among the hundreds of Untouchable men and women who came to Mahad every day for work from the surrounding villages about their rights to make use of public places.

In Mahad itself, several military pensioners and those who moved around in various social circles, belonging to the Untouchable castes, had in their own personal capacity striven to assert their rights by challenging old customs by fighting legal battles in courts and even by fighting battles to secure place in canoes for ferrying people of the upper castes across rivers. Another important landmark event that took place during the preparatory phase of the conference was a meeting of about 200-300 people from Veer, Dasgaon, and Goregaon in a *dharmashala* of Dasgaon convened at my initiative. Mamlatdar of Mahad and Police sub Inspector were present at this meeting. In their presence, people were made aware of the 'Bole' resolution and were appealed to assert their rights to use water from the Crawford Well and Tank. Accordingly, we began the programme of fetching water from these water sources right on the same day. Thinking that all this was happening with the permission of the government, no one from the village came forward to obstruct our proceedings or programme. Since then the people who were considered Untouchable have been enjoying their rights over these water sources at these places, along with people from the upper castes. This incident, although extremely important, has not been noted as such since it occurred in an isolated village. Whatever was happening in the Mahad region was inspired by Dr Babasaheb Ambedkar. Beyond this it may not be necessary to detail out to the people well versed with history—a long series of spontaneous and unorganized movement against untouchability since1885.

Conference Dates Finalized

Several factors encouraged Babasaheb to speed up the process of organizing the conference. Significant among them were: Subhedar Sawadkar undertaking the responsibility of financial assistance; Mahad Municipality's decision to support 'Bole' resolution of Bombay Legislative Council under the chairmanship of Surendranath Govind Tipnis; and persistence of Anantarao Chitre and other elderly activists from Konkan area that Babasaheb take up the leadership of the conference. Dr Ambedkar could clearly foresee the impact of all these developments on the future of Indian social life and immediately began to gather resources for the forthcoming struggle. One of the finest reflections of this foresight is the launch of a newspaper called *Bahishkrut Bharat* with my assistance in 1926. Even though Babasaheb had started *Mooknayak* before he was never its official editor. Nevertheless, he was the founder as well as the editor of *Bahishkrut Bharat*. Thus, it was the first newspaper under the editorship of Babasaheb. It had taken several days to decide upon the name and the motto of this newspaper. Once these things were decided, necessary permission for the publication was obtained from the Chief Presidency Magistrate. However, the newspaper was not launched for quite some time. Only after the conclusion of the Mahad conference, the first issue of the newspaper was published. This illustrates how Babasaheb paid systematic attention to the planning and strategy for the liberation war of the Dalit class to be fought in the near future.

It took a long period of three years to finalize the details of this much-awaited conference. The entire Dalit masses of Raigadh and Pratapgadh valley had been eagerly waiting for the conference and Dr Ambedkar's arrival. By this time, the information about the conference had reached the southern region of Kolaba district and northern region of Ratnagiri district by word of mouth. People from these regions also were looking forward to the conference for several reasons. Firstly, Mahad had always been historically important place in the Raigadh region. It was a capital during the reign of *Shivachhatrapati* and was situated almost at the centre of both, southern and northern regions. Secondly, since a majority of the people from this area had been working either as industrial workers in Bombay or in the military as soldiers, they were far more conscious about their human rights and very enraged about the inhuman practice of untouchability. They wanted to fight against this injustice. Thirdly, Bababasaheb's family belonged to this region. People of this area had heard of his intellectual achievements and therefore they had lots of adoration for him. This conference would give them an opportunity to see him and listen to his thoughts. People from the other regions of Maharashtra were not so much aware about this conference until it was over. However, people from certain areas did know about it through word of mouth. Under such circumstances, the dates for the conference were finalized with the consent of Babasaheb as 19 and 20 March 1927.

Activists all Set for Mahad

After learning about the final dates of the conference, Subhedar Sawadkar availed of 2-3 months leave from his platoon, arrived in the village, and began necessary preparation for the conference. Since he was a military officer, several former soldiers and military pensioners from 111 Mahar platoon, which was recently 'demobilized' by the British government, as well as several respected citizens belonging to the Mahar caste came forward to work for the conference, in deference to his call and example. Several activists of the *Konkanastha Mahar Samaj Seva Sangh,* specially formed in Bombay, to render voluntary service to the conference had left for their villages one month before the conference and began campaigning for it. Among them the prominent one was Shiringkar Shivram Gopal Jadhav from Thane who had relentlessly led the struggles against social exploitation in the form of untouchability. The campaign by these activists had created a new wave of enthusiasm among the masses.

The major question before the activists however, was about the premises for the conference. Earlier, several such conferences of the Touchables were held either in the courtyards of temples or similar other prominent premises. Who would provide the place for such a conference of the Untouchables? Leave aside the rabid orthodox; even the self-proclaimed social reformers had no courage to lend their premises for the conference. Nevertheless, as the old adage goes, 'once masses are determined, they can sail through all sorts of difficulties', the activists resolved this problem too. One contractor had erected a theatre made up of bamboos and twig impregnated mud walls at the Mahad bus depot (*gadital*). It bore a long name but was known as 'Vireshwar Theatre'. Famous Mahar Tamasha Artist Shivasambha Kolhapurkar had often performed at this theatre. The local activists approached the contractor and booked the theatre on rent for two days. Normally the theatre remained unused during the daytime. The contractor would earn profit instead of losing anything and therefore he immediately agreed to rent it out. Thus, the problem of the venue of conference was resolved.

Another issue was about the arrangement for lodging and boarding of the delegates. This was resolved by hiring some 4 to 5 small plots of land around the bus depot, close to the theatre. Huge pandals were erected on these plots for cooking as well as the stay of the delegates. The material required for these pandals, such as beams, bamboo, etc., were contributed by the people from near and far either at no cost or nominal cost. All types of big and small utensils necessary for cooking were organized by people from various villages. All these details were worked out at 'Mohoprekar's hotel'. During those days there was a teashop belonging to Deu Joshi located on the eastern side of the bridge in the old market. It may not be appropriate here to narrate the history of this 'Mahar' hotel but it was certainly noteworthy in the environment wherein untouchability was being practiced on a massive scale. This hotel in the market area had become the centre point of the movement. Another hotel was also opened by Raghoram Goyalkar but only after the conference was over.

Mohoprekar's hotel was practically used as the office of the conference. The entire planning for the erection of pandals as well as many other activities had taken place there. Subhedar Sawadkar and other activists used to come to Mahad from their villages early in the morning and leave back late in the evening. Those who could not go back to their villages camped in the nearby villages like Chambharkhind, Vadvali, Shirivli, Kemburly, Pale, Mohopre and Ladvali, just 2 to 3 miles away from Mahad. Some even stayed overnight at the Mohoprekar's hotel. Mahad always used to be full of people during those days. The upper caste Hindus at various levels had taken note of these activities and they had begun to discuss this amongst themselves. They developed a general impression that someone great from the Untouchable community was expected and all this was going on for his sake. Therefore, till this time there was no tension in the minds of the upper caste people about the Untouchables' activities.

Some 20 to 25 activists of Bombay's Mahar Samaj Seva Sangh including veterans like Sambhaji Tukaram Gaikwad and Govind Ramji Adrekar along with others such as Bhivaji Sambhaji Gaikwad, Changdeo Narayan Mohite, Mahadeo Tanaji Gudekar, Keshav Govind Adrekar, Tukaram Vargharker, Ganpatrao Kemburliker, Pandu Babaji Mandlekar, Lakhu Patankar, Sudam Kemburlikar, Pandurang Mahade Salvi,

Raghoram Goyalker, Balu Vamneker, arrived at Mahad, four days prior to the conference to work for its preparation. Only two or three among these activists are still alive [The text was written in 1963-64]. Since some of them were from the nearby villages, they would go back to their homes after working for the whole day. Some leaders like Jadhav and Gaikwad stayed in the hotel and hence it appeared like the base camp of the activists.

Dates of the conference were coming closer. Babasaheb's office was earlier situated in the building of the Damodar Hall. It was shifted to a corner room behind the Damodar Hall in a Marathi school. Another room was rented for the office of the *Bahishkrut Bharat* at Kavarana Building at the corner of Gokhale society lane and was handed over to me. We wished that some leaders of Touchable communities would accompany Dr Ambedkar for the conference. According to Babasaheb's suggestion, a noted lawyer and social worker of Bombay, Trivedi vakil, was requested to attend the conference. However, he gave some lame excuses and declined the invitation. Finally only two leaders form the upper caste communities agreed and attended the conference. One of them was Gangadhar Nilkanth Sahasrabuddhe, known as 'Agarkari Brahman'. He was also the main patron of the Social Service League and the co-operative movement. The other was Anantrao Vinayak Chitre alias Bhai Chitre. The invitation card of the conference bore only the names of Dr Bhimrao Ramji Ambedkar as president and Chitre and Sahasrabuddhe as main speakers. This was the first and the last printed card of the conference meant for the purpose of propaganda. It was sent to all the newspapers but not even one showed any goodwill to publish it.

Arrival of Babasaheb at the Conference

I was responsible for escorting Babasaheb and other leaders to Mahad. There were no facilities for public transport then. People used to travel by a few vehicles that plied on this route. On the early morning of 19 March we left from Bombay and reached the Dak Bungalow of Mahad by afternoon. Those who accompanied Babasaheb from Bombay were Shivram Namdev

Shivtarkar, Bapu Sahasrabuddhe, Bhai Chitre, Balaram Ramji Ambedkar, Ganpat Mahadeo Jadhav alias Madkebuwa, Wakhrikar Gaikwad, Devji Dagduji Dolas, Sitaram Kalu Hate, Dattatray Mahadeo Chitre. Among those who came from Pune included Shantaram Tipnis, Pandurang Nathuji Rajbhoj and others. Entire Mahad town was flooded with the Untouchable masses.

Hundreds of outstation delegates had arrived the previous night at the venue and were camping in the pandals. On the 19th, people poured into the town from all directions. By afternoon, a strong crowd of 5,000 people had already gathered. One striking feature of this congregation was that every delegate except for those who came from Bombay carried a stick in the hand. Those days a person belonging to the Mahar caste would not get out of the house without carrying a stick. Specially while travelling from their village to the other village, they would certainly carry a stick. As for those who cannot sign their name, a thumb impression is considered to be an authentic identification. Likewise, in those days each caste had its own marker that served as its identification in Maharashtra. For example, Kunbi farmers' marker was plough, that for the palanquin carriers' Bhoi was palanquin itself, and for the cobblers, it was a *Rapi* (a flat blade with wooden handle). Likewise, the marker for the Mahars' was their stick. Mahars considered this stick as one of their limbs or as one of their brothers. Therefore, it is obvious from the above description, as to why the huge crowd assembled there was lathi-wielding.

Proceedings Begin

On 19 March 1927, Dr Bhimrao and his colleagues entered Vireshwar theatre hall at 2 p.m. The hall was overflowing with people and several people had to squat outside the theatre. When the president of the Conference, Bhimrao ascended the platform, people did not clap but lifted their sticks and gave him a standing ovation. The entire sight looked awe-inspiring and festive with more than five thousand stocks going up in the air at the same time.

The conference began with my introduction of the important

delegates, who came from Bombay and Pune. After that, Dr Bhimrao, clad in a Bengali style *dhoti,* a shirt and a coat and his face beaming with radiance rose up and began to speak.

People listened to each and every word he spoke with rapt attention, as never before. They were certainly enlightened with a new insight to their life. As they listened to his speech, a conviction and a determination to fight against the perpetrators of injustice according to his teachings was building up within them. His speech made up of direct, but very simple words, continued for one hour. On the same day afternoon, Bhai Chitre and Bapu Sahasrabuddhe also spoke until nightfall. The proceedings of the first day thus came to an end.

Only two prominent citizens from the Touchable castes from Mahad shared seats on the platform with the guests who had come from Bombay. One was Purushottam Prabhakar Joshi alias Bapurao Joshi and other was Tulsaram Mitha. As said before, the other two guests from the upper castes, viz., Bapu Sahasrabuddhe and Bhai Chitre, had come from Bombay. Apart from these four persons from the Touchable communities, no one from either the Hindu or the Muslim community participated in the conference.

The Satyagraha of Chavadar Tank

On the second day of the conference, i.e., on 20 March, proceedings resumed at 9 a.m. People were made aware of their rights and duties through a number of resolutions that were proposed and adopted. Swami Shraddhanand, the founder and the leader of the *Arya Samaj* had recently been murdered. A resolution expressing grief over his death was also passed. Several people spoke on these resolutions. These speeches went on until 12 in the afternoon. Later, Bhai Chitre stood up and made the concluding remarks with the permission of the chair. After thanking the president and the others he said, "Our leader and the president of this conference Dr Ambedkar has ably guided us for the last two days. Among the many resolutions that we have passed there is one that relates with the exercise of our rights over the water from public wells and tanks, etc. We bought water from the Chavadar Tank for the purpose of our conference at the rate of one paisa per pitcher and spent Rs. 40. The Chavadar tank is a public tank. Now it is mid noon and we all are thirsty. So, let us follow our president to the tank and drink water there itself."

With that, the president declared the conclusion of the conference. All the delegates were arranged in files. President Bhimrao Ambedkar descended the platform and began to walk along with his colleagues. Behind him were thousands of lathi-wielding, brave Mahars heading towards the tank. This procession, which was to give a new turn to the history of India, reached the Chavadar Tank. Babasaheb glanced at the tank and then at the Brahman households around the tank. He shoved off the moss over the water with his own hands. By cupping his hands he took some water and drank it. All the people then followed him. The procession turned back. People moved to the pandals where food was being served. Sambhaji Gaikwad and Jadhav went to the base camp in the market and we went to the Dak Bungalow with Babasaheb. Neither any one from the government nor any one from the Touchable communities tried to obstruct the procession. By taking this step of establishing their rights, the Untouchable masses had challenged the thousand year old *varna* system and several regressive institutions which supported it and subjugated the Untouchables to the level of slaves. It had denied them their fundamental right to fetch water from public places. It thus inaugurated the new era of struggles for freedom and liberation.

Those who cherished conservative and rabid orthodox attitude however, could not digest the success of the Mahad conference. They sent their people to the various villages surrounding Mahad on foot and cycles to spread rumours among the farmer community that Mahars have already made the Tank impure and now they would enter the Vireshwara Temple. Falling prey to these rumours and insinuations from the upper caste *Khot-Savkars* (landlords and moneylenders), thousands of poor people from Touchable communities rushed to Mahad to protect their God and religion. They assembled in the premises of the Vireshwar Temple. Encouraged by their presence, some unruly persons in the groups began beating up

Untouchable individuals who wandered around in the market after the conference. This bashing up began two to three hours after the Untouchables had come back from the tank. By this time most of the people had finished their meals and were either leaving or had already left for their respective villages. Some were having their meals and had to leave it halfway as they heard of the attack. The Untouchable people also geared up themselves to face the attackers. They broke the pandals and took away the sticks from them. Some came to the dak bungalow and sought Babasaheb's permission to avenge the cowardly attack on the hapless masses. They were asked to calm down and return to their villages.

Towards the west side of the depot, thousands of Untouchables had assembled. The above-mentioned bands of goons were roaming around freely in the marketplace and in the lanes and the by lanes of the town to catch hold of lone and stray persons from the Untouchable community and beat them. Among those who faced such murderous attack was the young president of the Mahar Samaj Seva Sangh, Bhikaji Sambhaji Gaikwad and some others from Bombay. The streets of the town were sprinkled with the blood of innocent Dalits agitating for fundamental human rights. The goons had also sought to attack the base camp in the market seven times but they were challenged by two old but well-built Mahar activists– Shivram Gopal Jadhav and Sambhaji Tukaram Gaikwad, who stood at the doors with an axe and iron bar in their hands. Behind them was a strong mob of youngsters as back up. Sensing their infuriated demeanor, the goons could not muster courage to attack them. They also could not dare to attack the Untouchables who came in groups. They turned their attention to the shops of cobblers who had come from Khandesh and mercilessly thrashed not only men, but also young and old women. Even small children were not spared from these brutalities. Noted Untouchable leaders like Bhanudas Kambli and P.N. Rajbhoj were also injured seriously in these attacks.

The War Begins

Babasaheb was sitting along with his colleagues in the mango plantation in front of the dak bungalow to discuss the matter related to the news of the above attacks. Babasaheb immediately asked me and Datta Chitre to send a telegram to the D.S.P. He and his colleagues were engrossed in deep thoughts. Babasaheb seemed angry. People trickled in every five to ten minutes with different account of the scuffles. Someone brought the news that one group of goons had gone to the house of Surba and enquired about Chitre and had threatened to kill him with an iron bar. Chitre smiled over this and remarked, "why an iron bar? Even a small stick is enough to take my life!" Balaram Ambedkar, the elder brother of Babasaheb, and some other activists were also thinking over the future course of events. More and more people from the conference began to pour in there to protect their leaders. They were however asked to go back. At around 4.30 pm, Mamlatdar and the D.S.P. arrived at the dak bungalow. They informed Babasaheb that two large groups of agitated people, one from the Touchable and the other from the Untouchable communities had congregated in the town. The police force was inadequate and that they were trying their level best to restore peace. They also said that the leaders of the Touchables were ready for negotiation and asked his opinion. In response, Babasaheb said, "We are ready for the talks and you can ask the Touchable leaders to come to the dak bungalow." The officials however, said that the Touchables wanted Babasaheb to come there. It was a sensitive decision. Babasaheb gave consent to their request and began to go with them .We were about ten to twelve persons with him. As we approached the road close to Vireshwar temple, some among the thousands of Touchables who had assembled in the temple premises began to shout and scream. The government officials asked their leaders to stop the commotion and they stopped it. Dr Ambedkar and those with him stood on the road and under a weird setting, the discussions between the leaders of the Touchables, who had assembled in the temple premises, about 40 to 50 steps away, and of the Untouchables who were on the road, in the form of question-answers in the following manner:

Dinganker: Is it true that you went to the Chavadar tank and made it impure?

Ambedkar: Since that tank is a public property, we do have the right to use its water. It is true that we did execute our right.

Dingankar: Is it true that you would be entering the Vireshwar temple?

Ambedkar: No. We have not decided to enter the temple, nor do we need to enter the temple.

After this brief dialogue, the talks were over and we returned to the dak bungalow. These talks were held on the road, in the midst of thousands of people. This incident is worth writing in golden letters in the history of the struggle of the Untouchables. While these talks were on, two persons from our group were hurt by the stones hurled at us. This incident has been described by Babasaheb in *Bahishkrut Bharat* as 'Once we were in the jaws of death'.

After returning to the bungalow, we began to think about our travel plans to Bombay. There was no provision of going to Bombay from Mahad by ship and a trip to Dasgaon was necessary for that. Whichever way one thought, there was no option other than spending a night in Mahad. At about 5.30 p.m., Mamlatdar and the police officials came to the dak bungalow again and told us that though most of the Touchables and Untouchables had left the town, there was still some tension around. Many Untouchables had not left Mahad since Dr Ambedkar was around and so many others were also not leaving the market. Under such circumstances it would not be possible to provide adequate security at the bungalow. They further requested us to spend the night at the government office and assured that all the necessary arrangements would be made there. We told them that we did not need their security and we would leave Mahad the next day afternoon. They, however, pleaded that we should go to the government office. Eventually, we agreed with them. Our luggage was carried by the police in bullock carts. We all walked up along with Babasaheb to the police station. During that night, some sympathizers from the Touchable communities brought *jilebis* and other eatables for us. Alimia Kazi from Pale visited Babasaheb in the night and told him that he would provide his car to go to Bombay. Accordingly, he came with the car the next morning. On 21

March, we left by that car and reached Bombay in the afternoon. On the same day Dr Babasaheb Ambedkar declared his decision to hold the second conference in Mahad very shortly. Within just nine months, the second conference, widely known as the 'second historic conference', was organized on 25 December 1927.

The Second Satyagraha Conference

Within a week after the conclusion of the conference of *Bahishkrut Parishad* of Kolaba District, the first issue of the periodical, *Bahishkrut Bharat* was published. In this issue detail report of the events at Mahad conference was given. In the following issues of *Bahishkrut Bharat*, which began to come out regularly, Babasaheb wrote thought provoking and hard hitting editorials towards awakening of the Untouchable masses of Maharashtra. He instilled requisite consciousness in them to fight for their rights. At the same time, he successfully countered the protagonists of caste discrimination and untouchability from the Touchable castes, who openly voiced their orthodox thoughts in a blatant manner, and provoked them to introspect. He decided to organize a Satyagraha at Mahad and called it the 'Crusade of Mahad'. He wrote three editorials in *Bahishkrut Bharat* titled, 'Crusade of Mahad and Duties of the Untouchables', 'Crusade of Mahad and Duties of the Touchables' and 'Crusade of Mahad and Duties of the Government'. Through these editorials, he made everyone understand his altruistic vision, seeking a society based on the principles of equality. The activity for the publicity of the Satyagraha and awareness among Untouchable masses was not only carried out through *Bahishkrut Bharat*, but also through small and big propaganda meetings. Besides, the incidents related to the Mahad Satyagraha were also discussed through other newspapers. Obviously, not only young and enthusiastic Untouchable activist like Karmaveer Bhaurao Gaikwad, but several other activists from the Touchable communities also were attracted towards this peoples' movement launched by Babasaheb that was aimed at gaining self respect for the Untouchable masses. Several great figures like Acharya M.V.

Donde, Shyamrao Parulekar, P.G. Kanekar, S.C. Joshi, Barrister Samarth along with Bhai Chitre, Bapu Sahasrabuddhe came in close contact with Babasaheb. Activists of the *Samaj Samata Sangh*, which was formed after the first conference, like Devrao Naik, D.V. Pradhan, R.D. Kavli, Asaikar, Raghunath Kadrekar and Gupte also began to participate in the activities spearheaded by Babasaheb. Most of them had come for the Satyagraha Conference of Mahad held on 25th December 1927.

The entire task of preparation for the Satyagraha conference was being carried out under the direct leadership of Babasaheb. The liberation movement of the Untouchables had gained a renewed vigour by then. The bloodshed and the brutalities of 20 March could not shake the self confidence of the Untouchables. On the contrary, it strengthened their resolve to fight for their human rights and brightened up the flame of self confidence within them. They became more defiant. In accordance to the decisions taken in the first conference, people in that area gave up their traditional caste jobs assigned to them, such as skinning of dead cattle and other mandatory village duties. The Touchables termed this act as a strike declared by our community, which was not quite untrue. Enraged by the inconvenience caused by the Untouchables and their zealous assertion of their rights, many Touchable Hindus and Muslims harassed them in many different ways. However, the self respecting Mahar community did not budge. It used the language of tit for tat, abuse for abuse and lathi for lathi. They made their opponents aware of the spirit of self respect inculcated within them. However, in this process, several people had to abandon their households and villages. Nonetheless, they did not care and remained steadfast. While on the one hand they augmented their power of resistance in the face of atrocities, unleashed by the traditionalist, on the other they busied themselves in a dual task of preparation for the Satyagraha conference and the implementation of resolutions of the first conference. These tasks were complementary; they were the inseparable parts of the same activity.

Some rabid traditionalists and orthodox elements tried to go against the tide of time and discredit the civil and the peaceful movement launched by the Untouchable masses to restore their human rights. They purified the Chavadar tank by emptying out 108 earthen pots full of *gomutra* (cow's urine) into it. The Mahad Municipality cunningly withdrew the pompous resolution passed earlier, declaring the Chavadar tank open to all. Reactionary forces with their cloak and the dagger attitude sued Ambedkar for polluting the Chavadar tank. Pretending as the representatives of all the major castes, they obtained restraining order from the court that prohibited the Untouchables from the using the water of the Chavadar tank. The government imposed restraining orders on Babasaheb and thus, even the British government came forward to suppress the rights of the Untouchables by siding with the traditionalists. Naturally, the Untouchables had to fight on two fronts: firstly, against the religious traditionalist as well as the backwards from the majority Touchable community and secondly, against the foreign British rulers who had subjugated the Indian masses into political, economic and social slavery.

Ready for Sacrifice

Babasaheb was not at all affected by the restraining order of the government. In fact, he had already anticipated it. The activists of the conference too were undeterred by this. Leaders of the *Mahar Samaj Seva Sangh*, Sambhaji Tukaram Gaikwad, Shivram Gopal Jadhav, and Govind Ramji Adrekar were sent to the surrounding villages for campaigning for the conference two months earlier. Adrekar was determined to fight at the cost of his life and even went to the extent of carrying materials needed for his final rites. Later when he passed away in Bombay, Babasaheb had lent his shoulder to the coffin and walked up to the crematorium. Along with these campaigners from Bombay, Kamalakant Kashinath Tipnis and Wamanrao Patki also went from village to village for the publicity of the conference. Later they were felicitated by the Satyagraha Conference and rewarded with Gold medal for their exemplary services. During the preparatory phase of the previous Satyagraha conference, Dr Ambedkar Seva Dal was formed with this author's initiative. It was patterned on Dr Hardikar Seva Dal of the Indian National

Congress. According to Babasaheb's instruction, this band of volunteers was renamed as the *Samata Sainik Dal.* The first G.O.C. of the organization was Shankar Laxman Wadvalkar, an enthusiastic youth from Konkan and its Secretary was Uddhav Laxman Karandikar (Panch Mukh), a noted speaker from Pune district. Current veteran leaders of the *Bauddha Panchayat Committee,* Sakharam Bhivaji Lotekar and Arjun Gopal Jatekar were the main organizers of the *Samata Sainik Dal.* The main centers for the preparation for the conference were at Fort, Dhobitalav, Chandanwadi, chawls of Clark Road, and Poybawadi.

The Touchables of many villages had challenged the Untouchables by saying, "We will see how you will get out of the villages to drink the water of the Chavadar tank". The Untouchables also responded in similar vein and accepted the challenge. They would say, "This Satyagraha is not like the Satyagraha of Gandhi but it is like the one of Pandavas against Kauravas, inspired by Krishna in Bhagavad-Gita." This definition of the Satyagraha by Babasaheb had already reached the ears of people. Besides, [Untouchable] people were aware of the challenge thrown by the villagers and were ready to attend the conference with the determination to do or die. Several brave *Satyagrahis* left their houses one or two days before the conference after completing the religious rituals and praying to their family deity for success. Some also wiped off the vermilion mark from the foreheads of their wives before leaving their houses. Warm farewells were accorded to them from every village. These brave *satyagarahis,* who marched like disciplined soldiers from every village, neither faced any obstruction nor met with any challenge from the Touchables in their village. People were stunned with their organization and determination. They began to exclaim, "one cannot say what would happen if the path of these 'spirited Mahars is crossed!" By the time the first session of the conference began, over 15,000 *satyagrahis* had already assembled at the main camp.

The huge pandal of the conference and the main camp for the satyagrahis were located between the garden of Vaidyas on the Raigadh Road and the present *Bauddhawada.* Babasaheb was to stay at the house of Kamu More, a reputed citizen from Bauddhawada. Other Touchable and Untouchable leaders also were to stay at Bauddhawada. Since the conference was held in front of Bauddhawada, we could use water of the well there. Therefore, we did not have to buy water like we did for the first conference. This time food was also not prepared. Bags full of gram and puffed rice (*chana kurmura*) and jaggery that would last for a week for all the *satyagrahis* were brought from outside and stored. Because, the shopkeepers of Mahad had decided not to sell anything for the conference. Many of them along with many residents had abandoned the town as if plague was going to strike it. Seeing the defiant resolve of the Untouchables to come for the conference at Mahad, undermining the opposition from the Touchables and the restraint imposed by the government, they would not know what might happen. Another reason, which compelled people to leave Mahad, was the frequent visits of the government officials and police. Even before the Satyagraha could commence, hundreds of heavily guarded armed police were protecting the Chavadar tank from all sides round the clock. English D.S.P. and other police officials inspected this security arrangement minutely at frequent intervals. Due to all these happening, there was an atmosphere of palpable fear that prevailed in Mahad.

Apprehending that it might not be possible to reach Mahad if private vehicle owners operating on the Bombay-Mahad route were denied transportation and created hurdles (the entire situation could be easily foreseen), we decided to go to Mahad by ship. During those days, it was possible to go to Hareshwar port from Mumbai and then to Dasgaon through Bankot creek. A list of those who wished to attend the conference was prepared and arrangements were made to carry more than three hundred such people by ship. Several activists from various districts of Maharashtra had already arrived in Bombay to accompany Babasaheb for the conference. On 24 December, Bhimrao Ambedkar clad in a pure *khadi dhoti,* shirt (*sadra)* and *uparne* (a length of cloth worn across shoulder) left to board the ship with papers of the government order in his pocket. His outfit looked like that of Das Babu[2] at that time. Some of his

Touchable and Untouchable colleagues assembled at his office and left for *Bhaucha Dhakka* (pier to board the ship) in the afternoon. Two batches of the Dr Ambedkar Seva Dal from St. George Hospital Chawl and Parel Cement Chawl had already reached the wharf one hour before under the leadership of Sakharam Bhamgharkar, an educated youth. During those days, no one would wear Khaki uniform except for military men. When some Touchables saw volunteers of our organization in khaki uniform, they thought that Ambedkar was accompanied by military forces. As soon as Dr Ambedkar reached the wharf, volunteers blew and greeted him with military style salute. Thereafter they boarded the ship. The ship reached the port of Hareshwar at around 8 in the evening. Babasaheb was accorded a grand welcome by hundreds of people from Shrivardhan and Janjira area by blowing horn, thanks to the efforts of Pandurang Jadhav and Dharma Buwa Ostekar, leading activists from the *Mahar Samaj Seva Sangh*.

The Untouchables were disturbed over the rumours that the traditionalists were planning to murder Ambedkar when he reached the thinly populated sand belt of Hareshwar in the night. Therefore they had assembled there in large numbers with a strong determination to protect their leader even at the cost of their lives. They had made excellent lodging and boarding arrangement for the guests arriving by ship. Excited by the view of endless ocean and moonlit night, satyagrahis of Bombay could not realize how fast the night passed. Next morning our journey began by another boat from Bandkot to Dasgaon. Only delegates to the conference and the crew were present on this boat. While travelling, Babasaheb and his colleagues discussed issues among themselves. Entire atmosphere on the boat was fraught with joy and excitement. Babasaheb's village Ambawade (the real name is Ambadwe) is close to Nigade Port in this creek. Our boat anchored at Dasgaon port at around one o' clock in the afternoon. Hundreds of volunteers wearing badges of reception committee were present there. They welcomed Babasaheb by shouting slogans hailing him and the conference. At that juncture, a European D.S.P arrived with a police squad and he delivered a letter by the collector in Babasaheb's hands. Babasaheb read it and directly left for the collector's residence along with Bapu Sahasrabuddhe to Mahad by D.S.P.'s vehicle after leaving necessary instructions for us. Observing these things, a lot of people felt that Babasaheb was arrested. This misunderstanding was cleared by the author and Bhai Chitre. Later, all of us came to Dharmashala near Dasgaon road. Thousands of *satyagrahis* from Rohe, Mangaon and Goregaon areas had already camped there. They were told that we would be marching to Mahad in a procession. A three mile long procession lead by Bhai Chitre and followed by some other leaders as well as volunteers of Dr Ambedkar Seva Dal, who had come from Bombay, and the batches of satyagrahis reached the main camp of Mahad at about 6 'o clock in the evening. The necessary preparations to commence the proceedings of the conference were over by now. Important resolutions to be tabled at the conference and objectionable excerpts from *Manusmruti* were already compiled in Bombay. The guest delegates and the audience from various places had already gathered in Mahad. Arrangements of their stay and meals were already made. The main office of the conference was set up at the house where Babasaheb resided. Yet another office was set up in the *dharmashala* built for the Untouchables near Bauddhawada. The grand pandal where sessions of the conference were to be held was decorated with floral buntings and plaques with quotations. A special chair for the president, a beautifully covered table and some 15 to 20 chairs adorned the platform. It is understood that there were no loudspeakers then.

Proceedings of the Second Conference Begin

After Babasaheb returned from the collector's residence, the session of the conference began. He read his specially written speech. In his address, he mentioned that the conference was being ceremoniously convened in order to begin a new era of equality in India. More importantly and prophetically, he compared it with the French Revolution of 1789. That day's proceedings ended after certain declaration and resolutions. For dinner, everybody was served *channa-kurmura* and jaggery.

Babasaheb and his colleagues refused to eat the special food cooked for them and satisfied their hunger with *channa-kurmura* like others. At 10 in the night, Babasaheb called all the leading activists to discuss the next day's proceedings. He said, "Our proposed Satyagraha will happen tomorrow. Those who participate in the Satyagraha may have to go to jail. The government will put me behind the bars too. I have come prepared to go to jail. Now after taking into account the views of all gathered here we will have to decide whether to go ahead with the Satyagraha or not". After listening to these words some activists became restless. Shivtarkar said, "Doctor, if you go to jail, people would be demoralized. There would be no leader left behind you and the traditionalist Touchables and the government will crush our movement. So I feel that the Satyagraha should be withdrawn". I immediately reacted, "under no circumstances we should withdraw the Satyagraha". After that several people opined against the Satyagraha stating various reasons. Some of the reasons given were like they could not participate in Satyagraha as they were government servants, etc.

Bhaurao Gaikwad with his hard hitting speech silenced their voices. For the first time, I witnessed Bhaurao delivering a speech. Some people supported the plan of the Satyagraha but suggested that Babasaheb should not participate in it. Majority was in favor of the Satyagraha. Babasaheb was carefully listening to everyone's view in silence. Finally, he said, "If there are 1000 people who are ready to perform the Satyagraha and go to jail, we should go ahead with it". It was 12 in the night by the time this decision was taken. A draft of the pledge to be taken by the satyagrahis was prepared. The significant part of the draft ran as follows: "I am ready to go to jail, fight and die by performing Satyagraha". Several copies of this draft were prepared at the office in Dharmashala, and were distributed among the educated to collect the thumb impressions of the *satyagrahis*. By 4 o'clock in the morning 3,500 people had registered their consent.

In addition, more were coming forward. Therefore, the task of collecting signatures was suspended. The wads of signed papers were presented to Babasaheb at 4.30 a.m. when he was wide awake along with the entire camp of satyagrahis. At 7 o' clock in the morning Babasaheb asked me to deliver a letter to the collector. When I was going with the letter, I did not see a single soul on the road on my way to the dak bungalow. The entire market was looking desolate. As soon as I delivered the letter to the collector, he glanced at it and sent a verbal message through me that he would arrive there shortly and sent me back. I delivered the message to Bababsaheb. Bapu Sahasrabuddhe, who was close to Babasaheb, jokingly remarked, "How did they send you back without arresting?" I did not say anything. There were a few people around Babasaheb that time. Others had left for the meeting hall. That day's session began at 9 a.m. with the burning of the *Manusmruti*. A special place for the holy pyre was erected close to the pandal. Necessary material for ritualistic offering to the fire (*homa havana*) were organized. Babasaheb was standing in front of the fire and Bapu Sahasrabuddhe was dropping the sheets of objectionable excerpts from Manusmruti from Babasaheb's hand into the fire after reading them. There was a jubilant reaction among the people as this programme went on.

After this programme of burning *Manusmruti*, Babasaheb again occupied his chair. Huge mass of people sat peacefully with the intent of listening to his speech giving the future course of events. They knew they were witnessing a historic moment that would change the course of history. Around this time, the district collector Mr Hood came to the entrance of the Pandal. Subhedar Raghoram Ghatge received him and escorted him to the dais. The collector addressed the assembled crowd in Marathi. The gist of his speech was, "We do not believe in the discrimination between Touchables and Untouchables. We agree with your right of using the water of the public tank. However, Hindus have claimed that the Chavadar tank is not a public, but a private property. Till this claim is resolved, you shouldn't perform the proposed Satyagraha". Finally, he thanked the president and left the meeting after his speech.

At this stage, President asked those who were in favour of and those who were opposed to the Satyagraha to speak. Some

18 to 20 people spoke. Only four to five speakers opposed the plan of Satyagraha, whereas the rest of the speakers overwhelmingly supported it. Now the responsibility of taking the final decision came to Babasaheb after weighing the pros and cons of the prevailing situation. He rose to deliver his speech. Firstly, he appreciated the brave and selfless attitude of the people. He further said, "We are the vanguards of the war waged for our fundamental rights and equality. We have proved to our opponents that the strength of our organization is enormous. Our opponents are hiding behind the government by contending in the court that the Chavadar tank is a private property. It is proved that we are stronger than our opponents in the fight for our rights. When one wrestler is already declared stronger than the other in the arena, there is no need for the stronger wrestler to hit the weaker one to prove a point. So instead of performing the Satyagraha let us conserve our energy for future struggles. Not performing the Satyagraha today does not mean giving up the struggle. We have to fight many more battles in the future". This is not the full speech of Babasaheb but a gist of it. The conference agreed with this view of Babasaheb not to perform the Satyagraha. Later delegates marched to the Chavadar tank in a procession and came back to the pandal after taking a round of tank. The same night those who took special efforts to make the conference successful were felicitated and presented with badges and medals at the hands of Babasaheb in a special meeting. The conference concluded with this.

Second Conference and After

After the conference was over, Babasaheb along with other guests leisurely went on an excursion of the Buddhist caves at *Pale* and later on went to see Raigadh fort which was the capital of Shiva Chhatrapati at one time. Traditionalists knew that he would be spending the night there at the fort. They instigated poor Touchables in villages around Raigadh area by telling them false and fabricated stories. When the Untouchables got the wind of this news that a conspiracy was being hatched by the Touchables to go to the fort and murder Dr Ambedkar, they climbed up the fort through several hidden paths and blocked all the entrances to the fort. Some of the main activists went to the spot where Babasaheb was sleeping at midnight and woke everyone by sprinkling water. They cautioned against the possible danger and assured of full protection. This ever inspiring, illustrious history of brave Mahars from this area will live forever, and perhaps it would explain why Babasaheb chose this area to lay the foundation of his movement for equality.

After the above mentioned conferences at Mahad, more conferences of farmers opposing the *khoti* system, which was one of the worst forms of exploitation by the Indian *zamindari* and feudal system, were led by Babasaheb along with the *Bahishkrut* conferences organized to create awareness among the Untouchables. These conferences were attended by both the Touchable and the Untouchable farmers. Through this, he amply demonstrated that his movement was not against the Touchable masses but against the unjust societal order supporting reactionary caste and *varna* system. I worked in his movement with great zeal. During the entire movement, he published several periodicals. However, he sought my assistance exclusively in running the *Bahishkrut Bharat*.

Later Devrao Naik, and Bhaskar Raghunath Kadrekar came to the fore during the publication of *Samata* and *Janata*. Of course, although Babasaheb launched 'Samata' and 'Janata' later, during the entire tenure of *Bahishkrut Bharat*, right since its inception, he kept me actively associated with it. Even after the launch of *Janata*, he appointed me on its editorial board although had already become a communist by then. Later I left *Janata* willingly with the permission of Babasaheb due to the growing burden of activities of mass movement of the workers and peasants class. It would not be out of place to mention here that in the meanwhile I had launched a weekly periodical called *Avhan* and the government had clamped it down. Thus this author has participated with full faith and conviction as the front runner of the movement of the Untouchables for freedom and self-reliance launched by Babasaheb till the end of 1931. He later threw himself into the communist movement during the period of repression on the peasants-workers movement.

During all those years, I never verbally or in a written manner indulged in any false propaganda either against the freedom movement or against Babasaheb. Since my views were known to Babasaheb, he would often call me for discussions. Among many reasons, which made me to turn to the communist ideology, interestingly Babasaheb's own teaching was the main one. And I had openly told him about it. Due to this he felt satisfied when he saw as to how one of his trusted followers drew inspiration from him and accepted a life dedicated to public wellbeing by becoming a communist. This was very obvious from the affection that he showered upon me till the date of his *Mahaparinirvan* (death).

My analysis of Dr Babasaheb as a leader is that he was not merely a leader of the Untouchables but was a great national leader of the crores of Indians belonging to all the religions and speaking all the languages. He had realized that the caste discrimination was among the worst kind of slavery that existed in the world and a dark stain on humanity. So he firstly undertook the task of fighting against it and provided more attention to it. Without analysing him objectively, some political commentators and intellectuals, under the influence of casteism, ridicule him as a sectional leader of certain communities of people. The Indian people have lost their prospect of welfare and revolutionary change and suffered tremendous losses because his massive intellectual and organizational strength was not used to abolish social and economic slavery in this country. Had he been alive today, he would have impelled his followers to push the wheel of Indian social revolution with renewed vigour. He would have certainly moved that wheel himself and provided new vitality to India. This can be stated without any doubt, considering his vision for new India that he had always cherished.

NOTE AND REFERENCES

1. See, a sample letter reproduced by Khairmode, C.B., op. cit., p. 269.
2. Khairmode, C.B., op. cit., p. 273.

6

Looking Back, Moving Forward: Reflecting on Mahad

"History without politics descends to mere literature"

-Sir John Robert Seely

Mahad symbolizes a beacon for Dalits. With a respectable exception of Ayyankali's movement in Kerala as discussed earlier (See p. 56), which preceded Mahad by more than two decades, it is here that for the first time Dalits have shown their collective resolve to discard the yoke of caste slavery and assert their human rights. Mahad was preceded by even other movements against certain aspects of castes and for civil rights like right to temple entry or access to public water source. In fact, as part of the Mahad campaign, it was technically preceded by a successful access to the Crawford Well at Dasgaon, not very far from Mahad (See pp. 118, 289). They all are important as markers in Dalit movement and as the contributors to germination of Dalit consciousness. But they were mostly sporadic and remained localized without any articulation of their socio-historical significance. The difference between Mahad and them mainly lay in the organization and leadership; they lacked in elements of organization and the charismatic leadership of Dr Ambedkar. In the absence of these elements, they could not articulate their wider theoretical and historical significance beyond their locale. Even Vaikom Satyagraha (1924-25) for the civil rights of the lower castes to get access to a temple, which predates Mahad, lacked the aura of the latter despite its association with a galaxy of mainstream leaders including Mahatma Gandhi and the extent of publicity. (See Chapter 1,

p. 87). Although, it enjoyed prominence in the mainstream history, it failed to occupy the same iconic place as Mahad among Dalits. Of course, Vaikom was neither inspired nor led by Dalits. By the scale of its organization, articulation of vision, self-inspiration and leadership Mahad is unprecedented as the revolt of Dalits for their civil rights. As an instance in the civil rights movement of the downtrodden it must occupy a prominent place even in world history.

Like most things associated with Babasaheb Ambedkar, Mahad has become folklore among Dalits today. Apart from its earliest narrative, which also has been confined to Marathi, there is hardly any introspective review or analytical discussion of its form, content, and contribution in shaping the movement of Dalits. As it could be the tone setter for the future Dalit movement possibly embodying the philosophy and strategic orientation of Babasaheb Ambedkar, it is imperative to take a critical look at Mahad in order to understand the Dalit movement itself. In this chapter, an attempt is made to objectively reflect upon some of the salient dimensions of Mahad; firstly to situate it into the universal space of human emancipation and secondly to gain certain insights which may help in possible course correction in the contemporary Dalit movement.

1. Gandhian Influence in Mahad

In popular imagination Mahad is associated with Satyagraha. However, it is not fully true. The first conference did not have any reference to Satyagraha. Even when the decision to march to the Chavadar Tank was taken after conclusion of the first conference, it was not referred to as Satyagraha. The second conference was however consciously planned as a Satyagraha Conference. The organization of both the conferences had the full approval of Dr Ambedkar; the second being purely of his own conception. The first conference was presided over by him only after satisfying himself with its organizational details. The method of struggle adopted in both the conferences reflected the deep influence of Mahatma Gandhi. Later, Babasaheb Ambedkar became the most unsparing critic of Gandhi[1]. That image has almost eclipsed the little known fact that he was equally influenced by Gandhi during his early years. He was chosen as a singular ideal for the conference inasmuch as the only picture that adorned both the conference venues was that of Gandhi. Keeping in mind the state of the Dalits in those days, even a picture of some Hindu god or Shivaji Maharaj or even the British Emperor would have been easier choices. Dr Ambedkar those days can be seen as a normal Hindu, with *jai bhawani* printed on the top of his letterhead.[2] In an edit note under the title 'Discussion on Satyagraha' in *Bahishkrut Bharat* of 21 November 1927, just a few days before the historic Satyagraha at Mahad, he said that he had taken the ideology of Satyagraha from the *Bhagavad-Gita*. He wrote:

> Some people will be surprised that we take support of the Gita in respect of our Satyagraha. It is generally thought that Satyagraha is not the subject matter of the Gita. But in our opinion, this understanding is quite incorrect. Satyagraha is the only manifest subject matter of the Gita. If one carefully considered why the Gita was advised in the first place, one could easily realize the veracity of our statement. One needs to pay attention to the question asked by Arjuna and the answer given by Shrikrishna in the Gita. When Arjuna withdraws from the chariot and Lord Shrikrishna says to him, "Do not sit, Insist upon war against those who have taken away your ruling authority", Arjuna asks Shrikrishna a basic question: "tell me, how is this insistence (*agraha*) a Satyagraha?" The entire Gita is the answer to this single question given by the Lord God. There is no other manifest subject matter in the Gita beyond the Satyagraha.[3]

Later, during his cross examination in the suit filed by the caste Hindus on 27 March 1930, he had stated, "I do not consider the *Bhagavad-Gita* or any other scripture as divine or venerable. Though I do not follow *Veda*, I would like to be called a *sanatani* (orthodox) Hindu."[4] Therefore, a picture of some god indicative of divine blessings to the delegates who were beginning a battle for their freedom would have been just natural. Shivaji, whom Dr Ambedkar held in great esteem could have been another inspiring figure for the impending struggle that Mahad symbolized. Mahad being under the shadow of his Raigadh, he would have been a pertinent hero. Or George V, the then emperor of India, could have been another figurehead benefactor, whose protective power could be invoked against the orthodox Hindus. Or Mahatma Phule, or Gopal Baba Walangkar or even the contemporary local social reformers like Gopal Ganesh Agarkar could have been natural choice. Indeed, the slogans of victory were shouted in all their names during procession. But strangely, it was Gandhi, a *baniya* from Gujarat, who overshadowed all of them!

Gandhian influence could perhaps be discerned even in the way Dr Ambedkar dressed himself for the conference. He had worn a Bengali style khadi *dhoti-kurta*. What was it about Gandhi that impressed Ambedkar so much? It is true that Gandhi had returned to India with a halo of a nonviolent fighter against the racial discrimination by the British in South Africa. He had transformed the Congress which was a club of the high class and caste elites as a mass organization. It was he who first spoke against untouchability, and pushed it into the mainstream agenda of the Congress. And whatever has been his real contribution, he was credited with being on the side of the low castes in the Vaikom Satyagraha. These facts surely may have created a positive impact on Ambedkar's mind as they did on most people. Surprisingly, he has never spoken or written anything which would even remotely indicate this Gandhian influence on him prior to Mahad conference. Even in his speeches in the conference there has not been any mention of Gandhi's inspiration. Rather, writing in the context of Vaikom Satyagraha, he appears critical of Gandhi for not giving as much importance to the removal of untouchability as to the propagation of khadi and Hindu-Muslim unity. He wrote, "If he did, he would insist on the removal of untouchability as a precondition for entrance into Congress as he has insisted on spinning as a precondition for voting in Congress." But he also concluded, "... when no one else comes near us, even Mahatma Gandhi's sympathy is of no little importance".[5] Perhaps this logic informed his having Gandhi as the icon of inspiration during the Mahad struggle.

But it was not true that Gandhi alone came closer to Dalits.

There were others who spoke against untouchability and worked for the Dalits. What differentiated Gandhi from other reformers was his persona, his charisma and his moral power over Hindus. No other person could match him on this count. It was only Gandhi, who could influence the Hindus to adopt reforms in the Hindu society, if he wished. It was important for Dr Ambedkar, as then he did rear a hope of reforming the Hindu society from within. He had internalized the virtue of gradualism from his Fabian teachers in US and UK, which reflected in the focus on a single issue of untouchability in the agendas for the Mahad conferences. This reformist optimism informed his stratagem for the struggle at Mahad. He imagined that with agitations as in Mahad, the injustice and irrationalities of the Hindu customs and institutions would be exposed to the *savarna* Hindus, who would then be inspired to undertake reforms in the Hindu society. No one else better fitted the bill from this consideration. His mild complaint against Gandhi rather unwittingly, reveals his expectations from Gandhi. Even though he showed his disagreement with Gandhi's obsession about non-violence being the defining attribute of Satyagraha[6], nevertheless he would accept his method of Satyagraha.

2. Could Satyagraha be a Method for the Mahad Struggle?

Gandhian influence pervades the methodology of Satyagraha adopted for the Mahad struggle. However here, we are not discussing Gandhi's influence, the logic of which has been explicated in the previous pages, but the applicability and efficacy of the method of Satyagraha in a struggle by the people like Dalits.

The term 'Satyagraha', literally meaning 'insistence on truth' or 'soul force'[7], is a particular philosophy and practice within the broader category known as nonviolent resistance or passive resistance. It was coined and developed by Mahatma Gandhi[8], as a means of striving for truth and social justice through love, suffering, and conversion of the oppressor. Its tactic is active nonviolent resistance. Satyagraha relies on the notion that the moral appeal to the conscience and heart is more effective than an appeal based on threat and violence. In Gandhi's terminology, Satyagraha—truth-force—was an *outgrowth* of nonviolence, essentially relies upon the opponent melting under moral pressure exerted by sufferings of the satyagrahis. It is premised on the inveterate faith in the decency of human being and the strength of conscious. As a matter of fact, the change happens in Satyagraha in three ways: The first way is through *conversion*, in which the opponent becomes changed inwards. This is the true 'melting' that Gandhi would desire. The second is through *accommodation*, in which the opponent decides it is best to give in but still disagrees. This is what would happen in most cases; the opponent would just yield as a tactical escape. The third is through nonviolent *coercion*, in which the opponent disagrees and wants to continue the conflict, but is unable to do so.[9]

Satyagraha necessarily involves three things: (i) opponent, (ii) cause, and (iii) salience of self-suffering of a satyagrahi to his opponent. How does one identify these three elements in the case of the Mahad Satyagraha? The proposed Satyagraha of the Untouchables was for eradication of untouchability and identified its protagonists and practitioners, the caste Hindu society as an opponent. The goal of eradication of untouchability however, is amorphous; it could manifest through certain civil rights; rights not to be discriminated against in matters of access to various public amenities and other such. Who could grant these rights? Only some institution on behalf of the society could do it, as society itself, is an abstraction. Earlier, a religious body could do it as a hegemonic institution but today it is the state, which is vested with these powers. Therefore, the logical way to eradicate untouchability is to eradicate its manifestation through exercise of civil rights to be granted by the state. There could be struggles, including Satyagraha for demanding these civil rights. The operative dynamics of these rights (their exercise, resistance by the entrenched interests and state intervention in terms of protecting the former and punishing the latter) is expected to induce change in societal attitudes. Of course, if society proactively reforms itself to accept these rights, it would be so much better for their establishment. The change in society's attitude and culture can be brought about only over a long time with a sustained movement, which the Dalit movement could do. As for Chavadar Tank, the civil rights were already granted by the state to Dalits to access any public amenity. It was a matter of only exercising them. On 20 March 1927, when Dalits collectively marched to drink water from the Chavadar Tank in their exercise, it was the duty of the state to protect them. It failed in its duty, when the caste Hindu goons assaulted Dalits. The available documentation indicates that the state machinery just looked the other way, as it usually does, while orthodox elements had collected to avenge pollution of the Chavadar Tank and attacked Dalits. It is only on the complaints filed by Dalits that the police had arrested nine culprits.

When the Satyagraha[10] was planned at the Chavadar Tank, it was obviously against the caste Hindus and not the state[11], which was actually a culprit. Its objective remained unclear insofar as its terminability. If the objective was to establish Untouchables' right to take water from the Chavadar Tank, the question arises how it could be achieved and when could one say that it is accomplished. When the Untouchables went there they were not stopped. However, later, the caste Hindus avenged their defiling of the Tank and purified it by performing the *shastric* (scriptural) rituals. When the Untouchables planned a Satyagraha, the caste Hindus obtained a court injunction claiming that the tank was not a public property, to prevent the Satyagraha. But even if the Satyagraha had not been obstructed, how would one say that the Chavadar Tank was opened for the Untouchables? The caste Hindus were not expected to resist the satyagrahis during the Satyagraha. But as it happened in earlier instances, they would retaliate later and in any way, restore the status quo. There is thus no way to know when one would say that the rights were established. If the Chavadar Tank was the only source of water for the caste Hindus, the continued state of defilement of the tank would have broken the back of their orthodoxy. They would have been forced to consume water from the 'polluted' tank for sheer survival, ignoring their notions of caste. Of course, it would have been in *accommodation* mode of Satyagraha as referred above.[12] But if there was an alternate water source available for them, which indeed was there at Mahad, the episode after the first conference would have been repeated in all likelihood. After all, the Untouchable population in Mahad was less than 400 in the total population of Mahad town of seven to eight thousand.[13] They would have purified the tank and forced local Untouchables to keep away.

Could the sufferings of Untouchables have salience to the caste Hindus? This question would determine the appropriateness or efficacy of Satyagraha as a methodology for the Untouchables. The reasonable answer to this question may only be in the negative. Satyagraha is premised on melting of heart of the opponent with satyagrahi's suffering. The question is whether suffering of the Untouchables would melt the stony hearts of the majority of the caste Hindus, in whose world view the former were not even humans. Even in Mahad, it was glaringly seen that they did not have any objection to even animals drinking water from the Chavadar Tank, but mere touch of the Untouchables provoked them to violence. The method of Satyagraha may even be construed as shaming the adversary, but in their belief system, castes being created by divine ordinance, there was no question of shame. The mindset of the caste Hindus was moulded in the crucibles of religious (read 'divine') precepts, which would see the sufferings of the Untouchables as their destiny, a result of their own *karma*. They did not bear any responsibility for it. They were totally inured to their sufferings to which nothing more could be added to possibly shake their conscience. Satyagraha may work when it finds resonance with the opponent's own moral universe. But when the universe itself is filled with caste morals, there is no such resonance possible. Much of the appeal of Satyagraha is made to individuals who had hearts to feel the heat of conscience and melt; what was however, needed was the change in the society, which may not have even a heart to melt. Thus, all possible features of Satyagraha would seem to fail in resolving the issue at hand. Not only, in the specific case of the Untouchables, but also in generic terms, the efficacy of Satyagraha to resolve any issue is, disputable. Although highly eulogized in public rhetoric, there is hardly any evidence of its success in producing results. Not even in the case of Mahatma Gandhi, had Satyagraha really worked. Many scholars have disputed the very premise of Satyagraha.[14] One could see him using Satyagraha as a shrewd tactic[15] and at other times as pure coercion or worst, even blackmail; this, despite Gandhi having the might of money and mass following backing him. If the same acts were performed by an ordinary mortal, he would simply be ignored and allowed to die. As an empirical fact, none of the Satyagrahas that the Dalits performed, viz., Ambadevi Temple in Amravati, Parvati in Pune, and Kalaram Mandir in Nashik really brought them any results. The temples were opened either at the instance of Bajaj, dictated by the Gandhian strategy, or under the pressure of changed circumstances.

3. What if Dalits had retaliated the Attack on 20 March 1927?

While returning after exercising their legal right at the Chavadar Tank on 20 March, the Dalits were brutally attacked by caste Hindu hooligans. Those Dalits who still remained in Mahad were infuriated by this cowardly act and just wanted Ambedkar's nod to retaliate, which he refused. His biographer accurately captured this episode when he wrote:

> ... When Ambedkar returned to the bungalow, he saw about a hundred men impatiently awaiting his orders, their eyes literally blazing with fire and their hands itching for retaliation and revenge. Their leader, however appealed for peace and discipline. There was hushed silence for a while. A word of provocation would have turned Mahad into a pool of blood and destruction. The number of delegates still lingering in this town, in the pandal and in the bungalow together could have easily outnumbered the hooligans, and battered down their skulls. Hundreds among the Untouchables were men who had seen, fought, and moved actively in the theatre and battles of the First World War.[16]

R.B. More briefly, but more authentically presents the chronology of the incident. He tells us how just two youth armed with an axe and a crowbar stood guard at the entry of their base camp and scared off the attackers. The news of this cowardly attack infuriated the delegates so much that they broke the pandal to take out sticks and bamboos to thrash the attackers.

They just needed an approving nod from their leader.[17]

Babasaheb Ambedkar consciously avoided it. The folklorish explanation is that his decision was informed by the consideration of the consequences Dalits would have to face in other places. This was somewhat true. But it could be argued that even without retaliation, Dalits had to bear those consequences. The entire Chavadar Tank episode had angered the caste Hindus enough that at many places they boycotted Dalits, and unleashed various atrocities on them. Actually, although the first conference was not associated with Satyagraha, Gandhi's model held sway over the mind of Ambedkar. He simply would not allow violence to mar the moral standing of the movement.

At this point one could raise a hypothetical question, what if Dalits had retaliated. What would have been its consequence? There were about 3,000 delegates in the conference and even though some of them had begun to return to their villages, majority was still around in Mahad when the attack took place. Most of them were ex-military men, tempered in battles during World War I. In any case, for retaliation, what is required is the mental strength; physical attributes, experience of combat, and the number of combatants are only the secondary factors. The attackers were a handful, at most a few hundred in number. The total population of Mahad was given as 7,000 to 8,000 in 1937, which a decade before might not be more than 6,000. Considering the effective adult male population of the caste Hindus, and even in that, the hardened elements; their numbers would not exceed a few hundred. They could be easily taught a lesson by the delegates that they should not take the Untouchables for granted any longer. What could have been the worst possible consequence of this action? Surely, it would have enraged caste Hindus in surrounding areas to unleash atrocities on the Untouchables as Dr Ambedkar apprehended. At some places, they would impose social boycotts against Untouchables. Was there anything abnormal in this? Any act of defiance by Dalits met with such reactions from the caste Hindus throughout history. They were rather an integral part of the basic mechanism that preserved the Hindu social order.

As a matter of fact, all this kept happening even without Dalits raising their hands in resistance. Dalits were beaten at many places, social boycott was imposed on a few; they were variously humiliated, and so on. The collective defilement of the Chavadar Tank at Mahad brought them these sufferings. What more would have happened if the caste Hindus who had attacked Dalits had been beaten back? Perhaps, the scale of reaction would have differed. Perhaps, not; the opponent also would have taken a scare of this new phenomenon that Dalits would not take anything meekly as before. Indeed, nothing much would have happened beyond what was already happening to Dalits. Rather, there was a strong possibility that even what happened might not have happened if the Dalits had really retaliated.

Of course, the only new thing that would have happened was that some of the Untouchables would have been arrested for rioting and faced the law. Was it a huge price to be paid for discarding their slavish mentality? No sensible person having a little knowledge of history would say it was. It is an erroneous notion to expect that things can be had without paying for them. Even Gandhi's Satyagraha, which advocated nonviolence and passivity did not hold such an idiotic notion and provided for the costs in terms of self suffering. It was intrinsic to Satyagraha that satyagrahis suffered. It never feared police or jails. True, they had the backing of other resources which would not be there for Dalits. But that is overwhelmed by the logic for the Dalits, which was that in their case, jails were better than the outside caste prisons. The former just imprisoned their bodies but the outside caste prisons imprisoned their very spirit. In empirical terms too, they had comparatively little to lose.

But think of the possible gain from the retaliation. Mahad showed to the world that Dalits had mentally decided to discard the yoke of caste slavery. If they had retaliated against the attack that evening, it would have demonstrated their determination. It would have shown that their verbal proclamations were backed by concrete action. The mere symbolic act of raising a hand on caste Hindu bullies would have shattered the centuries-old notion that Dalits could be abused with impunity. The essence of the caste system lay in the victims internalizing their victimhood. Once they discarded it, it would mark the beginning of its end. The caste Hindus would have been shocked to their bones to see Dalits raising their hands. They had seen bouts of spiritual awakening among Dalits but they were inconsequential, as they did not dent their material interests. But never had they seen Dalit rebelliousness using their real latent strength, their bodily power. While the negative consequences of this physical retaliation considered above might not have materialized to the extent imagined, its positive impact would have surely spread like wildfire among Dalits. It would have certainly created qualitatively new awakening in them that they should resist if the caste Hindus misbehaved.

There was no virtue in passivity of Dalits. It was rather the cause of their pitiable state. If the objective was to prepare them for bringing about reforms in society, it was imperative to create congenial consciousness in them; create commensurate confidence in them. Mahad had brought them a golden opportunity for accomplishing this feat. Dr Ambedkar, at least principally, had not discounted the option of physical resistance by Dalits, singing paeans to nonviolence or passive struggles. He had not discounted the option of violence which as in the French Revolution squarely depended on the attitude of the adversary. He rather lamented that the weakness of Dalits to resist or retaliate the injustice done to them. A decade later, in his famous 1936 address, published with the title, *Mukti kon pathe?*, to the leading activists of his movement, he had presented his analysis that the caste Hindus dared to perpetrate atrocities on Dalits because of their lack of strength to retaliate. His proposal for religious conversion was basically meant to overcome this weakness by merging them into some existing religious community. Once they gained the consciousness to see the wrong, which Mahad got them, the most effective expression of it could have been in the form of physical resistance, the capacity for which they never lacked. Being kept away from education, they would not have been able to make sophisticated, cultured and constitutional counters against their oppression. The only asset they possessed was their physical body, which could match any other. Even in strategic terms, it would be prudent to make use of available strength to achieve the goal, than aspire for something which was not in sight.

Here one can appropriately recall the method of Ayyankali, who effectively used the representative strength of ordinary Dalits in asserting their civil rights which were not even granted by law. He first role-modeled by demonstrating the efficacy of his method. After the first incident, when the upper caste people who tried to prevent him were scared away by his violent action, no one dared to obstruct his path. While he frequented the marketplace in his cart, other Dalits would not even walk the path. In order to remove fear from their minds, he had to organize collective 'walk for freedom' to Puthen Market. Violence did break out resulting in *Chaliar* riots in which both sides suffered losses. One can easily imagine that the losses on the upper caste side would ordinarily be far more than those on the side of Dalits by the simple logic that the latter had both, better bodily strength as well as mental resolve. But even if they had more losses, even a few casualties, the cost would still be worth the cause. What the legal battle for years would not have achieved, they got it immediately. The Travancore state soon granted them the right to walk on public roads. It was not just the paper right as it comes through legal battles; it was the real right having paid the cost in blood.

Indeed, with hindsight though, one can reasonably see that Dalits should have retaliated the attack on them on 20 March 1927 demonstrating the prowess of their awakening. The greatest fallout of this act would have been in terms of imparting a very different image and orientation to the Dalit movement from the one it came to acquire. The Dalit movement reflects an amazing degree of passivity in confronting the real issues, whether they relate to their exploitation, oppression, discrimination or the increasing incidence of atrocities including rapes and murders of their women. It has shown a bewildering statist orientation, smacking of its misconception of the state as the benefactor of Dalits. Instead of realizing its strength, it only added to the historical disadvantage of Dalits while asking for concessions from the state. This overt statist orientation of the movement blinded it from knowing the true character of the state and its dynamics. The actual raising of Dalit hand on a caste Hindu oppressor in the evening on 20 March would have actually thwarted this future degeneration. Dalit defiance, not only in word but also in deed, would have kept even the state on tenterhooks. Except for the symbolic flash of such an attitude of Dalit movement during the short reign of the Dalit Panthers, which had sent shock waves through the entire ruling establishment, the Dalit movement never demonstrated this real prowess of Dalits.

4. What if, the Dalits had carried out the Satyagraha on 25 December 1927?

In a similar vein one can ask the question: what if the Satyagraha was conducted as planned on 25 December in defiance of the court injunction. Unlike the March conference, which ended with the caste Hindu goons attacking Untouchables for having polluted the Chavadar Tank, the December conference which was consciously planned as the Satyagraha conference, was not even allowed to start. It began and ended without performing the Satyagraha. The Satyagraha was supposed to be against the attitude of the caste Hindus, but as discussed, it should have been primarily against the failure of the government to protect Dalits from exercising their lawful civil rights, Nonetheless, the Satyagraha was prevented by a court injunction from taking place.

Unlike the first conference, massive preparations were made for the Satyagraha conference. The delegates came from all over the Marathi speaking region with huge enthusiasm and preparation as *satyagrahis*. But because of the court injunction fraudulently obtained by some Hindus, it ended as a non-event. The entire proceedings of the conference, apart from the burning of a copy of the *Manusmruti*, was devoted to the issue of whether to go ahead with the Satyagraha or not in the changed circumstances. The opinion of the conference heavily leaned in favour of the Satyagraha. Ultimately, only in deference to Dr Ambedkar's advice, people relented and agreed for suspending the Satyagraha. The basic argument Babasaheb Ambedkar put forth before the conference was that their struggle was against the caste Hindus; the objective to demonstrate the strength of their unity and determination was fulfilled; and if they went for the Satyagraha defying the court injunction, it would be direct confrontation with the state, which they ill afforded, particularly when the District Magistrate had assured them of his sympathies. The narrative of the conference indicates that people were not quite convinced by these arguments but out of respect to his plea they agreed to suspend the Satyagraha.

Hypothetically, we can ask ourselves what would have happened if they had decided to go ahead with the Satyagraha as planned. It was planned to have small teams of delegates go to the Chavadar Tank and drink the water. In normal circumstances, and in all probability, nothing would have happened to them as long as the Satyagraha continued. Because of the court injunction, there was no point in having a prolonged Satyagraha (in any case it is not clear for how many days the Satyagraha was planned) and the most prudent way of offering the Satyagraha would have been to get all delegates in a single procession, as in fact they did, by going round the Tank in a symbolic gesture, and take its water together. It could also be in a manner as planned or for that matter in any manner between these two options. The police would arrest them because they violated the law. What could the police do next? How and where would they take ten to fifteen thousand arrestees in a town of a population of about six to seven thousand? The sheer logistics of it would force them to take a lenient view and release all by the evening as it usually happens in cases of public protests. Even if the Satyagraha had happened in any other form, the police would do the same, albeit in a more managed way. The question again arises, what would they do next? The answer to the question could be given by anyone who has had a little brush with participating in mass agitations, which by definition have to necessarily violate some or the other section of the law. Unless there is some serious act of violence involved, police normally pick up the agitators, put them into their vans, take them to the police station, record their names, charge them under some sections of the law and let them go after a few hours. If they are vindictive, they put them behind bars, produce before court and the court would release them on bail.

This is what would have happened to the delegates in Mahad too if they had proceeded with the Satyagraha. Everyone, including the police, knew the context of the act and perhaps knew that the injunction was merely a technical device fraudulently contrived to thwart the Satyagraha. They also knew that public agitations, by definition, may not conform to the law. Moreover, it was not the first such protest that happened in the country; many having happened before, on a far bigger a scale . But there was nothing that the government could do. If it had jailed each protester, the Britishers would have been building only prisons all over the country. Nonetheless, these considerations did not even touch the delegates. All kinds of scares and forewarnings could not shake their determination to perform the Satyagraha and face the consequences. What if some of them faced imprisonment for a few months for the same? Would it have scared others, demoralized future generations or would it have become a beacon, an inspiration for others to resist without the fear of consequence? Even the narrative of Mahad itself could answer this question more conclusively than any speculation. All the delegates who enthusiastically came for the Satyagraha did know that their predecessors had their skulls broken in an attack by the Hindu goons. If they were to be scared by it, they would not have even come to the conference. The very fact that they came bubbling with enthusiasm and in numbers nearly four times their previous strength conclusively showed that such acts of valor only inspire people to make bigger and bigger sacrifices.

Indeed, the fallout of this action would have given an entirely different orientation to the movement. It was not a question of opening two fronts in a battle; it would have rather effectively communicated to both, Hindus as well as the Government the gravity of the issue and the determination of Dalits. Although the battle appeared to be against the caste Hindus, actually it was being fought with the purpose of having their legal rights guaranteed by the state. As contended before, the prime culprit in this episode was the state, which failed to protect Dalits while exercising their legal rights. The continuation with the Satyagraha would have exposed the double dealing of the state towards Dalits and dispelled the illusion about its being a friend of Dalits.

It is true that the colonial regime has been the boon for the lower castes as explained in the Chapter 1. But it should never be forgotten that this boon has come essentially as the unintended consequence of its expedient actions guided by intricate colonial logic. To exploit the existing communal and caste divide in the country was one easy way of managing such a huge landmass. We have already seen how it adopted the basic dictum of control theory that control necessitates measurement and went on a measurement spree in the form of various anthropological measurements, cultural mappings, documentation of customs and traditions and ultimately instituting castewise and communitywise censuses. Castes did exist with their viciousness through centuries but in a fluid form, as a life-world of people, which lived within their locale. But these measurements helped in concretizing them; extended them beyond their locales, created new caste equations and hierarchies and correspondingly germinating new consciousness that unleashed a novel dynamics which would be manipulated as per the strategic need of the colonial rule. Various castes may have benefitted or suffered in this dynamics but none of it was as such intended. If Dalits benefitted in process, it was also just incidental, as a byproduct of the process. With regard to castes, the underscoring attitude of the regime rather was to keep the existing social structure undisturbed (from cost minimization viewpoint), which necessarily meant favoring the entrenched castes vis-à-vis the lower castes. Therefore, it is grossly erroneous to take the state, even the colonial state, as the benefactor of Dalits and ignore its intrigues in the conflict with the caste Hindus.

We have seen how the state authorities instead of controlling caste Hindus approached Ambedkar with a request to control Dalits. Even in the second conference, the behavior of the state administration has been equally intriguing. The close reading of the archival documents indicates that the district administration was engrossed with how to avert the impending law and order problem in the wake of the Untouchables' Satyagraha at the Chavadar Tank. The collector of Kolaba indicates in his communiqué to the undersecretary the grounds in favour of the Touchable Hindus to prevent the Untouchables from entering the tank.[18] He however thinks that it would not succeed and might result in a serious riot. In a subsequent communiqué he writes, "I understand that some of the caste Hindus are at last beginning to talk of seeking an injunction to prevent the Untouchables from entering the tank. I think that the surest way of assuring that they shall translate this talk into action is to adopt the course previously recommended by me..." It appears that in order to diffuse the situation, the idea of injunction was given to the caste Hindus by none other than the collector himself. Not only was he anxious that they translate it into action, i.e., actually obtain the injunction but also was personally keen that it eventually succeeds in preventing the Satyagraha. He had sent for Dr Ambedkar to prepare the ground for suspending the Satyagraha and even went out of his way in addressing the delegates directly dissuading them from going ahead with the Satyagraha. One can reasonably suspect that the entire episode of preventing the Satyagraha in December 1927 and pushing Dr Ambedkar to squander his energies in a decade long inconsequential litigation was actually the misdoing of the state and not the caste Hindus.

5. The Issue of Violence in Satyagraha

In the wake of the Mahad Satyagraha, Dr Ambedkar had written an explanatory editorial in *Bahishkrut Bharat* of 21 November 1927 which discussed how the agitation of the Untouchables was just and hence a Satyagraha. He argued that the Hindu religion belonged to the Untouchables as much as it did to the caste Hindus. "If the Brahmans like Vasishtha, Kshatriyas like Krishna, Vaishyas like Harsh and Shudras like Tukaram upheld the prestige of *Hindutva*[19], there were Untouchables like Chokhamela and Rohidas, who also contributed to it." Thousands of Untouchables staked their lives for the defence of hindutva. The number of Untouchables, from the times of

Gita to the Shidnak Mahar in the battle of Kharda, who laid their lives for the sake of hindutva is large. Therefore, the temples constructed in the name of hindutva belong as much to the Untouchables as they do to the Touchables. After establishing equal right of the Untouchables over Hinduism, Dr Ambedkar argued that these rights do not disappear just because they were not being used for years. The Untouchables' struggle for restoration of these rights was therefore just, and thus a true Satyagraha.

Dr Ambedkar then moves to discuss the method of Satyagraha to be followed by the Untouchables. He wrote:

> Mahatma Gandhi is considered as the promoter of the movement of Satyagraha in modern times and hence the understanding has spread all over that the methodology of Satyagraha is the methodology propagated by Mahatma Gandhi. This methodology does not have any space for violence. Rather Mahatma Gandhi contends that where there is violence there is no Satyagraha. We feel that this contention of Mahatma Gandhi cannot be accepted by all as rational. Whether a struggle is Satyagraha or not is not dependent on the means adopted to accomplish the objective of the struggle but it depends on the moral standing of the objective. If the objective is based on truth, the struggle for it must be reckoned as Satyagraha. And if it is based on untruth, the insistence on accomplishing it must be taken as *duragraha* (insistence on untruth)
>
> Violence and non-violence are just the means of achieving the objective of a struggle. The moral form of struggle does not change according to the means deployed for it unlike the form of verb that changes according to the use of subject and object. Just because a person adopts a path of nonviolence for his unjust intent, his intrigues cannot be called a Satyagraha or the struggle of a person cannot be dismissed as *duragraha* just because she adopted a path of violence. If one dismissed violent struggle as *duragraha*, what would the Lord Krishna's advice in Gita be called that exhorted Arjun to resort to violence for the accomplishment of his just objective? Was Krishna a *Papatma* (opposite of *mahatma*, one with sinful soul)? We do not feel that any Hindu will be ever prepared to call him so and if any other person did it, one cannot say that it would be acceptable to all. Although, they say, *ahimsa paramodharmah* (nonviolence is the supreme religion), it is not

possible to observe nonviolence everywhere.

Although invisible with open eyes, logically we can understand the existence of numerous microscopic germs that fill our world, which might be getting killed even with minor movements of our eyelids. How can we stop killing of these all pervading microscopic organisms that fill our atmosphere, water, fruits, etc. The scientific research of Dr Jagdishchandra Bose has proved that even the plants also have life. Then what is the point in Brahmans who devour vegetables and Jain Tirthankars who wander with a cloth covering their nose and mouth making show of their nonviolence? It will not be correct to say that nonviolence can be practiced everywhere. What would we do if some evil person has come with weapons to kill us, or to rape our wife or daughter, or to set our house on fire, or to take away all our wealth and there is no one around to protect us? Do we shut our eyes and chant *ahinsa paramodharmah* and let this person do whatever he wanted, or resist him with whatever our strengths are if he does not listen to our sane counsel? Anybody will choose the latter option out of these two. No one can say that it is against the scriptures. Because the makers of the scriptures say that in such situations, the sin of killing does not come to the killer; rather the killed one dies because of his irreligiousness. Not only has the makers of ancient scriptures but also the modern criminal law admitted the right of violence in self defence with certain limitations.

Violence is inappropriate; nonetheless, it is justified when one cannot defend oneself without resorting to it. The killing of a young boy is considered unacceptable but nobody objects to cutting him into pieces if he comes to kill you. The same logic must apply to Satyagraha too. One will have to logically concede that the violence of a satyagrahi, if he had to commit it, is excusable. Viewed in this perspective, Gandhi's path of nonviolent Satyagraha, becomes impracticable. On the contrary, to call it nonviolent itself would be an illusion.

If one takes a constricted meaning of violence as killing, then only one would be able to differentiate violence from nonviolence. But violence is not only taking life but also includes causing hurt to others' mind or body. That means, nonviolence is not causing hurt to any sentient being. If one took this broad meaning of nonviolence, one will have to say that Gandhi's nonviolence itself is also a kind of violence. Because there is no doubt that the methodology he follows may not cause bodily injury to others

> but causes hurt to their minds. The satyagrahi of Gandhi might not kill a person but he surely disturbs the peace of mind of the adversary. One is thus compelled to say that the claim of Gandhi that there is no violence in his Satyagraha is not correct.
>
> As a matter of fact, from the viewpoint of accomplishing his objective, it is appropriate for a satyagrahi to adopt a policy of nonviolence to the extent possible and violence if necessary. It is also acceptable from moral viewpoint. The emphasis that Gandhi laid on nonviolence is not just because Gandhi is adherent to the ideology of nonviolence. The reason for his emphasis is entirely different. Mahatma Gandhi while speaking about his Santyagraha says that we cannot have a definite criterion that would help us determine what truth is. What we call Satyagraha, others could call it *duragraha*. This apprehension of Gandhi has been duly recorded in his testimony before the Hunter Committee.
>
> It is his opinion that where there is honest dispute about truth, it will not be proper to commit violence. This is the only reason that he has excluded violence from the repertoire of means for his Satyagraha. It is evident from this that Gandhi might not object to the violence if it had to be committed for achieving the Satyagraha's objective if someone ensured the truthfulness of the cause without any dispute. This entire discussion is just to stress the point that violence is not harmful to the moral aspects of Satyagraha. Although there cannot be any technical objection to discuss this matter beyond this point, nobody has time to spare for it in today's situation.

The purpose of providing such verbatim translation of this longish passage is to stress the point that violence and nonviolence were the strategic options for Ambedkar and not an ideological dogma. He clearly saw numerous situations wherein violence will necessarily come in. Later, while interpreting Buddha's nonviolence in his *Buddha and His Dhamma*, he wrote, "A proper understanding of these instances would show that the *Ahimsa* taught by the Blessed Lord was fundamental. But it was not absolute. He taught that evil should be cured by the return of good. But he never preached that evil should be allowed to overpower good. He stood for *Ahimsa*. He denounced *Himsa* [violence]. But he did not deny that *Himsa* may be the last resort to save good being destroyed by evil. Thus it is not that the Blessed Lord taught a dangerous doctrine.

It is the critics who failed to understand its significance and its scope."[20] Subsequently, in comparing Buddha with Marx, in his speech in Kathmandu[21] he characterized Marxism's violence against Buddha's nonviolence. He said that although the object of both Buddha and Marx was the same, the nonviolent and democratic path (he traces democracy to the Buddhist Sangha) was superior to the violent path of Marx that openly advocated 'dictatorship of proletariat'. His earlier arguments in *Bahishkrut Bharat* could easily convince him that the revolutionaries have a just cause and their situations are invariably such that nonviolence may just not work. The entrenched classes would not let go of their pelf and power merely because someone was asking for it.

That Ambedkar adopted nonviolence as a strategic option is evident in his further explanation as to why the Untouchables should adhere to the nonviolent method. He wrote:

> As the people of this country are without arms, there is only one path to accomplish the object of Satyagraha. The Untouchables prepared to do Satyagraha must move forward relying on this lone option. Moreover, there is no experiential evidence yet to prove that this option is inadequate to solve the problem of the Untouchables. The movement of Satyagraha to eradicate untouchability is just beginning. Therefore, the Satyagraha that is going to take place will be of the nonviolent type. People should firmly bear in mind that there is nothing more than that.

Ambedkar then explains the target of the Satyagraha. He cautioned that although, it seemed to be against the caste Hindus, it was actually against the state. Because, while exercising their legal right of accessing public water sources, the state was necessarily obligated to protect them from the ire of orthodox caste Hindus. He cautioned that in order to accomplish their objective, they would be compelled to break the prohibition orders of the government. The government will not spare those who broke the law and put them behind bars. The Untouchables, who come for the Satyagraha, must be determined to accept imprisonment. Ambedkar argued that untouchability was so insulting that one should not mind if its eradication demands a few lives.[22] Ambedkar had rightly construed that the Satyagraha of the Untouchables was actually against the state. He had gone so far as to threaten the state that if it opposed them, he would humiliate it in the International court of justice.[23]

If Ambedkar had this clear conception of violence and that the Satyagraha was essentially against the state, why did he abandon the Satyagraha much against the will of the people? Injunction or no injunction, the Satyagraha of the Untouchables was actually against the state as discussed before because, it was to establish the rights granted them by the state. People were prepared to go ahead with the Satyagraha knowing fully well that they would land up in jails, but they were dissuaded. Unusually, the District Magistrate, the minion of the state, was allowed to address the delegates and issue a veiled threat to them. Such was the determination of the delegates that they just ignored it and remained firm on their resolve to perform Satyagraha as planned. It was only when Babasaheb Ambedkar himself persuaded them to give it up that they reluctantly accepted it and returned home. The entire episode created a permanent misconception of the role of the state and made the movement excessively leader centric.

Ambedkar's views on violence were absolutely rational; inasmuch as violence or nonviolence was the matter of strategy and not ideology. He had gone to the extent of proving that there was nothing like nonviolence when the entire natural world was interdependent; every living being devouring another, every moment for sheer survival. He extended his conception of violence to mean hurting of minds and in that sense even the so-called nonviolent struggles also involved violence. In a nutshell, every struggle necessarily involved violence. The discussion of violence in the context of struggles for social change thus became meaningless. The negation of violence actually meant negation of struggle, negation of change and the affirmation of the status quo. If this message in *Bahishkrut Bharat* had been actualized in Mahad, the entire history of the Dalit movement and in turn the history of India would have been different!

6. Accomplishments of Mahad

The implicit strategic objective behind the Mahad struggle was to sensitize the Hindus about the unjust customs of untouchability and impel their advanced elements to come forward to initiate some reforms within the society. It was also aimed at galvanizing the Untouchables around their human rights, and motivating their struggle. The government had granted them civil rights to access public places like water sources, roads, temples, etc. These legal rights however were useless unless the larger section of civil society accepted them. After all, Mahad struggle was precisely for making the civil society accept these rights.

As Dr Ambedkar himself observed later, "The direct action in respect of the tank in Mahad, the Kalaram Temple in Nasik and the Guruyawur temple in Malabar have done in a few days what million days of preaching by reformers would never have done. I therefore strongly recommend this campaign of direct action for securing civic rights of the Depressed Classes for adoption by the Anti-Untouchability League".[24] Mahad had certainly awakened Dalits to their civil rights and inspired them to fight for their exercise. As a corollary, it also alarmed the larger Hindu society about the potential threat it faced if they did not address those raised by Dalits. However, the hope that they would come forward for reforms did not materialize. The impact on Dalits was visible right after the second conference. For instance, the women who came to see Dr Ambedkar had changed overnight following his advice. Considering the inertness of the Untouchables who had internalized their status as their destiny, this change could not be belittled. In many villages of Konkan, the Mahars had stopped begging for food, stopped dragging and skinning the dead animals, and doing their traditional *vethbegari* (the traditional duties of village servant without remuneration), *maharki* (degraded caste labour) and woken up the *savarnas* to their importance. Of course, while doing so they faced reprisal in the form of boycotts and physical attacks in many places, which they determinedly endured.

Mahad was also taken note of by Mahatma Gandhi. After the incident on 20 March, he wrote in his newspaper *Young*

India supporting Dr Ambedkar for having led a Satyagraha at Mahad and commended the Untouchables for their self-restraint, and him, for his leadership in refusing to get provoked by a stick-wielding mob of caste-Hindus.[25] It had its impact far and wide. Perhaps prompted by Gandhi, Jamnalal Bajaj, a Marwari millionaire and close confidant of Gandhi had opened his own temple- the Lakshminarayan Temple- in Wardha to the Untouchables in 1928. Next year, the Congress reconstituted the Anti-Untouchability Subcommittee with Pandit Malaviya as its president and Jamnalal Bajaj as its secretary. While Malaviya is not known to have contributed much, Bajaj toured many parts of India and persuaded the other temple owners and trustees to open their temples to Untouchables. Temple entry would be pursued by the Congress over the next decade, but on a voluntary basis. Vaikom Satyagraha was the first and last one in which Gandhi participated implicitly against the orthodox elements. Thereafter he had not even approved a Satyagraha for such issues because it created an atmosphere of "bitterness and distrust".[26]

Mahad gave a big fillip to the people who were already fighting for temple entry. While preparation for the Satyagraha conference was on, an agitation for the temple entry had broken out in Amravati in the then Berar part of CP & Berar. In 1925, Madhavrao Govind Meshram had made a demand for opening the ancient temple of Ambadevi in Amravati. He made several requests and applications but the management of the temple ignored them. This demand then was upheld by the likes of Dadasaheb Patil and Dr Panjabrao Deshmukh connected with the Satyashodhak Samaj and a huge public meeting was organized on 26 July 1927. In this meeting, a plan of Satyagraha for the temple entry was announced.[27] For the preparation of this Satyagraha, again a meeting was organized under the chairmanship of Dr. Ambedkar on 13-14 November 1927 a resolution was passed to defer the Satyagraha by three months as per the request of Ganesh Shrikrishna Khaparde[28], an elderly leader of Amravati, member of state council and president of the Ambadevi temple trust and it was declared that a Satyagraha would start if the temple was not opened by 15 February 1928.[29]

The Satyagraha accordingly started on 15 February 1928 but it was not carried out with enough force and enthusiasm. It dragged for many days and then stopped.[30]

Mahad Satyagraha was surely not for the temple entry. But with the awakening it created, the Untouchables at many places organized many Satyagrahas on their own. Curiously, they took the form of temple entry Satyagrahas. They did not aspire for access to the caste Hindus' water source. But they needed access to their Gods, indicative of their ideological enslavement. In 1929 two major Satyagrahas were noted. *Bahishkrut Bharat* of 12 July 1929 had published a brief news on them under the title, 'Untouchables' Satyagraha in Bengal: Arrest of Two satyagrahis'. On 9 July, two satyagrahis were arrested by police for having entered the Kali temple of Kapil Muni at Khulana (in the then East Bengal, now in Bangladesh) in defiance of the orders of the employees of the temple. Six Untouchables had performed this Satyagraha so as to open this temple for all castes. Personally however, Dr Ambedkar was quite disillusioned with the method of Satyagraha with the Mahad experience. He was least interested in entering temples but saw struggles for it as an opportunity for mobilizing masses and hence did not discourage when people voluntarily launched them.

Inspired by the Mahad Satyagraha, a public meeting was organized on 22 September 1929 under the chairmanship of Vinayakrao Bhuskute to discuss the Satyagraha for temple entry in Pune. A Satyagraha committee was formed for the purpose with S.J. Kamble as President, P.N. Rajbhoj as General Secretary and an Advisory Council comprising N.V. Gadgil, V.M. Bhuskute, V.V. Sathe, G.N. Kanitkar, and Keshavrao Jedhe. *Kesari*, the Marathi newspaper founded by Tilak published opinions of some prominent people with a heading "Do not do the Satyagraha." Some people had raised an issue of Parvati temple being a private property and hence the Untouchables should desist from doing Satyagraha there.[31] On 13 October 1929 the Satyagraha led by Gadgil, Rajbhoj and Bhuskute took place. The opponents of the Satyagraha launched an attack in which most people sustained injuries. Rajbhoj fell unconscious and had to be taken away. The upper caste people like Gadgil and Ranade were especially targeted by the orthodox people and were also wounded. One Aryasamaji Swami Yoganand, who had come in support of the satyagrahis, was also not spared. Ultimately with the collector's intervention the crowd disbursed. In the evening the Pune city Congress Committee, presided over by V.R. Shinde, organized a public meeting condemning the attack. Public meetings were organized at many places in its support. On 16 October 1929, a huge public meeting was held in Parel (Bombay) under the chairmanship of Dr Ambedkar. Among the prominent touchable people were Bhuskute, Devrao Naik, K.S. Thakre (father of Bal Thackeray), Pradhan, Khandke, Kavali, Kadrekar, Acharya Dr Suratkar, and among the Untouchables, were Shivtarkar, Mali, and Adrekar. On 22 October 1929, a huge public meeting was organized by the Untouchables at the Napier Park in Madras under the chairmanship of W.P. Saudagar Pandya Nadar, MLC. People who spoke in the meeting were N. Shivraj, SPI Balguru Shivam, Ellapa Thasser, and E.V. Ramaswami Naicker. The Parvati Satyagraha was ultimately called off on 20 January 1930 with the mediation of people like N.C. Kelkar, L.B. Bhopatkar, and Jamnalal Bajaj[32] without accomplishing its objective.

Like the Pune Untouchables, the leaders of the Untouchables in Nashik decided to launch a Satyagraha to enter the Kalaram temple there. When they came to consult Dr Ambedkar, he revealed to them for the first time his strategic thinking. He said, "I consider the political rights of the Untouchables more important than these Satyagrahas. One cannot say what conditions would emerge when the negotiation on these issues commence in India or in England. If the conditions turn out uncongenial to us, this Satyagraha will add to our difficulties. It will consume all our energies and we will be unable to face those conditions."[33] The Nashik people assured him that they would not bother him in his pursuit of the political rights. Rather, they would extend help whenever he needed. They requested him just to accept the leadership of the Satyagraha. In view of their enthusiasm, Dr Ambedkar accepted their request. Immediately a Satyagraha committee was formed with

Bhaurao Krishnaji Gaikwad (Dadasaheb Gaikwad) as Secretary and Patitpawan Das as President. Gaikwad issued a notice on behalf of the Committee to the Trustees of the Kalaram temple that the Untouchable people would enter the temple to worship the Ram idol. If they or any touchable Hindus opposed this move, the Untouchables would offer a Satyagraha for the temple entry. They requested their response. As the response did not come even after five months, the Satyagraha Committee declared that it would go ahead with the Satyagraha.

The Satyagraha began under the leadership of Dr Ambedkar on 2 March 1930. Over 16,000 satyagrahis marched to the Kalaram temple in procession to find all the doors of the temple locked and hence it was converted into a *dharna* (sit-in strike). The administration was taking side of the orthodox Hindus and threatening the satyagrahis. Even Dr Ambedkar's plea to the Governor for intervening as the temple was a public place to which the Untouchables had right to enter, did not work. The Governor declined to intervene in the matter. The collector was openly hostile; he even refused to meet Gaikwad and threatened to remove the satyagrahis.[34] When Gaikwad reported this to Ambedkar, he advised him, "My view is not to face a conflict with the Government if it can be avoided."[35] On 9 April, on the Ramnavami Day, when a chariot procession was to be taken out, Dr Ambedkar had personally gone to Nashik and requested the Police officer to conduct impartially when the Untouchables would seek to participate in pulling the chariot. But as the Untouchable touched the rope, the police cracked down on them and started beating them. While explaining the origin of this riot to the Governor, Ambedkar wrote to him on 11 April 1930, "But the immediate cause of the fight was the action of the Police Sepoys, a great majority of whom were caste Hindus, they at once started to assault those Untouchables who were struggling to hold a bit of the rope. The fight was started by the caste Hindu Police who openly took the side of the touchable Hindus".[36] Ambedkar assured the Governor that his complaint was not against the district magistrate or even the police officers, who according to him were just performing their duties, but against the policemen who being Hindu, were prejudiced against the

Untouchables.[37] On 23 March 1934, Gaikwad conveyed to Ambedkar that the local people had thought of relaunching the Satyagraha and sought his advice. Ambedkar replied vide his letter dated 3 March 1934 asking Gaikwad to stop the Satyagrahas. He wrote,

> ...I didn't launch the temple entry movement because I wanted the Depressed Classes to become worshipers of idols which they were prevented from worshiping or because I believed temple entry would make them equal members in and an integral part of the Hindu Society. ... I started temple entry *Satyagraha* only because I felt that was the best way of energizing the Depressed Classes and making them conscious of their position. As I believe I have achieved that purpose I have no more use for temple entry. I want the Depressed Classes to concentrate their energy and resource on politics and education and I hope that they will realize the importance of both.[38]

Like Mahad, both the Satyagrahas at Parvati and Kalaram temples ended without the Untouchable achieving their declared objectives of entering them. Although all these struggles with the method of Satyagraha thus appear to have ended in failure, they, as observed by Dr Ambedkar, had been tremendously successful in galvanizing the masses for fighting future political battles.

7. Mahad as the Strategy Deflector

The initial strategy of Dr Ambedkar was aimed at social reforms within the Untouchable community in terms of uplifting them educationally and culturally as well as within the caste Hindus in terms of doing away evil custom like untouchability and creating fellow feeling across castes. It involved sensitizing entire society, comprising both caste Hindus and Untouchables; Untouchables about their being humans with rights equal to anyone else and therefore they should struggle to restore them and the caste Hindus to make them realize the wickedness of their customs and traditions. The state was either not a factor or was seen as a benefactor to the Dalits. The founding of the *Bahishkrut Hitkarini Sabha* with many social elites at its helm; launching a paper, *Bahishkrut Bharat*; seeding many community activities; conducting public meetings; pleading with the government for helping Untouchables for their upliftment were the various components of that strategy. Initially, it appears, he was not in favour of direct actions such as Mahad Satyagraha.[39] But after accepting the leadership he would not look back. These direct actions supplemented the strategy in jolting caste Hindus into thinking and boosting the confidence of Untouchables to struggle.

However, Mahad shattered his hopes that Hindu society would ever undertake reforms. He had already turned his focus to the political arena which was fast unfolding along communal lines. With the signing of Lucknow Pact in 1916 between Congress and Muslim League as representatives of Hindus and Muslims respectively, the principle of sharing political power by communities had taken root.[40] While the Congress commanded bigger share of the political pie as the bigger partner, it was made aware by the Muslim League that its bigness was largely based on the population of the Untouchables (and Adivasis being considered as Hindus). Moreover, it was acutely aware that the Untouchables could not be taken for granted any more as they were getting conscious of their oppressed status in the Hindu society. The Untouchables could potentially topple the Congress applecart by claiming a separate political existence for themselves. While this fear impelled the Congress to take certain proactive steps in favour of the Untouchables[41], Dr Ambedkar read it as the most potent lever to make the caste Hindus behave.

If he could claim that the Untouchables were not Hindus, he would cause turmoil in both the contending political parties; the Congress representing the Hindus directly threatened by the possible loss of their share of political power and Muslim League enthused by the opportunity to increase their share of power. Both would start to lure them on their side with political concessions. Potentially, this single move would change the socio-political configuration of the subcontinent, leaving Hindus with their civilizational loss. With this strategy he could maximize the gain for the Untouchables. Therefore, immediately after Mahad, he began speaking of renouncing Hindu religion and hinted at embracing Islam. He had not developed the political argument yet (or kept it deliberately tacit).[42] Therefore the threat of conversion appeared to threaten the Hindus only socially (if the Untouchables became Muslims the Hindu social order would get disturbed) and somewhat economically (who would do the menial tasks if there are no Untouchables) so that they concede the demands of Untouchables. At his instance, Untouchables in the Berar area had issued a public notice to the Hindus that if they had not stopped observing untouchability before 1 June 1929, 5,000 people would become Musalmans.[43] The threat was palpable because already some people in Yavatmal and Akola districts had started becoming Musalmans. In a conference at Paturda Railway Station in Jalgaon (Jamod) taluka of district Buldana, that took place under his chairmanship on 29 May 1929, a formal resolution was unanimously passed that the Untouchables were prepared for conversion.[44] There was an immediate impact of the resolution in the area; the savarna people opened their four wells to the Untouchables at Paturda and began calling for a get-together. However, in accordance with the resolution, 12 Mahars converted themselves to Islam on 4 June. In response to the threat from the Untouchables to convert, 100-125 wells were opened up for them in that part and four district councils and 18 municipalities had passed resolutions that they should declare that all public wells were open to the Untouchables and they should put up such boards at all the wells. However, there was not much impact of it in practice.[45] Dr Ambedkar expected big ripples in the Hindu society but barring such localized reactions, it did not pay much heed. Soon thereafter he deflected his attention towards politics, and began seeing it as the key to most problems of the Untouchables. He would make rapid strides in this direction overpowering the mighty Mahatma, and get the Untouchables many political as well as economic concessions.

8. Mahad and the National Assembly in France in 1789

Babasaheb Ambedkar in his presidential speech in Mahad on 25 December 1927 compared Satyagraha conference with the constitution of National Assembly in France in 1789, which led to the French revolution. Years later he again repeated,

> The burning of the Manusmruti was a deed of great daring. It was an attack on the very citadel of Hinduism. The Manusmruti embodied the spirit of inequality which is at the base of Hindu life and thought just as the Bastille was the embodiment of the spirit of the Ancient regime in France. The burning of the Manusmruti by the Untouchables at Mahad in 1927 is an event which has the same significance and importance in the history of the emancipation of the Untouchables which the fall of Bastille had in the liberation of the masses in France and Europe.[46]

Metaphorically speaking this comparison sounds profound and there is a high risk of it being mistaken as reality, particularly by Dalits, who are reared on the staple food of metaphors and rhetoric. How did Mahad compare with the epochal events of French revolution? The French Revolution is much written about but unfortunately Mahad is not, beyond of course, what was reported in *Bahishkrut Bharat* . The formation of the National Assembly in France led to events that changed the course of world history. Mahad may have said to have changed the course of the Dalit movement. It set the attitude and orientation of the post-Mahad Dalit movement influencing the events that followed, positive as well as negative. Shorn of symbolism, it may be important to objectively assess Mahad vis-à-vis the benchmarks Dr Ambedkar himself provided.

As we know, before the revolution, France had a well entrenched feudal system, with three formal and distinct castelike estates, or social classes below the all powerful king, who enjoyed absolute power to make laws or was himself the law. The first estate comprised catholic clergy, (the really rich and influential clergy, such as bishops); the second estate, the nobles (the feudal lords, the seigneurs) and the third estate, the rest. The first estate was the smallest, occupying only 0.5 per cent of the population but owned nearly 10 per cent of the land. Many rural priests were as poor as their congregations; nonetheless were despised as a class by the majority of peasants. The second estate was made up of 1.5 per cent of the French population and comprised the richest class of the nobles who had right to tax local peasants and merchants, yet not to pay any taxes to the king. It owned nearly 40 per cent of the land. Both, the first and the second estates, enjoyed their specific legal and financial rights and prerogatives. The third estate was made up of the balance 98 per cent of the population but owned only 50 per cent of the land. It was virtually divided into two layers; the upper layer comprising the bourgeoisie, the middle class people and the bottom layer comprising the peasants, the rural poor and the city workers, the most exploited lot. While the bourgeoisie, by the year 1789 had become so rich as to be indistinguishable from nobility, the plight of peasants was very miserable. They had no vote. They were presumed guilty if arrested, had no right to legal representation if they could not afford it, could be tortured by the officials of the state; their property could be seized, and they could be made to work for their nobles for nothing. They had to pay heavy taxes, and had no say in how they were used. Apart from these estates, women of all classes had fewer rights than their male peers in feudal France.

When Ambedkar explained this structure of feudal France to his audience in Mahad in terms of castes, he was not far from the reality. The three estates could be roughly analogized with the *Brahmans*; *Kshatriyas*, and *Vaisyas*; and the *Shudras* and Untouchables, (*vaishyas* + *shudras* + *atishudras* or Untouchables together making one estate) of course without mobility. Although membership in the noble class was mainly passed down through hereditary rights, it was not a closed order like Indian caste system. The king could appoint new individuals to the nobility, or an individual could purchase rights and titles or join in by marriage. While most peasants worked on the lands of feudal lords, many of them owned land. But all peasants, whether landowners, tenants or share-croppers, had to pay feudal dues in money and in kind to the lord of the manor as well as tithes, payable in kind, to the church. Besides, they were obliged to use the lord's mill, bread oven and wine press rather than have their own, and pay for them.[47] Since the wealthy and rich comprising the big landowners, the church and the nobility were not taxed, the third estate had to bear heavy burden of taxes. Thus any fiscal crisis of the feudal regime directly burdened the peasants and the urban poor. France was deep in debt due to the costly wars and foreign policies of the previous kings. The treasury was almost drained in process of supporting the American rebels against its arch enemy, the English, in the American Revolution. While peasants were paying painfully for this profligacy, the nobility was indulging in conspicuous consumption and decadent lifestyle.

During the two decades preceding the revolution, this structural crisis was aggravated by various factors such as a spring drought, followed by a devastating hailstorm that ruined wheat crops in July 1788. By February 1789 the prices of bread had nearly doubled.[48] The situation was fast becoming explosive with pent up anger of masses. Distressed peasants had long been resentful of the privileges of their landlords and urban workers, who could not even feed their families, and were angry with the rich who reeled in comfort. The bourgeoisie that emerged from the Third Estate had more access to education and culture, leading to marriages between them and nobility. Although their economic progress raised them socially, it failed to get them commensurate political power; it only made them "more acutely sensitive to the inferior legal status to which they were still condemned."[49] In the Estates-General (a legislative body convened on rare occasion by the king) the votes were counted by estate, not by head, and as such the Third Estate to which they belonged was often outvoted by the First and Second Estate, usually voting together preserve and further their interests. They needed to change this.

One could find some parallel to this development in the Mahad revolt. Since the advent of colonial rule, many opportunities befell Dalits. Many Dalits entered the British army, educated themselves through military and missionary schools, took jobs in the emerging capitalist sectors, graduated to open petty businesses and slowly raised their economic status. Dr Ambedkar provided a glimpse of this development albeit referring to only the Mahars in Konkan area in his speech in the first conference. Quite like the bourgeoisie in France, this section also experienced that their educational and economic uplift did not make any change to their social status. It is this section of Dalits that came forward to constitute an incipient Dalit movement. The demand of the French bourgeoisie was expressed in terms of political power and manifested in constitution of the National Assembly. Unlike them the felt need of Dalits was social recognition and hence their struggle was aimed at social reforms. Moreover, as the French revolution was ignited by the subsistence crisis felt by the peasants and workers while the upper classes were indulging in profligate lifestyles, the Dalit revolt was ignited by the socio-psychological crisis experienced by a section of relatively educated and economically stable Dalits in major cities.

One aspect of the French revolution that often gets eclipsed by the estate discourse is the role played by the French women in general and those belonging to the third estate. Women were the most affected lot by subsistence crisis. They had virtually no civil or economic rights in feudal France. "By and large, women were legally totally subservient to their husbands or fathers in virtually all areas of marriage contracts, inheritance laws, property and tax laws, and child custody arrangements. Marriages were indissoluble."[50] Actually, it was they who fired the first salvo on 1 January, 1789 by presenting their charter of demands to King Louis XVI. The demands included right to send female deputies to the Estates-General, the right to adequate education, and the right to earn a respectable living (and thus avoid drifting into prostitution, which most lower-strata women were fated to). These demands were not especially radical as the petitioners themselves explained, "We ask to be enlightened, to have work, not in order to usurp men's authority, but in order to be better esteemed by them."[51] French women did not lack male support in their quest for human rights. The state of women in India was surely no better in 1920s than what is noted of the French women in 1789. But Mahad did not have women participation. Although Dalit women unlike the caste Hindu women shared more responsibility of running households than their menfolk, they did not get any prominence in social sphere. Ambedkar's emphasis on their importance did not make much difference.

On May 5, 1789, King Louis XVI convened the Estates-

General for its first meeting in 175 years to discuss solutions to France's economic woes. In the debate on how voting should proceed, when the first two estates refused to change the traditional methods of voting, the Third Estate walked out. On 10 June, the Third Estate (called Commons) issues an ultimatum to the other estates to join in or the Commons would go on alone. A few members of the First Estate (priests and clergy) join the Third Estate on 13 June. On June 17, the Third Estate held its own meeting and declared itself the National Assembly, claiming sovereign power. When the Royal Session opened on 23 June, the deputies of the National Assembly ignored it. On 25 June, Members of the Second Estate began to join the National Assembly. This was the beginning of the French revolution.[52] What the National Assembly accomplished was the dissolution of the Estates General that symbolized feudal authority; it effectively abolished monarchy and it adopted the Declaration of the Rights of Man and Citizen, codifying basic political, social, and civil rights as follows:

> The declaration of the Rights of Man and Citizen on August 26, 1789 was partly influenced by the American Declaration of Independence dated 4th July 1776. The French document is still considered unique and enduring in its own way. Historians have long agreed that the Declaration of the Rights of Man and Citizen has proved to be one of the most influential documents in history, one that has influenced the quest for human rights in not only Europe but throughout the world.[53]

Each node in the process of making of the National Assembly was momentous in its scale, intensity and repercussions. The Mahad Satyagraha conference, despite being an expression of revolt against the caste order, cannot be extended beyond symbolism. True, the structure of social power is far more intricate than that of political power, therefore it cannot be seen in isolation and fought against. Unless one struck at its roots, in the soil of political economy, it cannot be shaken. Dr Ambedkar focused only on the social and religious aspects of the French revolution and did not concern himself with the political and much less, economical.[54] Mahad targeted the social structure manifested into the evil of untouchability and its presumed source in religious scripture. The Estates, as Ambedkar explained could be seen as social stratification differentiating their constituents in all aspects of life, viz., economic, social, cultural, and political, although it might not be ascriptive as in castes. If the Third Estate had seen other two Estates as its adversaries and waged its war against them for some reforms, keeping the power structure untouched, it would not have achieved what it did. Mahad, which was happening after 138 years and a decade after another momentous revolution, the Bolshevik revolution in Russia, could have pitched itself far higher in the revolutionary scale than it did. Like the National Assembly, Mahad also passed certain resolutions which were far reaching in their import for the social relations within the Hindu society. But they were destined to stay just as statements, in the absence of 'political' backing, unlike the declaration by the National Assembly, which drove a series of revolutionary actions. Within a week the National Assembly effected certain decisions: Peasants were now free to earn their own wages without any feudal encumbrance; the economic element of human rights became a reality for the nation's rural poor; it widened economic freedom for urban laborers; abolished guilds; freed artisans from a complicated hierarchical system; workshops were established throughout cities as sources of employment for poor women; urban workers could go on strike for higher wages; and most importantly, making bread more affordable. Mahad missed two opportunities that came in its way for turning into political, viz., retaliating the caste Hindu attack on 20 March and going ahead with the Satyagraha on 25 December, and instead ended itself into an unclear aftermath.

Beyond the symbolic similarity between the two events as rebellion against the long established exploitative order (political-economic structure of French feudalism and religious cultural structure of the Hindu social order, respectively), there may be little that is comparable. The scale at which these two events had taken place was entirely different. They may be comparable in their defiant spirit, but not in their forms, contents, methods, or outcome. The comparison of Mahad in 1927 with the National Assembly of France in 1789 could have served as a benchmark for the future course of the Dalit movement.

9. Burning of Manusmruti and Storming of Bastille

The Bastille, a fortress in Paris that was basically built in fourteenth century to guard off the eastern entrance to the city from the English attack, had come to symbolize the King's absolute and arbitrary power. It played an important role in the internal conflicts of France and for most of its history was used as a state prison by the kings of France. Louis XIV (1638-1715) used it as a prison for upper-class members of French society who had opposed or angered him. Subsequent kings (Louis XV and XVI) used it to detain prisoners from more varied backgrounds, and to support the operations of the Parisian police, especially in enforcing government censorship of the printed media. Although inmates were kept in relatively good conditions, criticism of the Bastille grew during the 18th century, fueled by autobiographies written by former prisoners. Reforms were implemented in response and prisoner numbers were considerably reduced. In 1789, the significance of Bastille was purely symbolic, as there were no political prisoners inside.

In the wake of rumours of counter attack by the King's Army in response to the speech of Camille Desmoulins[55] in the gardens of the Palais Royale, urging the citizens of Paris to take up arms, a group of people, primarily residents of the Faubourg Saint-Antoine, decided to fight back and stole 28,000 rifles from 'Invalides' on 13 July. Since they did not find the gun powder, they decided to attack the Bastille, which was known to store arms and ammunition for the King. The Bastille was guarded only by a few soldiers. Since the crowd of attackers also was not big enough to impress the guards, the governor of the Bastille, the Marquis de Launay, accepted to meet their representatives inside the prison, hoping to buy time until a rescue team arrived. But when after some time a group of revolutionaries entered the Bastille, the guards were ordered to fire, killing more than one hundred people. The path of the revolt completely changed when the rescue team showed up and decided not to fight against, and rather be with the mob. With their canons and their professional soldier skills, they brought victory to the people of France against Louis XVI's guards in a few hours. At 4 pm, the Marquis de Launay surrendered and let the people enter the Bastille. The guards were violently killed and the Marquis de Launay was beheaded, with his head then put on a stake, and carried all over the city as a sign of victory. There weren't many prisoners in the Bastille at the time of the storming; only seven people were freed. That very night, 800 men began to destroy the Bastille. The Bastille was demolished by order of the Committee of the Hôtel de Ville. Souvenirs of the fortress were transported around France and displayed as icons of the overthrow of despotism. It marked the beginning of the French Revolution which would shake the earth.

Babasaheb Ambedkar likened the burning of Manusmruti in the Satyagraha conference at Mahad with the storming of the Bastille in Paris. In what way were these two events comparable? Obviously, what is implied in Ambedkar's comparison is the metaphor of a citadel of casteism based on the code of Manusmruti, which was demolished by the symbolic burning of Manusmruti as the storming of Bastille did to the fortress of absolutism of the monarchy in France. This could only be valid at the metaphorical level. The storming of Bastille entailed bloodshed, burning of Manusmruti did not even evoke as much reaction as for instance drinking water from the Chavadar Tank.

Bastille was a fortress that was captured and demolished by the revolutionaries. Manusmruti was assumed as the foundation of casteism, which, even if true, would not be shaken just by burning a copy of it. It only represented the denouncement of the Untouchables. With the fall of Bastille, the monarchy in France literally collapsed paving way for the republic. With the burning of Manusmruti, nothing happened except probably awakening the Untouchables that they should cast away the mental yoke of caste code and angering certain sections of the caste Hindus. Castes, whatsoever their origin might have been, had become the life world of people and that world could not be shaken by such a symbolic act. Rather it created a false consciousness in Dalits that castes were the product of Hindu scriptures, which needed to be destroyed for their annihilation. It led them to completely ignore their material aspects which were shaped and reshaped by the contemporary structures of political economy. This consciousness has conditioned their orientation that valorizes ideal over the material, the virtual over the real and the abstract over the concrete. The capture of the Chavadar Tank at Mahad was thus a more significant event than burning of Manusmruti, although two could imply different things: the former as assertion of human rights and not necessarily negation of the caste code, which burning of Manusmruti meant. Nonetheless in terms of impact, the former would prove far more consequential than the latter. The attacks on both reflected culmination of consciousness in defying their respective authorities. But beyond this point, they were incomparable. The burning of Manusmruti did not cause the caste structure to collapse. The Bastille raid was something physical that literally ended monarchy in France.

One may not be sure whether to call Mahad a revolution. Even Dr Ambedkar was cautious in not calling it so. He had just compared the instances within it and the French Revolution. The minimalist definition of revolution is the fundamental change in power or organization structure taking place within a compressed period of time. The French Revolution was certainly a revolution, or rather its exemplar. Mahad neither aimed at nor did it achieve any such revolutionary change. It was limited to realizing the rights which already existed in law. It was not even demanding its expansion or any new right. The resolutions it passed were radical enough, akin to the declaration of human rights. Mahad certainly raised consciousness of the Untouchables to new higher plane. Now they could think and speak the language of rights. It galvanized them into action and manifested into a series of satyagrahis undertaken voluntarily by them to exercise their legal rights. The attack on Bastille was the harbinger of the earth shattering revolution. It changed the entire complexion of politics in France. Manusmruti might have informed the caste culture in the past but empirically it was not even identified as such in public imagination as revealed by the relative absence of any harsh reaction to its burning. The demolition of the Bastille would reverberate for centuries, in public memory, inspiring them to revolt against oppressive regimes.

10. Mahad and the Civil Rights Struggle of the African Americans in the USA

If Mahad is to be compared with any other struggle, it should necessarily be the civil rights struggles of the African Americans in the United States. Although, caste is not race, the racial discrimination suffered by the Blacks in the US, comes very close to that of Dalits. Of course, they do not suffer from ritualistic untouchability but their existential segregation comes close to the segregation of Dalits. Likewise, Dalits did not suffer chattel slavery like the Blacks but their caste bondage may not be materially different from the slavery the Blacks suffered. It is unfortunate that the Dalit movement has practically no reference to these glorious struggles of the African Americans, except for a very brief one in relation to the Dalit Panthers. Also, the similarity extends to their communities too. As Dalits are not a homogenous people and are divided into numerous castes, the African societies from where African Americans came are also not homogenous in any sense; many of them follow social segregation of certain tribes and even practice untouchability.[56] These problems however had never surfaced as civil rights issue in African past; at least there being no account of the victim tribals having waged any struggle against their discrimination. However, there is a documented history of resistance by the Blacks against their racial discrimination by the Whites.

The Whites looked down upon them as inferior race and believed they were liberating them from heathenism.[57] The Spanish and Portuguese explorers took them to the USA and so did the French. In 1517, when the slavery was established in the New World[58], their real troubles started. What strikes one while reading their history is that they never meekly submitted to the force of slave catchers. Unlike Dalits who had internalized their state as divine ordained, the Africans never really accepted their inferiority. The accounts of their carriage from Africa as in Alex Haley's *Roots*[59] and many others' are fraught with their deadly resistance. They were 'so willful and loathe to leave their own country that they have often leaped out of the canoes, boats and ships into the sea, and kept under water till they were drowned. They preferred a watery grave or to be devoured by sharks to enslavement in some faraway land.'[60] One has to just glance through Herbert Aptheker's *American Negro Slave Revolts*[61] or E.D. Genovese's *From Rebellion to Revolution: Afro-American Slave Revolts in the Making of Modern World*[62] to get the glimpse of fierce fights the Blacks waged against their tormentors; how many of them preferred death to painful existence of slavery.

Kapoor (2004) also provides details of many cases of the 'organized resistance' and the bloody rebellions of the slaves in the US and their brutal retaliations by the racist establishment.[63] Such revolts on the part of slaves and repression by whites continued down to the Civil War, which came to be associated with anti-slavery movement. In 1865 chattel slavery was abolished and in 1866 Civil Rights Act was passed. Even thereafter, the response of the African Americans alternated "between demands for Civil Rights and outright violence."[64] One wonders why Dalit history is conspicuous with total absence of such a reaction to their oppression. Understandably, their early phase of resistance is lost in the distant murky past, and over centuries thereafter, they lived their internalized serfdom. But even in modern times when they regained their lost consciousness, there is still not the slightest evidence of such natural reaction to the monumental wrong inflicted upon them.[65] Even today, the response of Dalits to the spate of atrocities being committed on them does not transcend the outcries of self-pity or techno-legal boundaries drawn by their tormentors or still meandering in religio-cultural sphere.

It may be explained to some degree by the fact that the consciousness of being wronged dawned early on African Americans. Since their oppression began with their uprooting from their homelands and enslavement with visible force, the Blacks had gained the consciousness of free land and articulated response in terms of force. In the case of Dalits, since their oppression was part of a complex caste system with its continuum of discrimination supported by an ideology with divine sanction, it became their life-world over the centuries, blocking clear sight of oppressor or self-realization as oppressed. Their consciousness was correspondingly hazy and ideologically mundane and lazy. Unlike the Blacks, who from day one had the consciousness of being wronged, Dalits through a long history had internalized their oppression. It is only in the mid-twentieth century that they became conscious of their oppression being manmade that needed to be resisted.[66] But that surely is not the complete explanation. The difference perhaps is in the kind of consciousness in both movements. The consciousness of being wronged germinated naturally in ordinary Black people as they were being exploited or put to ignominy by their white masters and they agitated to resist it in the manner they thought feasible. Many individuals have spontaneously resisted racist excesses; some of these instances assuming organized form. It was thus largely a bottoms-up process. In contrast, Dalit protest appears to be top-down in its making. It germinated in the relatively better off Dalits, as explained earlier, and then it spread downward. In view of this it still appears constricted by the class outlook of the people who spearhead the Dalit movement. The development of consciousness in these communities has been therefore at variance, which manifests some way in the nature of their developments. It is not just the scaling of tangible progress, the self confidence with which African American conduct themselves is still not seen in the state-reliant and self-deprecating Dalits.

The resistance of the African Americans has been multi-stranded and essentially decentralized. Right from their transportation from West Africa, they rebelled against it. One of the first acts of resistance in later history took place in 1890s. Homer A Plessy, an Afro-Creole businessman[67], one-eighth black by racial stock, but still black under the United States Constitution had entered a 'only white' coach of a East Louisiana railroad train in New Orleans and refused to move from it. After the Civil War, when slavery was formally abolished, many

Southern states were determined to try and limit the rights of former slaves. They wanted to maintain segregation to stave off the possibility of mixing of races. The government succeeded enacting segregation laws, such as the one passed by Florida in 1887, which required railroads operating in the state or passing through the state to house black passengers in separate cars from the whites. It was soon after this that separate car laws were in force in most of the South. The incident was planned by a group of New Orleans black businessmen, members of the Citizens Committee, (an organization devoted to challenging Segregation Laws) to fight these laws along with railroads who were also against the law. The group decided to test the case and found a volunteer in Plessy to break the law. Plessy was arrested on 7 June 1892 under the Louisiana Separate Car Act 111 and was charged with a 25 dollar fine. The case went to the Supreme Court and the law was upheld as constitutional. "Separate but Equal" remained the law of the land for fifty-eight years, until 1954 when the Court held in *Brown v. Board of Education*[68] that separate was inherently unequal.

The march to the Chavadar Tank can be likened to African Americans' participation in the desegregation campaign following the 1954 Supreme Court judgment in the famous *Brown v. Board of Education* case which ended the legal segregation of black and white students in public schools and ordered admission to public schools be done on a racially non-discriminatory basis with all deliberate speed, i.e., to desegregate all schools speedily. This ruling, which overruled a Supreme Court decision of 1896 upholding segregation, became a tool for the African Americans with which to challenge white supremacy. They enthusiastically worked for the campaign to desegregate schools in different parts of the country. Although in terms of outcome, even ten years after the decision, 96 per cent of the African American children in the United States still attended segregated schools, mobilization of African American in large numbers produced valuable experience and consciousness that began to change race relations. The march to the Chavadar Tank to drink its water likewise was not *per se* important as Dalits were not getting anything new; the right to take water from public sources already being on the statute. However it was organizationally important in mobilizing Dalits for future struggles for their rights. As in the desegregation campaign, it took ten long years of a court battle for the realization of legal right to access water from the Chavadar Tank. In both the cases the reality completely contradicted the claims of 'justice'. While the experience with the Desegregation judgment ironically contributed to the erosion of black people's belief in legalism as a method of struggle, nothing of the kind, or rather exactly the opposite happened in the case of Dalits. They became increasingly legalistic and constitutional in their orientation.

Although the circumstances, the locale and the histories of Dalits and African Americans were too dissimilar to expect similarities among their movements the conspicuous absence of a militant stream in the Dalit movement is definitely surprising. Because, when racism, casteism, or any such ideology that severally denies people their dues operates in societies as hegemonic ideology, it is intrinsically violent because it promotes the interests of the entrenched classes at the cost of others. The embedded violence surfaces in the face of resistance by victims but otherwise it is always there. Were procurement, transportation and sale of Africans as slaves without violence? Was cultivated mass conformity and compliance in favour of caste hierarchy and institutionalization of mass illiteracy, superstition and irrationality in India without violence? Brahmanism has used castes with the strategy of 'brahman precept and kshatriya arm' which reflects the role of violence within the system. It is not for nothing that all the Hindu gods are fully loaded with deadly weapons and are linked to macabre violence. They depicted the response to the lower castes thinking of defying the caste code. The caste system being thus inherently violent, it would not be unnatural to have a violent response to it. Most times the well entrenched systems react with extra violence if they sense danger to their continuance. After the civil war, when slavery was abolished, the racist South had reacted with more violence than ever before. Similarly, the caste Hindus when they see threat to their domination, react with horrendous atrocities on the Dalits. It may therefore be imperative to have a violent component to the strategy to combat casteism. In Mahad, the caste Hindus also had acted violently when Dalits had physically gone to the Chavadar Tank and took its water and not when the bill according Dalits this right was passed by the Legislature. If the Dalits had a contingent strategy to respond to such incipient violence, they would have never dared to try it as explained above.

Violence or non-violence should be a matter of strategy and not ideology. By basing it on ideology, one innocuously enters the enemy's trap; he continues with violence but forbids it for others. It is often argued that violent methods do not succeed. May be they do not as an exclusive strategy, but their role cannot be undermined in effectualizing the non-violent strategies. There may not be any example of pure non-violent strategy ever succeeding either. The non-violent stream of civil rights movement appears to have succeeded in getting the Civil Rights Act in place but one cannot ignore the contributions of the armed resistance of the African Americans in the process. It is only when the state has seen the intensity of reactions of the African Americans that it was impelled to speak with the non-violent stream which could strategically serve its contingent purpose of debilitating violent movement and containing reaction within its own confines. It may be best exemplified by the case of Indian freedom from colonial rule which is customarily projected as the triumph of Gandhian methods of non-violence. The fact remains that it was the result of a series of armed struggles of revolutionaries and such violent events as naval mutiny and Indian National Army's march into its north-eastern borders during the World War II that directly threatened the loyalty of Indian soldiers in British army coupled with weakening of war devastated Britain. Obviously, it is strategically convenient for the ruling classes to side by those who are moderate, malleable and 'reasonable' among the lower classes and wipe out those who speak of violence. After the Civil Rights movement, this is what precisely happened. The federal government unleashed violence on the militant groups like Black Panther and almost wiped it out along with all others.

Epilogue

Mahad marks the birth of the Dalit movement and therefore has indelible imprint on its later history. Apart from being one of the earliest instances in the history of the civil rights movement, it can be an important treasure trove of learning for any movement of the oppressed people in general and of the Dalits in particular. Unfortunately, there has been a strong tendency among the latter to iconize its historical instances and make them unavailable for such learnings. History is potentially capable of teaching us many things: helping us understand our present in its evolutionary context, making us see the sources of our problems, encouraging us to seek solutions to them, and keep doing course corrections towards our goals.

It only demands of the present generation critical thinking and ruthless objectivity as it dissects its past but at the same time an acute awareness that it is doing this with hindsight. If it finds fault with the past, as part of the essential process of learning, it is merely because it is standing at the higher pedestal which it reached by the very efforts of the previous generations. There is no irreverence involved to the heroes who made this past. On the contrary, they are brought alive with veneration for having left behind so much to learn from. The opposite could be to entomb them for their gradual deification, which is the surest way of stripping them off their content. It is what humans uncritically do if they are not on guard against these natural tendencies. The pathetic state of Dalits in India, notwithstanding the bravados of a minuscule section comprising less than one-tenth of the Dalit population overshadowing the reality of the rest of Dalits, nearly nine decades after the Mahad struggle and its glorious sequel should certainly drive us to examine the building blocks of the movement. Insofar as Mahad constitutes the foundational episode, it needs to be looked at as the possible source of its ethos, orientations and attitudes.

Mahad undoubtedly marks a glorious moment for Dalits but at the same time reflects many infirmities of the contemporary Dalit movement in their embryonic forms. The traces of the contemporary Dalit movement's obsession with the socio-cultural issues and persistent ignorance of political and economic problems; its excessive reliance on the state as the benefactor or neutral arbiter betraying its erroneous conception of that institution; its excessive poetic mode of expression far beyond its inspirational utility to propel itself away from harsh realities into the virtual spaces; its obsessive leader-centricism and top-down orientations smacking of simultaneous feudal ethos and petty-bourgeois orientation; its penchant for abstract and avoidance of concrete; its persistence lack of strategic outlook in identifying its own strengths and weaknesses as well its friends and foes, which makes it available to be exploited by the enemy camp; its inability to take up appropriate issues and formulate apt forms of struggle; its identitarian streak and lack of willingness to acknowledge objective realities and so on can be variously sensed in Mahad. There lies the importance of Mahad.

NOTES AND REFERENCES

1. In fact, in an editorial written on 21 November 1927 in *Bahishkrut Bharat*, a few days before the conference, Ambedkar had discussed the method of Satyagraha and disagreed with Gandhi on his irrational insistence on Satyagraha to be nonviolent. This part is discussed in details under the subtitle "The Issue of Violence" in this chapter.
2. See, a sample letter reproduced by C.B. Khairmode, *Dr. Bhimrao Ramji Ambedkar yanche Charitra*, Vol. 3, Pratap Prakashan, Mumbai. 1964, p. 269.
3. Ibid., p. 112.
4. Ibid., p. 273.
5. C.B. Khairmode, *Dr Bheemrao Ramji Ambedkar yanche Charitra*, Vol. 2, pp. 117-18.
6. See, the end note 1 above.
7. John P. McKay, et al., *A History of World Societies: From 1775 to Present*, Volume C, Bedford/St. Martin's: Boston/New York, 2009. "..., Gandhi was searching for a spiritual theory of social action. He studied Hindu and Christian teachings, and gradually developed a weapon for the weak that he called Satyagraha." Ibild., p. 859.
8. Uma Majmudar, *Gandhi's Pilgrimage of Faith: From Darkness to Light*, SUNY Press, New York, 2005, p. 138.
9. Jai Narain Sharma, *Satyagraha: Gandhi's Approach to Conflict*

Resolution, Concept Publishing, New Delhi, 2008, p. 91. Gandhi might violently disagree with the third one as associated with his *Satyagraha*. He refused to acknowledge any coercion contained within Satyagraha. Actually, in most cases, what he practiced was nothing but coercion. For instance, his epic fast against the communal award in 1932 that compelled Dr Ambedkar to give up his hard won separate electorates for Dalits to sign the Poona Pact was coercion pure and simple. But, the adherent of truth would still maintain this untruth that Satyagraha did not contain coercion.

10. The march to the Chavadar Tank during the first conference was not called a Satyagraha.
11. Although, Dr Ambedkar was aware that actually it was against the state. See Khairmode C.B. op. cit. p. 121.
12. It can be repeatedly seen that such cultural notions, howsoever entrenched, do not last in the face of physical necessities. If today the castes are not as rigid as before, the credit only goes to the changes in political economy than all the efforts put in the cultural sphere. The caste Hindus, when forced to take water from the polluted tank, they would not have had any other option than reconciling with the changed conditions.
13. See Appendix 7: The Order of M/s. Broomfield and N. J. Wadia, dated 17 March 1937.
14. Mark Shephard for instance says, "As far as I can tell, no civil disobedience campaign of Gandhi's ever succeeded *chiefly* through a change of heart in his opponents." See, Mark Shepard, *Mahatma Gandhi and His Myths: Civil Disobedience, Nonviolence, and Satyagraha in the Real World*, Shepard Publications, Los Angeles, 2002.
15. Some problems of coercion in Gandhian tactics are dealt with in G. Sharp, Mechanisms of change in nonviolent action in Harvey A. Hornstein (ed.): *Strategies for Social Intervention*, Free Press., New York, 1971; and J. Galtung and A. Ness, Gandhi and Group Conflict: An Exploration of Satyragraha, Universitetsforlaget, Oslo cited in Robert E. Klitgaard, Gandhi's Non-Violence as a Tactic, *Journal of Peace Research*, Vol. 8, No. 2, 1971, pp. 143-153.
16. D. Keer, *Dr Ambedkar, Life and Mission*, Popular Prakashan, 2nd edition, Bombay: 1962, p. 76.
17. See chapter 5 for these details.
18. J.R. Hood, DM, Kolaba's letter No. MSC 192 dated 14 October 1927 to H.L. Painter, Commissioner, Southern Division, Belgaum. FN 324.

19. Interestingly, this usage of the term *hindutva* preceded Savarkar's *Hindutva: Who is a Hindu?* (Bharat Publications, Nagpur, 1928), which publicized it, although Savarkar's brief treatise titled "Essentials of Hindutva" written in 1922 predates it. Available at www.savarkar.org/content/pdfs/en/essentials_of_hindutva.v001.pdf. [Last accessed on 14 April 2015].
20. B.R. Ambedkar, Buddha and His Dhamma in Vasant Moon (ed), *Dr Babasaheb Ambedkar: Writings and Speeches*, Vol. 11, p. 509.
21. B.R. Ambedkar, Buddha or Karl Marx, in Vasant Moon (ed), *Dr Babasaheb Ambedkar: Writings and Speeches*, Vol. 3, p. 449.
22. C.B. Khairmode, C.B., op. cit., p. 121.
23. Ibid., p. 122.
24. B.R. Ambedkar, What Congress and Gandhi have Done to the Untouchables (Chapter V), in Vasant Moon (ed), *Dr Babasaheb Ambedkar: Writings and Speeches*, Vol. 9, Government of Maharashtra, Mumbai, 1991, p. 136.
25. Harold Coward, (ed), *Indian Critiques of Gandhi*, State University of New York Press, New York, 2003, p, 9.
26. Eleanor Zelliot, *Dr. Babasaheb Ambedkar and the Untouchable Movement*, Blumoon Books, New Delhi, 2004, p. 187.
27. *Bahishkrut Bharat*, 12 August 1927.
28. Khaparde had sent a letter to Satyagraha committee asking for three months time within which he would convince the caste Hindus to accept demands of the Satyagraha. C.B. Khairmode, op. cit., p. 108.
29. Hari Narke (ed), *Dr Babasaheb yanche Bahishkrut Bharat ani Mooknayak*, 2nd edition, Government of Maharashtra, Mumbai, 2008, p. 138(12).
30. C.B. Khairmode, Vol. 3, op. cit., p. 126.
31. See for instance an interview of G.N. Mujumdar, MLC reported in the Evening News, 16.10.1929, referred to by C.B. Khairmode, op. cit., p. 270.
32. Ibid., p. 306.
33. Ibid., pp. 334-5.
34. Ibid., pp. 316-7.
35. Dr Ambedkar's letter to B.K. Gaikwad dated 28 March 1930. See, C.B. Khairmode, Vol. 3, op. cit., p. 345.
36. Khairmode, Vol. 3, op. cit., p. 321.
37. Ibid., p. 350.
38. Ibid., p. 389
39. Anant Chitre writes that Dr Ambedkar was reluctant to participate in the Mahad Conference, saying that he wanted to

become a district judge. He needed to be persuaded by him (Chitre) and Sahasrabuddhe to accept the chairmanship of the Conference. See end note 9 to Chapter 3, p. 168.

40. As such the Indian Councils Act 1909 (Morley-Minto Reforms), which sought to restore stability to the British Raj against the armed uprisings in Bengal, had accepted the communal principle in granting the Muslims 25 per cent reservation of seats in the Municipal and District Boards; Provincial Councils and in the Imperial legislature with separate electorates. See, Tarique Mohammad, *Modern India History*, Tata McGraw Hill, New Delhi, 2008, pp. 16-8.
41. Gandhi was among the first to speak against the practice of untouchability in a speech on 5 June 1916, in Ahmedabad although he justified the caste system. M.K. Gandhi, Speech on Caste System in *Collected Works of Mahatma Gandhi*, 1916, Vol. 15, the CD-Rom "Mahatma Gandhi - Interactive Multimedia - Electronic Book" by the Publications Division in 1999, p. 226.
42. As a matter of fact, the dimension of religious conversion was included in the plan of Mahad. Ambedkar wrote that if the caste Hindus took adamant position, then the Satyagraha would certainly fail. But it would be entirely at their peril because then the Untouchables would be provoked to renounce Hinduism itself. However, he said that he would not expect the caste Hindus to go to that extent. It was certainly meant to forewarn the Hindus in socio-religious terms, but not yet politically. C.B. Khairmode, op. cit., p. 123.
43. Vasant Moon (ed), *Dr Babasaheb Ambedkar, Writings and Speeches*, Vol. 20, 2012, pp. 448-9.
44. Hari Narke (ed.), op. cit., p. 286(2).
45. Ibid., p. 302(8).
46. B.R. Ambedkar, Essays on Untouchables and Untouchability: Political in Vasant Moon (ed), *Dr Babasaheb Ambedkar, Writings and Speeches*, Vol. 5, Government of Maharashtra, Mumbai, 1989, p. 255.
47. Rodney Hilton, *Warriors and Pesants*, Available at: newleftreview.org/ static/assets/archive/pdf/NLR08207.pdf. [Last Accessed on 14 April 2015].
48. Simon Schama, *Citizens: A Chronicle of the French Revolution*, Penguin Press, London, 2004, p. 239.
49. Darline Gay Levy, Branson Harriet Applewhite and Mary Durham Johnson, *Women in Revolutionary Paris, 1789-1795*, University of Illinois Press, 1979, p. 20.

50. Ibid., p. 20.
51. Nora Temple, *The Road to 1789: From Reform to Revolution in France*, University of Wales Press, Cardiff, 1992, p. 51.
52. Abdul Matin, *Social Change and Planning*, Dorling Kindersley, New Delhi, p. 68.
53. Hari Narke, op. cit., p. 182(2)
54. Lucie Simplice Camille Benoît Desmoulins (1760–1794), a childhood friend of Maximilien Robespierre and a political ally of Georges Danton, both leading figures in the French Revolution, was tried and executed alongside Danton in response to Dantonist opposition to the Committee of Public Safety, the *de facto* executive government in France during the Reign of Terror (1793–1794). Sloan, Stephen, *Terrorism: The Present Threat in Context*, Bloomsbury, Oxford, 2006, p. 41.
55. See, discussions on this in Chapter 1 and see end note 14, p. 19.
56. George M. Fredrickson, and Edgar E. Robinson, *Black Liberation: A Comparative History of Black Ideologies in the United States and South Africa*, Oxford University Press, London, 1955, p. 79.
57. There is no definite date for the start of slavery in America. In 1517, under Charles V, Bishop las Casas said to have drawn up a plan of assisted migration to America and asked the right for immigrants to import twelve Negro slaves. As such Charles V had authorized the export of 15,000 slaves to san Domingo, and thus priest and King launched on the world the American slave trade and slavery. W.E. William Edward Burghardt Du Bois, "The Trade in Men" in Phil Zuckerman (ed), *The Social Theory of W.E.B. Du Bois*, Sage, London, 2004, p. 78.
58. Alex Haley, *Roots: The Saga of an American Family*, Vanguard Press, New York, 2007.
59. John Hope Franklin, A Brief History of the Negro in the United States in John P. Davis (ed), *The American Negro Reference Book*, Prentice Hall, New Jersey, 1967, p. 5.
60. First published in 1943 by Columbia University Press and the latest Sixth Edition by International Publishers, New York.
61. Louisiana State University Press, 1992.
62. S.D. Kapoor, *Dalits and African American: A Study in Comparison*, Kalpaz, Delhi, 2004, pp. 45-67.
63. Ibid., p. 49.
64. One gets a glimpse of the resistance in pre-modern times, expressed in the form of poetry of the Dalit saints like Chokhamela in the Bhakti movement. Probably, it was inevitable because of the homomorphous nature of the oppressive structure.

65. S.D. Kapoor, op. cit., p. 69.
66. Afro-Creoles were the highly educated free Blacks that had enjoyed the privileges of freedom dating back to French colonial days. See, Dixie Ray Haggard (ed), *African Americans in the Nineteenth Century: People and Perspectives*, ABC-Clio, Santa Barbara, 2010, p. 130.
67. The 1954 Supreme Court decision in respect of many cases of the admission of Black children to public schools that permitted segregation based on race in states of Kansas, South Carolina, Virginia, and Delaware. The Supreme Court held that the race-based segregation of children into 'separate but equal' public schools violated the Equal Protection Clause of the Fourteenth Amendment and as such was unconstitutional. The Fourteenth Amendment was one of three amendments to the Constitution adopted after the Civil War to guarantee black rights. The Thirteenth Amendment abolished slavery, the Fourteenth granted citizenship to people once enslaved, and the Fifteenth guaranteed black men the right to vote. The Fourteenth Amendment was passed by Congress in June 1866 and ratified by the states in 1868. See, James T. Patterson, *Brown v. Board of Education: A Civil Rights Milestone and its Troubled Legacy*, Oxford University Press, New York, 2001.

Appendix 1

Resolutions Passed in the Conference

Class 1

1. If the upper class Hindus desire that the movement of the boycotted classes for their self emancipation should not create antagonism between them and the boycotted classes, this conference is making the following suggestions to them:
   a) When people from the boycotted classes try to exercise their rights of citizenship by making use of public and water sources, people from the upper classes resort to stopping of all transactions with them and declare social boycott against them. Rather than doing so, people from the upper classes should actively help the people of boycotted classes in their endeavors
   b) People from the upper classes should accept people from the boycotted class as their domestic servants.
   c) They should promote inter caste marriages as the method of abolition of casteism.
   d) They should accept poor students from boycotted classes on daily terms for meals or arrange for their food and help them.
   e) They should not rely on the boycotted classes to drag their dead animals and should arrange for the same themselves.

Class 2

1. In the Bombay Legislative Council, Shri S.K. Bole has brought out a resolution regarding the opening of

public wells and tanks to the Untouchables. The Government should implement it and display notices to that effect at those places. If necessary, they should impose Criminal Procedure Code (CrPC) section 144 and arrange for anticipatory bails for the local leaders in the process of helping the Untouchables to exercise their rights.

2. This conference appeals to the Government to make arrangement for removal of the extreme inconvenience that the Untouchables have to go through to get drinking water in so many of the villages.
3. The government should allot forest lands to the boycotted class people for their economic development.
4. The government should pay attention to the following things in order to ameliorate the sufferings and to raise the economic status of the extremely backward people from the boycotted classes:
   a) Provide Government service to the unqualified persons from the Untouchable classes, wherever possible.
   b) Recruit Untouchable people in military.
   c) Take the Untouchable candidates in navy.
   d) The second year trained teachers should be given the post of supervisor in the education department.
   e) The literate people belonging to the Untouchable class should be given suitable positions in the local police force.
   f) As much as possible the Untouchable people should be recruited to the police department.
5. The method of paying *balute* from villagers for the government service should be stopped and in its place a kind of cess should be levied on them as in other provinces like the Central Provinces. Village servants should be given a monthly salary from this cess.
6. The custom of people from the boycotted classes consuming meat of dead animals should be prohibited

through law by the government because it causes serious damage to their health and lowers their social status.

7. The government should apply force in respect of education and 'liquor-ban'.
8. This conference feels sad for not giving the post of deputy collector to Shri M.K. Jadhav.
9. There is money available in the earlier fund raised by Platoon No. 111 contributed by the employees from Mahad taluka. This money should be utilized to start a boarding for the students belonging to the Untouchable class of this taluka.
10. The following things should be implemented for the progress of the boycotted classes whose condition has been pathetic in respect of education:
    a) A committee should be appointed to enquire into how to achieve progress in their education.
    b) A boarding should be opened in every district.
    c) A grant of Rs. 10 per month, per student be given to boardings run by private institutions
    d) A school should be opened in villages with more than 30 boys/girls.
    e) Scholarships should be given.

Class 3

1. This conference requests the *Panchas* of the boycotted classes that they should implement the following things in respect of marriages of children :
    a) They should stop the custom of marrying the boy below 20 years and the girl below 15 years of age.
    b) Wherever schools are available, they should make it compulsory for the people to educate their children. If they violate this dictum they should be made liable for punishment.
    c) They should not execute re-marriage without proper enquiry into both, bride as well as groom.
    d) In re-marriages a tax of Rs. 7 should be collected. There should not be any other tax from the *Panchas*

except for the clothes and ornaments for the couple and meals for the *Panchas*.

2. a) The Untouchable people should give up menial vocations like *Maharki* and speedily adopt the independent professions like farming, etc...
   b) They should start cooperative banks necessary for farming.
   c) This conference makes an earnest request to boycotted classes for establishing 'cooperative dens' to escape the trap of moneylenders and to face difficulties in times of famine and excessive rains.

Class 4

1. This conference condoles the inhumane assassination of Swami Shraddhanandji and feels that the Hindu castes should annihilate caste as he preached.

Appendix 2

Order of the Sub-Judge Vaidya granting injunction

ORDER

This is an application asking the Court to grant to the applicants a temporary injunction restraining the opponents from going to the Chaudar Tank or taking water therefrom. The applicants have, on 12th December 1927, filed in this Court, Regular Suit No. 405 of 1927, for obtaining a Declaration that the said Chaudar Tank is of the nature of private property of the touchable classes only and that the Untouchable classes have no right to go to that tank, or take water from there and also for obtaining a perpetual injunction restraining the defendants from doing any of these acts.

The applicants, by this application pray that pending the disposal of the suit a temporary injunction may be issued against the Defendants. The application states, among other things, that for hundreds of years since the tank has been in the exclusive enjoyment of the touchable classes only, that on 19th March 1927, a number of persons of the Untouchable classes led by the defendant, entered the tank all of a sudden, washed their hands and faces with the water and thus contaminated it, that in consequence of this contamination, the touchable classes could not take water from the tank for over 24/25 hours, i.e., until the water was purified, at a great cost, by performing ceremonies laid down by the Hindu Shastras. A great hardship was thus caused to the touchable classes, that the Untouchable classes have issued a manifesto proclaiming their intention of again entering the tank and taking water therefrom, that if they are allowed to do that, the touchable classes will be debarred by the *Shastras*, from using the water of the tank. This would cause serious hardship to them and that if a temporary injunction as asked for, is not granted and the defendants allowed to contaminate the water of plaintiffs, even if they finally succeed in the suit, would not reap the benefit of the decree.

The application is supported by the affidavits of several persons besides Plaintiff No. 1. Plaintiffs have also produced with exhibit 4, a notice issued by the municipality against one Divakar Joshi (one of the persons making an affidavit) calling upon him to repair his stone *Dhakkas* (dams) which adjoined the side of the Chaudar Tank, and also a deed of partition of Dharap family alleged to be more than a hundred years old. This deed contains a reference to the Pal of the tank as being one of the properties partitioned. Both these documents raise a '*Prima facie*' presumption of the tank being a private property.

The question now is, whether it would be more just to grant a temporary injunction to refuse it. The law regarding temporary injunctions is contained in order 39 of the Civil Procedure Code. Rule 1 of this order is as follows:- Where in any suit it is proved by an affidavit or otherwise (a) that any property in dispute in suit is in danger of being wasted, damaged or alienated by any party to the suit, or wrongfully said in execution of a decree or (b) that the defendant threatens, or intends, to remove or dispose off his property with a view to defraud his creditors, the court may by order grant a temporary injunction. Clause (b) has obviously, no application to the present case. The present case appears to come within clause (a).

Here is a tank which has, for years since, been in the exclusive enjoyment of the touchable classes. The manifesto issued over the signatures of the defendants 1 and others also shows that the Untouchable classes were until now under the impression that they had no right of access to the tank. It thus appears that the tank has been until now in the exclusive enjoyment of the touchable classes. The question now is, whether the ends of justice would be better met by disturbing this old state of things or by allowing it to continue until the rights of the parties have been finally decided.

The principles governing temporary injunctions have been summarised under part 2 of Mulla's Commentary on the Civil Procedure Code, 8th edition page 892. One of these is that the Court must see that there is a bona-fide contention between the parties About this there appears to me to be very little doubt. The second principle is, 'on which side, in the event of success, will lie the balance of inconvenience if the injunction does not issue.' To me it appears that the balance of inconvenience will lie, and lie very heavily, on the side of the Plaintiffs if an injunction is not issued. The point is so clear that I do not think I need to labour it at all.

If the Defendants are allowed to enter the tank and thus (according to the religious notions of the Plaintiffs) contaminate the water and render it until for further use, a large section of the population will be put to hardship and inconvenience, which will be so severe that only those living in places where there are no copious supply of water, can realise it. On the other hand, the defendants will not be put to any inconvenience what so ever, if they are asked to far-bear from exercising what they consider to be their right, until the first decision to the suit. This course appears to me not only just and equitable, but the only right course under the circumstances in order to maintain the status quo which it is imperative to do. Vide the remark appearing at I.L.R. 46, Calcutta, page 1030. It is also contended by the applicants (Plaintiffs) that if a temporary injunction as asked for is not granted and the water of the tank is allowed to be contaminated, irreparable injury would result to the Plaintiffs. Taking into consideration, how sensitive the touchable classes generally are on this point, both on account of their religious susceptibilities, as well as the wide gulf which has existed between the two communities from time immemorial, I am inclined to attach very great weight to this condition. I have no doubt that the spread of education will, in course of time, materially alter these conditions and bring the two communities in a clear and friendly contact with each other and that untouchability will be a thing of the past. But as things stand at present, I am bound to attach great weight to, the sentiment of the applicants who feel that the injury they will sustain if the water is allowed to be contaminated. It will be that it would not admit of being adequately compensated by damages.

Taking all these circumstances into consideration, I think I would be failing in duty if I were not to refuse the injunction prayed for. It is a very painful duty that I am called upon to perform, but the call of duty leaves no room for choice. I, therefore order that a temporary injunction as asked for, with notice do issue.

14-12-27 Sd/- G.V. Vaidya

Appendix 3

Communication to the Untouchables

Pamphlet*

Under the Aegis of Bahishkrut Hitkarini Sabha,
A Satyagraha will begin at Mahad from 25 December 1927!

Help Mahad Satyagraha

jene kulwant mhanave II *tehi vegi hajir vhave* II
hajir na hota kashtave II *lagel pudhe* II
(those who are called well-born, should present themselves fast without presenting so, they may have to struggle ahead)

All the Untouchable brothers are hereby notified that it has been decided to hold a conference on 25 December at Mahad. When we had already held a conference at Mahad recently, on 19 March, why is this conference being held at the same place? This is the natural question that may be asked by some people. The answer to this question is that when our Untouchable brothers attempted to exercise their right of drinking water from the Chavadar tank, the touchable people had brutally attacked them with the intention of preventing them from doing so. The assaulters among the touchable people have been sentenced to four month of *sakt majuri* (forced labour). The court verdict is important for both the parties.

The notion among the touchable people that it was their right not to let the Untouchables access the Chavadar tank, has lost its basis. There is no doubt that if they ventured to oppose us in future like madmen, they will have to see the prison gates again. Likewise there is no hitch in saying that the belief among the Untouchables that they had the right to go to the Chavadar

---

* Translated from C.B. Khairmode, *Dr. Bhimrao Ramji Ambedkar Yandhe Charitra*, Khand 3, Pratap Prakashan, Pune, 1964, pp. 149-151.

tank has been established. If it had not been so, instead of sentencing those who had obstructed us from going to the tank, they would have sentenced us for having gone to the tank. The work of operationalization of this right of ours, which has been established by law, still remains unexercised. The conference, which has been planned on 25 December, is meant to accomplish this objective.

In this connection, nobody needs to feel threatened to attend the conference. And also nobody needs to listen to the advice of any orthodox person. This issue concerns humanity. We have to wash off the blot put on us by the touchable people that we are born impure.

This is the blot not only on ourselves, but also on our parents. To remove it is our prime duty as their offspring. It is therefore requested that all should attend the conference.

We need funds for this. Therefore, those who wish to make contribution in the form of either money or grains should do it. Volunteers have been touring with the receipt books with my signature and stamp to collect such donations. Whatever you wish to give, you can hand over to these volunteers against a receipt. You may also send it to the Secretary, Bahishkrut Hitkarini Sabha, Damodar Hall, Parel, Mumbai.

Yours sincerely,

Dr Bhimrao Ambedkar, MA, PhD, DSc, Bar-at-Law, MLC, President

Members:

Shivram Gopal Jadhav, Sambhaji Tukaram Poudkar, Balaram Ramji Ambedkar, Nirmal Limbaji Gangawane, Ragho Narayan Vanmali, Ganapat Mahadev Jadhav, Govond Ramji Adrekar Pandurang Mahadev Vavurkar, Laxman Ganu Pusainkar, Sakharam Ratnaji Nagavkar, Arjun Ramji Nagavkar, Changdev Ramayan Mohite, Pandurang Babaji Mandlekar, Bhaguram Ramji Shirgavkar, Sonu Sajan Sandirkar, Vitthal Laxman Tidkar, Bhau Balu Jadhav, Bhaviknath Ratnu Salve, Pandharinath Ramchandra Aasudkar.

Sitaram Namdev Shivtarkar
Secretary, Satyagraha Committee

(Co. Op. Press, Bombay 12)

Appendix 4

The Original Pamphlet

महाड सत्याग्रहास जाणाऱ्या लोकांस

जाहीर खबर.

ता. २५-१२-२७ पासून महाड येथें सुरू होणाऱ्या सत्याग्रहास जाणाऱ्या मंडळीस विनंतिपूर्वक कळविण्यांत येतें कीं, त्यांनी आपल्याबरोबर ताट, तांब्या, कांबळी व तीन दिवस पुरेल इतकी भोजनाची सामुग्री जरूर आणावी. आम्ही तेथें भोजनाची व्यवस्था करणार आहोंत तरीपण प्रत्येकानें आपापली तयारी ठेवावी. **डॉ. आंबेडकर** व इतर सत्याग्रह कमिटीचें लोक मुंबईहून ता. २४-१२-२७ रोजी आगबोटीनें निघणार आहेत. तर ज्यांना त्यांच्याबरोबर येणें असेल त्यांनी ता. १५-१२-२७ पूर्वी आपल्या जाण्यायेण्याच्या खर्चाकरितां ५ रुपये बहिष्कृत हितकारिणी सभेच्या ऑफिसांत आणून दिल्यास त्यांच्याकरितां स्वतंत्र बोटीची व्यवस्था करण्यांत येणार आहे. तरी ही सोय ज्यांना पसंत असेल त्यांनी तावतोब आपली नांवें बहिष्कृत हितकारिणी सभेच्या ऑफिसांत नोंदवावी व सेक्रेटरीकडे ५ रुपये देऊन पावती घ्यावी. व ज्यांना कमिटीच्या मंडळीबरोबर यावयाचें नसेल त्यांनी दासगांवला उतरण्याची खबरदारी घ्यावी.

महाड येथें सत्याग्रहाच्यावेळीं अलोट गर्दी होणार आहे. म्हणून त्यावेळी गर्दीमध्यें आपला मनुष्य अचुक ओळखता यावा या करितां सत्याग्रहांत भाग घेणाऱ्या स्वयंसेवकानें **बहिष्कृत हितकारिणी** सभेच्या नांवाचें पदक छातीवर लाविलें पाहिजे. ज्यांच्या छातीवर सभेच्या नांवाचें पदक नसेल त्यांच्या संरक्षणाची किंवा इतर कसल्याही प्रकारची जबाबदारी सत्याग्रह कमिटी आपल्यावर घेणार नाही. सदरहू पदकाची किंमत फक्त दोन आणे ठेवण्यांत आली आहे व ते बहिष्कृत हितकारिणी सभेच्या ऑफिसांत विकत मिळेल.

आपला,

सिताराम नामदेव शिवतरकर.

---

* *Source*: Old papers of Babasaheb Ambedkar at Rajgruha, Mumbai

(Translation of the Marathi Pamphlet)

PUBLIC NOTICE

Those who are going for the Satyagraha at Mahad, starting on 25 December 1927 are earnestly requested that they should bring a plate, a tumbler, a blanket and food for three days along with them. We are going to make arrangements for meals there. But still everyone must be prepared for himself. Dr Ambedkar and other members of the Satyagraha committee will leave Mumbai on 24 December by a boat. Those who wish to come with them, must deposit Rs 5/- towards transport expenses in the office of the Bahishkrut Hitkarini Sabha before 15 December 1927 so that a separate boat could be arranged for them. Those who like this arrangement should immediately register their names in the office of the Bahishkrut Hitkarini Sabha and pay Rs 5 to the secretary and obtain the receipt. Those who do not want to travel with the committee members should ensure they alight at Dasgaon.

There is going to be a huge crowd at Mahad during the Satyagraha. Therefore, in order to recognize our people in the crowd, all participants in the Satyagraha should wear the badge of Bahishkrut Hitkarini Sabha on their chest. The committee will not take responsibility for the security or any other thing of those who do not bear the badge. This badge is priced nominally at just 2 annas and shall be available in the office of the Bahishkrut Hitkarini Sabha.

Yours sincerely

Sitaram Namdev Shivtarkar
Secretary, Satyagraha Committee

Appendix 5

Formal Programme of the Satyagraha Conference

25 December 1927 (day 1)

10.00 AM: Presidential speech. Thereafter, march to the Chavadar tank to fetch water.

12.30 PM: Lunch.

3.00 PM: Burning of *Manusmruti* and topical speeches. Thereafter, march to the Chavadar tank to fetch water.

7.30 PM: Light refreshment followed by *Kirtan* and then *Satyashodhak Tamasha.*

26 December 1927 (Day 2)

10.00 AM: Resolution for reform in the internal structure of the castes. Thereafter, march to the Chavadar tank to fetch water.

12.30 PM: Lunch.

3.00 PM: Public resolutions. Thereafter, march to the Chavadar tank to fetch water.

7.30 PM: Light refreshment; *Kirtan and Satyashodhak* Tamasha. Thereafter the conclusion of the conference.

Only 250 people will be asked to stay back and through them the programme of fetching water from the tank would be continued until 2 January 1928.

Special notice: The Satyagraha committee requests all the delegates to conduct themselves with extreme humility and peace during the course of the Satyagraha and hopes that on no occasion they will allow peace to be compromised.

Yours sincerely
Sitaram Namdeo Shivtarkar
Secretary, Satyagraha Committee

Appendix 6

Resolutions of the Satyagraha Conference

Resolution 1: It is the firm opinion of this conference that the Hindu society is the prominent example of how nations fall because of social injustice, religious degeneration, political regression and economic slavery. The main reason for the fallen state of the Hindu religion is the apathy of the majority people in knowing what inherent rights of human beings are, not being alert about preserving them and not arresting the intrigues of selfish people. It is the sacred duty of every human being to understand our birthrights, to protect them when they are endangered, and to ensure that they would not be violated in our interaction with others. In order to place the birthrights of the Hindus always in front of their eyes, with the omnipresent, almighty God as the witness, and with his blessings we are publishing this manifesto for the information of all.

1. All human beings are of equal status since birth and they are of equal status until they die. According to their utility for the society, difference in their status may creep in. Otherwise, their equal status should stay forever. This conference is of the firm opinion that no policy should be upheld that will violate the principle of equality in political and public affairs.
2. The ultimate aim of the political and the social order should be to ensure the above birthrights stay forever. Therefore, this conference intensely condemns the ancient and modern scriptures that promote inequality prevailing in the Hindu social structure.
3. People are the source of all kinds of authority and power.

If the special rights of any class or person or collective are not given by the majority of people, then they cannot be accepted on any other basis, no matter whether it is based on politics or religion. Therefore, this conference is not prepared to accept the basis or the authority of the *Shrutis, Smritis and Purans*, etc. in respect of social order.

4. Every person has the basic freedom to operate in accordance with his birthright. If that is limited, it could only be to the extent of the conflicts, with the enjoyment of similar rights by others. The limitation should be decided by laws made by the people. It cannot be decided by religious scriptures or any other source. Therefore, this conference condemns the order that sanctions inequality of rights between castes.
5. The law should prohibit only those things which are injurious to the society. The thing which is not proscribed by law should be free for all. Similarly, the thing which is not decided by law as necessary should not be compelled to be done by anyone. Therefore, there should not be any proscription on the use of public roads, public schools, public water sources and temples by anyone. Therefore, this conference considers the people who seek to proscribe such usage as the enemies of a well organized social structure and justice.
6. Law is not the limits determined by any particular class. The right to determine how the law should be, must be vested in people or their representatives. This law should be equally applicable to all, irrespective of whether it is related to defence or governance. And since social structure is to be based on the principle of equality, caste should not come in the way of exercising dignity, authority or vocation. If at all discrimination is inevitable, it should be based on attributes of a person; it should not be just by birth. Therefore, this conference condemns the prevailing custom of caste discrimination and the inequality stemming from it.

Proposer: Sitaram Namdeo Shivtarkar Seconded by: Bhau Krushnrao Gaikwad Supported by: N.T. Jadhav

Concurred by: Smt Gangabai Sawant

Resolution No. 2: It is the firm opinion of this conferencethat *Manusmruti,* taking into consideration its verses (statements) which undermined the *shudra* caste, thwarted their progress, and made their social, political, and economic slavery permanent, and by comparing them with the principles enunciated in the above part of the manifesto of birthrights of the Hindus, is not worthy of becoming a religious or a sacred book. And in order to give expression to this opinion, this conference is performing the cremation rites of such a religious book which has been divisive of people and destroyer of humanity.

Proposed by: Gangadhar Nilkanth Sahasrabuddhe Seconded by: P.N. Rajbhoj

Supported by: Thorat[41]

Resolution No. 3: This conference thinks that all the peoplefollowing the Hindu religion should be considered as a single class; they should all be identified as 'Hindus'. There should be a legal ban on identification by the *varna* indicative terms like *Brahman, Kshatriya, Vaishya, Shudra,* etc. or caste indicative termslike *Agar, Mahar, Mang,* etc. If necessary, there may not be any objection to identify people by their profession like *Shimpi* (tailor), *Sonar* (goldsmith), *Mali* (gardner), etc. or by their region or country indicative terms like *Maratha, Kokanastha, Deshastha,* etc.

Proposed by: Kondiram Kholwadikar Seconded by: Subhedar Ghatge Supported by: Nirmal Gangawane
Concurred by: Dhondiram Narayan Gaikwad

Resolution 4: It is the considered opinion of this conferencethat

(i) Institution of religious authority should be subject to peoples' opinion and appointed by people,

(ii) the right and the opportunity of acceptance of this profession (religious authority) and to make oneself capable of it should be given to all the Hindus,

(iii) The aspirants for the religious authority should be examined and they should be issued certificates, if qualified. The law should prohibit all those who failed to get these certificates to act as religious authority or perform any rites in the name of that authority,

(iv) the religious authority should be generally divided into village, taluka and provincial religious authority,

(v) the religious authority appointed as per the above terms should not have the right to demand *Dakshina*, or to take any other type of honorarium or accept any type of reward in exchange of performing religious rites. Instead, like any officer in other departments, these religious authorities, big or small, should be considered as Government servants, and accordingly be paid salary for their service.

Proposed by: Patitpawndas Buwa
Seconded by: Girjashankar Shivdas
Supported by: Chavare Master
Concurred by: Ragho Narayan Vanmali

Appendix 7

Final Order of the Bombay High Court

APPEAL NO. 462 OF 1933 FROM APPELLATE DECREE

Narhari Damodar Vaidya; and the others
(Original Plaintiffs Nos. 2 to 6)..............................Appellants.

Dr Bhimrao Ramji Ambedkar, Member of Joint Parliamentary Committee, London; and others (Original Deefendants)

..................................Respondents.

Second Appeal against the decision of S.M. Kaikini, Esquire, Second Assistant Judge at Thana in Appeal No. 32 of 1931.

Mr V.B. Virkar for the Appellants, Counsel Mr S.V. Gupte, with Mr B.G. Modak for Respondent No. 1.

17th March 1937
Coram:- Broomfield and N.J. Wadia J.
Oral Judgement (Per Broomfield J.):-

The appellants, on behalf of the caste Hindus of the town of Mahad, sued the respondents, who represented the so-called 'Untouchables' for a declaration that the Choudhari Tank near the town belongs to them and that they alone have a right to use it and the respondents are not entitled to use it, and for an injunction against the respondents not to us it. The claim to ownership is not now persisted in and it is conceded that, as found by the trial court, the tank belonged to the Government under the provisions of Section 37 of the Land Revenue Code and has now vested in the Municipality of Mahad under Section 50 of the District Municipalities Act. It is also conceded now that the caste Hindus are not entitled to use the tank exclusively by as against all the world, since Mohamedans may, and do use it. It is contended nevertheless that the appellants have the right to use it themselves and to exclude the 'Untouchables' from the use of it, and this right is said to be based on immemorial custom.

The trial Judge found that the plaintiffs have proved a long-standing custom (he does not describe it as immemorial) of using the tank water to the exclusion of the 'Untouchables'. He held however, that the custom conferred no legal right upon the plaintiffs because "mere user of a public tank by one-class and non-user by another would not clothe the class, making the user with any legal rights or rights of ownership." On appeal the Assistant Judge confirmed the finding that the caste Hindus have not proved that they have any legal right to exclude the 'Untouchables'. He has relied to some extent on a judgemnt of Sir Sadashiv Ayar V. Vaithilinga, a case not reported apparently in the authorised *reports* but to be found in 1913 Mad. W. N. 247 and 18 Indian cases 979; but his main reason seems to be that he held that the custom is not shown to be immemorial.

The Chowdhari tank is a small lake or a large pool; between four and five acres in extent, on the outskirts of the town. It is surrounded on all sides by municipal roads beyond which are houses occupied by caste Hindus (and very few Mohamedans}, and the owners of these houses also own in many cases strips of land on the edge of the tank, ghats or flights of steps to get to the water and the masonry embankments along the sides. There are no houses of 'Untouchables' anywhere near. It is not known how old the tank is, except that it is admittedly not less than 250 years old. There is no evidence as to its origin. It is not even clear that it is artificial. The Trial Judge took the view that it was "a natural excavation in the bed of the earth, of course repaired and remodelled by human agency." If it is so—and the point was not disputed in the argument before us—it is probably many centuries old. The water-supply comes from the monsoon and a few natural springs. The population of the town Mahad is between seven and eight thousand, of whom less then 400/- are 'Untouchables'. The Municipality was established in 1865, but there is no evidence available, at any rate on the record of this case, as to the early history of the town or as to the time when the side was first inhabited.

The Plaintiffs have examined a number of witnesses, many of them old inhabitants, whose evidence may be said to have established that within the period of living memory the tank has been used exclusively by the caste Hindus (and a few Mohamedans) and has never been used by the 'Untouchables'. It is in fact admitted that the latter never used it, before the year 1927, when a campaign against the doctrines of 'untouchability' was carried out by defendant N.I., and some of the 'Untouchables' went and drank water as a mask of protest. They were assaulted and beaten by the caste Hindus and there were criminal prosecutions which led to the present suit. As there is no record of any attempt having been made by the 'Untouchables' to use the tank before that there is no evidence of any positive acts of exclusion. What is provided is user by the one party and absence of user by the other. This was, undoubtedly not any accidental causes, but to—the mutual acceptance of the doctrine of 'Untouchability'—which until recent years was not openly challenged.

The learned Assistant Judge comments out the fact that there is no evidence of the exclusion of the 'Untouchables' in pre-British times, nothing to show that the exclusion or exclusive user was in force in the days of the Maratha rule or the Musalman rule, It is of course not always necessary to produce evidence going back beyond the memory of living persons. On proof of enjoyment for a period even less than that the courts have frequently felt justified in holding, in the absence of evidence to the contrary that a custom has existed from time immemorial. Nor, of course, is it necessary in a case of this kind to have evidence of positive acts of exclusion of one party by the other. There could be no such evidence as long as the enjoyment of the caste Hindus was not challenged, and it would not be likely to be challenged as long as the doctrine of 'untouchability' prevailed and was accepted. But a custom proved to have existed during the period of living memory can only be presumed to have existed from before the period of legal memory in case where conditions may be assumed to have been permanent and stable. It is reasonable to infer that what has happened during the period covered by the evidence also has that what has happened during the period covered by the evidence has also happened from time immemorial. This is where the plaintiffs' case in our opinion breaks down. As long as conditions were at all similar, as long as the houses of the caste Hindus have surrounded the tank, (which is not necessarily very long as the tank is on the outskirts of the town and the land around it was not likely to be occupied until after considerable expansion of the original settlement) it may be safely presumed that the practice was the same as at present. It would not be safe to presume, however, that conditions have been similar for a period long enough to establish the alleged custom. The Konkan has had a chequered history, even in comparatively modern times, and to suppose that the caste Hindus have been in a position to exercise exclusive control over this large natural reservoir, situated as it is, from time immemorial, would be contrary to reasonable probability.

In this connection some of the observations of Sir Sadashiv Ayar in Mariappa V. Vaithilinga are very instructive. He cites a saying of Manu's; "waters are pure as long as a cow goes to quench her thirst in and they have a good scent, colour and taste", and he points out that the *Shastric* writings "make a distinction between rivers, tanks and other receptacle which are more easily contaminated and where purification by time, atmospheric conditions and movement of the water is much more difficult." The learned Judge suggests that the dictates of the Hindu religion would not require any elaborate precautions against the pollution of water in a large open tank, and he was dealing with a tank in a village site considerably smaller than the Choudhari Tank at Mahad. The doctrine of 'Untouchability' therefore does not appear to go far enough to lend very much support to the appellants' case and it is doubtful whether any attempt would be made to secure exclusive user of the water until such time as the tank came to be surrounded by the houses of the caste Hindus.

This is the only case to which our attention has been drawn

dealing with a claim to exclude 'Untouchables' from the use of a watering-place of this description. The temple-entry cases, e.g., Anandrav N. Shankar, (1883) I.L.R., 7 Born. 323, and Sankaralinga V. Rajeswara, (1908) I.L.R., 31 Mad, 236, P.C., are not really on all fours. In such case long practice acquiesced in by the other castes and communities may naturally give rise to a presumption of dedication to the exclusive use of the higher castes, and may throw upon the "Untouchables" the burden of proving that they are among the people for whose worship a particular temple exists. No such presumption of a lawful origin of the custom can be said to arise here.

We therefore agree with the learned Assistant Judge that the appellants have not established the immemorial custom' which they allege. Had they succeeded on this point it might have been necessary to consider whether the custom were unreasonable or contrary to public policy (though strictly speaking. that he was not pleaded in the lower courts). It would certainly have been necessary to consider the legal effect of the vesting of the Choudhari Tank in the Municipality, and the question whether in any case the appellants could be granted any relief in this suit in which the legal owner is not a party. But as it is not necessary to decide these questions in the view we take of the case, and as they have not been very fully or effectively argued, we prefer to express no opinion.

Appeal dismissed with costs.

The Seal of the High Court at Bombay.	By order of the Court Sd/- R.S. Bavdekar Registrar
	Sd/-
High Court Appellate Side certified copy Bombay	For Deputy Registrar the 28th day of June I960

Appendix 8

Bio-sketches of Some Prominent Heroes of Mahad

1. DR BHIMRAO RAMJI ALIAS BABASAHEB AMBEDKAR (1891-1956)

Dr Ambedkar was born on April 14, 1891 at Mhow, where his father was a subhedar in the British army. After his retirement, the family shifted to Dapoli, Satara, and then to Bombay, where he finished his schooling and graduation. With a scholarship from the Baroda state, he went to Columbia University in 1913 where he completed his studies for MA and Ph D. degrees and soon enrolled himself at London School of Economics and Grey's Inn in London for D Sc and barristership respectively.

He had to return to India in the midst of his studies as the tenure of his scholarship had ended in 1917.

Despite being amongst the most educated, he faced many humiliations in India because of his caste. With the financial help from the Maharaja of Kolhapur he started a Marathi fortnightly—*Mooknayak* (The Leader of the Dumbs) and began participating in Depressed Classes conferences. After managing money from various sources he returned to London and completed his studies. Returning in 1923, he plunged into social work by founding 'Bahishkrit Hitkarini Sabha' in 1924 and presided over two historical conferences at Mahad. After his bitter experiences in Mahad, he gave up his hopes of reforming Hindu society and turned his sight to politics which was fast unfolding along communal lines.

On the basis of his testimony to the Simon Commission, sent to India to study constitutional reforms, he was invited to the round table conferences in England where he won Dalits separate electorates with reserved seats. However, he was blackmailed by Gandhi into signing the Poona Pact that gave Dalits more reserved seats in exchange of separate electorates. Later, he formed the Independent Labour Party on the lines of the British Labor Party, which he had to dissolve and form the Scheduled Caste Federation. He served as Member in Viceroy's Executive Council and when the constituent assembly was formed he became chairman of the drafting committee for which he earned the epithet of Chief Architect of the Constitution. He was also inducted as a Law Minister in the first cabinet led by Nehru. However, he soon got dejected and resigned from it and also disowned the constitution. Just before his death on 6 December 1956, he embraced Buddhism along with half a million of his followers.

2. COMRADE RAMCHANDRA BABAJI MORE (1903-1972)

R.B More, born on 1 March 1903 at Ladwali, near Mahad, was the brain behind the Mahad conference. He studied in a primary school for children of Dalits in the British army in Dasgaon. A brilliant student, he had won a scholarship but was summarily denied admission to the Mahad high school because he was a Dalit. He wrote letters to the government to withdraw grant to the school and published them in a newspaper. The school had to admit him forthwith. Inspired by this, he began taking up cases of injustice to Dalits in the area. He started a small hotel in Mahad, which became a regular meeting place for retired Dalit soldiers and for other Dalit activists. He founded the *Kokanastha Mahar Seva Sangh*, which decided to organize a conference, which Dr Ambedkar presided over. The previous year (December 1926), he had led the Crawford lake Satyagraha successfully asserting Dalits rights to water source. He had formed *Ambedkar Seva Dal*, an organization of Dalit youth, on the lines of the Congress Seva Dal, which was renamed by Ambedkar to *Samata Sainik Dal*.

Soon after the Mahad Satyagraha, More came in contact with the movement of textile workers in Mumbai. He was one of the founder-members of the *Girni Kamgar Union* (GKU) which, under communist leadership, organised massive strikes of the textile workers of Mumbai. He joined the Communist Party in 1930 and started a Marathi weekly *Aavhan* (Challenge) which was banned by the government the very next year. More led innumerable agitations of the working class and the peasantry, and also the struggles against caste oppression. He was thus a remarkable link between the Dalit and the communist movements, and truly deserved the later epithet as a 'Red Star in the Blue Sky'. The most enduring tribute to his memory is *Jeevanmarg*, the weekly organ of the CPI (M) Maharashtra state committee, of which he was the founder editor. Even after joining the communist party, More maintained his relationship with Dr Ambedkar. He remained a staunch and selfless communist revolutionary for over four decades, and was one of the most respected leaders of the CPI (M) till his death on May 11, 1972.

3. ANANT VINAYAK ALIAS BHAI CHITRE (1894-1959)

A.V. Chitre was born in Dapoli on 1 May 1894 in the Chandraseniya Kayastha Prabhu (CKP) caste. He completed his primary education in Poladpur, Dapoli and Mahad as Anant Vinayak Kondhvikar; his secondary schooling in New English School at Pune and college education from Fergusson College, Pune and Wilson College, Mumbai.

During his college education in Mumbai he started participating in social activities. Chitre took the initiative in organizing a youth convention on 11 March 1911, which led to the foundation of the *Social Service League*, a platform for youth to take up social causes. It was presided over by Justice Narayanrao Chandavarkar. It was he who had suggested to the young R.B. More to write to the government when he was denied admission in Mahad School and arranged for its publication in a newspaper.

After graduation, Chitre took a job of a teacher in Wilson High School in 1917. He started the Gokhale Night School for the working youth. In 1918, he started the Marathi periodical, *Maharashtra Sahitya,* to create social awareness in the society. His association with the Sir Currimbhoy Ibrahim Workmen's Institute, brought him in direct contact with workers. In the workers' strike of 1920, he played an active role in founding the Bombay Labour Settlement Committee, which catalysed the unity among the Mill Hands Association, *Kamgar Hitwardhak Sabha* and Social Service League.

Chitre was closely associated with Dr Ambedkar and played a very important role in organizing the Mahad conferences, and later in shaping the Independent Labour Party (ILP). He was among the few upper caste candidates put up by the ILP, who got elected at the second place. He made many spirited speeches in the Legislative Assembly in support of the Khoti and the Mahar Watan Bills. He had established the Kolaba District Peasants' Union in 1930 and successfully organized two conferences to mobilize peasantry. Due to his uncompromising struggle he was arrested and barred from entering Mumbai. He was attracted to the Peasants and Workers' Party in 1951 and eventually joined the communist party in 1954. He contracted epilepsy and died on 26 January 1959.

4. SAMBHAJI TUKARAM GAIKWAD ALIAS DADASAHEB GAIKWAD (1864-1949)

Gaikwad was born in 1864 at Poud in Kolaba district. Due to poverty he could not get any formal education. He came to Bombay at the age of 20, learnt the job of a motor mechanic and started working in a motor company, the Highland Motor Factory in Bombay on a handsome salary of Rs. 350 per month. Inspired by Gopal Baba Walangkar, of whom he was one of the torch bearers in the Konkan region he started taking an active part in the movements for uplifting Dalits. He lived in the Bombay Improvement Trust (BIT) Chawl at Sat Rasta, in Central Bombay, where he had started a library, which became an important centre of the *Bahiskrut Hitkarini Sabha*. He, along with his associates, founded the *Mahar Samaj Seva Sangh* on 10 August 1926. He had a lion's share in the organization of the first conference at Mahad, for which he was the chairman of the reception committee. He had toured all over the places around Mahad to canvass for the Satyagraha. He also enlisted support of the Untouchable saints belonging to various sects such as Kabir Panth, Ramanand Panth, Nath Panth and Warkari Panth to the Mahad Satyagraha. On 15 November 1929, he gave evidence before the Starte Committee which was appointed by the Government of Bombay to look into the socioeconomic condition of the Depressed Classes. He organized the first *vedic* wedding in the Untouchable community. He was an active participant in the Kalaram temple Satyagraha. He was also the vice president of the conference of the *Mumbai Ilakha Mahar Parishad* (Bombay Region Mahar Conference) organized in 1936 to discuss the declaration of Dr Ambedkar in Yeole to renounce Hinduism and convert to some other religion.

Under the banner of the ILP, he worked relentlessly among peasantry, especially in the movement for abolition of the Khoti System. He encouraged his son to participate in the movement but unfortunately he died at the young age of 26 in 1929. He established one more organization, named *Mahar Dnyati Panchayat Samiti* in 1942, which would become the *Bouddhajana Panchayat Samiti*, after conversion to Buddhism. He breathed his last on 7 March 1949 at the ripe age of 85.

5. SUBHEDAR VISHRAM GANGARAM SAWADKAR (1889-1939)

Sawadkar was born on 20 August 1889 at Telge village of Mahad taluka. He had a lineage of service in the armed forces that stretched back to five generations. He joined the British Army as a soldier in the 2/9 Jat Regiment and rose through the ranks to become a Subhedar.

While serving in the armed forces he grew attracted to the Ambedkarite movement. He had very good relations with his superiors as well as his juniors in the regiment, which came in handy for him to get help from this regiment for the Mahad conferences. He started a hostel for the Untouchable students in 1928 at Mahad. Much of his salary used to go in feeding the students in the hostel.

Subhedar Savadkar enjoyed the confidence of Dr Ambedkar all through his life. He played a significant role in convincing Dr Ambedkar to accept the presidentship of the first Depressed Classes Conference at Mahad and was the main fund collector for it. Whenever Dr Ambedkar went to Mahad, he would invariably go along with his companions to Savadkar's home at Veer, some eight kilometers away from Mahad. Later he worked as a Treasurer for the *Mumbai Ilaka Mahar Parishad* and as an organizer of the ILP. He was a member of the Mahad Parishad from 1936 to 1939. On 14 January 1939, in Mumbai, he succumbed to tuberculosis.

6. SITARAM NAMDEV SHIVTARKAR ALIAS SHIVTARKAR MASTER (1891-1966)

Sitaram Namdev Shivtarkar was born on 15 July 1891 in the Kamathipura area of Mumbai. His father was a teacher.

Shivtarkar completed his vernacular final in 1909 and was appointed as a teacher in a Marathi school at Parel, Mumbai. Later, in 1926, he was promoted as head master and subsequently as an educational supervisor. He retired in 1949.

He came close to Dr Ambedkar in 1914. When Dr Ambedkar went to England to complete his studies, he and D.D. Gholap managed the affairs of *Mooknayak* in his absence. In 1923 he became the Personal Secretary of Dr Ambedkar and secretary of the *Bahishkrut Hitkarini Sabha* when it was formed the next year. In the movement he was popularly known as "Shivtarkar master", who competently assisted Dr Ambedkar in his organizational activities and particularly the periodicals he started, *Mooknayak, Bahishkrit Bharat* and *Janata*. He played a leading role in Mahad struggles and actively participated in most agitations under the leadership of Dr Ambedkar. In 1952 he founded the *Rohidas Samaj Panchayat Sangh*. In the same year he was elected to the Mumbai Legislative Assembly. On 29 March 1966, he died in Mumbai in a private hospital.

7. SURENDRANATH GOVINDRAO TIPNIS ALIAS SURBANANA (1898–1978)

Surendranath Govindrao Tipnis was born in 1898 at Mahad. Although he was himself a Khot (landlord), belonging to the

Chandraseniya Kayastha Prabhus, he was a lifelong supporter of the Dalit movement started by Dr Ambedkar. In 1923, when he went to Mumbai and stayed with his brother-in-law, Anantrao Chitre, Chitre introduced him to Dr Ambedkar in the office of Social Service League, which was situated in Damodar Hall. He kept on meeting Dr Ambedkar thereafter and generously acknowledged his debt for having shaped him. He was progressive at the core and remained so with exemplary courage and conviction. Because of his status as Khot, he was not ostracized by his caste for having participated in the Chavadar tank march, but he still could not escape its impact. His Maratha tenants and other upper castes stopped taking food at his place, the housemaid and other domestic servants also left him. But nothing could shake him from his convictions. It was under his chairmanship that the Mahad Municipality had adopted a resolution to open all water sources within its jurisdiction (resolution No. 67 of 1927) to all castes. This resolution served as the basis for the Untouchables to assert their right over the Chavadar tank water. He was among the leaders in the march to the Chavadar tank. It was he who had provided the crucial evidence in the case in the form of documents from Government's Military Engineering Department that sought explanation as to why Rs. 500 sanctioned by the Government for dredging the tank was not spent, proving thereby that the tank belonged to the public and was not private property as claimed by the complainants. Later, when the Independent Labour Party was formed by Dr Ambedkar, he became the chief organizer in Konkan. Although he was a Khot himself, he actively participated in Dr Ambedkar's anti-Khoti agitation. He later participated in the *Samyukt Maharashtra Movement*. He was the Vice President of the People's Education Society founded by Dr Ambedkar from 1972 to 1974. He met his end in a road traffic accident on 22nd June 1978.

8. GANGADHAR NEELKANTH SAHASRABUDHE ALIAS BAPU (NOT AVAILABLE-1958)

Gangadhar Neelkanth Sahasrabudhe, popularly known as "Bapu" among the associates of Dr. Ambedkar, was very close to him. He was a Brahman by caste but was aware of the injustice Brahmans did to the lower castes. He genuinely attempted to create awareness in the society against the evil customs like untouchability and associated with Dr Ambedkar. He is said to have been instrumental in making Dr. Ambedkar accept the invitation to preside over the first Mahad conference. He was in the forefront in proposing the burning of Manusmriti in the programme for the Satyagraha Mahad on 25 December 1927, which incidentally was carried out at his hand. He was involved in working class movement as the secretary of *Ambarnath Kamgar Sangh* and *Municipal Kamgar Sangh* founded by Dr Ambedkar and was also the editor of Janata for a brief period. He died in Mumbai on 2 April 1958.

9. BHASKAR RAGHUNATH KADREKAR (1902-1975)

Kadrekar was born on 7 July 1902. He had participated in most struggles launched by Dr Ambedkar. In Kalaram Temple Satyagraha, he distinguished himself for his bravery and dedication to the cause. The biographer of Dr Ambedkar writes about it: "… a daring Bhandari youth by name Kadrekar broke the cordon of the armed police who were awaiting orders to fire, and in a moment crowds of Untouchables pursued the chariot amidst showers of stones and captured it. Dangerously wounded Kadrekar fell down in a pool of blood." [Dhananjay Keer, *Dr Amabedkar: Life and Mission*, Popular Prakashan, Mumbai, 2005, p. 138]. He was among the close lieutenants of Dr Ambedkar, who as per his wishes had started a fortnightly paper called *Janata* (the People) along with Deorao Naik. Dr Ambedkar was very appreciative of his dedication and sacrifices as he wrote to him in one of his letters: "I quite understand the difficulties you are undergoing and I have always felt, and this is no flattering that we all, and particularly myself, owe you a very great debt of gratitude for the way you are slaving yourself for a paltry pittance." [Dhananjay Keer, op. cit., p. 239]. He worked as editor and publisher of *Janata* and *Prabudha Bharat*. All booklets written by Dr. Ambedkar were printed at Bharat Bhushan Press by him. He was credited to bring out a special issue of Janata in 1933, an important document describing and analyzing the Ambedkarite movement. Kadrekar remained bachelor and completely dedicated to the Ambedkarite movement. After Dr. Ambedkar's passing, he ran a fortnightly *Buddhayaan* to spread Dr. Ambedkar's thought and Buddhism. He died on 28 August 1975.

10. BHAURAO KRISHNAJI ALIAS DADASAHEB GAIKWAD (1902-1971)

Gaikwad was born on 15 October 1902 at Ambe village of Didori taluka of Nashik district. He served for a year in the Telegraph Office, after completion of his education. Later, he joined the British Excise Department but was immediately transferred to Karachi (now in Pakistan). In 1924 he got introduced to Dr. Ambedkar, and quickly became one of his trusted lieutenants. He participated in the second Mahad Satyagraha and headed one of the divisions of satyagrahis..

He was one of the main organizers of the Kalaram Mandir Satyagraha (1930-35). Of all the Dalit leaders of his times, by his attire and demeanor he most genuinely represented the common Dalit folk. Perhaps for this reason, Dr Ambedkar had reposed his faith in him and intimately expressed his thoughts on major and minor aspects of the Dalit movement.

After Dr Ambedkar's death in 1956, he emerged as the biggest leader. The Republican Party of India, which was formed after the dissolution of the Scheduled Caste Federation, according to the wishes of Dr Ambedkar had gained significant radical orientation with him at its helm. It joined socialists and communists (under Nana Patil) in land Satyagraha in 1956 and 1965 aimed at gaining access to forest lands and village 'common' lands for cultivation by Dalits and other landless. He was imprisoned for four months along with many others.

This glorious struggle, reorienting the Dalit movement to focus on genuine caste-class issues had tremendous strategic import. The Congress Party, shaken by the possible threat this unity of the Dalit and Left posed to the ruling establishment, strategized to co-opt the radical Dalit leadership. Gaikwad was targeted through Yashwantrao Chauhan, the then chief minister of Maharashtra. Gaikwad, even though conscious of the strategic content of this offer, however fell prey and became the Rajya Sabha member, opening the floodgates for other opportunists to tag themselves to the ruling parties. He had also participated in the Samyukta Maharashtra movement. He was honoured by Padma Shri in 1968 for his dedicated service to society. He died on 29 December 1971 in Delhi.

11. PANDURANG NATHUJI RAJBHOJ ALIAS BAPUSAHEB RAJBHOJ (1905-1984)

Rajbhoi was born on 15 March 1905 at Kanashi, Nashik district. After completing his high school education at Pune he joined government service. However, due to consistent experience of caste discrimination he quit his job in 1925 and went on to work for *Bahishkrit Hitkarni Sabha* in its unit at Pune. At the instance of Dr Ambedkar, he called the first conference of Dhor and Chambhar castes in 1926 at Pune. He participated in Mahad struggles of 1927 and was badly injured in the attack by the caste Hindus after the Chavadar tank march. He led the Parvati temple entry Satyagraha at Pune and was injured in this Satyagraha too. He also took part in Kalaram Mandir Satyagraha at Nashik. He founded the *Bharat Dalit Sevashram* in Pune.

In 1930, he became Gandhi's follower, supporting the proposal of joint electorate for the Depressed Classes under the Rajah-Moonje Pact of 1931 and opposing the conversion move of Dr Ambedkar. Rajbhoj was one of the signatories of the said Pact. In 1936 he came back to Ambedkar. He was the founding General Secretary of the All India Scheduled Castes Federation founded in 1942. On 15 May 1950, he took part in the World Buddhist Conference held at Colombo in Sri Lanka along with Dr Ambedkar.

He edited periodicals such as *Dalit Bandhu* and *Samata* in Marathi and *Indian States* in English. In the first general elections of 1952, he was elected as a MP from Sholapur constituency on the SCF ticket. Owning to differences with Dr Ambedkar, he again left the SCF on 11 April 1955. After the death of Ambedkar in 1956, he joined the Congress and became a member of the Rajya Sabha. On 2 February 1956, he contested the election for President of India but lost to the Congress candidate Dr Zakir Hussain.

He converted to Buddhism at Bangkok in Thailand on 17 May 1957 and remained a staunch Buddhist till his end. He made a forceful demand for extending all the constitutional and statutory facilities for the SCs to the Neo-Buddhists and undertook a hunger strike from 9-18 December 1966 and again from 19-25 November 1977. Rajbhoj had also supported the agitation for renaming of Marathwada University after Babasaheb Ambedkar. He breathed his last on 22 July 1984 at the age of 79.

12. TANAJI MAHADEVRAO GUDEKAR ALIAS GUDEKARBABA (1894-1953)

Gudekar was born in 1894 at Gude. His father, Mahadevrao had served in the British army and was constantly on the move from one camp to the other. During the First World War, the British government started recruiting soldiers to the army and so he got an opportunity to join the Mahar Battalion of the British army in 1914.

In 1924, he left the army and tried to settle in his village, but very soon moved back to Mumbai. There, he came in contact with Sambhaji Tukaram Gaikwad, Govind Ramji Adrekar, Balaram Bhivaji Lotekar among others. He joined the *Mahar Samaj Seva Sangh* and played a prominent role in the Mahad Satyagraha. He also played a vital role along with Adrekar, Shivram Gopal Jadhav, Gaikwadbaba in making various conferences successful which were held at Thane (1926), Dapoli (1928), and Chiplun (1929). He undertook stormy tours in the district of Ratnagiri and tried to establish units of the Mahar Samaj Seva Sangh. He formed various social organizations to empower the Depressed Classes, viz., *Koknasth Mahar Dnyati Sanstha* (1941), a hostel for Untouchable students at Chiplun (1946), Mata Ramabai Ambedkar Boarding (1947-48), etc. He died on 10 February 1953 due to a heart attack.

13. C.N. MOHITE (1899-1984)

Changdeo Narayan (C.N.) Mohite Guruji was born on 18 May 1899 in Mumbai. He studied in municipal Marathi school in Kamathipura (red district of Mumbai) where he became a teacher. He was active in Mahar Samaj Seva sangh and participated in Mahad and Kalaram Mandir Satyagraha. He redrafted the constitution of the Kokanashtha Mahar Dnyati Panchayat, which was appreciated by Dr Ambedkar. He was involved in various social and political struggles. He Died on 13 April 1984.

14. BHIKAJI SAMBHAJI GAIKWAD

He was son of Sambahji Tukaram Gaikwad. with encouragement from his father he led the youth organization. He was first president of the *Bahishkrit Aikya Sanwardhak Mahar Samajseva Sangh* (formed on 10 august 1926). When the upper caste people attacked the delegates after the Chavadar tank march, he was in the forefront and was badly beaten. He succumbed to his injury (due to sepsis) in 1929, when he was just 26 years old.

15. GOVIND RAMJI ADAREKAR (NOT AVAILABLE-1936)

Adarekar was forerunner in organizing and forming the *Mahar Dnyati Paṇchayat Samiti* with the objective to culturally and educationally empower the Untouchables. He had played leading role in Mahad Satyagraha. "Bahishkrit Aikya Sanwardhak Mahar Samaj Sevasangh" the first organization of Untouchables of this kind was formed at Malabar Hill, the residence of Keshavrao Govindrao Adarekar (son of Govindrao Adarekar) on 10 August 1926 and the same was renamed to Mahar Samaj Seva Sangh. It was made clear right at the beginning that though the organization's name is caste based; its aim is not to promote casteism but to abolish it. The office of this organization was at Hanuman Building, Bazaar Gate Street, Fort, Mumbai. Govind Ramji Adarekar was the first person to start union of transporters along with Usuf Meahrali. He campaigned for Mahad Satyagraha in Konkan region along with other leading organizers. He died in 1936.

Index